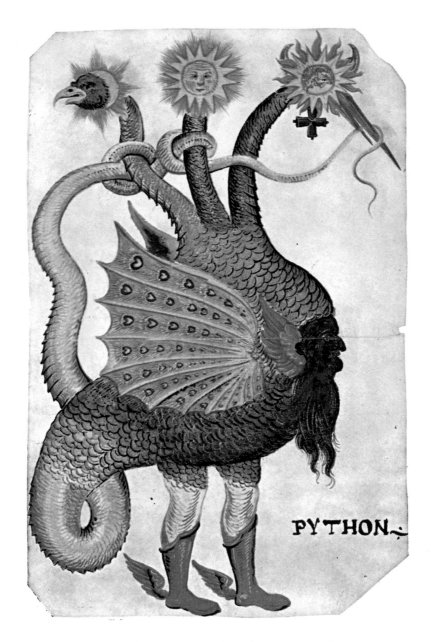

The *spiritus mercurialis* and his transformations represented as a monstrous dragon. It is a quaternity, in which the fourth is at the same time the unity of the three, the unity being symbolized by the mystagogue Hermes. The three (above) are (left to right): Luna, Sol, and coniunctio Solis et Lunae in Taurus, the House of Venus. Together they form $\breve{\varphi}$ = Mercurius. Illuminated drawing in a German alchemical ms., *c.* 1600

# ALCHEMICAL STUDIES

## C. G. JUNG

*TRANSLATED BY R. F. C. HULL*

*54 ILLUSTRATIONS*

BOLLINGEN SERIES XX

PRINCETON UNIVERSITY PRESS

*Second printing, 1970*
*Third printing, 1976*
*First Princeton / Bollingen Paperback printing, 1983*

THIS EDITION IS BEING PUBLISHED IN THE
UNITED STATES OF AMERICA BY PRINCETON
UNIVERSITY PRESS AND IN ENGLAND BY
ROUTLEDGE & KEGAN PAUL, LTD. IN THE
AMERICAN EDITION, ALL THE VOLUMES
COMPRISING THE COLLECTED WORKS CON-
STITUTE NUMBER XX IN BOLLINGEN SERIES.
THE PRESENT VOLUME IS NUMBER 13 OF
THE COLLECTED WORKS AND WAS THE FIF-
TEENTH TO APPEAR.

8    10    9
10

LIBRARY OF CONGRESS CATALOGUE CARD NUMBER: 75-156
ISBN 0-691-09760-7
ISBN 0-691-01849-9 pbk.
MANUFACTURED IN THE U.S.A.

HTTP:// PUP.PRINCETON.EDU

# EDITORIAL NOTE

When we compare the essays in the present volume with Jung's monumental *Mysterium Coniunctionis,* with *Psychology and Alchemy* and to a lesser extent *Aion,* we realize their special value as an introduction to his researches into alchemy. The three longer works, published earlier in this edition, have an impact which to the uninitiated is well-nigh overwhelming. After them these shorter and more manageable works will be turned to, if not for relaxation—their erudition forbids that—at least with a feeling of lively interest, as preliminary studies for the weightier volumes which they now appear to summarize. Much of the symbolic matter has been referred to in other earlier publications: the visions of Zosimos in "Transformation Symbolism in the Mass," and Mercurius in all the above-mentioned works but more especially in "The Psychology of the Transference," while "The Philosophical Tree" develops the theme of the tree symbol discussed sporadically in *Symbols of Transformation.* The "Commentary on *The Secret of the Golden Flower*" is of considerable historical interest. Jung says in *Memories, Dreams, Reflections* (ch. 7): "Light on the nature of alchemy began to come to me only after I had read the text of the *Golden Flower,* that specimen of Chinese alchemy which Richard Wilhelm sent me in 1928. I was stirred by the desire to become more closely acquainted with the alchemical texts." "Paracelsus as a Spiritual Phenomenon" stands out as a separate study with a powerful appeal, perhaps because Jung could identify himself rather closely and sympathetically with that dynamic and explosive personage, his own countryman. Because of its emphasis on alchemical sources, it is included in the present volume rather than in Volume 15 with two shorter essays on Paracelsus as a personality and physician.

The Editors and the translator are greatly indebted to the late Mr. A. S. B. Glover for the translation of the Latin, Greek, and French passages in the text, as well as for his tireless work in checking the references and bibliographical data, which continued until shortly before his death in January 1966.

For assistance in explicating Noël Pierre's poem, grateful acknowledgment is made to Comte Pierre Crapon de Caprona (Noël Pierre), to Miss Paula Deitz, and to Mr. Jackson Mathews.

For help and co-operation in obtaining the photographs for the plates in this volume the Editors are much indebted to the late Mrs. Marianne Niehus-Jung, who made materials available from Professor Jung's collection; to Dr. Jolande Jacobi and Dr. Rudolf Michel, in charge of the picture collection at the C. G. Jung Institute, Zurich; and to Mr. Hellmut Wieser, of Rascher Verlag, Zurich. The frontispiece, an almost exact coloured replica of a woodcut published by the author in *Paracelsica,* was discovered fortuitously in a manuscript in the Mellon Collection of the Alchemical and Occult. It is reproduced by courtesy of Mr. Paul Mellon and the Yale University Library. The Editors are indebted also to Mr. Laurence Witten for his advice and assistance in regard to it.

# TABLE OF CONTENTS

Translated from the "Europäischer Kommentar" to *Das Geheimnis der goldenen Blüte: Ein chinesisches Lebensbuch,* 5th edn. (Zurich: Rascher, 1957).

vii

## I I

## I I I

# IV

## The Spirit Mercurius     191

Translated from "Der Geist Mercurius," *Symbolik des Geistes* (Zurich: Rascher, 1948).

## *Part I*

## *Part II*

# V

## The Philosophical Tree     251

Translated from "Der philosophische Baum," *Von den Wurzeln des Bewusstseins* (Zurich: Rascher, 1954).

# CONTENTS

xi

# LIST OF ILLUSTRATIONS

## For "Commentary on *The Secret of the Golden Flower*"

**Four stages of meditation**  30–33

Drawings from the *Hui Ming Ching,* as reproduced in the original Swiss edition of *Das Geheimnis der goldenen Blüte* (1929).

**A1–A10. Examples of European mandalas**

Drawings or paintings by patients in analysis. Author's collection, except A4: C. G. Jung Institute.

*all following page* 56

## For "Paracelsus as a Spiritual Phenomenon"

**The *spiritus mercurialis* represented as a monstrous dragon**  *frontispiece*

Illuminated drawing from a German alchemical ms., *c.* 1600, in the collection of Paul Mellon (now in the Yale University Library). It replaces an almost identical woodcut from Nazari, *Della tramutatione metallica sogni tre* (Brescia, 1599), reproduced in *Paracelsica.* P: Yale Univ. Library.

**B1. A fish meal, with statue of the hermaphrodite**

Miniature from "Le livre des ansienes estoires," in British Museum MS. Add. 15268 (13th cent.), fol. 242ᵛ. P: British Museum.

**B2. The *filius* or *rex* in the form of a hermaphrodite**

Woodcut from *Rosarium philosophorum* (second part of *De alchimia,* 1550), fol. X, iiiᵛ (copy in author's collection).

**B3. The Rebis**

Painting from "Das Buch der hl. Dreifaltigkeit . . . und Beschreibung der Heimlichkeit von Veränderung der Metallen"

xiii

(1420), in the Codex Germanicus 598, Staatsbibliothek, Munich. P: Staatsbibliothek.

B4. Melusina as the *aqua permanens*
Woodcut in Reusner, *Pandora* (1588), p. 249 (copy in author's collection).

B5. The anima as Melusina
Drawing from a variant of the Ripley *Scrowle* (1588), British Museum MS. Sloane 5025. P: British Museum.

B6. The King's Son and Hermes on a mountain
Engraving from Lambspringk, "De lapide philosophico," fig. XII, in *Musaeum hermeticum* (1678), p. 365. P: C. G. Jung Institute.

B7. The Pelican, in which the distillation takes place
Page from Rhenanus, *Solis e puteo* (1613), as reproduced in *Paracelsica.*

*all following page* 152


For "The Philosophical Tree"

Figs. 1–32. Drawings, paintings, etc., by patients in analysis
Author's collection, except Fig. 9: from Gerhard Adler, *Studies in Analytical Psychology*, pl. 12, reproduced by courtesy of Dr. Adler; Figs. 22, 25, 27, 30, and 31 (a design in embroidery): C. G. Jung Institute.

*all following page* 272

# I

# COMMENTARY ON
# "THE SECRET OF THE GOLDEN
# FLOWER"

[In late 1929, in Munich, Jung and the sinologist Richard Wilhelm published *Das Geheimnis der goldenen Blüte: Ein chinesisches Lebensbuch,* consisting of Wilhelm's translation of an ancient Chinese text, *T'ai I Chin Hua Tsung Chih* (Secret of the Golden Flower), with his notes and discussion of the text, and a "European commentary" by Jung. Earlier the same year, the two authors had published in the *Europäische Revue* (Berlin), V: 2/8 (Nov.), 530–42, a much abbreviated version entitled "Tschang Scheng Schu; Die Kunst das menschliche Leben zu verlängern" (i.e., "Ch'ang Sheng Shu; The Art of Prolonging Life"), an alternative title of the "Golden Flower."

[In 1931, Jung's and Wilhelm's joint work appeared in English as *The Secret of the Golden Flower: A Chinese Book of Life,* translated by Cary F. Baynes (London and New York), containing as an appendix Jung's memorial address for Wilhelm, who had died in 1930. (For "In Memory of Richard Wilhelm," see Vol. 15 of the *Collected Works.*)

[A second, revised edition of the German original was published in 1938 (Zurich), with a special foreword by Jung and his Wilhelm memorial address. Two more (essentially unaltered) editions followed, and in 1957 appeared a fifth, entirely reset edition (Zurich), which added a related text, the *Hui Ming Ching,* and a new foreword by Salome Wilhelm, the translator's widow.

[Mrs. Baynes prepared a revision of her translation, and this appeared in 1962 (New York and London), including Jung's foreword and the additional Wilhelm material. (Her revised translation of Jung's commentary alone had appeared in an anthology, *Psyche and Symbol,* edited by Violet S. de Laszlo, Anchor Books, New York, 1958.)

[The following translation of Jung's commentary and his foreword is based closely on Mrs. Baynes' version, from which some of the editorial notes have also been taken over. Four pictures of the stages of meditation, from the *Hui Ming Ching,* which accompanied the "Golden Flower" text, have been reproduced because of their pertinence to Jung's commentary; and the examples of European mandalas have been retained, though most of them were published, in a different context, in "Concerning Mandala Symbolism," Vol. 9, part i, of the *Collected Works.* The chapters have been given numbers.

—EDITORS.]

# FOREWORD TO THE SECOND GERMAN EDITION

My deceased friend, Richard Wilhelm, co-author of this book, sent me the text of *The Secret of the Golden Flower* at a time that was crucial for my own work. This was in 1928. I had been investigating the processes of the collective unconscious since the year 1913, and had obtained results that seemed to me questionable in more than one respect. They not only lay far beyond everything known to "academic" psychology, but they also overstepped the bounds of any medical, purely personal, psychology. They confronted me with an extensive phenomenology to which hitherto known categories and methods could no longer be applied. My results, based on fifteen years of effort, seemed inconclusive, because no possibility of comparison offered itself. I knew of no realm of human experience with which I might have backed up my findings with some degree of assurance. The only analogies—and these, I must say, were far removed in time —I found scattered among the reports of the heresiologists. This connection did not in any way ease my task; on the contrary, it made it more difficult, because the Gnostic systems consist only in small part of immediate psychic experiences, the greater part being speculative and systematizing recensions. Since we possess only very few complete texts, and since most of what is known comes from the reports of Christian opponents, we have, to say the least, an inadequate knowledge of the history as well as the content of this strange and confused literature, which is so difficult to evaluate. Moreover, considering the fact that a period of not less than seventeen to eighteen hundred years separates us from that age, support from that quarter seemed to me extraordinarily risky. Again, the connections were for the most part of a subsidiary nature and left gaps at just the most important points, so that I found it impossible to make use of the Gnostic material.

3

The text that Wilhelm sent me helped me out of this difficulty. It contained exactly those items I had long sought for in vain among the Gnostics. Thus the text afforded me a welcome opportunity to publish, at least in provisional form, some of the essential results of my investigations.

At that time it seemed to me a matter of no importance that *The Secret of the Golden Flower* is not only a Taoist text concerned with Chinese yoga, but is also an alchemical treatise. A deeper study of the Latin treatises has taught me better and has shown me that the alchemical character of the text is of prime significance, though I shall not go into this point more closely here. I would only like to emphasize that it was the text of the *Golden Flower* that first put me on the right track. For in medieval alchemy we have the long-sought connecting link between Gnosis and the processes of the collective unconscious that can be observed in modern man.[1]

I would like to take this opportunity to draw attention to certain misunderstandings to which even well-informed readers of this book have succumbed. Not infrequently people thought that my purpose in publishing it was to put into the hands of the public a recipe for achieving happiness. In total misapprehension of all that I say in my commentary, these readers tried to imitate the "method" described in the Chinese text. Let us hope these representatives of spiritual profundity were few in number!

Another misunderstanding gave rise to the opinion that, in my commentary, I was to some extent describing my own therapeutic method, which, it was said, consisted in my instilling Eastern ideas into my patients for therapeutic purposes. I do not believe there is anything in my commentary that lends itself to that sort of superstition. In any case such an opinion is altogether erroneous, and is based on the widespread view that psychology was invented for a specific purpose and is not an empirical science. To this category belongs the superficial as well as unintelligent opinion that the idea of the collective unconscious is "metaphysical." On the contrary, it is an *empirical* concept to

---

[1] The reader will find more about this in two essays published by me in the *Eranos Jahrbuch 1936* and *1937*. [This material is now contained in *Psychology and Alchemy*, Parts II and III.—EDITORS.]

be put alongside the concept of instinct, as is obvious to anyone who will read with some attention.

C. G. J.

*Küsnacht/Zurich, 1938*

# 1. DIFFICULTIES ENCOUNTERED BY A EUROPEAN IN TRYING TO UNDERSTAND THE EAST

1     A thorough Westerner in feeling, I cannot but be profoundly impressed by the strangeness of this Chinese text. It is true that some knowledge of Eastern religions and philosophies helps my intellect and my intuition to understand these things up to a point, just as I can understand the paradoxes of primitive beliefs in terms of "ethnology" or "comparative religion." This is of course the Western way of hiding one's heart under the cloak of so-called scientific understanding. We do it partly because the *misérable vanité des savants* fears and rejects with horror any sign of living sympathy, and partly because sympathetic understanding might transform contact with an alien spirit into an experience that has to be taken seriously. Our so-called scientific objectivity would have reserved this text for the philological acumen of sinologists, and would have guarded it jealously from any other interpretation. But Richard Wilhelm penetrated too deeply into the secret and mysterious vitality of Chinese wisdom to allow such a pearl of intuitive insight to disappear into the pigeon-holes of specialists. I am greatly honoured that his choice of a psychological commentator has fallen upon me.

2     This, however, involves the risk that this precious example of more-than-specialist insight will be swallowed by still another specialism. Nevertheless, anyone who belittles the merits of Western science is undermining the foundations of the Western mind. Science is not indeed a perfect instrument, but it is a superb and invaluable tool that works harm only when it is taken as an end in itself. Science must serve; it errs when it usurps the throne. It must be ready to serve all its branches, for each, because of its insufficiency, has need of support from the others. Science is the tool of the Western mind, and with it one can open more doors than with bare hands. It is part and parcel of

our understanding, and it obscures our insight only when it claims that the understanding it conveys is the only kind there is. The East teaches us another, broader, more profound, and higher understanding—understanding through life. We know this only by hearsay, as a shadowy sentiment expressing a vague religiosity, and we are fond of putting "Oriental wisdom" in quotation marks and banishing it to the dim region of faith and superstition. But that is wholly to misunderstand the realism of the East. Texts of this kind do not consist of the sentimental, overwrought mystical intuitions of pathological cranks and recluses, but are based on the practical insights of highly evolved Chinese minds, which we have not the slightest justification for undervaluing.

3    This assertion may seem bold, perhaps, and is likely to cause a good deal of head-shaking. Nor is that surprising, considering how little people know about the material. Its strangeness is indeed so arresting that our puzzlement as to how and where the Chinese world of thought might be joined to ours is quite understandable. The usual mistake of Western man when faced with this problem of grasping the ideas of the East is like that of the student in *Faust.* Misled by the devil, he contemptuously turns his back on science and, carried away by Eastern occultism, takes over yoga practices word for word and becomes a pitiable imitator. (Theosophy is our best example of this.) Thus he abandons the one sure foundation of the Western mind and loses himself in a mist of words and ideas that could never have originated in European brains and can never be profitably grafted upon them.

4    An ancient adept has said: "If the wrong man uses the right means, the right means work in the wrong way." [1] This Chinese saying, unfortunately only too true, stands in sharp contrast to our belief in the "right" method irrespective of the man who applies it. In reality, everything depends on the man and little or nothing on the method. The method is merely the path, the direction taken by a man; the way he acts is the true expression of his nature. If it ceases to be this, the method is nothing more than an affectation, something artificially pieced on, rootless and sapless, serving only the illegitimate goal of self-deception. It becomes a means of fooling oneself and of evading what may

1 [*The Secret of the Golden Flower* (1962 edn.), p. 63.]

7

perhaps be the implacable law of one's being. This is far removed from the earthiness and self-reliance of Chinese thought.
It is a denial of one's own nature, a self-betrayal to strange and
unclean gods, a cowardly trick for the purpose of feigning mental
superiority, everything in fact that is profoundly contrary to the
spirit of the Chinese "method." For these insights spring from a
way of life that is complete, genuine, and true to itself; from
that ancient, cultural life of China which grew logically and organically from the deepest instincts, and which, for us, is forever
inaccessible and impossible to imitate.

5      Western imitation is a tragic misunderstanding of the psychology of the East, every bit as sterile as the modern escapades
to New Mexico, the blissful South Sea islands, and central Af-
rica, where "the primitive life" is played at in deadly earnest
while Western man secretly evades his menacing duties, his *Hic
Rhodus hic salta*. It is not for us to imitate what is foreign to our
organism or to play the missionary; our task is to build up our
Western civilization, which sickens with a thousand ills. This
has to be done on the spot, and by the European just as he is,
with all his Western ordinariness, his marriage problems, his
neuroses, his social and political delusions, and his whole philosophical disorientation.

6      We should do well to confess at once that, fundamentally, we
do not understand the utter unworldliness of a text like this—
that actually we do not want to understand it. Have we, perhaps,
a dim suspicion that a mental attitude which can direct the
glance inward to that extent is detached from the world only
because these people have so completely fulfilled the instinctive
demands of their natures that there is nothing to prevent them
from glimpsing the invisible essence of things? Can it be that the
precondition for such a vision is liberation from the ambitions
and passions that bind us to the visible world, and does not this
liberation come from the sensible fulfilment of instinctive demands rather than from the premature and fear-ridden repression of them? Are our eyes opened to the spirit only when the
laws of the earth are obeyed? Anyone who knows the history of
Chinese culture and has carefully studied the *I Ching*, that book
of wisdom which for thousands of years has permeated all Chinese thought, will not lightly wave these doubts aside. He will
be aware that the views set forth in our text are nothing extraor-

dinary to the Chinese, but are actually inescapable psychological conclusions.

7    For a long time the spirit, and the sufferings of the spirit, were positive values and the things most worth striving for in our peculiar Christian culture. Only in the course of the nineteenth century, when spirit began to degenerate into intellect, did a reaction set in against the unbearable dominance of intellectualism, and this led to the unpardonable mistake of confusing intellect with spirit and blaming the latter for the misdeeds of the former. The intellect does indeed do harm to the soul when it dares to possess itself of the heritage of the spirit. It is in no way fitted to do this, for spirit is something higher than intellect since it embraces the latter and includes the feelings as well. It is a guiding principle of life that strives towards superhuman, shining heights. Opposed to this *yang* principle is the dark, feminine, earthbound *yin,* whose emotionality and instinctuality reach back into the depths of time and down into the labyrinth of the physiological continuum. No doubt these are purely intuitive ideas, but one can hardly dispense with them if one is trying to understand the nature of the human psyche. The Chinese could not do without them because, as the history of Chinese philosophy shows, they never strayed so far from the central psychic facts as to lose themselves in a one-sided over-development and over-valuation of a single psychic function. They never failed to acknowledge the paradoxicality and polarity of all life. The opposites always balanced one another—a sign of high culture. One-sidedness, though it lends momentum, is a mark of barbarism. The reaction that is now beginning in the West against the intellect in favour of feeling, or in favour of intuition, seems to me a sign of cultural advance, a widening of consciousness beyond the narrow confines of a tyrannical intellect.

8    I have no wish to depreciate the tremendous differentiation of the Western intellect; compared with it the Eastern intellect must be described as childish. (Naturally this has nothing to do with intelligence.) If we should succeed in elevating another, and possibly even a third psychic function to the dignified position accorded to the intellect, then the West might expect to surpass the East by a very great margin. Therefore it is sad indeed when the European departs from his own nature and

imitates the East or "affects" it in any way. The possibilities open to him would be so much greater if he would remain true to himself and evolve out of his own nature all that the East has brought forth in the course of the millennia.

9      In general, and looked at from the incurably externalistic standpoint of the intellect, it would seem as if the things the East values so highly were not worth striving for. Certainly the intellect alone cannot comprehend the practical importance Eastern ideas might have for us, and that is why it can classify them as philosophical and ethnological curiosities and nothing more. The lack of comprehension goes so far that even learned sinologists have not understood the practical use of the *I Ching*, and consider the book to be no more than a collection of abstruse magic spells.

## 2. MODERN PSYCHOLOGY OFFERS A POSSIBILITY OF UNDERSTANDING

10     Observations made in my practical work have opened out to me a quite new and unexpected approach to Eastern wisdom. In saying this I should like to emphasize that I did not have any knowledge, however inadequate, of Chinese philosophy as a starting point. On the contrary, when I began my career as a psychiatrist and psychotherapist, I was completely ignorant of Chinese philosophy, and only later did my professional experience show me that in my technique I had been unconsciously following that secret way which for centuries had been the preoccupation of the best minds of the East. This could be taken for a subjective fancy—which was one reason for my previous reluctance to publish anything on the subject—but Richard Wilhelm, that great interpreter of the soul of China, enthusiastically confirmed the parallel and thus gave me the courage to write about a Chinese text that belongs entirely to the mysterious shadowland of the Eastern mind. At the same time—and this is the extraordinary thing—its content forms a living parallel to what takes place in the psychic development of my patients, none of whom is Chinese.

11     In order to make this strange fact more intelligible to the reader, it must be pointed out that just as the human body shows a common anatomy over and above all racial differences, so, too, the human psyche possesses a common substratum transcending all differences in culture and consciousness. I have called this substratum the collective unconscious. This unconscious psyche, common to all mankind, does not consist merely of contents capable of becoming conscious, but of latent predispositions towards identical reactions. The collective unconscious is simply the psychic expression of the identity of brain structure irrespective of all racial differences. This explains the analogy, sometimes even identity, between the various myth motifs and

11

symbols, and the possibility of human communication in general. The various lines of psychic development start from one common stock whose roots reach back into the most distant past. This also accounts for the psychological parallelisms with animals.

12      In purely psychological terms this means that mankind has common instincts of ideation and action. All conscious ideation and action have developed on the basis of these unconscious archetypal patterns and always remain dependent on them. This is especially the case when consciousness has not attained any high degree of clarity, when in all its functions it is more dependent on the instincts than on the conscious will, more governed by affect than by rational judgment. This ensures a primitive state of psychic health, but it immediately becomes lack of adaptation when circumstances arise that call for a higher moral effort. Instincts suffice only for a nature that remains more or less constant. An individual who is guided more by the unconscious than by conscious choice therefore tends towards marked psychic conservatism. This is the reason why the primitive does not change in the course of thousands of years, and also why he fears anything strange and unusual. It might easily lead to maladaptation, and thus to the greatest psychic dangers—to a kind of neurosis, in fact. A higher and wider consciousness resulting from the assimilation of the unfamiliar tends, on the other hand, towards autonomy, and rebels against the old gods who are nothing other than those mighty, primordial images that hitherto have held our consciousness in thrall.

13      The stronger and more independent our consciousness becomes, and with it the conscious will, the more the unconscious is thrust into the background, and the easier it is for the evolving consciousness to emancipate itself from the unconscious, archetypal pattern. Gaining in freedom, it bursts the bonds of mere instinctuality and finally reaches a condition of instinctual atrophy. This uprooted consciousness can no longer appeal to the authority of the primordial images; it has Promethean freedom, but it also suffers from godless hybris. It soars above the earth and above mankind, but the danger of its sudden collapse is there, not of course in the case of every individual, but for the weaker members of the community, who then, again like Prometheus, are chained to the Caucasus of the unconscious. The

wise Chinese would say in the words of the *I Ching*: When *yang* has reached its greatest strength, the dark power of *yin* is born within its depths, for night begins at midday when *yang* breaks up and begins to change into *yin*.

14    The doctor is in a position to see this cycle of changes translated literally into life. He sees, for instance, a successful businessman attaining all his desires regardless of death and the devil, and then, having retired at the height of his success, speedily falling into a neurosis, which turns him into a querulous old woman, fastens him to his bed, and finally destroys him. The picture is complete even to the change from masculine to feminine. An exact parallel to this is the story of Nebuchadnezzar in the Book of Daniel, and Caesarean madness in general. Similar cases of one-sided exaggeration of the conscious standpoint, and the resultant *yin*-reaction from the unconscious, form no small part of the psychiatrist's clientele in our time, which so overvalues the conscious will as to believe that "where there's a will there's a way." Not that I wish to detract in the least from the high moral value of the will. Consciousness and the will may well continue to be considered the highest cultural achievements of humanity. But of what use is a morality that destroys the man? To bring the will and the capacity to achieve it into harmony seems to me to require more than morality. Morality *à tout prix* can be a sign of barbarism—more often wisdom is better. But perhaps I look at this with the eyes of a physician who has to mend the ills following in the wake of one-sided cultural achievements.

15    Be that as it may, the fact remains that a consciousness heightened by an inevitable one-sidedness gets so far out of touch with the primordial images that a breakdown ensues. Long before the actual catastrophe, the signs of error announce themselves in atrophy of instinct, nervousness, disorientation, entanglement in impossible situations and problems. Medical investigation then discovers an unconscious that is in full revolt against the conscious values, and that therefore cannot possibly be assimilated to consciousness, while the reverse is altogether out of the question. We are confronted with an apparently irreconcilable conflict before which human reason stands helpless, with nothing to offer except sham solutions or dubious compromises. If these evasions are rejected, we are faced with the

question as to what has become of the much needed unity of the personality, and with the necessity of seeking it. At this point begins the path travelled by the East since the beginning of things. Quite obviously, the Chinese were able to follow this path because they never succeeded in forcing the opposites in man's nature so far apart that all conscious connection between them was lost. The Chinese owe this all-inclusive consciousness to the fact that, as in the case of the primitive mentality, the yea and the nay have remained in their original proximity. Nonetheless, it was impossible not to feel the clash of opposites, so they sought a way of life in which they would be what the Indians call *nirdvandva,* free of opposites.

16     Our text is concerned with this way, and the same problem comes up with my patients also. There could be no greater mistake than for a Westerner to take up the direct practice of Chinese yoga, for that would merely strengthen his will and consciousness against the unconscious and bring about the very effect to be avoided. The neurosis would then simply be intensified. It cannot be emphasized enough that we are not Orientals, and that we have an entirely different point of departure in these matters. It would also be a great mistake to suppose that this is the path every neurotic must travel, or that it is the solution at every stage of the neurotic problem. It is appropriate only in those cases where consciousness has reached an abnormal degree of development and has diverged too far from the unconscious. This is the *sine qua non* of the process. Nothing would be more wrong than to open this way to neurotics who are ill on account of an excessive predominance of the unconscious. For the same reason, this way of development has scarcely any meaning before the middle of life (normally between the ages of thirty-five and forty), and if entered upon too soon can be decidedly injurious.

17     As I have said, the essential reason which prompted me to look for a new way was the fact that the fundamental problem of the patient seemed to me insoluble unless violence was done to one or the other side of his nature. I had always worked with the temperamental conviction that at bottom there are no insoluble problems, and experience justified me in so far as I have often seen patients simply outgrow a problem that had destroyed others. This "outgrowing," as I formerly called it, proved on

further investigation to be a new level of consciousness. Some higher or wider interest appeared on the patient's horizon, and through this broadening of his outlook the insoluble problem lost its urgency. It was not solved logically in its own terms, but faded out when confronted with a new and stronger life urge. It was not repressed and made unconscious, but merely appeared in a different light, and so really did become different. What, on a lower level, had led to the wildest conflicts and to panicky outbursts of emotion, from the higher level of personality now looked like a storm in the valley seen from the mountain top. This does not mean that the storm is robbed of its reality, but instead of being in it one is above it. But since, in a psychic sense, we are both valley and mountain, it might seem a vain illusion to deem oneself beyond what is human. One certainly does feel the affect and is shaken and tormented by it, yet at the same time one is aware of a higher consciousness looking on which prevents one from becoming identical with the affect, a consciousness which regards the affect as an object, and can say, "I *know* that I suffer." What our text says of indolence, "Indolence of which a man is conscious, and indolence of which he is unconscious, are a thousand miles apart," [1] holds true in the highest degree of affect.

18      Now and then it happened in my practice that a patient grew beyond himself because of unknown potentialities, and this became an experience of prime importance to me. In the meantime, I had learned that all the greatest and most important problems of life are fundamentally insoluble. They must be so, for they express the necessary polarity inherent in every self-regulating system. They can never be solved, but only outgrown. I therefore asked myself whether this outgrowing, this possibility of further psychic development, was not the normal thing, and whether getting stuck in a conflict was pathological. Everyone must possess that higher level, at least in embryonic form, and must under favourable circumstances be able to develop this potentiality. When I examined the course of development in patients who quietly, and as if unconsciously, outgrew themselves, I saw that their fates had something in common. The new thing came to them from obscure possibilities either outside or inside themselves; they accepted it and grew with its

1 [*The Golden Flower* (1962 edn.), p. 42.]

help. It seemed to me typical that some took the new thing from outside themselves, others from inside; or rather, that it grew into some persons from without, and into others from within. But the new thing never came exclusively either from within or from without. If it came from outside, it became a profound inner experience; if it came from inside, it became an outer happening. In no case was it conjured into existence intentionally or by conscious willing, but rather seemed to be borne along on the stream of time.

19    We are so greatly tempted to turn everything into a purpose and a method that I deliberately express myself in very abstract terms in order to avoid prejudicing the reader in one way or the other. The new thing must not be pigeon-holed under any heading, for then it becomes a recipe to be used mechanically, and it would again be a case of the "right means in the hands of the wrong man." I have been deeply impressed by the fact that the new thing prepared by fate seldom or never comes up to conscious expectations. And still more remarkable, though the new thing goes against deeply rooted instincts as we have known them, it is a strangely appropriate expression of the total personality, an expression which one could not imagine in a more complete form.

20    What did these people do in order to bring about the development that set them free? As far as I could see they did nothing (*wu wei*[2]) but let things happen. As Master Lü-tsu teaches in our text, the light circulates according to its own law if one does not give up one's ordinary occupation. The art of letting things happen, action through non-action, letting go of oneself as taught by Meister Eckhart, became for me the key that opens the door to the way. We must be able to let things happen in the psyche. For us, this is an art of which most people know nothing. Consciousness is forever interfering, helping, correcting, and negating, never leaving the psychic processes to grow in peace. It would be simple enough, if only simplicity were not the most difficult of all things. To begin with, the task consists solely in observing objectively how a fragment of fantasy develops. Nothing could be simpler, and yet right here the difficulties begin. Apparently one has no fantasy fragments—or yes, there's one, but it is too stupid! Dozens of good reasons are brought against

2 [The Taoist idea of action through non-action.—C.F.B.]

it. One cannot concentrate on it—it is too boring—what would come of it anyway—it is "nothing but" this or that, and so on. The conscious mind raises innumerable objections, in fact it often seems bent on blotting out the spontaneous fantasy activity in spite of real insight and in spite of the firm determination to allow the psychic process to go forward without interference. Occasionally there is a veritable cramp of consciousness.

21    If one is successful in overcoming the initial difficulties, criticism is still likely to start in afterwards in the attempt to interpret the fantasy, to classify it, to aestheticize it, or to devalue it. The temptation to do this is almost irresistible. After it has been faithfully observed, free rein can be given to the impatience of the conscious mind; in fact it must be given, or obstructive resistances will develop. But each time the fantasy material is to be produced, the activity of consciousness must be switched off again.

22    In most cases the results of these efforts are not very encouraging at first. Usually they consist of tenuous webs of fantasy that give no clear indication of their origin or their goal. Also, the way of getting at the fantasies varies with individuals. For many people, it is easiest to write them down; others visualize them, and others again draw or paint them with or without visualization. If there is a high degree of conscious cramp, often only the hands are capable of fantasy; they model or draw figures that are sometimes quite foreign to the conscious mind.

23    These exercises must be continued until the cramp in the conscious mind is relaxed, in other words, until one can let things happen, which is the next goal of the exercise. In this way a new attitude is created, an attitude that accepts the irrational and the incomprehensible simply because it is happening. This attitude would be poison for a person who is already overwhelmed by the things that happen to him, but it is of the greatest value for one who selects, from among the things that happen, only those that are acceptable to his conscious judgment, and is gradually drawn out of the stream of life into a stagnant backwater.

24    At this point, the way travelled by the two types mentioned earlier seems to divide. Both have learned to accept what comes to them. (As Master Lü-tsu teaches: "When occupations come to us, we must accept them; when things come to us, we must un-

17

derstand them from the ground up." [3]) One man will now take chiefly what comes to him from outside, and the other what comes from inside. Moreover, the law of life demands that what they take from outside and inside will be the very things that were always excluded before. This reversal of one's nature brings an enlargement, a heightening and enrichment of the personality, if the previous values are retained alongside the change—provided that these values are not mere illusions. If they are not held fast, the individual will swing too far to the other side, slipping from fitness into unfitness, from adaptedness into unadaptedness, and even from rationality into insanity. The way is not without danger. Everything good is costly, and the development of personality is one of the most costly of all things. It is a matter of saying yea to oneself, of taking oneself as the most serious of tasks, of being conscious of everything one does, and keeping it constantly before one's eyes in all its dubious aspects—truly a task that taxes us to the utmost.

25    A Chinese can always fall back on the authority of his whole civilization. If he starts on the long way, he is doing what is recognized as being the best thing he could possibly do. But the Westerner who wishes to set out on this way, if he is really serious about it, has all authority against him—intellectual, moral, and religious. That is why it is infinitely easier for him to imitate the Chinese way and leave the troublesome European behind him, or else to seek the way back to the medievalism of the Christian Church and barricade himself behind the wall separating true Christians from the poor heathen and other ethnographic curiosities encamped outside. Aesthetic or intellectual flirtations with life and fate come to an abrupt halt here: the step to higher consciousness leaves us without a rearguard and without shelter. The individual must devote himself to the way with all his energy, for it is only by means of his integrity that he can go further, and his integrity alone can guarantee that his way will not turn out to be an absurd misadventure.

26    Whether his fate comes to him from without or from within, the experiences and happenings on the way remain the same. Therefore I need say nothing about the manifold outer and inner events, the endless variety of which I could never exhaust in any case. Nor would this be relevant to the text under discus-

3 [*The Golden Flower* (1962 edn.), p. 51.]

sion. On the other hand, there is much to be said about the psychic states that accompany the process of development. These states are expressed symbolically in our text, and in the very same symbols that for many years have been familiar to me from my practice.

# 3. THE FUNDAMENTAL CONCEPTS

## A. TAO

27     The great difficulty in interpreting this and similar texts[1] for the European is that the author always starts from the central point, from the point we would call the goal, the highest and ultimate insight he has attained. Thus our Chinese author begins with ideas that demand such a comprehensive understanding that a person of discriminating mind has the feeling he would be guilty of ridiculous pretension, or even of talking utter nonsense, if he should embark on an intellectual discourse on the subtle psychic experiences of the greatest minds of the East. Our text, for example, begins: "That which exists through itself is called the Way." The *Hui Ming Ching* begins with the words: "The subtlest secret of the Tao is human nature and life."

28     It is characteristic of the Western mind that it has no word for Tao. The Chinese character is made up of the sign for "head" and the sign for "going." Wilhelm translates Tao by *Sinn* (Meaning). Others translate it as "way," "providence," or even as "God," as the Jesuits do. This illustrates our difficulty. "Head" can be taken as consciousness,[2] and "going" as travelling a way, and the idea would then be: to go consciously, or the conscious way. This is borne out by the fact that the "light of heaven" which "dwells between the eyes" as the "heart of heaven" is used synonymously with Tao. Human nature and life are contained in the "light of heaven" and, according to the *Hui Ming Ching,* are the most important secrets of the Tao. "Light" is the symbolical equivalent of consciousness, and the nature of consciousness is expressed by analogies with light. The *Hui Ming Ching* is introduced with the verses:

1 Cf. the *Hui Ming Ching* (Book of Consciousness and Life) in *The Secret of the Golden Flower* (1962 edn.), pp. 69ff.
2 The head is also the "seat of heavenly light."

> If thou wouldst complete the diamond body with no outflowing,
> Diligently heat the roots of consciousness[3] and life.
> Kindle light in the blessed country ever close at hand,
> And there hidden, let thy true self always dwell.

29 These verses contain a sort of alchemical instruction as to the method or way of producing the "diamond body," which is also mentioned in our text. "Heating" is necessary; that is, there must be an intensification of consciousness in order that light may be kindled in the dwelling place of the true self. Not only consciousness, but life itself must be intensified: the union of these two produces conscious life. According to the *Hui Ming Ching*, the ancient sages knew how to bridge the gap between consciousness and life because they cultivated both. In this way the *sheli,* the immortal body, is "melted out" and the "great Tao is completed." [4]

30 If we take the Tao to be the method or conscious way by which to unite what is separated, we have probably come close to the psychological meaning of the concept. At all events, the separation of consciousness and life cannot very well be understood as anything else than what I described earlier as an aberration or uprooting of consciousness. There can be no doubt, either, that the realization of the opposite hidden in the unconscious—the process of "reversal"—signifies reunion with the unconscious laws of our being, and the purpose of this reunion is the attainment of conscious life or, expressed in Chinese terms, the realization of the Tao.

### B. THE CIRCULAR MOVEMENT AND THE CENTRE

31 As I have pointed out, the union of opposites[5] on a higher level of consciousness is not a rational thing, nor is it a matter of will; it is a process of psychic development that expresses itself in symbols. Historically, this process has always been represented in symbols, and today the development of personality is still depicted in symbolic form. I discovered this fact in the following way. The spontaneous fantasy products I discussed earlier

---

[3] In the *Hui Ming Ching,* "human nature" (*hsing*) and "consciousness" (*hui*) are used interchangeably.
[4] *The Golden Flower* (1962 edn.), p. 70.
[5] Cf. *Psychological Types,* ch. V.

become more profound and gradually concentrate into abstract structures that apparently represent "principles" in the sense of Gnostic *archai*. When the fantasies take the form chiefly of thoughts, intuitive formulations of dimly felt laws or principles emerge, which at first tend to be dramatized or personified. (We shall come back to these again later.) If the fantasies are drawn, symbols appear that are chiefly of the *mandala*[6] type. *Mandala* means "circle," more especially a magic circle. Mandalas are found not only throughout the East but also among us. The early Middle Ages are especially rich in Christian mandalas; most of them show Christ in the centre, with the four evangelists, or their symbols, at the cardinal points. This conception must be a very ancient one, because Horus and his four sons were represented in the same way by the Egyptians.[7] It is known that Horus with his four sons has close connections with Christ and the four evangelists. An unmistakable and very interesting mandala can be found in Jakob Böhme's book *XL Questions concerning the Soule*.[8] It is clear that this mandala represents a psychocosmic system strongly coloured by Christian ideas. Böhme calls it the "Philosophical Eye" [9] or the "Mirror of Wisdom," by which is obviously meant a *summa* of secret knowledge. Most mandalas take the form of a flower, cross, or wheel, and show a distinct tendency towards a quaternary structure reminiscent of the Pythagorean *tetraktys,* the basic number. Mandalas of this sort also occur as sand paintings in the religious ceremonies of the Pueblo and Navaho Indians.[10] But the most beautiful mandalas are, of course, those of the East, especially the ones found in Tibetan Buddhism, which also contain the symbols mentioned in our text. Mandala drawings are often produced by the mentally ill, among them persons who certainly

6 [For a fuller discussion of the *mandala,* see "A Study in the Process of Individuation" and "Concerning Mandala Symbolism" in *The Archetypes and the Collective Unconscious*. For examples of European mandalas, see below, after p. 56.—EDITORS.]

7 Cf. Wallis Budge, *The Gods of the Egyptians*.

8 [The mandala is reproduced in "A Study in the Process of Individuation," p. 297.]

9 Cf. the Chinese concept of the heavenly light between the eyes.

10 Matthews, "The Mountain Chant: A Navajo Ceremony" (1887), and Stevenson, "Ceremonial of Hasjelti Dailjis" (1891).

did not have the least idea of any of the connections we have discussed.[11]

32     Among my patients I have come across cases of women who did not draw mandalas but danced them instead. In India there is a special name for this: *mandala nrithya*, the mandala dance. The dance figures express the same meanings as the drawings. My patients can say very little about the meaning of the symbols but are fascinated by them and find that they somehow express and have an effect on their subjective psychic state.

33     Our text promises to "reveal the secret of the Golden Flower of the great *One*." The golden flower is the light, and the light of heaven is the Tao. The golden flower is a mandala symbol I have often met with in the material brought me by my patients. It is drawn either seen from above as a regular geometric pattern, or in profile as a blossom growing from a plant. The plant is frequently a structure in brilliant fiery colours growing out of a bed of darkness, and carrying the blossom of light at the top, a symbol recalling the Christmas tree. Such drawings also suggest the origin of the golden flower, for according to the *Hui Ming Ching* the "germinal vesicle" is the "dragon castle at the bottom of the sea." [12] Other synonyms are the "yellow castle," the "heavenly heart," the "terrace of living," the "square inch field of the square foot house," the "purple hall of the city of jade," the "dark pass," the "space of former heaven." [13] It is also called the "boundary region of the snow mountains," the "primordial pass," the "kingdom of greatest joy," the "boundless country," the "altar upon which consciousness and life are made." "If a dying man does not know this germinal vesicle," says the *Hui Ming Ching*, "he will not find the unity of consciousness and life in a thousand births, nor in ten thousand aeons." [14]

34     The beginning, where everything is still one, and which therefore appears as the highest goal, lies at the bottom of the sea, in the darkness of the unconscious. In the germinal vesicle, consciousness and life (or human nature and life, *hsing-ming*) are still a "unity, inseparably mixed like the sparks in the

11 The mandala of a somnambulist is reproduced in *Psychiatric Studies*, p. 40.
12 *The Golden Flower* (1962 edn.), p. 70.
13 [Ibid., p. 22.]
14 [Ibid., p. 70.]

refining furnace." "Within the germinal vesicle is the fire of the ruler." "All the sages began their work at the germinal vesicle." [15] Note the fire analogies. I know a series of European mandala drawings in which something like a plant seed surrounded by membranes is shown floating in the water. Then, from the depths below, fire penetrates the seed and makes it grow, causing a great golden flower to unfold from the germinal vesicle.

35    This symbolism refers to a quasi-alchemical process of refining and ennobling. Darkness gives birth to light; out of the "lead of the water region" grows the noble gold; what is unconscious becomes conscious in the form of a living process of growth. (Indian Kundalini yoga offers a perfect analogy.[16]) In this way the union of consciousness and life takes place.

36    When my patients produce these mandala pictures, it is naturally not the result of suggestion; similar pictures were being made long before I knew their meaning or their connection with the practices of the East, which, at that time, were wholly unknown to me. The pictures arise quite spontaneously, and from two sources. One source is the unconscious, which spontaneously produces fantasies of this kind; the other is life, which, if lived with utter devotion, brings an intuition of the self, of one's own individual being. When the self finds expression in such drawings, the unconscious reacts by enforcing an attitude of devotion to life. For in complete agreement with the Eastern view, the mandala is not only a means of expression but also produces an effect. It reacts upon its maker. Age-old magical effects lie hidden in this symbol, for it is derived from the "protective circle" or "charmed circle," whose magic has been preserved in countless folk customs.[17] It has the obvious purpose of drawing a *sulcus primigenius*, a magical furrow around the centre, the temple or *temenos* (sacred precinct), of the innermost personality, in order to prevent an "outflowing" or to guard by apotropaic means against distracting influences from outside. Magical practices are nothing but projections of psychic events, which then exert a counter-influence on the psyche and put a

[15] [Ibid., p. 71.]
[16] Cf. Avalon, *The Serpent Power.*
[17] Cf. the excellent collection in Knuchel, *Die Umwandlung in Kult, Magie und Rechtsbrauch.*

kind of spell upon the personality. Through the ritual action, attention and interest are led back to the inner, sacred precinct, which is the source and goal of the psyche and contains the unity of life and consciousness. The unity once possessed has been lost, and must now be found again.

37    The unity of the two, life and consciousness, is the Tao, whose symbol would be the central white light, also mentioned in the *Bardo Thödol*.[18] This light dwells in the "square inch" or in the "face," that is, between the eyes. It is a visualization of the "creative point," of that which has intensity without extension, in conjunction with the "field of the square inch," the symbol for that which has extension. The two together make the Tao. Human nature (*hsing*) and consciousness (*hui*) are expressed in light symbolism, and therefore have the quality of intensity, while life (*ming*) would coincide with extensity. The one is *yang*-like, the other *yin*-like. The afore-mentioned mandala of a somnambulist girl, aged fifteen and a half, whom I had under observation some thirty years ago, shows in its centre a spring of "Primary Force," or life energy without extension, whose emanations clash with a contrary spatial principle—in complete analogy with the basic idea of our Chinese text.

38    The "enclosure," or *circumambulatio,* is expressed in our text by the idea of "circulation." The circulation is not merely movement in a circle, but means, on the one hand, the marking off of the sacred precinct and, on the other, fixation and concentration. The sun-wheel begins to turn; the sun is activated and begins its course—in other words, the Tao begins to work and takes the lead. Action is reversed into non-action; everything peripheral is subordinated to the command of the centre. Therefore it is said: "Movement is only another name for mastery." Psychologically, this circulation would be the "movement in a circle around oneself," so that all sides of the personality become involved. "The poles of light and darkness are made to rotate," that is, there is an alternation of day and night.

39    The circular movement thus has the moral significance of activating the light and dark forces of human nature, and together with them all psychological opposites of whatever kind they may be. It is nothing less than self-knowledge by means of self-

18 Evans-Wentz, *The Tibetan Book of the Dead.*

25

brooding (Sanskrit *tapas*). A similar archetypal concept of a perfect being is that of the Platonic man, round on all sides and uniting within himself the two sexes.

40    One of the best modern parallels is the description which Edward Maitland, the biographer of Anna Kingsford,[19] gave of his central experience. He had discovered that when reflecting on an idea, related ideas became visible, so to speak, in a long series apparently reaching back to their source, which to him was the divine spirit. By concentrating on this series, he tried to penetrate to their origin. He writes:

> I was absolutely without knowledge or expectation when I yielded to the impulse to make the attempt. I simply experimented on a faculty . . . being seated at my writing-table the while in order to record the results as they came, and resolved to retain my hold on my outer and circumferential consciousness, no matter how far towards my inner and central consciousness I might go. For I knew not whether I should be able to regain the former if I once quitted my hold of it, or to recollect the facts of the experience. At length I achieved my object, though only by a strong effort, the tension occasioned by the endeavour to keep both extremes of the consciousness in view at once being very great.
>
> Once well started on my quest, I found myself traversing a succession of spheres or belts . . . the impression produced being that of mounting a vast ladder stretching from the circumference towards the centre of a system, which was at once my own system, the solar system, the universal system, the three systems being at once diverse and identical. . . . Presently, by a supreme, and what I felt must be a final effort . . . I succeeded in polarizing the whole of the convergent rays of my consciousness into the desired focus. And at the same instant, as if through the sudden ignition of the rays thus fused into a unity, I found myself confronted with a glory of unspeakable whiteness and brightness, and of a lustre so intense as well-nigh to beat me back. . . . But though feeling that I had to explore further, I resolved to make assurance doubly sure by piercing if I could the almost blinding lustre, and seeing what it enshrined. With a great effort I succeeded, and the glance revealed to me that which I had felt must be there. . . . It was the dual form of the Son . . . the unmanifest made manifest, the unformulate formulate, the unindividuate individuate, God as the Lord, proving through His duality that God is Substance as well as Force, Love

---

19 *Anna Kingsford, Her Life, Letters, Diary, and Work*, pp. 129f. I am indebted for this reference to my colleague, Dr. Beatrice Hinkle, New York.

as well as Will, Feminine as well as Masculine, Mother as well as Father.

41     He found that God is two in one, like man. Besides this he noticed something that our text also emphasizes, namely "suspension of breathing." He says ordinary breathing stopped and was replaced by an internal respiration, "as if by breathing of a distinct personality within and other than the physical organism." He took this being to be the "entelechy" of Aristotle and the "inner Christ" of the apostle Paul, the "spiritual and substantial individuality engendered within the physical and phenomenal personality, and representing, therefore, the rebirth of man on a plane transcending the material."

42     This genuine[20] experience contains all the essential symbols of our text. The phenomenon itself, the vision of light, is an experience common to many mystics, and one that is undoubtedly of the greatest significance, because at all times and places it proves to be something unconditioned and absolute, a combination of supreme power and profound meaning. Hildegard of Bingen, an outstanding personality quite apart from her mysticism, writes in much the same way about her central vision:

> Since my childhood I have always seen a light in my soul, but not with the outer eyes, nor through the thoughts of my heart; neither do the five outer senses take part in this vision. . . . The light I perceive is not of a local kind, but is much brighter than the cloud which supports the sun. I cannot distinguish height, breadth, or length in it. . . . What I see or learn in such a vision stays long in my memory. I see, hear, and know in the same moment. . . . I cannot recognize any sort of form in this light, although I sometimes see in it another light that is known to me as the living light. . . . While I am enjoying the spectacle of this light, all sadness and sorrow vanish from my memory.[21]

43     I myself know a few individuals who have had personal experience of this phenomenon. So far as I have been able to understand it, it seems to have to do with an acute state of consciousness, as intense as it is abstract, a "detached" consciousness

---

[20] Such experiences are genuine, but their genuineness does not prove that all the conclusions or convictions forming their content are necessarily sound. Even in cases of lunacy one comes across perfectly valid psychic experiences. [Author's note added in the first (1931) English edition.]

[21] [*Acta S. Hildegardis*, in Migne, *P.L.*, vol. 197, col. 18.]

(see infra, pars. 64ff.), which, as Hildegard implies, brings into awareness areas of psychic happenings ordinarily covered in darkness. The fact that the general bodily sensations disappear during the experience suggests that their specific energy has been withdrawn and has apparently gone towards heightening the clarity of consciousness. As a rule, the phenomenon is spontaneous, coming and going on its own initiative. Its effect is astonishing in that it almost always brings about a solution of psychic complications and frees the inner personality from emotional and intellectual entanglements, thus creating a unity of being which is universally felt as "liberation."

44      Such a symbolic unity cannot be attained by the conscious will because consciousness is always partisan. Its opponent is the collective unconscious, which does not understand the language of the conscious mind. Therefore it is necessary to have the magic of the symbol which contains those primitive analogies that speak to the unconscious. The unconscious can be reached and expressed only by symbols, and for this reason the process of individuation can never do without the symbol. The symbol is the primitive exponent of the unconscious, but at the same time an idea that corresponds to the highest intuitions of the conscious mind.

45      The oldest mandala drawing known to me is a palaeolithic "sun-wheel," recently discovered in Rhodesia. It, too, is based on the quaternary principle. Things reaching so far back into human history naturally touch upon the deepest layers of the unconscious, and can have a powerful effect on it even when our conscious language proves itself to be quite impotent. Such things cannot be thought up but must grow again from the forgotten depths if they are to express the supreme insights of consciousness and the loftiest intuitions of the spirit, and in this way fuse the uniqueness of present-day consciousness with the age-old past of life.

## 4. PHENOMENA OF THE WAY

### A. THE DISINTEGRATION OF CONSCIOUSNESS

46    The meeting between the narrowly delimited, but intensely clear, individual consciousness and the vast expanse of the collective unconscious is dangerous, because the unconscious has a decidedly disintegrating effect on consciousness. According to the *Hui Ming Ching,* this effect belongs to the peculiar phenomena of Chinese yoga. It says: "Every separate thought takes shape and becomes visible in colour and form. The total spiritual power unfolds its traces. . . ." [1] The relevant illustration in the text [stage 4] shows a sage sunk in contemplation, his head surrounded by tongues of fire, out of which five human figures emerge; these five again split up into twenty-five smaller figures.[2] This would be a schizophrenic process if it were to become a permanent state. Therefore the *Hui Ming Ching,* as though warning the adept, continues: "The shapes formed by the spirit-fire are only empty colours and forms. The light of human nature (*hsing*) shines back on the primordial, the true."

47    So we can understand why the figure of the protecting circle was seized upon. It is intended to prevent the "outflowing" and to protect the unity of consciousness from being burst asunder by the unconscious. The text seeks to mitigate the disintegrating effect of the unconscious by describing the thought-figures as "empty colours and forms," thus depotentiating them as much as possible. This idea runs through the whole of Buddhism (especially the Mahayana form) and, in the instructions to the dead in *The Tibetan Book of the Dead,* it is even pushed to the point of explaining the favourable as well as the unfavourable gods as illusions still to be overcome. It is certainly not within the com-

---

[1] *The Golden Flower* (1962 edn.), pp. 76f. [For elucidation of the four pictures from the *Hui Ming Ching* reproduced here, see ibid., pp. 75–77.—EDITORS.]
[2] These are recollections of earlier incarnations that arise during contemplation.

坐禪圖

Stage 1: Gathering the light

*Pages 30–33:*
Four stages of meditation,
with inspirational texts,
from the *Hui Ming Ching*

嬰兒現形圖

此時丹熱更須慈母惜嬰兒

氣穴法名無盡藏
藏包於寂寂包空
我問空中誰氏子
他云是你主人翁

術泯坐卧
擁護守雛
綿綿若存
念茲在茲

夫婦媾之真
子娠孕之子
傳其情交媾
持泯其氣樹
其神隨加大
小俱得其真

潛龍今已化飛龍
變現神通不可窮
一朝跳出珠光外
渾身直到紫微宮

神水浴液
沆瀣根休
內外無塵
長養聖胎

他日雲飛方見真人朝上帝

Stage 2: Origin of a new being in the place of power

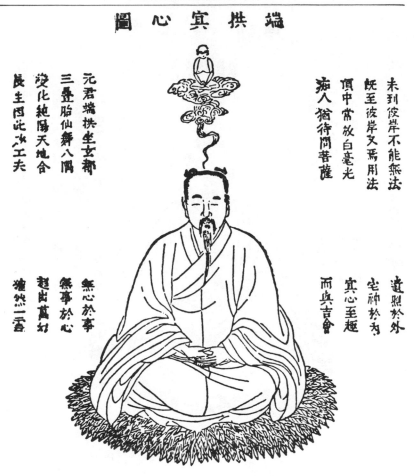

圖心宊拱端

Stage 3: Separation of the spirit-body for independent existence

32

Stage 4: The centre in the midst of conditions

petence of the psychologist to establish the metaphysical truth or untruth of this idea; he must be content to determine so far as possible its psychic effect. He need not bother himself whether the shape in question is a transcendental illusion or not, since faith, not science, has to decide this point. In any case we are moving on ground that for a long time has seemed to be outside the domain of science and was looked upon as wholly illusory. But there is no scientific justification for such an assumption; the substantiality of these things is not a scientific problem since it lies beyond the range of human perception and judgment and thus beyond any possibility of proof. The psychologist is concerned not with the substantiality of these complexes but with psychic experience. Without a doubt they are psychic contents that can be experienced, and their autonomy is equally indubitable. They are fragmentary psychic systems that either appear spontaneously in ecstatic states and evoke powerful impressions and effects, or else, in mental disturbances, become fixed in the form of delusions and hallucinations and consequently destroy the unity of the personality.

48    Psychiatrists are always ready to believe in toxins and the like, and even to explain schizophrenia in these terms, putting next to no emphasis on the psychic contents as such. On the other hand, in psychogenic disturbances (hysteria, obsessional neurosis, etc.), where toxic effects and cell degeneration are out of the question, split-off complexes are to be found similar to those occurring in somnambulistic states. Freud would like to explain these spontaneous split-offs as due to unconscious repression of sexuality, but this explanation is by no means valid in all cases, because contents that the conscious mind cannot assimilate can emerge just as spontaneously out of the unconscious, and in these cases the repression theory is inadequate. Moreover, their autonomy can be observed in daily life, in affects that obstinately obtrude themselves against our will and, in spite of the most strenuous efforts to repress them, overwhelm the ego and force it under their control. No wonder the primitive sees in these moods a state of possession or sets them down to a loss of soul. Our colloquial speech reflects the same thing when we say: "I don't know what has got into him today," "he is possessed of the devil," "he is beside himself," etc. Even legal practice recognizes a degree of diminished responsibility in a state of affect.

Autonomous psychic contents are thus quite common experiences for us. Such contents have a disintegrating effect upon consciousness.

49      But besides the ordinary, familiar affects there are subtler, more complex emotional states that can no longer be described as affects pure and simple but are fragmentary psychic systems. The more complicated they are, the more they have the character of personalities. As constituents of the psychic personality, they necessarily have the character of "persons." Such fragmentary systems are to be found especially in mental diseases, in cases of psychogenic splitting of the personality (double personality), and of course in mediumistic phenomena. They are also encountered in the phenomenology of religion. Many of the earlier gods developed from "persons" into personified ideas, and finally into abstract ideas. Activated unconscious contents always appear at first as projections upon the outside world, but in the course of mental development they are gradually assimilated by consciousness and reshaped into conscious ideas that then forfeit their originally autonomous and personal character. As we know, some of the old gods have become, via astrology, nothing more than descriptive attributes (martial, jovial, saturnine, erotic, logical, lunatic, and so on).

50      The instructions of *The Tibetan Book of the Dead* in particular help us to see how great is the danger that consciousness will be disintegrated by these figures. Again and again the dead are instructed not to take these shapes for truth, not to confuse their murky appearance with the pure white light of *Dharma-kaya* (the divine body of truth). That is to say, they are not to project the *one* light of highest consciousness into concretized figures and dissolve it into a plurality of autonomous fragmentary systems. If there were no danger of this, and if these systems did not represent menacingly autonomous and disintegrative tendencies, such urgent instructions would not be necessary. Allowing for the simpler, polytheistic attitude of the Eastern mind, these instructions would be almost the equivalent of warning a Christian not to let himself be blinded by the illusion of a personal God, let alone by the Trinity and the host of angels and saints.

51      If tendencies towards dissociation were not inherent in the human psyche, fragmentary psychic systems would never have

35

been split off; in other words, neither spirits nor gods would ever have come into existence. That is also the reason why our time has become so utterly godless and profane: we lack all knowledge of the unconscious psyche and pursue the cult of consciousness to the exclusion of all else. Our true religion is a monotheism of consciousness, a possession by it, coupled with a fanatical denial of the existence of fragmentary autonomous systems. But we differ from the Buddhist yoga doctrines in that we even deny that these systems are experienceable. This entails a great psychic danger, because the autonomous systems then behave like any other repressed contents: they necessarily induce wrong attitudes since the repressed material reappears in consciousness in a spurious form. This is strikingly evident in every case of neurosis and also holds true for the collective psychic phenomena. Our time has committed a fatal error; we believe we can criticize the facts of religion intellectually. Like Laplace, we think God is a hypothesis that can be subjected to intellectual treatment, to be affirmed or denied. We completely forget that the reason mankind believes in the "daemon" has nothing whatever to do with external factors, but is simply due to a naïve awareness of the tremendous inner effect of autonomous fragmentary systems. This effect is not abolished by criticizing it—or rather, the name we have given it—or by describing the name as false. The effect is collectively present all the time; the autonomous systems are always at work, for the fundamental structure of the unconscious is not affected by the deviations of our ephemeral consciousness.

52      If we deny the existence of the autonomous systems, imagining that we have got rid of them by a mere critique of the name, then the effect which they still continue to exert can no longer be understood, nor can they be assimilated to consciousness. They become an inexplicable source of disturbance which we finally assume must exist somewhere outside ourselves. The resultant projection creates a dangerous situation in that the disturbing effects are now attributed to a wicked will outside ourselves, which is naturally not to be found anywhere but with our neighbour *de l'autre côté de la rivière*. This leads to collective delusions, "incidents," revolutions, war—in a word, to destructive mass psychoses.

53      Insanity is possession by an unconscious content that, as

such, is not assimilated to consciousness, nor can it be assimilated since the very existence of such contents is denied. This attitude is equivalent to saying: "We no longer have any fear of God and believe that everything is to be judged by human standards." This hybris or narrowness of consciousness is always the shortest way to the insane asylum. I recommend the excellent account of this problem in H. G. Wells's novel *Christina Alberta's Father*, and Schreber's *Memoirs of My Nervous Illness*.

54 It must stir a sympathetic chord in the enlightened European when it is said in the *Hui Ming Ching* that the "shapes formed by the spirit-fire are only empty colours and forms." That sounds thoroughly European and seems to suit our reason to a T. We think we can congratulate ourselves on having already reached such a pinnacle of clarity, imagining that we have left all these phantasmal gods far behind. But what we have left behind are only verbal spectres, not the psychic facts that were responsible for the birth of the gods. We are still as much possessed by autonomous psychic contents as if they were Olympians. Today they are called phobias, obsessions, and so forth; in a word, neurotic symptoms. The gods have become diseases; Zeus no longer rules Olympus but rather the solar plexus, and produces curious specimens for the doctor's consulting room, or disorders the brains of politicians and journalists who unwittingly let loose psychic epidemics on the world.

55 So it is better for Western man if he does not know too much about the secret insights of the Oriental sages to begin with, for, as I have said, it would be a case of the "right means in the hands of the wrong man." Instead of allowing himself to be convinced once more that the daemon is an illusion, he ought to experience once more the reality of this illusion. He should learn to acknowledge these psychic forces anew, and not wait until his moods, nervous states, and delusions make it clear in the most painful way that he is not the only master in his house. His dissociative tendencies are actual psychic personalities possessing a differential reality. They are "real" when they are not recognized as real and consequently projected; they are relatively real when they are brought into relationship with consciousness (in religious terms, when a cult exists); but they are unreal to the extent that consciousness detaches itself from its contents. This last stage, however, is reached only when life has been lived so

37

exhaustively and with such devotion that no obligations remain unfulfilled, when no desires that cannot safely be sacrificed stand in the way of inner detachment from the world. It is futile to lie to ourselves about this. Wherever we are still attached, we are still possessed; and when we are possessed, there is one stronger than us who possesses us. ("Verily I say unto thee, thou shalt by no means come out thence, until thou hast paid the uttermost farthing.") It is not a matter of indifference whether one calls something a "mania" or a "god." To serve a mania is detestable and undignified, but to serve a god is full of meaning and promise because it is an act of submission to a higher, invisible, and spiritual being. The personification enables us to see the relative reality of the autonomous system, and not only makes its assimilation possible but also depotentiates the daemonic forces of life. When the god is not acknowledged, egomania develops, and out of this mania comes sickness.

56    Yoga takes acknowledgment of the gods as something self-evident. Its secret instruction is intended only for those whose consciousness is struggling to disentangle itself from the dae-monic forces of life in order to enter into the ultimate undivided unity, the "centre of emptiness," where "dwells the god of ut-most emptiness and life," as our text says.[3] "To hear such a teaching is difficult to attain in thousands of aeons." Evidently the veil of Maya cannot be lifted by a merely rational resolve; it requires a most thoroughgoing and persevering preparation consisting in the full payment of all debts to life. For as long as unconditional attachment through *cupiditas* exists, the veil is not lifted and the heights of a consciousness free of contents and free of illusion are not attained; nor can any trick nor any deceit bring this about. It is an ideal that can ultimately be realized only in death. Until then there are the real and relatively real figures of the unconscious.

### B. ANIMUS AND ANIMA

57    According to our text, among the figures of the unconscious there are not only the gods but also the animus and anima. The word *hun* is translated by Wilhelm as animus. And indeed, the term "animus" seems appropriate for *hun,* the character for

3 [*The Golden Flower,* p. 22.]

which is made up of the sign for "clouds" and that for "demon." Thus *hun* means "cloud-demon," a higher breath-soul belonging to the *yang* principle and therefore masculine. After death, *hun* rises upward and becomes *shen,* the "expanding and self-revealing" spirit or god. "Anima," called *p'o,* and written with the characters for "white" and "demon," that is, "white ghost," belongs to the lower, earthbound, bodily soul, the *yin* principle, and is therefore feminine. After death, it sinks downward and becomes *kuei* (demon), often explained as "the one who returns" (i.e., to earth), a revenant, a ghost. The fact that the animus and anima part after death and go their ways independently shows that, for the Chinese consciousness, they are distinguishable psychic factors; originally they were united in "the one effective, true human nature," but in the "house of the Creative" they are two. "The animus is in the heavenly heart." "By day it lives in the eyes [i.e., in consciousness]; at night it houses in the liver." It is "that which we have received from the great emptiness, that which is identical in form with the primal beginning." The anima, on the other hand, is the "energy of the heavy and the turbid"; it clings to the bodily, fleshly heart. Its effects are "sensuous desires and impulses to anger." "Whoever is sombre and moody on waking . . . is fettered to the anima." [4]

58     Many years ago, before Wilhelm acquainted me with this text, I used the term "anima" [5] in a way quite analogous to the Chinese definition of *p'o,* and of course entirely apart from any metaphysical premise. To the psychologist, the anima is not a transcendental being but something quite within the range of experience, as the Chinese definition makes clear: affective states are immediate experiences. Why, then, speak of the anima and not simply of moods? The reason is that affects have an autonomous character, and therefore most people are under their power. But affects are delimitable contents of consciousness, parts of the personality. As such, they partake of its character and can easily be personified—a process that still continues today, as I have shown. The personification is not an idle invention, since a person roused by affect does not show a neutral character but a quite distinct one, entirely different from his ordinary character. Careful investigation has shown that the

4 [*The Golden Flower,* pp. 26 and 28.]
5 Cf. *Two Essays on Analytical Psychology,* pars. 296ff.

affective character of a man has feminine traits. From this psychological fact derives the Chinese doctrine of the *p'o* soul as well as my own concept of the anima. Deeper introspection or ecstatic experience reveals the existence of a feminine figure in the unconscious, hence the feminine name: anima, psyche, *Seele.* The anima can be defined as the image or archetype or deposit of all the experiences of man with woman. As we know, the poets have often sung the anima's praises.[6] The connection of anima with ghost in the Chinese concept is of interest to parapsychologists inasmuch as mediumistic "controls" are very often of the opposite sex.

59     Although Wilhelm's translation of *hun* as "animus" seems justified to me, nonetheless I had important reasons for choosing the term "Logos" for a man's "spirit," for his clarity of consciousness and his rationality, rather than the otherwise appropriate expression "animus." Chinese philosophers are spared certain difficulties that aggravate the task of the Western psychologist. Like all mental and spiritual activity in ancient times, Chinese philosophy was exclusively a component of the masculine world. Its concepts were never understood psychologically, and therefore were never examined as to how far they also apply to the feminine psyche. But the psychologist cannot possibly ignore the existence of woman and her special psychology. For these reasons I would prefer to translate *hun* as it appears in man by "Logos." Wilhelm in his translation uses Logos for *hsing,* which can also be translated as "essence of human nature" or "creative consciousness." After death, *hun* becomes *shen,* "spirit," which is very close, in the philosophical sense, to *hsing.* Since the Chinese concepts are not logical in our sense of the word, but are intuitive ideas, their meanings can only be elicited from the ways in which they are used and from the constitution of the written characters, or from such relationships as obtain between *hun* and *shen. Hun,* then, would be the light of consciousness and reason in man, originally coming from the *logos spermatikos* of *hsing,* and returning after death through *shen* to the Tao. Used in this sense the expression "Logos" would be especially appropriate, since it includes the idea of a universal being, and thus covers the fact that man's clarity of consciousness and rationality are something universal rather than indi-

6 Cf. *Psychological Types,* ch. V.

40

vidually unique. The Logos principle is nothing personal, but is in the deepest sense impersonal, and thus in sharp contrast to the anima, which is a personal demon expressing itself in thoroughly personal moods ("animosity"!).

60    In view of these psychological facts, I have reserved the term "animus" strictly for women, because, to answer a famous question, *mulier non habet animam, sed animum*. Feminine psychology exhibits an element that is the counterpart of a man's anima. Primarily, it is not of an affective nature but is a quasi-intellectual factor best described by the word "prejudice." The conscious side of woman corresponds to the emotional side of man, not to his "mind." Mind makes up the "soul," or better, the "animus" of woman, and just as the anima of a man consists of inferior relatedness, full of affect, so the animus of woman consists of inferior judgments, or better, opinions. As it is made up of a plurality of preconceived opinions, the animus is far less susceptible of personification by a single figure, but appears more often as a group or crowd. (A good example of this from parapsychology is the "Imperator" group in the case of Mrs. Piper.[7]) On a low level the animus is an inferior Logos, a caricature of the differentiated masculine mind, just as on a low level the anima is a caricature of the feminine Eros. To pursue the parallel further, we could say that just as *hun* corresponds to *hsing*, translated by Wilhelm as Logos, so the Eros of woman corresponds to *ming*, "fate" or "destiny," interpreted by Wilhelm as Eros. Eros is an interweaving; Logos is differentiating knowledge, clarifying light. Eros is relatedness, Logos is discrimination and detachment. Hence the inferior Logos of woman's animus appears as something quite unrelated, as an inaccessible prejudice, or as an opinion which, irritatingly enough, has nothing to do with the essential nature of the object.

61    I have often been accused of personifying the anima and animus as mythology does, but this accusation would be justified only if it could be proved that I concretize these concepts in a mythological manner for psychological use. I must declare once and for all that the personification is not an invention of mine,

---

[7] Cf. Hyslop, *Science and a Future Life*, pp. 113ff. [Mrs. Leonora Piper, an American psychic medium active about 1890–1910 in the U.S. and England, was studied by William James, Mrs. Henry Sidgwick, Hyslop, and others. A group of five of her psychic controls had the collective name "Imperator."—EDITORS.]

but is inherent in the nature of the phenomena. It would be unscientific to overlook the fact that the anima is a psychic, and therefore a personal, autonomous system. None of the people who make the charge against me would hesitate for a second to say, "I dreamed of Mr. X," whereas, strictly speaking, he dreamed only of a representation of Mr. X. The anima is nothing but a representation of the personal nature of the autonomous system in question. What the nature of this system is in a transcendental sense, that is, beyond the bounds of experience, we cannot know.

62    I have defined the anima as a personification of the unconscious in general, and have taken it as a bridge to the unconscious, in other words, as a function of relationship to the unconscious. There is an interesting point in our text in this connection. The text says that consciousness (that is, the personal consciousness) comes from the anima. Since the Western mind is based wholly on the standpoint of consciousness, it must define the anima in the way I have done. But the East, based as it is on the standpoint of the unconscious, sees consciousness as an effect of the anima. And there can be no doubt that consciousness does originate in the unconscious. This is something we are apt to forget, and therefore we are always attempting to identify the psyche with consciousness, or at least to represent the unconscious as a derivative or an effect of consciousness (as in the Freudian repression theory). But, for the reasons given above, it is essential that we do not detract from the reality of the unconscious, and that the figures of the unconscious be understood as real and effective factors. The person who has understood what is meant by psychic reality need have no fear that he has fallen back into primitive demonology. If the unconscious figures are not acknowledged as spontaneous agents, we become victims of a one-sided belief in the power of consciousness, leading finally to acute tension. A catastrophe is then bound to happen because, for all our consciousness, the dark powers of the psyche have been overlooked. It is not we who personify them; they have a personal nature from the very beginning. Only when this is thoroughly recognized can we think of depersonalizing them, of "subjugating the anima," as our text expresses it.

63    Here again we find an enormous difference between Buddhism and the Western attitude of mind, and again there is a

dangerous semblance of agreement. Yoga teaching rejects all fantasy products and we do the same, but the East does so for entirely different reasons. In the East there is an abundance of conceptions and teachings that give full expression to the creative fantasy; in fact, protection is needed against an excess of it. We, on the other hand, regard fantasy as worthless subjective day-dreaming. Naturally the figures of the unconscious do not appear in the form of abstractions stripped of all imaginative trappings; on the contrary, they are embedded in a web of fantasies of extraordinary variety and bewildering profusion. The East can reject these fantasies because it has long since extracted their essence and condensed it in profound teachings. But we have never even experienced these fantasies, much less extracted their quintessence. We still have a large stretch of experience to catch up with, and only when we have found the sense in apparent nonsense can we separate the valuable from the worthless. We can be sure that the essence we extract from our experience will be quite different from what the East offers us today. The East came to its knowledge of inner things in childlike ignorance of the external world. We, on the other hand, shall explore the psyche and its depths supported by an immense knowledge of history and science. At present our knowledge of the external world is the greatest obstacle to introspection, but the psychological need will overcome all obstructions. We are already building up a psychology, a science that gives us the key to the very things that the East discovered—and discovered only through abnormal psychic states.

## 5. THE DETACHMENT OF CONSCIOUSNESS FROM THE OBJECT

<sup>64</sup> By understanding the unconscious we free ourselves from its domination. That is really also the purpose of the instructions in our text. The pupil is taught to concentrate on the light of the innermost region and, at the same time, to free himself from all outer and inner entanglements. His vital impulses are guided towards a consciousness void of content, which nevertheless permits all contents to exist. The *Hui Ming Ching*[1] says of this detachment:

A halo of light surrounds the world of the law.
We forget one another, quiet and pure, all-powerful and empty.
The emptiness is irradiated by the light of the heart of heaven.
The water of the sea is smooth and mirrors the moon in its surface.
The clouds disappear in blue space; the mountains shine clear.
Consciousness reverts to contemplation; the moon-disk rests alone.

<sup>65</sup> This description of fulfilment depicts a psychic state that can best be characterized as a detachment of consciousness from the world and a withdrawal to a point outside it, so to speak. Thus consciousness is at the same time empty and not empty. It is no longer preoccupied with the images of things but merely contains them. The fullness of the world which hitherto pressed upon it has lost none of its richness and beauty, but it no longer dominates. The magical claim of things has ceased because the interweaving of consciousness with world has come to an end. The unconscious is not projected any more, and so the primordial *participation mystique* with things is abolished. Consciousness is no longer preoccupied with compulsive plans but dissolves in contemplative vision.

<sup>66</sup> How did this effect come about? (We assume, of course, that the Chinese author was first of all not a liar; secondly, that he was of sound mind; and thirdly, that he was an unusually intel-

[1] [*The Golden Flower* (1962 edn.), pp. 77f.]

ligent man.) To understand and explain this detachment, we must proceed by a roundabout way. It is an effect that cannot be simulated; nothing would be more childish than to make such a psychic state an object of aesthetic experiment. I know this effect very well from my practice; it is the therapeutic effect *par excellence,* for which I labour with my students and patients, and it consists in the dissolution of *participation mystique.* By a stroke of genius, Lévy-Bruhl singled out what he called *participation mystique* as being the hallmark of the primitive mentality.[2] What he meant by it is simply the indefinitely large remnant of non-differentiation between subject and object, which is still so great among primitives that it cannot fail to strike our European consciousness very forcibly. When there is no consciousness of the difference between subject and object, an unconscious identity prevails. The unconscious is then projected into the object, and the object is introjected into the subject, becoming part of his psychology. Then plants and animals behave like human beings, human beings are at the same time animals, and everything is alive with ghosts and gods. Civilized man naturally thinks he is miles above these things. Instead of that, he is often identified with his parents throughout his life, or with his affects and prejudices, and shamelessly accuses others of the things he will not see in himself. He too has a remnant of primitive unconsciousness, of non-differentiation between subject and object. Because of this, he is magically affected by all manner of people, things, and circumstances, he is beset by disturbing influences nearly as much as the primitive and therefore needs just as many apotropaic charms. He no longer works magic with medicine bags, amulets, and animal sacrifices, but with tranquillizers, neuroses, rationalism, cult of the will, etc.

67    But if the unconscious can be recognized as a co-determining factor along with consciousness, and if we can live in such a way that conscious and unconscious demands are taken into account as far as possible, then the centre of gravity of the total personality shifts its position. It is then no longer in the ego, which is merely the centre of consciousness, but in the hypothetical point between conscious and unconscious. This new centre might be called the self. If the transposition is successful, it does away with the *participation mystique* and results in a personality that

2 Lévy-Bruhl, *Primitive Mentality.*

suffers only in the lower storeys, as it were, but in its upper storeys is singularly detached from painful as well as from joyful happenings.

68    The production and birth of this superior personality is what is meant when our text speaks of the "holy fruit," the "diamond body," or any other kind of incorruptible body. Psychologically, these expressions symbolize an attitude that is beyond the reach of emotional entanglements and violent shocks—a consciousness detached from the world. I have reasons for believing that this attitude sets in after middle life and is a natural preparation for death. Death is psychologically as important as birth and, like it, is an integral part of life. What happens to the detached consciousness in the end is a question the psychologist cannot be expected to answer. Whatever his theoretical position he would hopelessly overstep the bounds of his scientific competence. He can only point out that the views of our text in regard to the timelessness of the detached consciousness are in harmony with the religious thought of all ages and with that of the overwhelming majority of mankind. Anyone who thought differently would be standing outside the human order and would, therefore, be suffering from a disturbed psychic equilibrium. As a doctor, I make every effort to strengthen the belief in immortality, especially with older patients when such questions come threateningly close. For, seen in correct psychological perspective, death is not an end but a goal, and life's inclination towards death begins as soon as the meridian is passed.

69    Chinese yoga philosophy is based upon this instinctive preparation for death as a goal. In analogy with the goal of the first half of life—procreation and reproduction, the means of perpetuating one's physical existence—it takes as the goal of spiritual existence the symbolic begetting and birth of a "spirit-body," or "breath-body," which ensures the continuity of detached consciousness. It is the birth of the pneumatic man, known to the European from antiquity, but which he seeks to produce by quite other symbols and magical practices, by faith and a Christian way of life. Here again we stand on a foundation quite different from that of the East. Again the text sounds as though it were not so very far from Christian ascetic morality, but nothing could be more mistaken than to assume that it actually means the same thing. Behind our text is a civilization thou-

sands of years old, one which is built up organically on primitive instincts and knows nothing of that brutal morality so suited to us as recently civilized Teutonic barbarians. For this reason the Chinese are without the impulse towards violent repression of the instincts that poisons our spirituality and makes it hysterically exaggerated. The man who lives with his instincts can also detach from them, and in just as natural a way as he lived with them. Any idea of heroic self-conquest would be entirely foreign to the spirit of our text, but that is what it would infallibly amount to if we followed the instructions literally.

70      We must never forget our historical antecedents. Only a little more than a thousand years ago we stumbled out of the crudest beginnings of polytheism into a highly developed Oriental religion which lifted the imaginative minds of half-savages to a height that in no way corresponded to their spiritual development. In order to keep to this height in some fashion or other, it was inevitable that the instinctual sphere should be largely repressed. Thus religious practice and morality took on a decidedly brutal, almost malignant, character. The repressed elements naturally did not develop, but went on vegetating in the unconscious, in their original barbarism. We would like to scale the heights of a philosophical religion, but in fact are incapable of it. To grow up to it is the most we can hope for. The Amfortas wound and the Faustian split in the Germanic man are still not healed; his unconscious is still loaded with contents that must first be made conscious before he can be free of them. Recently I received a letter from a former patient which describes the necessary transformation in simple but trenchant words. She writes:

Out of evil, much good has come to me. By keeping quiet, repressing nothing, remaining attentive, and by accepting reality—taking things as they are, and not as I wanted them to be—by doing all this, unusual knowledge has come to me, and unusual powers as well, such as I could never have imagined before. I always thought that when we accepted things they overpowered us in some way or other. This turns out not to be true at all, and it is only by accepting them that one can assume an attitude towards them.[3] So now I intend to play the game of life, being receptive to whatever comes to me, good and bad, sun and shadow forever alternating, and, in

3 Dissolution of *participation mystique*.

this way, also accepting my own nature with its positive and negative sides. Thus everything becomes more alive to me. What a fool I was! How I tried to force everything to go according to the way I thought it ought to!

71    Only on the basis of such an attitude, which renounces none of the Christian values won in the course of Christian development, but which, on the contrary, tries with Christian charity and forbearance to accept even the humblest things in one's own nature, will a higher level of consciousness and culture become possible. This attitude is religious in the truest sense, and therefore therapeutic, for all religions are therapies for the sorrows and disorders of the soul. The development of the Western intellect and will has given us an almost fiendish capacity for aping such an attitude, with apparent success, despite the protests of the unconscious. But it is only a matter of time before the counterposition asserts itself all the more harshly. Aping an attitude always produces an unstable situation that can be overthrown by the unconscious at any time. A safe foundation is found only when the instinctive premises of the unconscious win the same respect as the views of the conscious mind. No one should blind himself to the fact that this necessity of giving due consideration to the unconscious runs violently counter to our Western, and in particular the Protestant, cult of consciousness. Yet, though the new always seems to be the enemy of the old, anyone with a more than superficial desire to understand cannot fail to discover that without the most serious application of the Christian values we have acquired, the new integration can never take place.

## 6. THE FULFILMENT

72    A growing familiarity with the spirit of the East should be taken merely as a sign that we are beginning to relate to the alien elements within ourselves. Denial of our historical foundations would be sheer folly and would be the best way to bring about another uprooting of consciousness. Only by standing firmly on our own soil can we assimilate the spirit of the East.

73    Speaking of those who do not know where the true springs of secret power lie, an ancient adept says, "Worldly people lose their roots and cling to the treetops." The spirit of the East has grown out of the yellow earth, and our spirit can, and should, grow only out of our own earth. That is why I approach these problems in a way that has often been charged with "psychologism." If "psychology" were meant, I should indeed be flattered, for my aim as a psychologist is to dismiss without mercy the metaphysical claims of all esoteric teachings. The unavowed purpose of gaining power through words, inherent in all secret doctrines, ill accords with our profound ignorance, which we should have the modesty to admit. I quite deliberately bring everything that purports to be metaphysical into the daylight of psychological understanding, and do my best to prevent people from believing in nebulous power-words. Let the convinced Christian believe, by all means, for that is the duty he has taken upon himself; but whoever is not a Christian has forfeited the charisma of faith. (Perhaps he was cursed from birth with not being able to believe, but merely to know.) Therefore, he has no right to put his faith elsewhere. One cannot grasp anything metaphysically, one only can do so psychologically. Therefore I strip things of their metaphysical wrappings in order to make them objects of psychology. In that way I can at least extract something understandable from them and avail myself of it, and I also discover psychological facts and processes that before were veiled in symbols and beyond my comprehension. In doing so I

49

may perhaps be following in the footsteps of the faithful, and may possibly have similar experiences; and if in the end there should be something ineffably metaphysical behind it all, it would then have the best opportunity of showing itself.

74      My admiration for the great philosophers of the East is as genuine as my attitude towards their metaphysics is irreverent.[1] I suspect them of being symbolical psychologists, to whom no greater wrong could be done than to take them literally. If it were really metaphysics that they mean, it would be useless to try to understand them. But if it is psychology, we can not only understand them but can profit greatly by them, for then the so-called "metaphysical" comes within the range of experience. If I assume that God is absolute and beyond all human experience, he leaves me cold. I do not affect him, nor does he affect me. But if I know that he is a powerful impulse of my soul, at once I must concern myself with him, for then he can become important, even unpleasantly so, and can affect me in practical ways—which sounds horribly banal, like everything else that is real.

75      The epithet "psychologism" applies only to a fool who thinks he has his soul in his pocket. There are certainly more than enough such fools, for although we know how to talk big about the "soul," the depreciation of everything psychic is a typically Western prejudice. If I make use of the concept "autonomous psychic complex," my reader immediately comes up with the ready-made prejudice that it is "nothing but a psychic complex." How can we be so sure that the soul is "nothing but"? It is as if we did not know, or else continually forgot, that everything of which we are conscious is an image, and that image *is* psyche. The same people who think that God is depreciated if he is understood as something moved in the psyche, as well as the moving force of the psyche—i.e., as an autonomous complex —can be so plagued by uncontrollable affects and neurotic states that their wills and their whole philosophy of life fail them miserably. Is that a proof of the impotence of the psyche? Should Meister Eckhart be accused of "psychologism" when he says, "God must be born in the soul again and again"? I think the accusation of "psychologism" can be levelled only at an intellect

1 The Chinese philosophers—in contrast to the dogmatists of the West—are only grateful for such an attitude, because they also are masters of their gods. [Note by Richard Wilhelm in original edn.]

that denies the genuine nature of the autonomous complex and seeks to explain it rationalistically as the consequence of known causes, i.e., as something secondary and unreal. This is just as arrogant as the metaphysical assertion that seeks to make a God outside the range of our experience responsible for our psychic states. Psychologism is simply the counterpart of this metaphysical presumption, and is just as childish. Therefore it seems to me far more reasonable to accord the psyche the same validity as the empirical world, and to admit that the former has just as much "reality" as the latter. As I see it, the psyche is a world in which the ego is contained. Maybe there are fishes who believe that they contain the sea. We must rid ourselves of this habitual illusion of ours if we wish to consider metaphysical assertions from the standpoint of psychology.

76     A metaphysical assertion of this kind is the idea of the "diamond body," the incorruptible breath-body which grows in the golden flower or in the "field of the square inch." [2] This body is

2 Our text is somewhat unclear as to whether by "continuation of life" a survival after death or a prolongation of physical existence is meant. Expressions such as "elixir of life" and the like are exceedingly ambiguous. In the later additions to the text it is evident that the yoga instructions were also understood in a purely physical sense. To a primitive mind, there is nothing disturbing in this odd mixture of the physical and the spiritual, because life and death are by no means the complete opposites they are for us. (Particularly interesting in this connection, apart from the ethnological material, are the communications of the English "rescue circles" with their thoroughly archaic ideas.) The same ambiguity with regard to survival after death is found in early Christianity, where immortality depends on very similar assumptions, i.e., on the idea of a breath-body as the carrier of life. (Geley's paraphysiological theory would be the latest incarnation of this ancient idea.) But since in our text there are warnings about the superstitious use of it—warnings, for example, against the making of gold—we can safely insist on the spiritual purport of the instructions without contradicting their meaning. In the states which the instructions seek to induce the physical body plays an increasingly unimportant part anyway, since it is replaced by the breath-body (hence the importance of breath control in all yoga exercises). The breath-body is not something "spiritual" in our sense of the word. It is characteristic of Western man that he has split apart the physical and the spiritual for epistemological purposes. But these opposites exist together in the psyche and psychology must recognize this fact. "Psychic" means physical *and* spiritual. The ideas in our text all deal with this "intermediate" world which seems unclear and confused because the concept of psychic reality is not yet current among us, although it expresses life as it actually is. Without soul, spirit is as dead as matter, because both are artificial abstractions; whereas man originally regarded spirit as a volatile body, and matter as not lacking in soul.

a symbol for a remarkable psychological fact which, precisely because it is objective, first appears in forms dictated by the experience of biological life—that is, as fruit, embryo, child, living body, and so on. This fact could be best expressed by the words "It is not I who live, it lives me." The illusion of the supremacy of consciousness makes us say, "I live." Once this illusion is shattered by a recognition of the unconscious, the unconscious will appear as something objective in which the ego is included. The attitude towards the unconscious is then analogous to the feeling of the primitive to whom the existence of a son guarantees continuation of life—a feeling that can assume grotesque forms, as when the old Negro, angered at his son's disobedience, cried out, "There he stands with my body, but does not even obey me!"

77     It is, in fact, a change of feeling similar to that experienced by a father to whom a son has been born, a change known to us from the testimony of St. Paul: "Yet not I, but Christ liveth in me." The symbol "Christ" as "son of man" is an analogous psychic experience of a higher spiritual being who is invisibly born in the individual, a pneumatic body which is to serve us as a future dwelling, a body which, as Paul says, is put on like a garment ("For as many of you as have been baptized into Christ have put on Christ"). It is always a difficult thing to express, in intellectual terms, subtle feelings that are nevertheless infinitely important for the individual's life and well-being. It is, in a sense, the feeling that we have been "replaced," but without the connotation of having been "deposed." It is as if the guidance of life had passed over to an invisible centre. Nietzsche's metaphor, "in most loving bondage, free," would be appropriate here. Religious language is full of imagery depicting this feeling of free dependence, of calm acceptance.

78     This remarkable experience seems to me a consequence of the detachment of consciousness, thanks to which the subjective "I live" becomes the objective "It lives me." This state is felt to be higher than the previous one; it is really like a sort of release from the compulsion and impossible responsibility that are the inevitable results of *participation mystique*. This feeling of liberation fills Paul completely; the consciousness of being a child of God delivers one from the bondage of the blood. It is also a feeling of reconciliation with all that happens, for which

reason, according to the *Hui Ming Ching,* the gaze of one who has attained fulfilment turns back to the beauty of nature.

79  In the Pauline Christ symbol the supreme religious experiences of West and East confront one another: Christ the sorrow-laden hero, and the Golden Flower that blooms in the purple hall of the city of jade. What a contrast, what an unfathomable difference, what an abyss of history! A problem fit for the crowning work of a future psychologist!

80  Among the great religious problems of the present is one which has received scant attention, but which is in fact the main problem of our day: the evolution of the religious spirit. If we are to discuss it, we must emphasize the difference between East and West in their treatment of the "jewel," the central symbol. The West lays stress on the human incarnation, and even on the personality and historicity of Christ, whereas the East says: "Without beginning, without end, without past, without future." [3] The Christian subordinates himself to the superior divine person in expectation of his grace; but the Oriental knows that redemption depends on the work he does on himself. The Tao grows out of the individual. The *imitatio Christi* has this disadvantage: in the long run we worship as a divine example a man who embodied the deepest meaning of life, and then, out of sheer imitation, we forget to make real our own deepest meaning—self-realization. As a matter of fact, it is not altogether inconvenient to renounce one's own meaning. Had Jesus done so, he would probably have become a respectable carpenter and not a religious rebel to whom the same thing would naturally happen today as happened then.

81  The imitation of Christ might well be understood in a deeper sense. It could be taken as the duty to realize one's deepest conviction with the same courage and the same self-sacrifice shown by Jesus. Happily not everyone has the task of being a leader of humanity, or a great rebel; and so, after all, it might be possible for each to realize himself in his own way. This honesty might even become an ideal. Since great innovations always begin in the most unlikely places, the fact that people today are not nearly as ashamed of their nakedness as they used to be might be the beginning of a recognition of themselves as they really are. Hard upon this will follow an increasing recognition

3 *The Golden Flower* (1962 edn.), p. 77.

of many things that formerly were strictly taboo, for the reality of the earth will not forever remain veiled like the *virgines velandae* of Tertullian. Moral unmasking is but a step further in the same direction, and behold, there stands man as he is, and admits to himself that he is as he is. If he does this in a meaningless way he is just a muddled fool; but if he knows the significance of what he is doing he could belong to a higher order of man who makes real the Christ symbol, regardless of the suffering involved. It has often been observed that purely concrete taboos or magical rites in an early stage of a religion become in the next stage something psychic, or even purely spiritual symbols. An outward law becomes in the course of time an inward conviction. Thus it might easily happen to contemporary man, especially Protestants, that the person Jesus, now existing outside in the realm of history, might become the higher man within himself. Then we would have attained, in a European way, the psychological state corresponding to Eastern enlightenment.

82      All this is a step in the evolution of a higher consciousness on its way to unknown goals, and is not metaphysics as ordinarily understood. To that extent it is only "psychology," but to that extent, too, it is experienceable, understandable and—thank God—real, a reality we can do something with, a living reality full of possibilities. The fact that I am content with what can be experienced psychically, and reject the metaphysical, does not amount, as any intelligent person can see, to a gesture of scepticism or agnosticism aimed at faith and trust in higher powers, but means approximately the same as what Kant meant when he called the thing-in-itself a "merely negative borderline concept." Every statement about the transcendental is to be avoided because it is only a laughable presumption on the part of a human mind unconscious of its limitations. Therefore, when God or the Tao is named an impulse of the soul, or a psychic state, something has been said about the knowable only, but nothing about the unknowable, about which nothing can be determined.

# 7. CONCLUSION

83    The purpose of my commentary is to attempt to build a bridge of psychological understanding between East and West. The basis of every real understanding is man, and therefore I had to speak of human beings. This must be my excuse for having dealt only with general aspects, and for not having entered into technical details. Technical directions are valuable for those who know, for example, what a camera is, or a combustion engine, but they are useless for anyone who has no idea of such apparatus. Western man for whom I write is in an analogous position. Therefore it seemed to me important above all to emphasize the agreement between the psychic states and symbolisms of East and West. These analogies open a way to the inner chambers of the Eastern mind, a way that does not require the sacrifice of our own nature and does not confront us with the threat of being torn from our roots. Nor is it an intellectual telescope or microscope offering a view of no fundamental concern to us because it does not touch us. It is the way of suffering, seeking, and striving common to all civilized peoples; it is the tremendous experiment of becoming conscious, which nature has laid upon mankind, and which unites the most diverse cultures in a common task.

84    Western consciousness is by no means the only kind of consciousness there is; it is historically conditioned and geographically limited, and representative of only one part of mankind. The widening of our consciousness ought not to proceed at the expense of other kinds of consciousness; it should come about through the development of those elements of our psyche which are analogous to those of the alien psyche, just as the East cannot do without our technology, science, and industry. The European invasion of the East was an act of violence on a grand scale, and it has left us with the duty—*noblesse oblige*—of understanding the mind of the East. This is perhaps more necessary than we realize at present.

## EXAMPLES OF EUROPEAN MANDALAS

The pictures that now follow were produced in the way described in the text, by patients during the course of treatment.[1] The earliest picture dates from 1916. All the pictures were done independently of any Eastern influence. The *I Ching* hexagrams in picture No. 4 come from Legge's translation in the Sacred Books of the East series, but they were put into the picture only because their content seemed, to the university-trained patient, especially meaningful for her life. No European mandalas known to me (I have a fairly large collection) achieve the conventionally and traditionally established harmony and perfection of the Eastern mandala. I have made a choice of ten pictures from among an infinite variety of European mandalas, and they ought, as a whole, to illustrate clearly the parallelism between Eastern philosophy and the unconscious mental processes in the West.

[1] [The following mandalas are also published, with more detailed comments, in "Concerning Mandala Symbolism": A1 (fig. 9), A3 (fig. 6), A5 (fig. 25), A6 (fig. 28), A7 (fig. 38), A8 (fig. 37), A9 (fig. 26), A10 (fig. 36); in "A Study of the Process of Individuation": A4 (Picture 9). A2 is not republished. In *Memories, Dreams, Reflections,* Jung tells of painting the pictures reproduced in A3 and A10 (see the N.Y. edn., p. 197 and Pl. XI; London edn., pp. 188f. and facing p. 241). Cross reference in "Concerning Mandala Symbolism" indicates that he also painted the picture in A6.—EDITORS.]

♀ The Golden Flower represented as the most splendid of all flowers

A1

♀ In the centre, the Golden Flower; radiating out from it, fishes as fertility symbols (corresponding to the thunderbolts of Lamaic mandalas)

♂ A luminous flower in the centre, with stars rotating about it. Around the flower, walls with eight gates. The whole conceived as a transparent window

A3

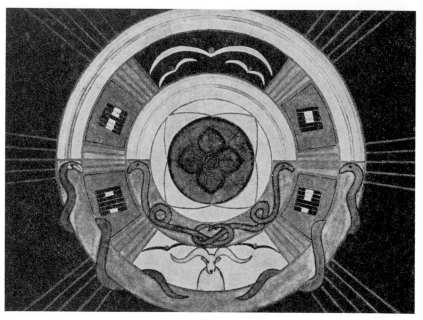

♀ Separation of the air-world and the earth-world. (Birds and serpents.) In the centre, a flower with a golden star

A4

♀ Separation of the light from the dark world; the heavenly from the earthly soul. In the centre, a representation of contemplation

♂ In the centre, the white light, shining in the firmament; in the first circle, proto-plasmic life-seeds; in the second, rotating cosmic principles which contain the four primary colours; in the third and fourth, creative forces working inward and out-ward. At the cardinal points, the masculine and feminine souls, both again divided into light and dark

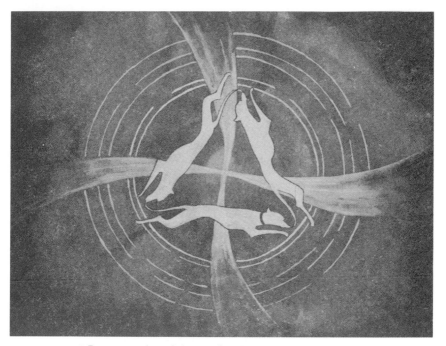

♀ Representation of the *tetraktys* in circular movement

♀ A child in the germinal vesicle with the four primary colours included in the circular movement

♀ In the centre, the germinal vesicle with a human figure nourished by blood vessels which have their origin in the cosmos. The cosmos rotates around the centre, which attracts its emanations. Around the outside is spread nerve tissue indicating that the process takes place in the solar plexus

♂ A mandala as a fortified city with wall and moat. Within, a broad moat surrounding a wall fortified with sixteen towers and with another inner moat. This moat encloses a central castle with golden roofs whose centre is a golden temple

# II

# THE VISIONS OF ZOSIMOS

[Originally given as a lecture to the Eranos Conference at Ascona, Switzer-land, in August 1937, and published under the title "Einige Bemerkungen zu den Visionen des Zosimos," *Eranos-Jahrbuch 1937* (Zurich, 1938). Re-vised and considerably expanded, as "Die Visionen des Zosimos," in *Von den Wurzeln des Bewusstseins: Studien über den Archetypus* (Psycholo-gische Abhandlungen, Vol. IX; Zurich, 1954), which version is translated here.—EDITORS.]

# I

## THE TEXTS

85    I must make clear at once that the following observations on the visions of Zosimos of Panopolis, an important alchemist and Gnostic of the third century A.D., are not intended as a final explanation of this extraordinarily difficult material. My psychological contribution is no more than an attempt to shed a little light on it and to answer some of the questions raised by the visions.

86    The first vision occurs at the beginning of "The Treatise of Zosimos the Divine concerning the Art." [1] Zosimos introduces the treatise with some general remarks on the processes of nature and, in particular, on the "composition of the waters" (θέσις ὑδάτων) and various other operations, and closes with the words: ". . . and upon this simple system of many colours is based the manifold and infinitely varied investigation of all things." Thereupon the text begins:[2]

(III, i, 2.) And as I spoke thus I fell asleep, and I saw a sacrificer[3] standing before me, high up on an altar, which was in the shape of a bowl. There were fifteen steps leading up to the altar. And the priest stood there, and I heard a voice from above saying to me: "I have performed the act of descending the fifteen steps into the darkness, and of ascending the steps into the light. And he who renews me is the sacrificer, by casting away the grossness of the body;

1 "Ζωσίμου τοῦ θείου περὶ ἀρετῆς." Ἀρετή here should not be translated as "virtue" or "power" ("vertu" in Berthelot) but as "the Art," corresponding to the Latin *ars nostra*. The treatise has nothing whatever to do with virtue.

2 Berthelot, *Collection des anciens alchimistes grecs,* with translations into French by C. E. Ruelle. [The present translation is by A. S. B. Glover from the Greek text in Berthelot, with reference also to Ruelle's French and Jung's German. The section numeration is Berthelot's.—EDITORS.]

3 The ἱερουργός is the sacrificial priest who performs the ceremonies. The ἱερεύς is rather the ἱεροφάντης, the prophet and revealer of the mysteries. No difference is made between them in the text.

and by compelling necessity I am sanctified as a priest and now stand in perfection as a spirit." And on hearing the voice of him who stood upon the altar, I inquired of him who he was. And he answered me in a fine voice, saying: "I am Ion,[4] the priest of the inner sanctuaries, and I submit myself to an unendurable torment.[5] For there came one in haste at early morning, who overpowered me, and pierced me through with the sword, and dismembered me in accordance with the rule of harmony.[6] And he drew off the skin of my head with the sword, which he wielded with strength, and mingled the bones with the pieces of flesh, and caused them to be burned upon the fire of the art, till I perceived by the transformation of the body that I had become spirit. And that is my unendurable torment." And even as he spoke thus, and I held him by force to converse with me, his eyes became as blood. And he spewed forth all his own flesh. And I saw how he changed into the opposite of himself, into a mutilated anthroparion,[7] and he tore his flesh with his own teeth, and sank into himself.

(III, i, 3.) Full of fear I awoke from sleep, and I thought to myself: "Is not this the composition of the waters?" And I was assured that I had well understood, and again I fell asleep. I saw the same bowl-shaped altar and, on the upper part, boiling water, and a numberless multitude of people in it. And there was no one near the altar whom I could question. Then I went up to the altar to see this sight. And I perceived an anthroparion, a barber[8] grown grey

[4] Ion occurs in the Sabaean tradition as Jûnân ben Merqûlius (son of Mercury), the ancestor of the Ionians (el-Jûnâniûn). [Cf. Eutychius, *Annales*, in Migne, *P.G.*, vol. 111, col. 922.] The Sabaeans consider him the founder of their religion. Cf. Chwolsohn, *Die Ssabier und der Ssabismus*, I, pp. 205, 796, and II, p. 509. Hermes, too, was considered a founder (I, p. 521).

[5] Κόλασις, literally 'punishment.' Here it means the torment which the prima materia has to undergo in order to be transformed. This procedure is called *mortificatio*. [For an example, see the *mortificatio* of the "Ethiopian" in *Psychology and Alchemy*, par. 484. Also infra, "The Philosophical Tree," ch. 17.—Editors.]

[6] Διασπάσας κατὰ σύστασιν ἁρμονίας. Berthelot has "démembrant, suivant les règles de la combinaison." It refers to the division into four bodies, natures, or elements. Cf. Berthelot, *Alch. grecs*, II, iii, 11 and *Chimie au moyen âge*, III, p. 92. Also "Visio Arislei," *Artis auriferae*, I, p. 151, and "Exercitationes in Turbam IX," ibid., p. 170.

[7] εἶδον αὐτὸν ὡς τοὐναντίον ἀνθρωπάριον κολοβόν. If I am not mistaken, the concept of the *homunculus* appears here for the first time in alchemical literature.

[8] I read ξυρουργός instead of the meaningless ξηρουργός in the text. Cf. III, v, 1, where the barber does in fact appear as an anthroparion. (Or should it be taken adjectivally: ξυρουργὸν ἀνθρωπάριον?) The anthroparion is grey because, as we shall see, he represents the lead.

with age, who said to me: "What are you looking at?" I replied that I was astonished to see the seething of the water, and the men burning and yet alive. He answered me thus: "The sight that you see is the entrance, and the exit, and the transformation." I asked him: "What transformation?" and he answered: "This is the place of the operation called embalming. Those who seek to obtain the art[9] enter here, and become spirits by escaping from the body." Then I said to him: "And you, are you a spirit?" And he answered: "Yes, a spirit and a guardian of spirits." As we spoke, while the boiling continued and the people uttered distressful cries, I saw a brazen man holding a leaden tablet in his hand. And he spoke with a loud voice, looking upon the tablet: "I command all those who are undergoing the punishment to be calm, to take each of them a leaden tablet, to write with their own hand, and to keep their eyes upraised in the air and their mouths open, until their uvula swell." [10] The deed followed the word, and the master of the house said to me: "You have beheld, you have stretched your neck upward and have seen what is done." I replied that I had seen, and he continued: "This brazen man whom you see is the priest who sacrifices and is sacrificed, and spews forth his own flesh. Power is given him over this water and over the people who are punished." [11]

(III, v, 1.) At last I was overcome with the desire to mount the seven steps and to see the seven punishments, and, as was suitable,

9 Or "moral perfection."

10 Evidently a particularly convulsive opening of the mouth is meant, coupled with a violent contraction of the pharynx. This contraction was a kind of retching movement for bringing up the inner contents. These had to be written down on the tablets. They were inspirations coming from above that were caught, as it were, by the upraised eyes. The procedure might be compared with the technique of active imagination.

11 [In the Swiss edition (*Von den Wurzeln des Bewusstseins*, pp. 141–45) this section, though numbered III, i, 3 only, continues into III, i, 4, 5, and 6 without a break, the whole being run together as a single section. III, i, 5 then reappears at the end of the sequence of visions (par. 87), but in variant form, as a "résumé," and the reasons for its placement there are explained in the commentary (pars. 93, 111, 121). As no explanation is given for its duplication under III, i, 3, and the variations are in the main merely stylistic, we have omitted it at this point and reconstituted III, i. 4–6 at the end of the sequence. The wording of Jung's interpolation at par. 87 has been altered to account for this change. The sections are presented in the order III, i, 5, III, i, 4, III, i, 6 on the assumption that III, i, 4 is not meant to form a part of the "résumé" proper, but, as stated in the Eranos version of "Transformation Symbolism in the Mass," is rather "Zosimos' own commentary on his visions" and "a general philosophical conclusion" (*The Mysteries*, pp. 311f.).—EDITORS.]

in a single day; so I went back in order to complete the ascent. Passing it several times, I at length came upon the path. But as I was about to ascend, I lost my way again; greatly discouraged, and not seeing in which direction I should go, I fell asleep. And while I was sleeping, I saw an anthroparion, a barber clad in a robe of royal purple, who stood outside the place of punishments. He said to me: "Man, what are you doing?" and I replied: "I have stopped here because, having turned aside from the road, I have lost my way." And he said: "Follow me." And I turned and followed him. When we came near to the place of punishments, I saw my guide, this little barber, enter that place, and his whole body was consumed by the fire.

(III, v, 2.) On seeing this, I stepped aside, trembling with fear; then I awoke, and said within myself: "What means this vision?" And again I clarified my understanding, and knew that this barber was the brazen man, clad in a purple garment. And I said to myself: "I have well understood, this is the brazen man. It is needful that first he must enter the place of punishments."

(III, v, 3.) Again my soul desired to mount the third step also. And again I followed the road alone, and when I was near the place of punishments, I again went astray, not knowing my way, and I stopped in despair. And again, as it seemed, I saw an old man whitened by years, who had become wholly white, with a blinding whiteness. His name was Agathodaimon. Turning himself about, the old man with white hair gazed upon me for a full hour. And I urged him: "Show me the right way." He did not come towards me, but hastened on his way. But I, running hither and thither, at length came to the altar. And when I stood at the top of the altar, I saw the white-haired old man enter the place of punishments. O ye demiurges of celestial nature! Immediately he was transformed by the flame into a pillar of fire. What a terrible story, my brethren! For, on account of the violence of the punishment, his eyes filled with blood. I spoke to him, and asked: "Why are you stretched out there?" But he could barely open his mouth, and groaned: "I am the leaden man, and I submit myself to an unendurable torment." Thereupon, seized with great fear, I awoke and sought within myself the reason for what I had seen. And again I considered and said to myself: "I have well understood, for it means that the lead is to be rejected, and in truth the vision refers to the composition of the liquids."

(III, v^bis.) Again I beheld the divine and holy bowl-shaped altar, and I saw a priest clothed in a white robe reaching to his feet, who was celebrating these terrible mysteries, and I said: "Who is this?" And the answer came: "This is the priest of the inner sanctuaries. It is he who changes the bodies into blood, makes the eyes clairvoyant, and raises the dead." Then, falling again to earth, I again fell asleep. And as I was ascending the fourth step, I saw, to the east, one approaching, holding a sword in his hand. And another [came] behind him, bringing one adorned round about with signs, clad in white and comely to see, who was named the Meridian of the Sun.[12] And as they drew near to the place of punishments, he who held the sword in his hand [said]: "Cut off his head, immolate his body, and cut his flesh into pieces, that it may first be boiled according to the method,[13] and then delivered to the place of punishments." Thereupon I awoke and said: "I have well understood, this concerns the liquids in the art of the metals." And he who bore the sword in his hand said again: "You have completed the descent of the seven steps." And the other answered, as he caused the waters to gush forth from all the moist places: "The procedure is completed."

(III, vi, 1.) And I saw an altar which was in the shape of a bowl, and a fiery spirit stood upon the altar, and tended the fire for the seething and the boiling and the burning of the men who rose up from it. And I inquired about the people who stood there, and I said: "I see with astonishment the seething and the boiling of the water, and the men burning and yet alive!" And he answered me, saying: "This boiling that you see is the place of the operation

---

[12] Καὶ ἄλλος ὀπίσω αὐτοῦ φέρων περιηκονισμένον τινὰ λευκοφόρον καὶ ὡραῖον τὴν ὄψιν, οὗ τὸ ὄνομα ἐκαλεῖτο μεσουράνισμα ἡλίου. Berthelot: "Un autre, derrière lui, portait un objet circulaire, d'une blancheur éclatante, et très beau à voir appelé Méridien du Cinnabre." It is not clear why μεσουράνισμα ἡλίου is translated as "meridian of the cinnabar," thus making it a chemical analogy. περιηκονισμένον τινά must refer to a person and not to a thing. Dr. M.-L. von Franz has drawn my attention to the following parallels in Apuleius. He calls the *stola olympiaca* with which the initiate was clad a "precious scarf with sacred animals worked in colour on every part of it; for instance, Indian serpents and Hyperborean griffins." "I . . . wore a white palm-tree chaplet with its leaves sticking out all round like rays of light." The initiate was shown to the people "as when a statue is unveiled, dressed like the sun." The sun, which he now was, he had seen the previous night, after his figurative death. "At midnight I saw the sun shining as if it were noon." (*The Golden Ass*, trans. Graves, p. 286.)

[13] Literally, ὀργανικῶς.

63

called embalming. Those who seek to obtain the art enter here, and they cast their bodies from them and become spirits. The practice [of the art] is explained by this procedure; for whatever casts off the grossness of the body becomes spirit."

87    The Zosimos texts are in a disordered state. At III, i, 5 there is a misplaced but obviously authentic résumé or amplification of the visions, and at III, i, 4 a philosophical interpretation of them. Zosimos calls this whole passage an "introduction to the discourse that is to follow" (III, i, 6).

(III, i, 5.) In short, my friend, build a temple from a single stone, like to white lead, to alabaster, to Proconnesian marble,[14] with neither end nor beginning in its construction.[15] Let it have within it a spring of the purest water, sparkling like the sun. Note carefully on what side is the entrance to the temple, and take a sword in your hand; then seek the entrance, for narrow is the place where the opening is. A dragon lies at the entrance, guarding the temple. Lay hold upon him; immolate him first; strip him of his skin, and taking his flesh with the bones, separate the limbs; then, laying [the flesh of] the limbs[16] together with the bones at the entrance of the temple, make a step of them, mount thereon, and enter, and you will find what you seek.[17] The priest, that brazen man, whom you see seated in the spring and composing the substance, [look on] him not as the brazen man, for he has changed the colour of his nature and has become the silver man; and if you will, you will soon have him [as] the golden man.

(III, i, 4.) And after I had seen this apparition, I awoke, and I said to myself: "What is the cause of this vision? Is not that boiling white and yellow water the divine water?" And I found that I had well understood. And I said: "Beautiful it is to speak and beautiful to hear, beautiful to give and beautiful to receive, beautiful to be poor and beautiful to be rich. How does nature teach giving and receiving? The brazen man gives and the hydrolith receives; the metal gives and the plant receives; the stars give and the flowers receive; the heavens give and the earth receives; the thunderclaps give forth darting fire. And all things are woven together and all things are undone again; all things are mingled together and all

14 The island of Prokonnesos was the site of the famous Greek marble quarry, now called Marmara (Turkey).
15 That is, circular.
16 The Greek has only μέλος. I follow the reading of codex Gr. 2252 (Paris).
17 The res quaesita or quaerenda is a standing expression in Latin alchemy.

things combine; and all things unite and all things separate; all things are moistened and all things are dried; and all things flourish and all things fade in the bowl of the altar. For each thing comes to pass with method and in fixed measure and by exact[18] weighing of the four elements. The weaving together of all things and the undoing of all things and the whole fabric of things cannot come to pass without method. The method is a natural one, preserving due order in its inhaling and its exhaling; it brings increase and it brings decrease. And to sum up: through the harmonies of separating and combining, and if nothing of the method be neglected, all things bring forth nature. For nature applied to nature transforms nature. Such is the order of natural law throughout the whole cosmos, and thus all things hang together."

(III, i, 6.) This introduction is the key which shall open to you the flowers of the discourse that is to follow, namely, the investigation of the arts, of wisdom, of reason and understanding, the efficacious methods and revelations which throw light upon the secret words.

[18] Οὐγγιασμῷ.

## II

## COMMENTARY

### 1. GENERAL REMARKS ON THE INTERPRETATION

88    Although it looks as if this were a series of visions following one after the other, the frequent repetitions and striking similarities suggest rather that it was essentially a single vision which is presented as a set of variations on the themes it contains. Psychologically at least, there is no ground for supposing that it is an allegorical invention. Its salient features seem to indicate that for Zosimos it was a highly significant experience which he wished to communicate to others. Although alchemical literature contains a number of allegories which without doubt are merely didactic fables and are not based on direct experience,[1] the vision of Zosimos may well have been an actual happening. This seems to be borne out by the manner in which Zosimos himself interprets it as a confirmation of his own preoccupation: "Is not this the composition of the waters?" Such an interpretation seems—to us at any rate—to leave out of account the most impressive images in the vision, and to reduce a far more significant complex of facts to an all too simple common denominator. If the vision were an allegory, the most conspicuous images would also be the ones that have the greatest significance. But it is characteristic of any subjective dream interpretation that it is satisfied with pointing out superficial relationships which take no account of the essentials. Another thing to be considered is that the alchemists themselves testify to the occurrence of dreams and visions during the opus.[2] I am inclined to think that the vision or visions of Zosimos were experiences of this kind,

---

[1] For example, the "Visio Arislei" (*Art. aurif.*, I, pp. 146ff.) and the visions in the "Book of Krates" (Berthelot, *Chimie au moyen âge,* III, pp. 44–75).
[2] Cf. *Psychology and Alchemy,* pars. 347ff.

which took place during the work and revealed the nature of the psychic processes in the background.[3] In these visions all those contents emerge which the alchemists unconsciously projected into the chemical process and which were then perceived there, as though they were qualities of matter. The extent to which this projection was fostered by the conscious attitude is shown by the somewhat overhasty interpretation given by Zosimos himself.

89 Even though his interpretation strikes us at first as somewhat forced, indeed as far-fetched and arbitrary, we should nevertheless not forget that while the conception of the "waters" is a strange one to us, for Zosimos and for the alchemists in general it had a significance we would never suspect. It is also possible that the mention of the "water" opened out perspectives in which the ideas of dismemberment, killing, torture, and transformation all had their place. For, beginning with the treatises of Democritus and Komarios, which are assigned to the first century A.D., alchemy, until well into the eighteenth century, was very largely concerned with the miraculous water, the *aqua divina* or *permanens,* which was extracted from the lapis, or prima materia, through the torment of the fire. The water was the *humidum radicale* (radical moisture), which stood for the *anima media natura* or *anima mundi* imprisoned in matter,[4] the

---

[3] The opus extended over a period with no fixed limits. During this time the artifex had to devote himself "religiously" to the process of transformation. Since the process was subjective as well as objective, it is not surprising that it included dream-experiences. G. Battista Nazari (*Della tramutatione metallica sogni tre,* 1599) actually represented the opus in the form of (allegorical) dreams. "The philosophic water is sometimes manifested to thee in sleep," says the "Parabola" of Sendivogius (*Bibliotheca chemica,* II, p. 475). We cannot suppose that the author had any knowledge of the visions of Zosimos; the reference is probably to the "Visio Arislei," as suggested by the following (p. 475 b): "Solum fructum arboris Solaris vidi in somniis Saturnum Mercurio nostro imponere" (I saw in dreams the sole fruit of the tree of the sun impose Saturn on our Mercurius). Cf. the end of the "Visio Arislei": "Vidimus te magistrum in somniis. Petiimus ut nobis subsidium Horfolto discipulo tuo offeras, qui nutrimenti auctor est" (We saw thee, the master, in dreams. We besought that thou wouldst offer us for our help thy disciple Horfoltus, who is the author of nourishment).—Codex Q. 584 (Berlin), fol 21ᵛ. Ruska, ed., *Turba Philosophorum,* pp. 327f. The beginning of the "Visio" shows how the fruit of "that immortal tree" may be gathered.

[4] In our text (III, v. 3) it is the Agathodaimon itself that suffers transformation.

67

soul of the stone or metal, also called the *anima aquina*. This anima was set free not only by means of the "cooking," but also by the sword dividing the "egg," or by the *separatio*, or by dissolution into the four "roots" or elements.[5] The *separatio* was often represented as the dismemberment of a human body.[6] Of the *aqua permanens* it was said that it dissolved the bodies into the four elements. Altogether, the divine water possessed the power of transformation. It transformed the *nigredo* into the *albedo* through the miraculous "washing" (*ablutio*); it animated inert matter, made the dead to rise again,[7] and therefore possessed the virtue of the baptismal water in the ecclesiastical rite.[8] Just as, in the *benedictio fontis*, the priest makes the sign of the cross over the water and so divides it into four parts,[9] so the mercurial serpent, symbolizing the *aqua permanens*, undergoes dismemberment, another parallel to the division of the body.[10]

90      I shall not elaborate any further this web of interconnected meanings in which alchemy is so rich. What I have said may suffice to show that the idea of the "water" and the operations connected with it could easily open out to the alchemist a vista in which practically all the themes of the vision fall into place. From the standpoint of Zosimos' conscious psychology, there-

[5] Division into four elements after the *mortificatio* occurs in "Exercitationes in Turbam IC" (*Art. aurif.*, I, p. 170), also in "Aenigma" VI (ibid., p. 151). For division of the egg into four, see the Book of El-Habib (Berthelot, *Moyen âge*, III, p. 92). The division into four was known as τετραμερεῖν τὴν φιλοσοφίαν (Berthelot, *Alch. grecs*, III, xliv, 5).

[6] For example, in Trismosin, *Splendor solis* (*Aureum vellus*, p. 27). The same in *Splendor Solis* (London, 1920, repr.), Pl. X, and Lacinius, *Pretiosa margarita novella* (Venice, 1546), fol. *** xii.

[7] "It is the water that kills and vivifies" (*Rosarium philosophorum*, in *Art. aurif.*, II, p. 214).

[8] Just as baptism is a pre-Christian rite, according to the testimony of the gospels, so, too, the divine water is of pagan and pre-Christian origin. The Praefatio of the Benedictio Fontis on Easter Eve says: "May this water, prepared for the rebirth of men, be rendered fruitful by the secret inpouring of his divine power; may a heavenly offering, conceived in holiness and reborn into a new creation, come forth from the stainless womb of this divine font; and may all, however distinguished by age in time or sex in body, be brought forth into one infancy by the motherhood of grace" (*The Missal in Latin and English*, p. 429).

[9] "The priest divides the water crosswise with his hand" (ibid.).

[10] Cf. *Psychology and Alchemy*, pars. 334, 530.

fore, his interpretation seems rather less forced and arbitrary. A Latin proverb says: *canis panem somniat, piscator pisces* (the dog dreams of bread, the fisherman of fish). The alchemist, too, dreams in his own specific language. This enjoins upon us the greatest circumspection, all the more so as that language is exceedingly obscure. In order to understand it, we have to learn the psychological secrets of alchemy. It is probably true what the old Masters said, that only he who knows the secret of the stone understands their words.[11] It has long been asserted that this secret is sheer nonsense, and not worth the trouble of investigating seriously. But this frivolous attitude ill befits the psychologist, for any "nonsense" that fascinated men's minds for close on two thousand years—among them some of the greatest, e.g., Newton and Goethe[12]—must have something about it which it would be useful for the psychologist to know. Moreover, the symbolism of alchemy has a great deal to do with the structure of the unconscious, as I have shown in my book *Psychology and Alchemy*. These things are not just rare curiosities, and anyone who wishes to understand the symbolism of dreams cannot close his eyes to the fact that the dreams of modern men and women often contain the very images and metaphors that we find in the medieval treatises.[13] And since an understanding of the biological compensation produced by dreams is of importance in the treatment of neurosis as well as in the development of consciousness, a knowledge of these facts has also a practical value which should not be underestimated.

11 Cf. "Hortulanus super Epistolum Hermetis" in *Rosarium, Art. aurif.*, II, p. 270. *Aurora Consurgens* (ed. von Franz), pp. 39–41: "For she [this science] is clear to them that have understanding . . . she seemeth easy to them that have knowledge of her." Maier, *Symbola aureae mensae*, p. 146: ". . . that they should not understand his words, save those who are judged worthy of this very great magistery."

12 Cf. Gray, *Goethe the Alchemist.*

13 It has often been objected that symbols of this sort do not occur in dreams at all. Naturally they do not occur in all dreams or in just any dreams, but only in special ones. The differences between dreams are as great as those between individuals. A particular constellation of the unconscious is needed to produce such dreams, i.e., archetypal dreams containing mythological motifs. (Examples in *Psychology and Alchemy*, Part II.) But they cannot be recognized without a knowledge of mythology, which not all psychologists possess.

## 2. THE SACRIFICIAL ACT

91    The central image in our dream-vision shows us a kind of sacrificial act undertaken for the purpose of alchemical transformation. It is characteristic of this rite that the priest is at once the sacrificer and the sacrificed. This important idea reached Zosimos in the form of the teachings of the "Hebrews" (i.e., Christians).[1] Christ was a god who sacrificed himself. An essential part of the sacrificial act is dismemberment. Zosimos must have been familiar with this motif from the Dionysian mystery-tradition. There, too, the god is the victim, who was torn to pieces by the Titans and thrown into a cooking pot,[2] but whose heart was saved at the last moment by Hera. Our text shows that the bowl-shaped altar was a cooking vessel in which a multitude of people were boiled and burned. As we know from the legend and from a fragment of Euripides,[3] an outburst of bestial greed and the tearing of living animals with the teeth were part of the Dionysian orgy.[4] Dionysius was actually called ὁ ἀμέριστος καὶ μεμερισμένος νοῦς (the undivided and divided spirit).[5]

92    Zosimos must also have been familiar with the flaying motif. A well-known parallel of the dying and resurgent god Attis[6] is the flayed and hanged Marsyas. Also, legend attributes death by flaying to the religious teacher Mani, who was a near-contemporary of Zosimos.[7] The subsequent stuffing of the skin with straw is a reminder of the Attic fertility and rebirth ceremonies. Every year in Athens an ox was slaughtered and skinned, and its pelt

[1] Provided, of course, that the passages in question are not interpolations by copyists, who were mostly monks.

[2] Preller, *Griechische Mythologie*, I, p. 437.

[3] Fragment 472 N2, "The Cretans." Cited in Dieterich, *Mithrasliturgie*, p. 105.

[4] Cf. "Transformation Symbolism in the Mass," pp. 231f. For dismemberment, transformation, and recomposition in a case of schizophrenia, see Spielrein, "Ueber den psychologischen Inhalt eines Falles von Schizophrenie," pp. 358ff. Dismemberment is a practically universal motif of primitive shamanistic psychology. It forms the main experience in the initiation of a shaman. Cf. Eliade, *Shamanism*, pp. 53ff.

[5] Firmicus Maternus, *Liber de errore profanarum religionum* (ed. Halm), ch. 7, p. 89.

[6] Attis has close affinities with Christ. According to tradition, the birthplace at Bethlehem was once an Attis sanctuary. This tradition has been confirmed by recent excavations.

[7] Frazer, *The Golden Bough*, Part IV: *Adonis, Attis, Osiris*, pp. 242ff.

stuffed with straw. The stuffed dummy was then fastened to a plough, obviously for the purpose of restoring the fertility of the land.[8] Similar flaying ceremonies are reported of the Aztecs, Scythians, Chinese, and Patagonians.[9]

93    In the vision, the skinning is confined to the head. It is a scalping as distinct from the total ἀποδερμάτωσις (skinning) described in III, i, 5. It is one of the actions which distinguish the original vision from the description of the process given in this résumé. Just as cutting out and eating the heart or brain of an enemy is supposed to endow one with his vital powers or virtues, so scalping is a *pars pro toto* incorporation of the life principle or soul.[10] Flaying is a transformation symbol which I have discussed at greater length in my essay "Transformation Symbolism in the Mass." Here I need only mention the special motif of torture or punishment (κόλασις), which is particularly evident in the description of the dismemberment and scalping. For this there is a remarkable parallel in the Akhmim manuscript of the Apocalypse of Elijah, published by Georg Steindorff.[11] In the vision it is said of the leaden homunculus that "his eyes filled with blood" as a result of the torture. The Apocalypse of Elijah says of those who are cast "into eternal punishment": "their eyes are mixed with blood";[12] and of the saints who were persecuted by the Anti-Messiah: "he will draw off their skins from their heads." [13]

94    These parallels suggest that the κόλασις is not just a punishment but the torment of hell. Although κόλασις would have to be translated as *poena,* this word nowhere occurs in the Vulgate, for in all the places where the torments of hell are mentioned the word used is *cruciare* or *cruciatus,* as in Revelation 14 : 10, "tormented with fire and brimstone," or Revelation 9 : 5, "the torment of a scorpion." The corresponding Greek word is βασανίζειν or βασανισμός, 'torture'. For the alchemists it had a

8 Ibid., p. 249.
9 Ibid., p. 246.
10 Among the Thompson and Shuswap Indians in British Columbia the scalp signifies a helpful guardian spirit. Frazer, *Totemism and Exogamy,* III, pp. 417, 427.
11 *Die Apokalypse des Elias.*
12 Ibid., p. 43, 5, line 1.
13 P. 95, 36, line 8.

double meaning: βασανίζειν also meant 'testing on the touchstone' (βάσανος). The *lapis Lydius* (touchstone) was used as a synonym for the *lapis philosophorum*. The genuineness or incorruptibility of the stone is proved by the torment of fire and cannot be attained without it. This *leitmotiv* runs all through alchemy.

95      In our text the skinning refers especially to the head, as though signifying an extraction of the soul (if the primitive equation *skin = soul* is still valid here). The head plays a considerable role in alchemy, and has done so since ancient times. Thus Zosimos names his philosophers the "sons of the Golden Head." I have dealt with this theme elsewhere,[14] and need not go into it again now. For Zosimos and the later alchemists the head had the meaning of the "omega element" or "round element" (στοιχεῖον στρογγύλον), a synonym for the arcane or transformative substance.[15] The decapitation in section III, v[bis] therefore signifies the obtaining of the arcane substance. According to the text, the figure following behind the sacrificer is named the "Meridian of the Sun," and his head is to be cut off. This striking off of the golden head is also found in the manuscripts of *Splendor solis* as well as in the Rorschach printing of 1598. The sacrifice in the vision is of an initiate who has undergone the experience of the *solificatio*. In alchemy, sun is synonymous with gold. Gold, as Michael Maier says, is the "circulatory work of the sun," "shining clay moulded into the most beauteous substance, wherein the solar rays are gathered together and shine forth." [16] Mylius says that the "water comes from the rays of the sun and moon." [17] According to the "Aurelia occulta," the sun's rays are gathered together in the quicksilver.[18] Dorn derives all metals from the "invisible rays" of heaven,[19] whose spherical shape is a prototype of the Hermetic vessel. In view of all this, we shall hardly go wrong in supposing that the initiate named the "Meridian of the Sun" himself represents the arcane substance. We shall come back to this idea later.

14 "Transformation Symbolism in the Mass," pp. 240ff.
15 Ibid.
16 *De circulo physico quadrato*, pp. 15f.
17 *Philosophia reformata*, p. 313.
18 *Theatrum chemicum*, IV (1659), p. 496.
19 "Speculativa philosophia," ibid., I (1659), p. 247.

96     Let us turn now to other details of the vision. The most striking feature is the "bowl-shaped altar." It is unquestionably related to the *krater* of Poimandres. This was the vessel which the
demiurge sent down to earth filled with Nous, so that those who
were striving for higher consciousness could baptize themselves
in it. It is mentioned in that important passage where Zosimos
tells his friend and *soror mystica,* Theosebeia: "Hasten down to
the shepherd and bathe yourself in the *krater,* and hasten up to
your own kind (γένος)." [20] She had to go down to the place of
death and rebirth, and then up to her "own kind," i.e., the twice-
born, or, in the language of the gospels, the kingdom of heaven.

97     The *krater* is obviously a wonder-working vessel, a font or
piscina, in which the immersion takes place and transformation
into a spiritual being is effected. It is the *vas Hermetis* of later
alchemy. I do not think there can be any doubt that the *krater*
of Zosimos is closely related to the vessel of Poimandres in the
*Corpus Hermeticum.*[21] The Hermetic vessel, too, is a uterus of
spiritual renewal or rebirth. This idea corresponds exactly to
the text of the *benedictio fontis,* which I quoted earlier in a
footnote.[22] In "Isis to Horus," [23] the angel brings Isis a small
vessel filled with translucent or "shining" water. Considering
the alchemical nature of the treatise, we could take this water as
the divine water of the art,[24] since after the prima materia this
is the real arcanum. The water, or water of the Nile, had a special significance in ancient Egypt: it was Osiris, the dismembered god *par excellence.*[25] A text from Edfu says: "I bring you
the vessels with the god's limbs [i.e., the Nile] that you may
drink of them; I refresh your heart that you may be satisfied." [26]
The god's limbs were the fourteen parts into which Osiris was

---

[20] Berthelot, *Alch. grecs,* III, li, 8.

[21] Scott, *Hermetica,* I, Book IV, and Reitzenstein, *Poimandres,* pp. 8ff.

[22] See supra, par. 89, n. 8.

[23] Berthelot, *Alch. grecs,* I, xiii, 1f.

[24] The arcanum is here symbolized by the sowing of the grain and the begetting
of man, lion, and dog. In chemical usage it refers to the fixation of quicksilver
(ibid., I, xiii, 6–9). Quicksilver was one of the older symbols for the divine water
on account of its silvery-white sheen. In *Rosarium* it is called "aqua clarissima"
(*Art. aurif.,* II, p. 213).

[25] Budge, *The Gods of the Egyptians,* II, pp. 122ff.

[26] Jacobsohn, *Die dogmatische Stellung des Königs in der Theologie der alten
Aegypter,* p. 50.

divided. There are numerous references to the hidden, divine nature of the arcane substance in the alchemical texts.[27] According to this ancient tradition, the water possessed the power of resuscitation; for it was Osiris, who rose from the dead. In the "Dictionary of Goldmaking," [28] Osiris is the name for lead and sulphur, both of which are synonyms for the arcane substance. Thus lead, which was the principal name for the arcane substance for a long time, is called "the sealed tomb of Osiris, containing all the limbs of the god." [29] According to legend, Set (Typhon) covered the coffin of Osiris with lead. Petasios tells us that the "sphere of the fire is restrained and enclosed by lead." Olympiodorus, who quotes this saying, remarks that Petasios added by way of explanation: "The lead is the water which issues from the masculine element." [30] But the masculine element, he said, is the "sphere of fire."

98    This train of thought indicates that the spirit which is a water, or the water which is a spirit, is essentially a paradox, a pair of opposites like water and fire. In the *aqua nostra* of the alchemists, the concepts of water, fire, and spirit coalesce as they do in religious usage.[31]

99    Besides the motif of water, the story that forms the setting of the Isis treatise also contains the motif of violation. The text says:[32]

Isis the Prophetess to her son Horus: My child, you should go forth to battle against the faithless Typhon for the sake of your father's kingdom, while I retire to Hormanuthi, Egypt's [city] of the sacred art, where I sojourned for a while. According to the circumstances of the time and the necessary consequences of the movement of the

27 Cf. the identification of the Agathodaimon with the transformative substance, supra, III, v, 3.

28 Berthelot, *Alch. grecs*, I, ii.

29 Ὄσιρίς ἐστιν ἡ ταφὴ ἐσφιγμένη, κρύπτουσα πάντα τὰ Ὀσίριδος μέλη: Treatise of Olympiodorus of Alexandria (ibid., II, iv, 42). Here Osiris is the "principle of all moisture" in agreement with Plutarch. This refers to the relatively low melting point of lead.

30 Ibid., II, iv, 43.

31 Cf. the hymn of St. Romanus on the theophany: ". . . him who was seen of old in the midst of three children as dew in the fire, now a fire flickering and shining in the Jordan, himself the light inaccessible" (Pitra, *Analecta sacra*, I, 21).

32 Berthelot, *Alch. grecs*, I, xiii, 1–4.

spheres,[33] it came to pass that a certain one among the angels, dwelling in the first firmament, watched me from above and wished to have intercourse with me. Quickly he determined to bring this about. I did not yield, as I wished to inquire into the preparation of the gold and silver. But when I demanded it of him, he told me he was not permitted to speak of it, on account of the supreme importance of the mysteries; but on the following day an angel, Amnael, greater than he, would come, and he could give me the solution of the problem. He also spoke of the sign of this angel—he bore it on his head and would show me a small, unpitched vessel filled with a translucent water. He would tell me the truth. On the following day, as the sun was crossing the midpoint of its course, Amnael appeared, who was greater than the first angel, and, seized with the same desire, he did not hesitate, but hastened to where I was. But I was no less determined to inquire into the matter.[34]

100    She did not yield to him, and the angel revealed the secret, which she might pass only to her son Horus. Then follow a number of recipes which are of no interest here.

101    The angel, as a winged or spiritual being, represents, like Mercurius, the volatile substance, the pneuma, the ἀσώματον (disembodied). Spirit in alchemy almost invariably has a relation to water or to the radical moisture, a fact that may be explained simply by the empirical nature of the oldest form of "chemistry," namely the art of cooking. The steam arising from boiling water conveys the first vivid impression of "metasomatosis," the transformation of the corporeal into the incorporeal, into spirit or pneuma. The relation of spirit to water resides in the fact that the spirit is hidden in the water, like a fish. In the "Allegoriae super librum Turbae" [35] this fish is described as "round" and endowed with "a wonder-working virtue." As is evident from the text,[36] it represents the arcane substance. From the alchemical transformation, the text says, is produced a collyrium (eyewash)

---

33 Instead of φευρικῆς in the text.

34 The secrets of the art.

35 Art. aurif., I, pp. 141f.

36 "There is in the sea a round fish, lacking bones and scales [?], and it has in itself a fatness, a wonder-working virtue, which if it be cooked on a slow fire until its fatness and moisture have wholly disappeared, and then be thoroughly cleansed, is steeped in sea water until it begins to shine. . . ." This is a description of the transformation process. [Cf. Aion, pars. 195ff.]

which will enable the philosopher to see the secrets better.[37] The "round fish" seems to be a relative of the "round white stone" mentioned in the *Turba*.[38] Of this it is said: "It has within itself the three colours and the four natures and is born of a living thing." The "round" thing or element is a well-known concept in alchemy. In the *Turba* we encounter the *rotundum:* "For the sake of posterity I call attention to the *rotundum,* which changes the metal into four." [39] As is clear from the context, the *rotundum* is identical with the *aqua permanens*. We meet the same train of thought in Zosimos. He says of the round or omega element: "It consists of two parts. It belongs to the seventh zone, that of Kronos,[40] in the language of the corporeal ($\kappa\alpha\tau\grave{\alpha}$ $\tau\grave{\eta}\nu$ $\check{\epsilon}\nu\sigma\omega\mu o\nu$ $\varphi\rho\acute{\alpha}\sigma\iota\nu$); but in the language of the incorporeal it is something different, that may not be revealed. Only Nikotheos knows it, and he is not to be found.[41] In the language of the corporeal it is named Okeanos, the origin and seed, so they say, of all the gods." [42] Hence the *rotundum* is outwardly water, but inwardly the arcanum. For the Peratics, Kronos was a "power having the colour of water," [43] "for the water, they say, is destruction."

102      Water and spirit are often identical. Thus Hermolaus Barbarus[44] says: "There is also a heavenly or divine water of the alchemists, which was known both to Democritus and to Hermes Trismegistus. Sometimes they call it the divine water, and sometimes the Scythian juice, sometimes pneuma, that is spirit, of the nature of aether, and the quintessence of things." [45] Ruland calls the water the "spiritual power, a spirit of heavenly nature." [46] Christopher Steeb gives an interesting explanation of the origin of this idea: "The brooding of the Holy Spirit

[37] ". . . whose anointed eyes could easily look upon the secrets of the philosophers."

[38] Codex Vadiensis 390 (St. Gall), 15th cent. (mentioned by Ruska, *Turba*, p. 93). Concerning the fish, see *Aion*, ch. X.

[39] Sermo XLI.

[40] That is, Saturn, who was regarded as the dark "counter-sun." Mercurius is the child of Saturn, and also of the sun and moon.

[41] Cf. *Psychology and Alchemy*, par. 456, §6.

[42] Berthelot, *Alch. grecs*, III, xix, 1.

[43] Δύναμις γάρ φησίν ὑδατόχρους, ἥντινα δύναμιν, φησί, τουτέστι τόν κρόνον. Hippolytus, *Elenchos*, V, 16, 2 (trans. Legge, *Philosophumena*, I, p. 154).

[44] 1454–1493. Cardinal archbishop of Aquileia, and a great humanist.

[45] *Corollarium in Dioscoridem*. Cited in Maier, *Symb. aur. mens.*, p. 174.

[46] *Lexicon alchemiae*, pp. 46f.

upon the waters above the firmament brought forth a power which permeates all things in the most subtle way, warms them, and, in conjunction with the light, generates in the mineral kingdom of the lower world the mercurial serpent, in the plant kingdom the blessed greenness, and in the animal kingdom the formative power; so that the supracelestial spirit of the waters, united with the light, may fitly be called the soul of the world." [47] Steeb goes on to say that when the celestial waters were animated by the spirit, they immediately fell into a circular motion, from which arose the perfect spherical form of the *anima mundi*. The *rotundum* is therefore a bit of the world soul, and this may well have been the secret that was guarded by Zosimos. All these ideas refer expressly to Plato's *Timaeus*. In the *Turba*, Parmenides praises the water as follows: "O ye celestial natures, who at a sign from God multiply the natures of the truth! O mighty nature, who conquers the natures and causes the natures to rejoice and be glad! [48] For she it is in particular, whom God has endowed with a power which the fire does not possess. . . . She is herself the truth, all ye seekers of wisdom, for, liquefied with her substances, she brings about the highest of works." [49]

103    Socrates in the *Turba* says much the same: "O how this nature changes body into spirit! . . . She is the sharpest vinegar, which causes gold to become pure spirit." [50] "Vinegar" is synonymous with "water," as the text shows, and also with the "red spirit." [51] The *Turba* says of the latter: "From the compound that is transformed into red spirit arises the principle of the world," which again means the world soul.[52] *Aurora consurgens*

---

[47] *Coelum Sephiroticum*, p. 33.

[48] An allusion to the axiom of pseudo-Democritus.

[49] Ruska, p. 190.

[50] P. 197.

[51] Pp. 200f. *Aqua nostra* is "fire, because it burns all things and reduces them to powder; quicksilver is vinegar" (Quotation from Calid in *Rosarium*, p. 218). "Our water is mightier than fire. . . . And fire in respect thereto is like water in respect to common fire. Therefore the philosophers say: Burn our metal in the mightiest fire" (ibid., p. 250). Hence the "water" is a kind of superfire, an *ignis coelestis*.

[52] Contrary to Ruska (*Turba*, p. 201, n. 3), I adhere to the reading in the MSS. because it is simply a synonym for the moist soul of the prima materia, the radical moisture. Another synonym for the water is "spiritual blood" (ibid., p. 129), which Ruska rightly collates with πυρρὸν αἷμα (fire-coloured blood) in the Greek

says: "Send forth thy Spirit, that is water . . . and thou wilt renew the face of the earth." And again: "The rain of the Holy Spirit melteth. He shall send out his word . . . his wind shall blow and the waters shall run." [53] Arnaldus de Villanova (1235–1313) says in his "Flos Florum": "They have called water spirit, and it is in truth spirit." [54] The *Rosarium philosophorum* says categorically: "Water is spirit." [55] In the treatise of Komarios (1st cent. A.D.), the water is described as an elixir of life which wakens the dead sleeping in Hades to a new springtime.[56] Apollonius says in the *Turba*:[57] "But then, ye sons of the doctrine, that thing needs the fire, until the spirit of that body is transformed and left to stand through the nights, and turns to dust like a man in his grave. After this has happened, God will give it back its soul and its spirit, and, the infirmity being removed, that thing will be stronger and better after its destruction, even as a man becomes stronger and younger after the resurrection than he was in the world." The water acts upon the substances as God acts upon the body. It is coequal with God and is itself of divine nature.

104　　As we have seen, the spiritual nature of the water comes from the "brooding" of the Holy Spirit upon the chaos (Genesis 1 : 3). There is a similar view in the *Corpus Hermeticum:* "There was darkness in the deep and water without form; and there was a subtle breath, intelligent, which permeated the things in Chaos with divine power." [58] This view is supported in the first place by the New Testament motif of baptism by "water and spirit," and in the second place by the rite of the *benedictio fontis,* which is performed on Easter Eve.[59] But the

---

sources. The equation fire = spirit is common in alchemy. Thus, as Ruska himself remarks (p. 271), Mercurius (a frequent synonym for the *aqua permanens,* cf. Ruland's *Lexicon*) is called φάρμακον πύρινον (fiery medicine).

[53] Cf. *Aurora Consurgens* (ed. von Franz), pp. 85, 91.

[54] *Art. aurif.,* II, p. 482.　　[55] Ibid., II, p. 239.

[56] Berthelot, *Alch. grecs,* IV, xx, 8: "Make known to us how the blessed waters come down from above to awaken the dead, who lie round about in the midst of Hades, chained in the darkness; how the elixir of life comes to them and awakens them, rousing them out of their sleep. . . ."

[57] P. 139.　　　　[58] Scott, *Hermetica,* I, p. 147.

[59] Praefatio: "May the power of the Holy Ghost descend into this brimming font, and may it make the whole substance of the water fruitful in regenerative power" (*Missal,* p. 431).

idea of the wonder-working water derived originally from Hellenistic nature philosophy, probably with an admixture of Egyptian influences, and not from Christian or biblical sources. Because of its mystical power, the water animates and fertilizes but also kills.

105 In the divine water, whose dyophysite nature (τὸ στοιχεῖον τὸ διμερές)[60] is constantly emphasized, two principles balance one another, active and passive, masculine and feminine, which constitute the essence of creative power in the eternal cycle of birth and death.[61] This cycle was represented in ancient alchemy by the symbol of the uroboros, the dragon that bites its own tail.[62] Self-devouring is the same as self-destruction,[63] but the union of the dragon's tail and mouth was also thought of as self-fertilization. Hence the texts say: "The dragon slays itself, weds itself, impregnates itself." [64]

[60] It shares this quality with Mercurius duplex.

[61]         "In the floods of life, in the storm of work,
        In ebb and flow,
        In warp and weft,
        Cradle and grave,
        An eternal sea,
        A changing patchwork,
        A glowing life,
        At the whirring loom of Time I weave
        The living clothes of the Deity."
Thus the Earth Spirit, the *spiritus mercurialis*, to Faust. (Trans. by MacNeice, p. 23.)

[62] In Egypt the darkness of the soul was represented as a crocodile (Budge, *The Gods of the Egyptians*, I, p. 286).

[63] In the Book of Ostanes (Berthelot, *Chimie au moyen âge*, III, p. 120) there is a description of a monster with wings of a vulture, an elephant's head, and a dragon's tail. These parts mutually devour one another.

[64] Of the quicksilver (*aqua vitae, perennis*) it is said: "This is the serpent which rejoices in itself, impregnates itself, and brings itself forth in a single day; it slays all things with its venom, and will become fire from the fire (*et ab igne ignis fuerit*)." ("Tractatulus Avicennae," *Art. aurif.*, I, p. 406.) "The dragon is born in the *nigredo* and feeds upon its Mercurius and slays itself" (*Rosarium*, ibid., II, p. 230). "The living Mercurius is called the scorpion, that is, venom; for it slays itself and brings itself back to life" (ibid., pp. 271f.). The oft-cited saying, "The dragon dieth not save with its brother and sister," is explained by Maier (*Symb. aur. mens.*, p. 466) as follows: "For whenever the heavenly sun and moon meet in conjunction, this must take place in the head and tail of the dragon; in this comes about the conjunction and uniting of sun and moon, when an eclipse takes place."

106    This ancient alchemical idea reappears dramatically in the vision of Zosimos, much as it might in a real dream. In III, i, 2 the priest Ion submits himself to an "unendurable torment." The "sacrificer" performs the act of sacrifice by piercing Ion through with a sword. Ion thus foreshadows that dazzling white-clad figure named the "Meridian of the Sun" (III, v[bis]), who is decapitated, and whom we have connected with the *solificatio* of the initiate in the Isis mysteries. This figure corresponds to the kingly mystagogue or psychopomp who appears in a vision reported in a late medieval alchemical text, the "Declaratio et Explicatio Adolphi," which forms part of the "Aurelia occulta." [65] So far as one can judge, the vision has no connection whatever with the Zosimos text, and I also doubt very much whether one should attribute to it the character of a mere parable. It contains certain features that are not traditional but are entirely original, and for this reason it seems likely that it was a genuine dream-experience. At all events, I know from my professional experience that similar dream-visions occur today among people who have no knowledge of alchemical symbolism. The vision is concerned with a shining male figure wearing a crown of stars. His robe is of white linen, dotted with many-coloured flowers, those of green predominating. He assuages the anxious doubts of the adept, saying: "Adolphus, follow me. I shall show thee what is prepared for thee, so that thou canst pass out of the darkness into the light." This figure, therefore, is a true Hermes Psychopompos and initiator, who directs the spiritual *transitus* of the adept. This is confirmed in the course of the latter's adventures, when he receives a book showing a "parabolic figure" of the Old Adam. We may take this as indicating that the psychopomp is the second Adam, a parallel figure to Christ. There is no talk of sacrifice, but, if our conjecture is right, this thought would be warranted by the appearance of the second Adam. Generally speaking, the figure of the king is associated with the motif of the *mortificatio*.

107    Thus in our text the personification of the sun or gold is to be sacrificed,[66] and his head, which was crowned with the aure-

[65] *Theatr. chem.*, IV (1659), pp. 509ff.
[66] The killing (*mortificatio*) of the king occurs in later alchemy (cf. *Psychology and Alchemy*, Fig. 173). The king's crown makes him a kind of sun. The motif belongs to the wider context of the sacrifice of the god, which developed not

ole of the sun, struck off, for this contains, or is, the arcanum.[67] Here we have an indication of the psychic nature of the arcanum, for the head of a man signifies above all the seat of consciousness.[68] Again, in the vision of Isis, the angel who bears the secret is connected with the meridian of the sun, for the text says that he appeared as "the sun was crossing the midpoint of its course." The angel bears the mysterious elixir on his head and, by his relationship to the meridian, makes it clear that he is a kind of solar genius or messenger of the sun who brings "illumination," that is, an enhancement and expansion of consciousness. His indecorous behaviour may be explained by the fact that angels have always enjoyed a dubious reputation as far as their morals are concerned. It is still the rule for women to cover their hair in church. Until well into the nineteenth century, especially in Protestant regions, they had to wear a special hood [69] when they went to church on Sundays. This was not because of the men in the congregation, but because of the possible presence of angels, who might be thrown into raptures at the sight of a feminine coiffure. Their susceptibility in these matters goes back to Genesis 6 : 2, where the "sons of God" displayed a particular penchant for the "daughters of men," and bridled their enthusiasm as little as did the two angels in the Isis treatise. This treatise is assigned to the first century A.D. Its views reflect the Judaeo-Hellenistic angelology[70] of Egypt, and it might easily have been known to Zosimos the Egyptian.

108    Such opinions about angels fit in admirably with masculine

---

only in the West but also in the East, and particularly in ancient Mexico. There the personifier of Tezcatlipoca ("fiery mirror") was sacrificed at the festival of Toxcatl (Spence, *The Gods of Mexico*, pp. 97ff.). The same thing happened in the cult of Uitzilopochtli, the sun-god (ibid., p. 73), who also figured in the eucharistic rite of the *teoqualo*, "god-eating" (cf. "Transformation Symbolism in the Mass," pp. 223f.).

[67] The solar nature of the victim is confirmed by the tradition that the man destined to be beheaded by the priests of Harran had to have fair hair and blue eyes (ibid., p. 240).

[68] Cf. my remarks on the Harranite head mystery and the legendary head oracle of Pope Sylvester II (ibid., pp. 240f.).

[69] Its form can still be seen in the deacon's hood.

[70] According to Rabbinic tradition the angels (including Satan) were created on the second day of Creation (the day of the moon). They were immediately divided on the question of creating man. Therefore God created Adam in secret, to avoid incurring the displeasure of the angels.

as well as with feminine psychology. If angels are anything at all, they are personified transmitters of unconscious contents that are seeking expression. But if the conscious mind is not ready to assimilate these contents, their energy flows off into the affective and instinctual sphere. This produces outbursts of affect, irritation, bad moods, and sexual excitement, as a result of which consciousness gets thoroughly disoriented. If this condition becomes chronic, a dissociation develops, described by Freud as repression, with all its well-known consequences. It is, therefore, of the greatest therapeutic importance to acquaint oneself with the contents that underlie the dissociation.

109    Just as the angel Amnael brings the arcane substance with him, so the "Meridian of the Sun" is himself a representation of it. In alchemical literature, the procedure of transfixing or cutting up with the sword takes the special form of dividing the philosophical egg. It, too, is divided with the sword, i.e., broken down into the four natures or elements. As an arcanum, the egg is a synonym for the water.[71] It is also a synonym for the dragon (mercurial serpent)[72] and hence for the water in the special sense of the microcosm or monad. Since water and egg are synonymous, the division of the egg with the sword is also applied to the water. "Take the vessel, cut it through with the sword, take its soul . . . thus is this water of ours our vessel." [73] The vessel likewise is a synonym for the egg, hence the recipe: "Pour into a round glass vessel, shaped like a phial or egg." [74] The egg is a copy of the World-Egg, the egg-white corresponding to the "waters above the firmament," the "shining liquor," and the yolk to the physical world.[75] The egg contains the four elements.[76]

71 "They compared the water to an egg, because it surrounds everything that is within it, and has in itself all that is necessary" ("Consilium coniugii," *Ars chemica*, p. 140). "Having all that is necessary" is one of the attributes of God.
72 Maier, *Symb. aur. mens.*, p. 466. Cf. Senior, *De chemia*, p. 108: "The dragon is the divine water."
73 *Mus. herm.*, p. 785.
74 Ibid., p. 90.
75 Steeb, *Coelum Sephiroticum*, p. 33.
76 *Turba*, Sermo IV, p. 112. Cf. also the "nomenclature of the egg" in Berthelot, *Alch. grecs*, I, iv, and Olympiodorus on the egg, the tetrasomia, and the spherical phial (II, iv, 44). Concerning the identity of uroboros and egg, and the division into four, see the Book of El-Habib (Berthelot, *Moyen âge*, III, pp. 92, 104). There is a picture of the egg being divided with the sword in Emblem VIII of

110    The dividing sword seems to have a special significance in addition to those we have noted. The "Consilium coniugii" says that the marriage pair, sun and moon, "must both be slain by their own sword, imbibing immortal souls until the most hidden interior [i.e., the previous] soul is extinguished." [77] In a poem of 1620, Mercurius complains that he is "sore tormented with a fiery sword." [78] According to the alchemists, Mercurius is the old serpent who already in paradise possessed "knowledge," since he was closely related to the devil. It is the fiery sword brandished by the angel at the gates of paradise that torments him,[79] and yet he himself is this sword. There is a picture in the "Speculum veritatis" [80] of Mercurius killing the king and the snake with the sword—"gladio proprio se ipsum interficiens." Saturn, too, is shown pierced by a sword.[81] The sword is well suited to Mercurius as a variant of the *telum passionis*, Cupid's arrow.[82] Dorn, in his "Speculativa philosophia," [83] gives a long and interesting interpretation of the sword: it is the "sword of God's wrath," which, in the form of Christ the Logos, was hung upon the tree of life. Thus the wrath of God was changed to love, and "the water of Grace now bathes the whole world." Here again, as in Zosimos, the water is connected with the sacrificial act. Since the Logos, the Word of God, is "sharper than any two-edged sword" (Hebrews 4 : 12), the words

---

Maier's *Scrutinium chymicum* (p. 22), with the inscription: "Take the egg and pierce it with a fiery sword." Emblem XXV shows the killing of the dragon. Killing with the sword is also shown in Lambspringk's Symbol II (*Musaeum hermeticum*, p. 345), titled "Putrefactio." Killing and division into four go together. "Mortificatio (scl. Lapidis) separatio elementorum" ("Exercit. in Turb. IX"). Cf. the dramatic fights with the dragon in the visions of Krates (Berthelot, *Moyen âge*, III, pp. 73ff.).

77 *Ars chemica*, p. 259.

78 *Verus Hermes*, p. 16. [Cf. infra, par. 276.]

79 This motif also occurs in the Adam parable in "Aurelia occulta" (*Theatr. chem.*, IV, 1659, pp. 511f.), which describes how the angel had to deal Adam several bloody wounds with his sword because he refused to move out of Paradise. Adam is the arcane substance, whose "extraction from the garden" of Eve is finally accomplished by means of blood magic.

80 Codex Vat. Lat. 7286 (17th cent.). Fig. 150 in *Psychology and Alchemy*.

81 Codex Vossianus 29 (Leiden), fol. 73.

82 Ripley's "Cantilena," verse 17. [Cf. *Mysterium Coniunctionis*, p. 285.—EDITORS.]

83 *Theatr. chem.*, I (1659), p. 254. Cf. "Transformation Symbolism in the Mass," pp. 234f. [Also cf. infra, pars. 447f.]

of the Consecration in the Mass were interpreted as the sacrificial knife with which the offering is slain.[84] One finds in Christian symbolism the same "circular" Gnostic thinking as in alchemy. In both the sacrificer is the sacrificed, and the sword that kills is the same as that which is killed.

111 In Zosimos this circular thinking appears in the sacrificial priest's identity with his victim and in the remarkable idea that the homunculus into whom Ion is changed devours himself.[85] He spews forth his own flesh and rends himself with his own teeth. The homunculus therefore stands for the uroboros, which devours itself and gives birth to itself (as though spewing itself forth). Since the homunculus represents the transformation of Ion, it follows that Ion, the uroboros, and the sacrificer are essentially the same. They are three different aspects of the same principle. This equation is confirmed by the symbolism of that part of the text which I have called the "résumé" and have placed at the end of the visions. The sacrificed is indeed the uroboros serpent, whose circular form is suggested by the shape of the temple, which has "neither beginning nor end in its construction." Dismembering the victim corresponds to the idea of dividing the chaos into four elements or the baptismal water into four parts. The purpose of the operation is to create the beginnings of order in the *massa confusa,* as is suggested in III, i, 2: "in accordance with the rule of harmony." The psychological parallel to this is the reduction to order, through reflection, of apparently chaotic fragments of the unconscious which have broken through into consciousness. Without knowing anything of alchemy or its operations, I worked out many years ago a psychological typology based on the four functions of consciousness as the ordering principles of psychic processes in general. Unconsciously, I was making use of the same archetype which had led Schopenhauer to give his "principle of sufficient reason" a fourfold root.[86]

112 The temple built of a "single stone" is an obvious paraphrase of the lapis. The "spring of purest water" in the temple is a fountain of life, and this is a hint that the production of the

---

[84] Ibid., p. 215.

[85] The parallel to this is the old view that Christ drank his own blood (ibid., p. 211).

[86] Cf. my "A Psychological Approach to the Dogma of the Trinity," p. 167.

round wholeness, the stone, is a guarantee of vitality. Similarly, the light that shines within it can be understood as the illumination which wholeness brings.[87] Enlightenment is an increase of consciousness. The temple of Zosimos appears in later alchemy as the *domus thesaurorum* or *gazophylacium* (treasurehouse).[88]

113     Although the shining white "monolith" undoubtedly stands for the stone, it clearly signifies at the same time the Hermetic vessel. The *Rosarium* says: "One is the stone, one the medicine, one the vessel, one the procedure, and one the disposition." [89] The scholia to the "Tractatus aureus Hermetis" put it even more plainly: "Let all be one in one circle or vessel." [90] Michael Maier ascribes to Maria the Jewess ("sister of Moses") the view that the whole secret of the art lay in knowledge of the Hermetic vessel. It was divine, and had been hidden from man by the wisdom of the Lord.[91] *Aurora consurgens* II [92] says that the natural vessel is the *aqua permanens* and the "vinegar of the philosophers," which obviously means that it is the arcane substance itself. We should understand the "Practica Mariae" [93] in this sense when it says that the Hermetic vessel is "the measure of your fire" and that it had been "hidden by the Stoics";[94] it is the "toxic body" which transforms Mercurius and is therefore the water of the philosophers.[95] As the arcane substance the vessel is not only water but also fire, as the "Allegoriae sapientum" makes clear: "Thus our stone, that is the flask of fire, is created from fire." [96] We can therefore understand why Mylius[97] calls the vessel the "root and principle of our art." Laurentius

---

87 The shining of the vessel is often mentioned, as in "Allegoriae super librum Turbae" (*Art. aurif.*, I, p. 143): ". . . until you see the vessel gleam and shine like a jacinth."
88 *Ars chemica*, p. 9.
89 1550 edn., fol. A III.
90 *Bibl. chem.*, I, p. 442.
91 *Symb. aur. mens.*, p. 63.
92 *Art. aurif.*, I, p. 203.
93 Ibid., p. 323.
94 The "Stoics" are also mentioned in "Liber quartorum," *Theatr. chem.*, V (1660), p. 128.
95 Hoghelande, "De difficult. alch.," *Theatr. chem.*, I (1659), p. 177.
96 *Theatr. chem.*, V (1660), p. 60.
97 *Phil. ref.*, p. 32.

Ventura[98] calls it "Luna," the *foemina alba* and mother of the stone. The vessel that is "not dissolved by water and not melted by fire" is, according to the "Liber quartorum," [99] "like the work of God in the vessel of the divine seed (*germinis divi*), for it has received the clay, moulded it, and mixed it with water and fire." This is an allusion to the creation of man, but on the other hand it seems to refer to the creation of souls, since immediately afterwards the text speaks of the production of souls from the "seeds of heaven." In order to catch the soul God created the *vas cerebri*, the cranium. Here the symbolism of the vessel coincides with that of the head, which I have discussed in my "Transformation Symbolism in the Mass." [100]

114    The prima materia, as the radical moisture, has to do with the soul because the latter is also moist by nature[101] and is sometimes symbolized by dew.[102] In this way the symbol of the vessel gets transferred to the soul. There is an excellent example of this in Caesarius of Heisterbach:[103] the soul is a spiritual substance of spherical nature, like the globe of the moon, or like a glass vessel that is "furnished before and behind with eyes" and "sees the whole universe." This recalls the many-eyed dragon of alchemy and the snake vision of Ignatius Loyola.[104] In this connection the remark of Mylius[105] that the vessel causes "the whole firmament to rotate in its course" is of special interest because, as I have shown, the symbolism of the starry heaven coincides with the motif of polyophthalmia.[106]

115    After all this we should be able to understand Dorn's view that the vessel must be made "by a kind of squaring of the circle." [107] It is essentially a psychic operation, the creation of an

[98] *Theatr. chem.*, II (1659), p. 246.

[99] Ibid., V (1660), p. 132.

[100] Pp. 239ff.

[101] The moisture is "retentive of souls" ("Lib. quart.," *Theatr. chem.*, V, 1660, p. 132).

[102] Cf. the descent of the soul in my "Psychology of the Transference," pars. 483 and 497.

[103] *Dialogus miraculorum*, Dist. IV, ch. xxxix (Eng. edn., p. 42).

[104] Cf. my "On the Nature of the Psyche," p. 198.

[105] *Phil. ref.*, p. 33.

[106] "On the Nature of the Psyche," pp. 198f.

[107] *Theatr. chem.*, I (1659), pp. 506f.: "Our vessel . . . should be made according to true geometrical proportion and measure, and by a kind of squaring of the circle."

inner readiness to accept the archetype of the self in whatever subjective form it appears. Dorn calls the vessel the *vas pellican-icum*, and says that with its help the quinta essentia can be extracted from the prima materia.[108] The anonymous author of the scholia to the "Tractatus aureus Hermetis" says: "This vessel is the true philosophical Pelican, and there is none other to be sought for in all the world." [109] It is the lapis itself and at the same time contains it; that is to say, the self is its own container. This formulation is borne out by the frequent comparison of the lapis to the egg or to the dragon which devours itself and gives birth to itself.

116    The thought and language of alchemy lean heavily on mysticism: in the Epistle of Barnabas[110] Christ's body is called the "vessel of the spirit." Christ himself is the pelican who plucks out his breast feathers for his young.[111] According to the teachings of Herakleon, the dying man should address the demiurgic powers thus: "I am a vessel more precious than the feminine being who made you. Whereas your mother knew not her own roots, I know of myself, and I know whence I have come, and I call upon the imperishable wisdom which is in the Father[112]

---

108 Ibid., p. 442.

109 Ibid., IV (1659), p. 698. [Cf. infra, Fig. B7.]

110 Lake, *Apostolic Fathers*, I, p. 383.

111 Honorius of Autun, *Speculum de myst. eccl.* (Migne, *P.L.*, vol. 172, col. 936). Christ's tearing of the breast, the wound in his side, and his martyr's death are parallels of the alchemical *mortificatio*, dismemberment, flaying, etc., and pertain like these to the birth and revelation of the inner man. Cf. the report in Hippolytus (*Elenchos*, V, 9, 1–6) of the Phrygian system. The Phrygians taught that the Father of all things was called Amygdalos (almond-tree), was pre-existent, and bore in himself the "perfect fruit pulsating and stirring in the depths." He "tore his breast and gave birth to his invisible, nameless and unnameable child." That was the "Invisible One, through whom all things were made, and without whom nothing was made" (an allusion to John 1 : 3). He was "Syriktes, the piper," i.e., the wind (pneuma). He was "thousand-eyed, not to be comprehended," the Word ($\dot\rho\eta\mu\alpha$) of God, the Word of annunciation and great power." He was "hidden in the dwelling where the roots of all things are established." He was the "Kingdom of Heaven, the grain of mustard-seed, the indivisible point . . . which none know save the spiritual alone." (Cf. Legge trans., *Philosophumena*, I, pp. 140f.)

112 Herakleon taught that the Ground of the world was a Primordial Man named Bythos (depths of the sea), who was neither male nor female. From this being was produced the inner man, his counterpart, who "came down from the Pleroma on high."

and is the Mother of your mother, which has no mother, but also has no male companion." [113]

117    In the abstruse symbolism of alchemy we hear a distant echo of this kind of thinking, which, without hope of further development, was doomed to destruction under the censorship of the Church. But we also find in it a groping towards the future, a premonition of the time when the projection would be taken back into man, from whom it had arisen in the first place. It is interesting to see the strangely clumsy ways in which this tendency seeks to express itself in the phantasmagoria of alchemical symbolism. The following instructions are given in Johannes de Rupescissa: "Cause a vessel to be made in the fashion of a Cherub, which is the face of God, and let it have six wings, like to six arms folding back upon themselves; and above, a round head. . . ." [114] From this it appears that although the ideal distilling vessel should resemble some monstrous kind of deity, it nevertheless had an approximately human shape. Rupescissa calls the quintessence the "ciel humain" and says it is "comme le ciel et les étoiles." The Book of El-Habib [115] says: "Man's head likewise resembles a condensing apparatus." Speaking of the four keys for unlocking the treasure-house, the "Consilium coniugii" [116] explains that one of them is "the ascent of the water through the neck to the head of the vessel, that is like a living man." There is a similar idea in the "Liber quartorum": "The vessel . . . must be round in shape, that the artifex may be the transformer of the firmament and the brain-pan, just as the thing which we need is a simple thing." [117] These ideas go back to the head symbolism in Zosimos, but at the same time they are an intimation that the transformation takes place in the head and is a psychic process. This realization was not something that

---

113 Epiphanius, *Panarium* (ed. Holl), II, pp. 46f.
114 *La Vertu et propriété de la quinte essence*, p. 26.
115 Berthelot, *Moyen âge*, III, p. 80.
116 *Ars chemica*, p. 110.
117 *Theatr. chem.*, V (1660), p. 134. The *res simplex* refers, ultimately, to God. It is "insensible." The soul is simple, and the "opus is not perfected unless the matter is turned into the simple" (p. 116). "The understanding is the simple soul," and "knows also what is higher than it, and the One God surrounds it, whose nature it cannot comprehend" (p. 129). "That from which things have their being is the invisible and immoveable God, by whose will the understanding is created" (p. 129).

was clumsily disguised afterwards; the laborious way in which it was formulated proves how obstinately it was projected into matter. Psychological knowledge through withdrawal of projections seems to have been an extremely difficult affair from the very beginning.

118     The dragon, or serpent, represents the initial state of unconsciousness, for this animal loves, as the alchemists say, to dwell "in caverns and dark places." Unconsciousness has to be sacrificed; only then can one find the entrance into the head, and the way to conscious knowledge and understanding. Once again the universal struggle of the hero with the dragon is enacted, and each time at its victorious conclusion the sun rises: consciousness dawns, and it is perceived that the transformation process is taking place inside the temple, that is, in the head. It is in truth the inner man, presented here as a homunculus, who passes through the stages that transform the copper into silver and the silver into gold, and who thus undergoes a gradual enhancement of value.

119     It sounds very strange to modern ears that the inner man and his spiritual growth should be symbolized by metals. But the historical facts cannot be doubted, nor is the idea peculiar to alchemy. It is said, for instance, that after Zarathustra had received the drink of omniscience from Ahuramazda, he beheld in a dream a tree with four branches of gold, silver, steel, and mixed iron.[118] This tree corresponds to the metallic tree of alchemy, the *arbor philosophica,* which, if it has any meaning at all, symbolizes spiritual growth and the highest illumination. Cold, inert metal certainly seems to be the direct opposite of spirit—but what if the spirit is as dead and as heavy as lead? A dream might then easily tell us to look for it in lead or quicksilver! It seems that nature is out to prod man's consciousness towards greater expansion and greater clarity, and for this reason continually exploits his greed for metals, especially the precious ones, and makes him seek them out and investigate their properties. While so engaged it may perhaps dawn on him that not only veins of ore are to be found in the mines, but also kobolds and little metal men, and that there may be hidden in lead either a deadly demon or the dove of the Holy Ghost.[119]

[118] Reitzenstein and Schaeder, *Studien zum antiken Synkretismus aus Iran und Griechenland,* p. 45.     [119] [Cf. *Psychology and Alchemy,* par. 443.]

120    It is evident that some alchemists passed through this process of realization to the point where only a thin wall separated them from psychological self-awareness. Christian Rosencreutz is still this side of the dividing line, but with *Faust* Goethe came out on the other side and was able to describe the psychological problem which arises when the inner man, or greater personality that before had lain hidden in the homunculus, emerges into the light of consciousness and confronts the erstwhile ego, the animal man. More than once Faust had inklings of the metallic coldness of Mephistopheles, who had first circled round him in the shape of a dog (uroboros motif). Faust used him as a familiar spirit and finally got rid of him by means of the motif of the cheated devil; but all the same he claimed the credit for the fame Mephistopheles brought him as well as for the power to work magic. Goethe's solution of the problem was still medieval, but it nevertheless reflected a psychic attitude that could get on without the protection of the Church. That was not the case with Rosencreutz: he was wise enough to stay outside the magic circle, living as he did within the confines of tradition. Goethe was more modern and therefore more incautious. He never really understood how dreadful was the Walpurgisnacht of the mind against which Christian dogma offered protection, even though his own masterpiece spread out this underworld before his eyes in two versions. But then, an extraordinary number of things can happen to a poet without having serious consequences. These appeared with a vengeance only a hundred years later. The psychology of the unconscious has to reckon with long periods of time like this, for it is concerned less with the ephemeral personality than with age-old processes, compared with which the individual is no more than the passing blossom and fruit of the rhizome underground.

### 3. THE PERSONIFICATIONS

121    What I have taken as a résumé, namely the piece we have been discussing, Zosimos calls a προοίμιον, an introduction.[1] It is therefore not a dream-vision; Zosimos is speaking here in the conscious language of his art, and expresses himself in terms that are obviously familiar to his reader. The dragon, its sacrifice

1 [Supra, par. 87 (III, i, 6).]

and dismemberment, the temple built of a single stone, the miracle of goldmaking, the transmutation of the anthroparia, are all current conceptions in the alchemy of his day. That is why this piece seems to us a conscious allegory, contrasting with the authentic visions, which treat the theme of transmutation in an unorthodox and original way, just as a dream might do. The abstract spirits of the metals are pictured here as suffering human beings; the whole process becomes like a mystic initiation and has been very considerably psychologized. But Zosimos' consciousness is still so much under the spell of the projection that he can see in the vision nothing more than the "composition of the waters." One sees how in those days consciousness turned away from the mystic process and fastened its attention upon the material one, and how the projection drew the mind towards the physical. For the physical world had not yet been discovered. Had Zosimos recognized the projection, he would have fallen back into the fog of mystic speculation, and the development of the scientific spirit would have been delayed for an even longer time. For us, matters are different. It is just the mystic content of his visions that is of special importance for us, because we are familiar enough with the chemical processes which Zosimos was out to investigate. We are therefore in a position to separate them from the projection and to recognize the psychic element they contain. The résumé also offers us a standard of comparison which enables us to discern the difference between its style of exposition and that of the visions. This difference supports our assumption that the visions are more like a dream than an allegory, though there is little possibility of our reconstructing the dream from the defective text that has come down to us.

122 The representation of the "alchemystical" process by persons needs a little explanation. The personification of lifeless things is a remnant of primitive and archaic psychology. It is caused by unconscious identity,[2] or what Lévy-Bruhl called *participation mystique*. The unconscious identity, in turn, is caused by the projection of unconscious contents into an object, so that these contents then become accessible to consciousness as qualities apparently belonging to the object. Any object that is at all interesting provokes a considerable number of projections. The difference between primitive and modern psychology in this

2 Cf. *Psychological Types*, Def. 25.

respect is in the first place qualitative, and in the second place one of degree. Consciousness develops in civilized man by the acquisition of knowledge and by the withdrawal of projections. These are recognized as psychic contents and are reintegrated with the psyche. The alchemists concretized or personified practically all their most important ideas—the four elements, the vessel, the stone, the prima materia, the tincture, etc. The idea of man as a microcosm, representing in all his parts the earth or the universe,[3] is a remnant of an original psychic identity which reflected a twilight state of consciousness. An alchemical text[4] expresses this as follows:

Man is to be esteemed a little world, and in all respects he is to be compared to a world. The bones under his skin are likened to mountains, for by them is the body strengthened, even as the earth is by rocks, and the flesh is taken for earth, and the great blood vessels for great rivers, and the little ones for small streams that pour into the great rivers. The bladder is the sea, wherein the great as well as the small streams congregate. The hair is compared to sprouting herbs, the nails on the hands and feet, and whatever else may be discovered inside and outside a man, all according to its kind is compared to the world.

123     Alchemical projections are only a special instance of the mode of thinking typified by the idea of the microcosm. Here is another example of personification:[5]

Now mark further Best Beloved / how you should do / you should go to the house / there you will find two doors / that are shut / you should stand a while before them / until one comes / and opens the door / and goes out to you / that will be a Yellow Man / and is not pretty to look upon / but you should not fear him / because he is unshapely / but he is sweet of word / and will ask you / my dear what seekest thou here / when truly I have long seen no man / so near this house / then you should answer him / I have come here and seek the Lapidem Philosophorum / the same Yellow Man will answer you and speak thus / my dear friend since you now have

[3] Cf. the medieval *melothesiae*. [For a definition, see "Psychology and Religion," p. 67, n. 5.—EDITORS.]
[4] "Gloria mundi," *Mus. herm.*, p. 270.
[5] "Ein Philosophisches Werck und Gespräch, von dem Gelben und Rotten Mann Reverendissimi Domini Melchioris Cardinalis et Episcopi Brixiensis," reprinted in *Aureum vellus*, pp. 177f. After the Red Man he finds the Black Raven, and from this comes the White Dove.

come so far / I will show you further / you should go into the house / until you come to a running fountain / and then go on a little while / and there will come to you a Red Man / he is Fiery Red and has Red eyes / you should not fear him on account of his ugliness / for he is gentle of word / and he also will ask you / my dear friend / what is your desire here / when to me you are a strange guest / and you should answer him / I seek the Lapidem Philosophorum. . . .

124    Personifications of metals are especially common in the folktales of imps and goblins, who were often seen in the mines.[6] We meet the metal men several times in Zosimos,[7] also a brazen eagle.[8] The "white man" appears in Latin alchemy: "Accipe illum album hominem de vase." He is the product of the conjunction of the bridegroom and bride,[9] and belongs to the same context of thought as the oft-cited "white woman" and "red slave," who are synonymous with Beya and Gabricus in the "Visio Arislei." These two figures seem to have been taken over by Chaucer:[10]

> The statue of Mars upon a carte stood,
> Armed, and looked grym as he were wood;
> And over his heed ther shynen two figures
> Of sterres, that been cleped in scriptures,
> That oon Puella, that oother Rubeus.

125    Nothing would have been easier than to equate the love story of Mars and Venus with that of Gabricus and Beya (who were also personified as dog and bitch), and it is likely that astrological influences also played a part. Thanks to his unconscious identity with it, man and cosmos interact. The following passage, of the utmost importance for the psychology of alchemy, should be understood in this sense: "And as man is composed of the four elements, so also is the stone, and so it is [dug] out of man, and you are its ore, namely by working; and from you it is extracted, namely by division; and in you it remains inseparably,

6 Cf. the interesting examples in Agricola, *De animantibus subterraneis,* and Kircher, *Mundus subterraneus,* lib. VIII, cap. IV.

7 *Alch. grecs,* III, xxxv.

8 Ibid., III, xxix, 18f.

9 "Aenigma" VI, in *Art. aurif.,* I, p. 151.

10 *The Canterbury Tales* (ed. Robinson), p. 43 (The Knight's Tale, 2041–45).

namely through the science." [11] Not only do things appear personified as human beings, but the macrocosm personifies itself as a man too. "The whole of nature converges in man as in a centre, and one participates in the other, and man has not unjustly concluded that the material of the philosophical stone may be found everywhere." [12] The "Consilium coniugii" [13] says: "Four are the natures which compose the philosophical man." "The elements of the stone are four, which, when well proportioned to one another, constitute the philosophical man, that is, the perfect human elixir." "They say that the stone is a man, because one cannot attain to it [14] save by reason and human knowledge." The above statement "you are its ore" has a parallel in the treatise of Komarios:[15] "In thee [Cleopatra] is hidden the whole terrible and marvellous secret." The same is said of the "bodies" ($\sigma\acute{\omega}\mu\alpha\tau\alpha$, i.e., 'substances'): "In them the whole secret is concealed." [16]

### 4. THE STONE SYMBOLISM

126    Zosimos contrasts the body ($\sigma\acute{\alpha}\rho\xi$ in the sense of 'flesh') with the spiritual man ($\pi\nu\epsilon\upsilon\mu\alpha\tau\iota\kappa\acute{o}s$).[1] The distinguishing mark of the spiritual man is that he seeks self-knowledge and knowledge of God.[2] The earthly, fleshly man is called Thoth or Adam. He bears within him the spiritual man, whose name is light ($\phi\tilde{\omega}s$). This first man, Thoth-Adam, is symbolized by the four elements. The spiritual and the fleshly man are also named Prometheus and Epimetheus. But "in allegorical language" they "are but one man, namely soul and body." The spiritual man was seduced into putting on the body, and was bound to it by "Pandora,

11 "Rosinus ad Sarrat.," *Art. aurif.,* I, p. 311.
12 "Orthelii epilogus," *Theatr. chem.,* VI (1661), p. 438.
13 *Ars chemica,* pp. 247, 253, 254.
14 The text has "ad Deum" (instead of "ad eum"), which is meaningless. Statements like "our body is our Stone" ("Authoris ignoti opusculum," *Art. aurif.,* I, p. 392) are doubtful, because "corpus nostrum" can just as well mean the arcane substance.
15 *Alch. grecs,* IV, xx, 8.
16 IV, xx, 16.
1 III, xlix, 4.
2 The importance of self-knowledge is stressed in the alchemical texts. Cf. *Aion,* pp. 162ff.

whom the Hebrews call Eve." [3] She played the part, therefore, of the anima, who functions as the link between body and spirit, just as Shakti or Maya entangles man's consciousness with the world. In the "Book of Krates" the spiritual man says: "Are you capable of knowing your soul completely? If you knew it as you should, and if you knew what could make it better, you would be capable of knowing that the names which the philosophers gave it of old are not its true names." [4] This last sentence is a standing phrase which is applied to the names of the lapis. The lapis signifies the inner man, the ἄνθρωπος πνευματικός, the *natura abscondita* which the alchemists sought to set free. In this sense the *Aurora consurgens* says that through baptism by fire "man, who before was dead, is made a living soul." [5]

127    The attributes of the stone—incorruptibility, permanence, divinity, triunity, etc.—are so insistently emphasized that one cannot help taking it as the *deus absconditus* in matter. This is probably the basis of the lapis-Christ parallel, which occurs as early as Zosimos[6] (unless the passage in question is a later interpolation). Inasmuch as Christ put on a "human body capable of suffering" and clothed himself in matter, he forms a parallel to the lapis, the corporeality of which is constantly stressed. Its ubiquity corresponds to the omnipresence of Christ. Its "cheapness," however, goes against the doctrinal view. The divinity of Christ has nothing to do with man, but the healing stone is "extracted" from man, and every man is its potential carrier and creator. It is not difficult to see what kind of conscious situation the lapis philosophy compensates: far from *signifying* Christ, the lapis *complements* the common conception of the Christ figure at that time.[7] What unconscious nature was ultimately aiming at when she produced the image of the lapis can be seen most clearly in the notion that it originated in matter and in man, that it was to be found everywhere, and that its fabrication lay at least potentially within man's reach. These qualities all reveal what were felt to be the defects in the Christ image at that time: an air too rarefied for human needs, too great a remoteness, a

---

[3] For a translation of the entire text, see *Psychology and Alchemy*, par. 456.
[4] Berthelot, *Moyen âge*, III, p. 50.
[5] Cf. *Aurora Consurgens* (ed. M.-L. von Franz), p. 87.
[6] *Alch. grecs*, III, xlix, 4.
[7] Cf. infra, "The Spirit Mercurius," pars. 289ff.

place left vacant in the human heart. Men felt the absence of the "inner" Christ who belonged to every man. Christ's spirituality was too high and man's naturalness was too low. In the image of Mercurius and the lapis the "flesh" glorified itself in its own way; it would not transform itself into spirit but, on the contrary, "fixed" the spirit in stone, and endowed the stone with all the attributes of the three Persons. The lapis may therefore be understood as a symbol of the inner Christ, of God in man. I use the expression "symbol" on purpose, for though the lapis is a parallel of Christ, it is not meant to replace him. On the contrary, in the course of the centuries the alchemists tended more and more to regard the lapis as the culmination of Christ's work of redemption. This was an attempt to assimilate the Christ figure into the philosophy of the "science of God." In the sixteenth century Khunrath formulated for the first time the "theological" position of the lapis: it was the *filius macrocosmi* as opposed to the "son of man," who was the *filius microcosmi*. This image of the "Son of the Great World" tells us from what source it was derived: it came not from the conscious mind of the individual man, but from those border regions of the psyche that open out into the mystery of cosmic matter. Correctly recognizing the spiritual one-sidedness of the Christ image, theological speculation had begun very early to concern itself with Christ's body, that is, with his materiality, and had temporarily solved the problem with the hypothesis of the resurrected body. But because this was only a provisional and therefore not an entirely satisfactory answer, the problem logically presented itself again in the Assumption of the Blessed Virgin, leading first to the dogma of the Immaculate Conception and finally to that of the Assumption. Though this only postpones the real answer, the way to it is nevertheless prepared. The assumption and coronation of Mary, as depicted in the medieval illustrations, add a fourth, feminine principle to the masculine Trinity. The result is a quaternity, which forms a real and not merely postulated symbol of totality. The totality of the Trinity is a mere postulate, for outside it stands the autonomous and eternal adversary with his choirs of fallen angels and the denizens of hell. Natural symbols of totality such as occur in our dreams and visions, and in the East take the form of mandalas, are quaternities or multiples of four, or else squared circles.

128     The accentuation of matter is above all evident in the choice of the *stone* as a God-image. We meet this symbol in the very earliest Greek alchemy, but there are good reasons for thinking that the stone symbol is very much older than its alchemical usage. The stone as the birthplace of the gods (e.g., the birth of Mithras from a stone) is attested by primitive legends of stone-births which go back to ideas that are even more ancient—for instance, the view of the Australian aborigines that children's souls live in a special stone called the "child-stone." They can be made to migrate into a uterus by rubbing the "child-stone" with a *churinga*. *Churingas* may be boulders, or oblong stones artificially shaped and decorated, or oblong, flattened pieces of wood ornamented in the same way. They are used as cult instruments. The Australians and the Melanesians maintain that *churingas* come from the totem ancestor, that they are relics of his body or of his activity, and are full of *arunquiltha* or mana. They are united with the ancestor's soul and with the spirits of all those who afterwards possess them. They are taboo, are buried in caches or hidden in clefts in the rocks. In order to "charge" them, they are buried among the graves so that they can soak up the mana of the dead. They promote the growth of field-produce, increase the fertility of men and animals, heal wounds, and cure sicknesses of the body and the soul. Thus, when a man's vitals are all knotted up with emotion, the Australian aborigines give him a blow in the abdomen with a stone *churinga*.[8] The *churingas* used for ceremonial purposes are daubed with red ochre, anointed with fat, bedded or wrapped in leaves, and copiously spat on (spittle = mana).[9]

129     These ideas of magic stones are found not only in Australia and Melanesia but also in India and Burma, and in Europe itself. For example, the madness of Orestes was cured by a stone in Laconia.[10] Zeus found respite from the sorrows of love by sitting on a stone in Leukadia. In India, a young man will tread upon a stone in order to obtain firmness of character, and a bride will do the same to ensure her own faithfulness. According

8 Spencer and Gillen, *The Northern Tribes of Central Australia*, pp. 257ff.
9 Hastings, *Encyclopaedia of Religion and Ethics*, XI, p. 874b, and Frazer, *Magic Art*, I, pp. 160ff. Similar ochre-painted stones can still be seen in India today, for instance in the Kalighat at Calcutta.
10 Pausanias, *Descriptio Graeciae* (ed. Spiro), I, p. 300.

to Saxo Grammaticus, the electors of the king stood on stones in order to give their vote permanence.[11] The green stone of Arran was used both for healing and for taking oaths on.[12] A cache of "soul stones," similar to *churingas,* was found in a cave on the river Birs near Basel, and during recent excavations of the pole-dwellings on the little lake at Burgaeschi, in Canton Solothurn, a group of boulders was discovered wrapped in the bark of birch trees. This very ancient conception of the magical power of stones led on a higher level of culture to the similar importance attached to gems, to which all kinds of magical and medicinal properties were attributed. The gems that are the most famous in history are even supposed to have been responsible for the tragedies that befell their owners.

130    A myth of the Navaho Indians of Arizona gives a particularly graphic account of the primitive fantasies that cluster round the stone.[13] In the days of the great darkness,[14] the ancestors of the hero saw the Sky Father descending and the Earth Mother rising up to meet him. They united, and on the top of the mountain where the union took place the ancestors found a little figure made of turquoise.[15] This turned into (or in another version gave birth to) Estsánatlehi, "the woman who rejuvenates or transforms herself." She was the mother of the twin gods who slew the primordial monsters, and was called the mother or grandmother of the gods (*yéi*). Estsánatlehi is the most important figure in the matriarchal pantheon of the Navaho. Not only is she the "woman who transforms herself," but she also has two shapes, for her twin sister, Yolkaíestsan, is endowed with similar powers. Estsánatlehi is immortal, for though she grows into a withered old woman she rises up again as a young girl—a true Dea Natura. From different parts of her body four daughters were born to her, and a fifth from her spirit. The sun came from the turquoise beads hidden in her right breast, and from white shell beads in her left breast the moon. She issues reborn by roll-

11 So did the archons in Athens when taking their oath.
12 Frazer, *Magic Art,* I, p. 161.
13 Schevill, *Beautiful on the Earth,* pp. 24ff. and 38ff.
14 For the Australian aborigines, this would be the primeval *alcheringa* time, which means both the world of the ancestors and the world of dreams.
15 Cf. the treatise of Komarios (Berthelot, *Alch. grecs,* IV, xx, 2): "Go up into the highest cave on the thick-wooded mountain, and behold there a stone on the mountain top. And take from the stone the male. . . ."

ing a piece of skin from under her left breast. She lives in the west, on an island in the sea. Her lover is the wild and cruel Sun Bearer, who has another wife; but he has to stay at home with her only when it rains. The turquoise goddess is so sacred that no image may be made of her, and even the gods may not look on her face. When her twin sons asked her who their father was, she gave them a wrong answer, evidently to protect them from the dangerous fate of the hero.

131     This matriarchal goddess is obviously an anima figure who at the same time symbolizes the self. Hence her stone-nature, her immortality, her four daughters born from the body, plus one from the spirit, her duality as sun and moon, her role as paramour, and her ability to change her shape.[16] The self of a man living in a matriarchal society is still immersed in his unconscious femininity, as can be observed even today in all cases of masculine mother-complexes. But the turquoise goddess also exemplifies the psychology of the matriarchal woman, who, as an anima figure, attracts the mother-complexes of all the men in her vicinity and robs them of their independence, just as Omphale held Herakles in thrall, or Circe reduced her captives to a state of bestial unconsciousness—not to mention Benoît's Atlantida, who made a collection of her mummified lovers. All this happens because the anima contains the secret of the precious stone, for, as Nietzsche says, "all joy wants eternity." Thus the legendary Ostanes, speaking of the secret of the "philosophy," says to his pupil Cleopatra: "In you is hidden the whole terrible and marvellous secret. . . . Make known to us how the highest descends to the lowest, and how the lowest ascends to the highest, and how the midmost draws near to the highest, and is made one with it." [17] This "midmost" is the stone, the mediator which unites the opposites. Such sayings have no meaning unless they are understood in a profoundly psychological sense.

132     Widespread as is the motif of the stone-birth (cf. the creation myth of Deucalion and Pyrrha), the American cycle of legends seems to lay special emphasis on the motif of the stone-body, or animated stone.[18] We meet this motif in the Iroquois tale of the twin brothers. Begotten in a miraculous manner in

16 Cf. Rider Haggard's *She.*

17 *Alch. grecs*, IV, xx, 8.

18 I am indebted to Dr. M.-L. von Franz for this material.

the body of a virgin, a pair of twins were born, one of whom came forth in the normal way, while the other sought an abnormal exit and emerged from the armpit, thereby killing his mother. This twin had a body made of flint. He was wicked and cruel, unlike his normally born brother.[19] In the Sioux version the mother was a tortoise. Among the Wichita, the saviour was the great star in the south, and he performed his work of salvation on earth as the "flint man." His son was called the "young flint." After completing their work, both of them went back into the sky.[20] In this myth, just as in medieval alchemy, the saviour coincides with the stone, the star, the "son," who is "super omnia lumina." The culture hero of the Natchez Indians came down to earth from the sun, and shone with unendurable brightness. His glance was death-dealing. In order to mitigate this, and to prevent his body from corrupting in the earth, he changed himself into a stone statue, from which the priestly chieftains of the Natchez were descended.[21] Among the Taos Pueblos, a virgin was made pregnant by beautiful stones and bore a hero son,[22] who, owing to Spanish influence, assumed the aspect of the Christ child.[23] The stone plays a similar role in the Aztec cycle of legends. For instance, the mother of Quetzalcoatl was made pregnant by a precious green stone.[24] He himself had the cognomen "priest of the precious stone" and wore a mask made of turquoise.[25] The precious green stone was an animating principle and was placed in the mouth of the dead.[26] Man's original home was the "bowl of precious stone." [27] The motif of transformation into stone, or petrifaction, is common in the Peruvian and Colombian legends and is probably connected with a megalithic stone-cult,[28] and perhaps also with the palaeolithic cult of *churinga*-like soul-stones. The parallels here would be the menhirs of megalithic culture, which reached as far as the

19 Krickeberg, *Indianermärchen aus Nordamerika*, pp. 92ff.
20 Van Deursen, *Der Heilbringer*, p. 227.
21 Ibid., p. 238.
22 Cf. the fertility significance of the *churingas*.
23 Van Deursen, p. 286.
24 Krickeberg, *Märchen der Azteken, Inka, Maya und Muiska*, p. 36.
25 Ibid., p. 65.
26 P. 330.
27 P. 317.
28 P. 382.

Pacific archipelago. The civilization of the Nile valley, which originated in megalithic times, turned its divine kings into stone statues for the express purpose of making the king's *ka* everlasting. In shamanism, much importance is attached to crystals, which play the part of ministering spirits.[29] They come from the crystal throne of the supreme being or from the vault of the sky. They show what is going on in the world and what is happening to the souls of the sick, and they also give man the power to fly.[30]

133     The connection of the lapis with immortality is attested from very early times. Ostanes (possibly 4th cent. B.C.) speaks of "the Nile stone that has a spirit." [31] The lapis is the panacea, the universal medicine, the alexipharmic, the tincture that transmutes base metals into gold and gravel into precious stones. It brings riches, power, and health; it cures melancholy and, as the *vivus lapis philosophicus,* is a symbol of the saviour, the Anthropos, and immortality. Its incorruptibility is also shown in the ancient idea that the body of a saint becomes stone. Thus the Apocalypse of Elijah says of those who escape persecution by the Anti-Messiah:[32] "The Lord shall take unto him their spirit and their souls, their flesh shall be made stone, no wild beast shall devour them till the last day of the great judgment." In a Basuto legend reported by Frobenius,[33] the hero is left stranded by his pursuers on the bank of a river. He changes himself into a stone, and his pursuers throw him across to the other side. This is the motif of the *transitus:* the "other side" is the same as eternity.

## 5. THE WATER SYMBOLISM

134     Psychological research has shown that the historical or ethnological symbols are identical with those spontaneously produced by the unconscious, and that the lapis represents the idea of a transcendent totality which coincides with what analytical psychology calls the self. From this point of view we can understand without difficulty the apparently absurd statement of the

[29] Eliade, *Shamanism,* p. 52.
[30] Ibid., pp. 363f.
[31] *Alch. grecs,* III, vi, 5, 12ff.
[32] Steindorff, *Apokalypse des Elias,* 36, 17–37, 1, p. 97.
[33] *Das Zeitalter des Sonnengottes,* p. 106.

alchemists that the lapis consists of body, soul, and spirit, is a living being, a homunculus or "homo." It symbolizes man, or rather, the inner man, and the paradoxical statements about it are really descriptions and definitions of this inner man. Upon this connotation of the lapis is based its parallelism with Christ. Behind the countless ecclesiastical and alchemical metaphors may be found the language of Hellenistic syncretism, which was originally common to both. Passages like the following one from Priscillian, a Gnostic-Manichaean heretic of the fourth century, must have been extremely suggestive for the alchemists: "One-horned is God, Christ a rock to us, Jesus a cornerstone, Christ the man of men" [1]—unless the matter was the other way round, and metaphors taken from natural philosophy found their way into the language of the Church via the Gospel of St. John.

135    The principle that is personified in the visions of Zosimos is the wonder-working water, which is both water and spirit, and kills and vivifies. If Zosimos, waking from his dream, immediately thinks of the "composition of the waters," this is the obvious conclusion from the alchemical point of view. Since the long-sought water, as we have shown,[2] represents a cycle of birth and death, every process that consists of death and rebirth is naturally a symbol of the divine water.

136    It is conceivable that we have in Zosimos a parallel with the Nicodemus dialogue in John 3. At the time when John's gospel was written, the idea of the divine water was familiar to every alchemist. When Jesus said: "Except a man be born of water and of the spirit . . . ," an alchemist of that time would at once have understood what he meant. Jesus marvelled at the ignorance of Nicodemus and asked him: "Art thou a master in Israel, and knowest not these things?" He obviously took it for granted that a teacher ($\delta\iota\delta\acute{a}\sigma\kappa\alpha\lambda o\varsigma$) would know the secret of water and spirit, that is, of death and rebirth. Whereupon he went on to utter a saying which is echoed many times in the alchemical treatises: "We speak that we do know, and testify that we have seen." Not that the alchemists actually cited this passage, but they thought in a similar way. They talk as if they had touched the arcanum or gift of the Holy Spirit with their own hands,

1 Tractatus I, *Corp. Script. Eccl. Lat.*, XVIII, p. 24.
2 See supra, par. 105.

and seen the workings of the divine water with their own eyes.[3] Even though these statements come from a later period, the spirit of alchemy remained more or less the same from the earliest times to the late Middle Ages.

137    The concluding words of the Nicodemus dialogue, concerning "earthly and heavenly things," had likewise been the common property of alchemy ever since Democritus had written of the "physika and mystika," also called "somata and asomata," "corporalia and spiritualia." [4] These words of Jesus are immediately followed by the motif of the ascent to heaven and descent to earth.[5] In alchemy this would be the ascent of the soul from the mortified body and its descent in the form of reanimating dew.[6] And when, in the next verse, Jesus speaks of the serpent lifted up in the wilderness and equates it with his own self-sacrifice, a "Master" would be bound to think of the uroboros,

---

[3] ". . . which I have seen with my own eyes and touched with my hands" (*Rosarium,* in *Art. aurif.,* II, p. 205).

[4] It must be remembered, however, that John uses other terms than those found in the alchemy of the time: τὰ ἐπίγεια and τὰ ἐπιουράνια (*terrena* and *coelestia* in the Vulgate).

[5] The source for this is Hermes Trismegistus in the "Tabula smaragdina": "It ascends from earth to heaven and descends again to earth. . . . The wind hath borne it in his belly." This text was always interpreted as referring to the stone (cf. Hortulanus, "Commentariolum," *Ars chemica*). But the stone comes from the "water." A perfect alchemical parallel to the Christian mystery is the following passage from the "Consilium coniug." (ibid., p. 128): "And if I ascend naked into heaven, then will I come clothed to earth and perfect all minerals. And if we are baptized in the fountain of gold and silver, and the spirit of our body ascends to heaven with the father and the son, and descends again, our souls will revive, and my animal body will remain white." The anonymous author of "Liber de arte chymica" (*Art. aurif.,* I, pp. 612f.) speaks in the same way: "It is certain that the earth cannot ascend, except first the heaven descend, for the earth is said to be raised up to heaven, when, dissolved in its own spirit, it is at last united therewith. I will satisfy thee with this parable: The Son of God descending into the Virgin, and there clothed with flesh, is born as man, who having shown us the way of truth for our salvation, suffered and died for us, and after his resurrection returned into heaven, where the earth, that is mankind, is exalted above all the circles of the world, and is placed in the intellectual heaven of the most holy Trinity. In like manner, when I die, my soul, helped by the grace and the merits of Christ, will return to the fount of life whence it descended. The body returns to earth, and at the last judgment of the world the soul, descending from heaven, will carry it with her, purified, to glory."

[6] The motif of ascent and descent is based partly on the motion of water as a natural phenomenon (clouds, rain, etc.).

which slays itself and brings itself to life again. This is followed by the motif of "everlasting life" and the panacea (belief in Christ). Indeed, the whole purpose of the opus was to produce the incorruptible body, "the thing that dieth not," the invisible, spiritual stone, or *lapis aethereus*. In the verse, "For God so loved the world that he gave his only begotten Son . . . ," Jesus identifies himself with the healing snake of Moses; for the Monogenes is synonymous with the Nous, and this with the serpent-saviour or Agathodaimon. The serpent is also a synonym for the divine water. The dialogue may be compared with Jesus' words to the woman of Samaria in John 4 : 14: ". . . a well of water springing up into everlasting life." [7] Significantly enough, the conversation by the well forms the context for the teaching that "God is Spirit" (John 4 : 24).[8]

138    In spite of the not always unintentional obscurity of alchemical language, it is not difficult to see that the divine water or its symbol, the uroboros, means nothing other than the *deus absconditus,* the god hidden in matter, the divine Nous that came down to Physis and was lost in her embrace.[9] This mystery of the "god become physical" underlies not only classical alchemy but also many other spiritual manifestations of Hellenistic syncretism.[10]

[7] Justin Martyr says: "As a fount of living water from God . . . this Christ gushed forth" (cited in Preuschen, *Antilegomena*, p. 129). Gaudentius (Sermo XIX) compares Christ's humanity to water (Migne, *P.L.*, vol. 20, col. 983). Eucherius of Lyons (*Liber formularum spiritalis intelligentiae*) says that Christ "carried up to heaven the flesh he assumed for us" (ibid., vol. 50, col. 734). This idea coincides with the saying in the "Tab. smarag." that the arcanum "ascends from earth to heaven, and descends again to earth, and receives the power of Above and Below."

[8] "Spirit" in alchemy means anything volatile, all evaporable substances, oxides, etc., but also, as a projected psychic content, a *corpus mysticum* in the sense of a "subtle body." (Cf. Mead, *The Doctrine of the Subtle Body in Western Tradition*.) It is in this sense that the definition of the lapis as a *spiritus humidus et aereus* should be understood. There are also indications that spirit was understood as "mind," which could be refined by "sublimation."

[9] Cf. the fate of the "man of light" in Zosimos (*Psychology and Alchemy*, par. 456).

[10] In the oldest sources this mystery is expressed in symbolical terms. But from the 13th cent. on there are more and more texts which reveal the mystical side of the arcanum. One of the best examples is the German treatise *Der Wasserstein der Weysen*, "A Chymical Tract, wherein the Way is Shown, the Materia Named, and the Process Described."

## 6. THE ORIGIN OF THE VISION

139    Since alchemy is concerned with a mystery both physical and spiritual, it need come as no surprise that the "composition of the waters" was revealed to Zosimos in a dream. His sleep was the sleep of incubation, his dream "a dream sent by God." The divine water was the alpha and omega of the process, desperately sought for by the alchemists as the goal of their desire. The dream therefore came as a dramatic explanation of the nature of this water. The dramatization sets forth in powerful imagery the violent and agonizing process of transformation which is itself both the producer and the product of the water, and indeed constitutes its very essence. The drama shows how the divine process of change manifests itself to our human understanding and how man experiences it—as punishment, torment,[1] death, and transfiguration. The dreamer describes how a man would act and what he would have to suffer if he were drawn into the cycle of the death and rebirth of the gods, and what effect the *deus absconditus* would have if a mortal man should succeed by his "art" in setting free the "guardian of spirits" from his dark dwelling. There are indications in the literature that this is not without its dangers.[2]

140    The mystical side of alchemy, as distinct from its historical aspect, is essentially a psychological problem. To all appearances, it is a concretization, in projected and symbolic form, of the process of individuation. Even today this process produces

[1] The element of torture, so conspicuous in Zosimos, is not uncommon in alchemical literature. "Slay the mother, cutting off her hands and feet" ("Aenigma" VI, *Art. aurif.*, I, p. 151). Cf. *Turba*, Sermones XVIII, XLVII, LXIX. "Take a man, shave him, and drag him over a stone . . . until his body dies." "Take a cock, pluck it alive, then put its head in a glass vessel" ("Alleg. sup. lib. Turb.," *Art. aurif.*, I, pp. 139ff.). In medieval alchemy the torturing of the materia was an allegory of Christ's passion (cf. *Der Wasserstein der Weysen*, p. 97).

[2] "The foundation of this art, for whose sake many have perished" (*Turba*, Sermo XV). Zosimos mentions Antimimos, the demon of error (*Alch. grecs*, III, xlix, 9). Olympiodorus quotes the saying of Petasios that lead (prima materia) was so "shameless and bedevilled" that it drove the adepts mad (ibid., II, iv, 43). The devil caused impatience, doubt, and despair during the work (*Mus. herm.*, p. 461). Hoghelande describes how the devil deceived him and his friend with delusions ("De difficult. alchem.," *Theatr. chem.*, I, 1659, pp. 152ff.). The dangers that threatened the alchemists were obviously psychic. Cf. infra, pars. 429ff.

symbols that have the closest connections with alchemy. On this point I must refer the reader to my earlier works, where I have discussed the question from a psychological angle and illustrated it with practical examples.

141    The causes that set such a process in motion may be certain pathological states (for the most part schizophrenic) which produce very similar symbols. But the best and clearest material comes from persons of sound mind who, driven by some kind of spiritual distress, or for religious, philosophical, or psychological reasons, devote particular attention to their unconscious. In the period extending from the Middle Ages back to Roman times, a natural emphasis was laid on the inner man, and since psychological criticism became possible only with the rise of science, the inner factors were able to reach consciousness in the form of projections much more easily than they can today. The following text[3] may serve to illustrate the medieval point of view:

For as Christ says in Luke 11: The light of the body is the eye, but if your eye is evil or becomes so, then your body is full of darkness and the light within you becomes darkness. Moreover, in the seventeenth chapter he says also: Behold, the kingdom of God is within you—from which it is clearly seen that knowledge of the light in man must emerge in the first place from within and cannot be placed there from without, and many passages in the Bible bear witness to this, namely, that the external object (as it is usually called), or the sign written to help us in our weakness, is in Matthew 24 merely a testimony of the inner light of grace planted in and imparted to us by God. So, too, the spoken word is to be heeded and considered only as an indication, an aid and a guide to this. To take an example: a white and a black board are placed in front of you and you are asked which is black and which is white. If the knowledge of the two different colours were not previously within you, you would never be able to answer from these mere mute objects or boards the question put to you, since this knowledge does not come from the boards themselves (for they are mute and inanimate), but originates in and flows forth from your innate faculties which you exercise daily. The objects (as stated earlier) indeed stimulate the senses and cause them to apprehend, but in no way do they give knowledge. This must come from within, from the apprehender, and the knowledge of such colours must emerge in

3 *Der Wasserstein der Weysen*, pp. 73ff. [For this translation I am indebted to Dr. R. T. Llewellyn.—TRANSLATOR.]

an act of apprehension. Similarly, when someone asks you for a material and external fire or light from a flint (in which the fire or light is hidden) you cannot put this hidden and secret light into the stone, but rather you must arouse, awaken, and draw forth the hidden fire from the stone and reveal it by means of the requisite steel striker which must be necessarily at hand. And this fire must be caught and vigorously fanned up in good tinder well prepared for this purpose, if it is not to be extinguished and disappear again. Then, afterwards, you will obtain a truly radiant light, shining like fire, and as long as it is tended and preserved, you will be able to create, work, and do with it as you please. And, likewise hidden in man, there exists such a heavenly and divine light which, as previously stated, cannot be placed in man from without, but must emerge from within.

For not in vain and without reason has God bestowed on and given to man in the highest part of his body two eyes and ears in order to indicate that man has to learn and heed within himself a twofold seeing and hearing, an inward and an outward, so that he may judge spiritual things with the inward part and allot spiritual things to the spiritual (I Corinthians 2), but also give to the outward its portion.

142      For Zosimos and those of like mind the divine water was a *corpus mysticum.*[4] A personalistic psychology will naturally ask: how did Zosimos come to be looking for a *corpus mysticum?* The answer would point to the historical conditions: it was a problem of the times. But in so far as the *corpus mysticum* was conceived by the alchemists to be a gift of the Holy Spirit, it can be understood in a quite general sense as a visible gift of grace conferring redemption. Man's longing for redemption is universal and can therefore have an ulterior, personalistic motive only in exceptional cases, when it is not a genuine phenomenon but an abnormal misuse of it. Hysterical self-deceivers, and ordinary ones too, have at all times understood the art of misusing everything so as to avoid the demands and duties of life, and above all to shirk the duty of confronting themselves. They pretend to be seekers after God in order not to have to face the truth that they are ordinary egoists. In such cases it is well worth asking: Why are you seeking the divine water?

143      We have no reason to suppose that all the alchemists were

---

[4] This term occurs in alchemy, e.g.: "Congeal [the quicksilver] with its mystic body" ("Consilium coniug.," *Theatr. chem.*, I, 1659, p. 137).

self-deceivers of this sort. The deeper we penetrate into the obscurities of their thinking, the more we must admit their right to style themselves "philosophers." Throughout the ages, alchemy was one of the great human quests for the unattainable. So, at least, we would describe it if we gave rein to our rationalistic prejudices. But the religious experience of grace is an irrational phenomenon, and cannot be discussed any more than can the "beautiful" or the "good." Since that is so, no serious quest is without hope. It is something instinctive, that cannot be reduced to a personal aetiology any more than can intelligence or musicality or any other inborn propensity. I am therefore of the opinion that our analysis and interpretation have done justice to the vision of Zosimos if we have succeeded in understanding its essential components in the light of how men thought then, and in elucidating the meaning and purpose of its *mise en scène*. When Kékulé had his dream of the dancing pairs and deduced from it the structure of the benzol ring, he accomplished something that Zosimos strove for in vain. His "composition of the waters" did not fall into as neat a pattern as did the carbon and hydrogen atoms of the benzol ring. Alchemy projected an inner, psychic experience into chemical substances that seemed to hold out mysterious possibilities but nevertheless proved refractory to the intentions of the alchemist.

144     Although chemistry has nothing to learn from the vision of Zosimos, it is a mine of discovery for modern psychology, which would come to a sorry pass if it could not turn to these testimonies of psychic experience from ancient times. Its statements would then be without support, like novelties that cannot be compared with anything, and whose value it is almost impossible to assess. But such documents give the investigator an Archimedean point outside his own narrow field of work, and therewith an invaluable opportunity to find his bearings in the seeming chaos of individual events.

# III

## PARACELSUS AS A SPIRITUAL
## PHENOMENON

[Originally a lecture, "Paracelsus als geistige Erscheinung," which, revised
and expanded, was published in *Paracelsica: Zwei Vorlesungen über den
Arzt und Philosophen Theophrastus* (Zurich, 1942).

[In the present translation, chapter and section headings have been
added to elucidate the structure of the monograph. Two brief statements
found among Jung's posthumous papers have, because of their relevance
to the subject-matter, been added as footnotes on pp. 136 and 144.—
EDITORS.]

# FOREWORD TO "PARACELSICA"

This little book comprises two lectures delivered this year on the occasion of the four-hundredth anniversary of the death of Paracelsus.[1] The first, "Paracelsus the Physician,"[2] was delivered to the Swiss Society for the History of Medicine and the Natural Sciences at the annual meeting of the Society for Nature Research, Basel, September 7, 1941; the second, "Paracelsus as a Spiritual Phenomenon," was given at the Paracelsus celebrations in Einsiedeln, October 5, 1941. The first lecture goes into print unaltered except for a few minor changes. But the special nature of the theme has obliged me to take the second lecture out of its original framework and to expand it into a proper treatise. The stylistic form and scope of a lecture are not suited to portray the unknown and enigmatic Paracelsus who stands beside or behind the figure we meet in his prolific medical, scientific, and theological writings. Only when they are taken together do they give a picture of this contradictory and yet so significant personality.

I am aware that the title of this lecture is somewhat presumptuous. The reader should take it simply as a contribution to our knowledge of the arcane philosophy of Paracelsus. I do not claim to have said anything final or conclusive on this difficult subject, and am only too painfully aware of gaps and inadequacies. My purpose was confined to providing clues that might point the way to the roots and psychic background of his philosophy, if such it can be called. Besides all the other things he was, Paracelsus was, perhaps most deeply of all, an alchemical "philosopher" whose religious views involved him in an unconscious conflict with the Christian beliefs of his age in a way that seems to us inextricably confused. Nevertheless, in this confusion are to be found the beginnings of philosophical, psychological, and religious problems which are taking clearer shape in our own epoch. Because of this, I have felt it almost an historical duty to contribute what I may in appreciation of prescient ideas which he left behind for us in his treatise *De vita longa*.

*October 1941*                                                          C. G. J.

[1] [Philippus Aureolus Theophrastus Bombastus von Hohenheim, known as Paracelsus, born 1493, in Einsiedeln, died Sept. 21, 1541, in Salzburg.—Editors.]
[2] [In *Coll. Works*, Vol. 15.—Editors.]

# 1. THE TWO SOURCES OF KNOWLEDGE: THE LIGHT OF NATURE AND THE LIGHT OF REVELATION

145    The man whose death four hundred years ago we commemorate today exerted a powerful influence on all subsequent generations, as much by sheer force of his personality as by his prodigious literary activity. His influence made itself felt chiefly in the field of medicine and natural science. In philosophy, not only was mystical speculation stimulated in a fruitful way, but philosophical alchemy, then on the point of extinction, received a new lease of life and enjoyed a renaissance. It is no secret that Goethe, as is evident from the second part of *Faust*, still felt the impact of the powerful spirit of Paracelsus.

146    It is not easy to see this spiritual phenomenon in the round and to give a really comprehensive account of it. Paracelsus was too contradictory or too chaotically many-sided, for all his obvious one-sidedness in other ways. First and foremost, he was a physician with all the strength of his spirit and soul, and his foundation was a firm religious belief. Thus he says in his *Paragranum*:[1] "You must be of an honest, sincere, strong, true faith in God, with all your soul, heart, mind, and thought, in all love and trust. On the foundation of such faith and love, God will not withdraw his truth from you, and will make his works manifest to you, believable, visible, and comforting. But if, not having such faith, you are against God, then you will go astray in your work and will have failures, and in consequence people will have no faith in you." The art of healing and its demands were the supreme criterion for Paracelsus. Everything in his life was devoted to this goal of helping and healing. Around this cardinal principle were grouped all his experiences, all his

[1] Ed. Strunz, p. 97. [For the translation of the direct quotations from Paracelsus in the text and footnotes of this section I am indebted to Dr. R. T. Llewellyn. —TRANSLATOR.]

knowledge, all his efforts. This happens only when a man is actuated by some powerful emotional driving force, by a great passion which, undeterred by reflection and criticism, overshadows his whole life. The driving force behind Paracelsus was his compassion. "Compassion," he exclaims, "is the physician's schoolmaster." [2] It must be inborn in him. Compassion, which has driven many another great man and inspired his work, was also the supreme arbiter of Paracelsus's fate.

147      The instrument which he put at the service of his great compassion was his science and his art, which he took over from his father. But the dynamism at the back of his work, the compassion itself, must have come to him from the prime source of everything emotional, that is, from his mother, of whom he never spoke. She died young, and she probably left behind a great deal of unsatisfied longing in her son—so much that, so far as we know, no other woman was able to compete with that far-distant mother-imago, which for that reason was all the more formidable. The more remote and unreal the personal mother is, the more deeply will the son's yearning for her clutch at his soul, awakening that primordial and eternal image of the mother for whose sake everything that embraces, protects, nourishes, and helps assumes maternal form, from the Alma Mater of the university to the personification of cities, countries, sciences, and ideals. When Paracelsus says that the mother of the child is the planet and star, this is in the highest degree true of himself. To the mother in her highest form, Mater Ecclesia, he remained faithful all his life, despite the very free criticism he levelled at the ills of Christendom in that epoch. Nor did he succumb to the great temptation of that age, the Protestant schism, though he may well have had it in him to go over to the other camp. Conflict was deeply rooted in Paracelsus's nature; indeed, it had to be so, for without a tension of opposites there is no energy, and whenever a volcano, such as he was, erupts, we shall not go wrong in supposing that water and fire have clashed together.

148      But although the Church remained a mother for Paracelsus all his life, he nevertheless had two mothers: the other was Mater Natura. And if the former was an absolute authority, so too was the latter. Even though he endeavoured to conceal the conflict between the two maternal spheres of influence, he was

[2] "De caducis," ed. Huser, I, p. 589.

honest enough to admit its existence; indeed, he seems to have had a very good idea of what such a dilemma meant. Thus he says: "I also confess that I write like a pagan and yet am a Christian." [3] Accordingly he named the first five sections of his *Paramirum de quinque entibus morborum* "Pagoya." "Pagoyum" is one of his favourite neologisms, compounded of "paganum" and the Hebrew word "goyim." He held that knowledge of the nature of diseases was pagan, since this knowledge came from the "light of nature" and not from revelation.[4] "Magic," he says, is "the preceptor and teacher of the physician," [5] who derives his knowledge from the *lumen naturae*. There can be no doubt the "light of nature" was a second, independent source of knowledge for Paracelsus. His closest pupil, Adam von Bodenstein, puts it like this: "The Spagyric has the things of nature not by authority, but by his own experience." [6] The concept of the *lumen*

[3] "Therefore Christian knowledge is better than natural knowledge, and a prophet or an apostle better than an astronomer or a physician . . . but I am compelled to add that the sick need a physician not apostles, just as prognostications require an astronomer not a prophet" ("Von Erkantnus des Gestirns," ed. Sudhoff, XII, pp. 496f.).

[4] He says in the fourth treatise of *Paramirum primum* (ed. Sudhoff, I, p. 215), speaking of the "ens spirituale" of diseases: "If we are to talk of the *Ens Spirituale*, we admonish you to put aside the style which you call theological. For not everything which is called *Theologia* is holy and also not everything it treats of is holy. And, moreover, not everything is true which the uncomprehending deal with in theology. Now although it is true that theology describes this *Ens* most powerfully, it does not do so under the name and text of our fourth *Pagoyum*. And, in addition, they deny what we are proving. But there is one thing which you must understand from us, namely, that the ability to recognize this *Ens* does not come from Christian belief, for it is a *Pagoyum* to us. It is, however, not contrary to the belief in which we shall depart from this life. Accordingly, you must recognize that in no way are you to understand an *Ens* as being of the spirits, by saying they are all devils, for then you are talking nonsensically and foolishly like the Devil."

[5] Cf. "Labyrinthus medicorum," ed. Sudhoff, XI, pp. 207f.: "And as the Magi from the East found Christ in the star by means of this sign, so is fire found in the flint. Thus are the arts found in nature, and it is easier to see the latter than it was to look for Christ."

[6] *De vita longa* (1562), p. 56. In "Caput de morbis somnii" (ed. Sudhoff, IX, p. 360), Paracelsus says of the *lumen naturae*: "Look at Adam and Moses and others. They sought in themselves what was in man and have revealed it and all kabbalistic arts and they knew nothing alien to man neither from the Devil nor from the spirits, but derived their knowledge from the Light of Nature. This they nurtured in themselves . . . it comes from nature which contains its man-

*naturae* may derive from the *Occulta philosophia* of Agrippa von Nettesheim (1533), who speaks of a *luminositas sensus naturae* that extends even to the four-footed beasts and enables them to foretell the future.[7] Paracelsus says accordingly:

It is, therefore, also to be known that the auguries of the birds are caused by these innate spirits, as when cocks foretell future weather and peacocks the death of their master and other such things with their crowing. All this comes from the innate spirit and is the Light of Nature. Just as it is present in animals and is natural, so also it dwells within man and he brought it into the world with himself. He who is chaste is a good prophet, natural as the birds, and the prophecies of birds not contrary to nature but are of nature. Each, then, according to his own state. These things which the birds announce can also be foretold in sleep, for it is the astral spirit which is the invisible body of nature.[8] And it should be known that when a man prophesies, he does not speak from the Devil, not from Satan, and not from the Holy Spirit, but he speaks from the innate spirit of the invisible body which teaches *Magiam* and in which the *Magus* has his origin.[9]

The light of nature comes from the *Astrum:* "Nothing can be in man unless it has been given to him by the Light of Nature, and what is in the Light of Nature has been brought by the stars." [10] The pagans still possessed the light of nature, "for to

---

ner of activity within itself. It is active during sleep and hence things must be used when dormant and not awake—sleep is waking for such arts—for things have a spirit which is active for them in sleep. Now it is true that Satan in his wisdom is a Kabbalist and a powerful one. So, too, are these innate spirits in man . . . for it is the Light of Nature which is at work during sleep and is the invisible body and was nevertheless born like the visible and natural body. But there is more to be known than the mere flesh, for from this very innate spirit comes that which is visible . . . the Light of Nature which is man's mentor dwells in this innate spirit." Paracelsus also says that though men die, the mentor goes on teaching (*Astronomia magna*, ed. Sudhoff, XII, p, 23; "De podagricis," ed. Huser, I, p. 566).

[7] *Occulta philosophia*, p. lxviii. The *lumen naturae* also plays a considerable role in Meister Eckhart.

[8] Cf. the fine saying in "Fragmenta medica" (ed. Huser, I, p. 141): "Great is he whose dreams are right, that is, who lives and moves harmoniously in this kabbalistic, innate spirit."

[9] "Caput de morbis somnii," ed. Sudhoff, IX, p. 361.

[10] *Astronomia magna*, ed. Sudhoff, XII, p. 23; also "Lab. med.," ed. Sudhoff, ch. II, and "De pestilitate," Tract. I (ed. Huser, I, p. 327). The *astrum* theory

act in the Light of Nature and to rejoice in it is divine despite being mortal." Before Christ came into the world, the world was still endowed with the light of nature, but in comparison with Christ this was a "lesser light." "Therefore we should know that we have to interpret nature according to the spirit of nature, the Word of God according to the spirit of God, and the Devil according to his spirit also." "He who knows nothing of these things is a gorged pig and will not leave room for instruction and experience." The light of nature is the *quinta essentia,* extracted by God himself from the four elements, and dwelling "in our hearts." [11] It is enkindled by the Holy Spirit.[12] The light of nature is an intuitive apprehension of the facts, a kind of illumination.[13] It has two sources: a mortal and an immortal, which Paracelsus calls "angels." [14] "Man," he says, "is also an angel and has all the latter's qualities." He has a natural light, but also a light outside the light of nature by which he can search out supernatural things.[15] The relationship of this supernatural light to the light of revelation remains, however, obscure. Paracelsus seems to have held a peculiar trichotomous view in this respect.

149    The authenticity of one's own experience of nature against the authority of tradition is a basic theme of Paracelsan thinking. On this principle he based his attack on the medical schools, and his pupils[16] carried the revolution even further by attacking Aristotelian philosophy. It was an attitude that opened the way for the scientific investigation of nature and helped to emancipate natural science from the authority of tradition. Though this liberating act had the most fruitful consequences, it also led to that conflict between knowledge and faith which poisoned the spiritual atmosphere of the nineteenth century in particular. Paracelsus naturally had no inkling of the possibility of these late repercussions. As a medieval Christian, he still lived

---

had been foreshadowed in the *Occulta philosophia* of Agrippa, to whom Paracelsus was much indebted.

11 *Astronomia magna,* ed. Sudhoff, XII, pp. 36 and 304.

12 *Paramirum,* pp. 35f.

13 "Lab. med.," ed. Sudhoff, ch. VIII.

14 "De podagricis," ed. Huser, I, p. 566.

15 "De nymphis," prologue (ed. Sudhoff, XIV, p. 115).

16 Adam von Bodenstein and Gerard Dorn, for instance.

in a unitary world and did not feel the two sources of knowledge, the divine and the natural, as the conflict it later turned out to be. As he says in his "Philosophia sagax": "There are, therefore, two kinds of knowledge in this world: an eternal and a temporal. The eternal springs directly from the light of the Holy Spirit, but the other directly from the Light of Nature." In his view the latter kind is ambivalent: both good and bad. This knowledge, he says, "is not from flesh and blood, but from the stars in the flesh and blood. That is the treasure, the natural Summum Bonum." Man is twofold, "one part temporal, the other part eternal, and each part takes its light from God, both the temporal and the eternal, and there is nothing that does not have its origin in God. Why, then, should the Father's light be considered pagan, and I be recognized and condemned as a pagan?" God the Father created man "from below upwards," but God the Son "from above downwards." Therefore Paracelsus asks: "If Father and Son are one, how then can I honour two lights? I would be condemned as an idolater: but the number one preserves me. And if I love two and accord to each its light, as God has ordained for everyone, how then can I be a pagan?"

150      It is clear enough from this what his attitude was to the problem of the two sources of knowledge: both lights derive from the unity of God. And yet—why did he give the name "Pagoyum" to what he wrote in the light of nature? Was he playing with words, or was it an involuntary avowal, a dim presentiment of a duality in the world and the soul? Was Paracelsus really unaffected by the schismatic spirit of the age, and was his attack on authority really confined only to Galen, Avicenna, Rhazes, and Arnaldus de Villanova?

### A. MAGIC

151      Paracelsus's scepticism and rebelliousness stop short at the Church, but he also reined them in before alchemy, astrology, and magic, which he believed in as fervently as he did in divine revelation, since in his view they proceeded from the authority of the *lumen naturae*. And when he speaks of the divine office of the physician, he exclaims: "I under the Lord, the Lord under me, I under him outside my office, and he under me outside his

office." [17] What kind of spirit addresses us in these words? Do they not recall those of the later Angelus Silesius?

> I am as great as God,
> And he is small like me;
> He cannot be above,
> Nor I below him be.

152    There is no denying that the human ego's affinity with God here raises a distinct claim to be heard and also to be recognized as such. That is the spirit of the Renaissance—to give man in his mightiness, intellectual power, and beauty a visible place beside God. *Deus et Homo* in a new and unprecedented sense! Agrippa von Nettesheim, Paracelsus's older contemporary and an authority on the Cabala, declares in his sceptical and contumacious book *De incertitudine et vanitate scientiarum:*[18]

> Agrippa spares no man.
> He contemns, knows, knows not, weeps, laughs, waxes wroth,
> reviles, carps at all things;
> being himself philosopher, demon, hero, God,
> and all things.

Paracelsus to be sure did not rise to such unfortunate heights of modernity. He felt at one with God and with himself. Wholly and unremittingly engaged in the practical art of healing, his busy mind wasted no time on abstract problems, and his irrational, intuitive nature never pursued logical reflections so far that they resulted in destructive insights.

153    Paracelsus had one father, whom he held in love and respect, but, as we have said, like every true hero he had two mothers, a heavenly one and an earthly one—Mother Church and Mother Nature. Can one serve two mothers? And even if, like Paracelsus, one feels oneself a physician created by God, is there not something suspicious about pressing God into one's service inside the physician's office, so to speak? One can easily object that Paracelsus said this, like so much else, only in passing and that it is not to be taken all that seriously. He himself would probably have been astonished and indignant if he had been taken at his word. The words that flowed into his pen came less from deep reflection than from the spirit of the age in which he lived. No

[17] "De caducis," ed. Sudhoff, VIII, p. 267.
[18] I used the edition of 1584, "as finally revised by the author."

one can claim to be immune to the spirit of his own epoch or to possess anything like a complete knowledge of it. Regardless of our conscious convictions, we are all without exception, in so far as we are particles in the mass, gnawed at and undermined by the spirit that runs through the masses. Our freedom extends only as far as our consciousness reaches. Beyond that, we succumb to the unconscious influences of our environment. Though we may not be clear in a logical sense about the deepest meanings of our words and actions, these meanings nevertheless exist and they have a psychological effect. Whether we know it or not, there remains in each of us the tremendous tension between the man who *serves* God and the man who *commands* God to do his bidding.

154    But the greater the tension, the greater the potential. Great energy springs from a correspondingly great tension of opposites. It was to the constellation of the most powerful opposites within him that Paracelsus owed his almost daemonic energy, which was not an unalloyed gift of God but went hand in hand with his impetuous and quarrelsome temperament, his hastiness, impatience, discontentedness, and his arrogance. Not for nothing was Paracelsus the prototype of Faust, whom Jacob Burckhardt once called "a great primordial image" in the soul of every German. From Faust the line leads direct to Nietzsche, who was a Faustian man if ever there was one. What still maintained the balance in the case of Paracelsus and Angelus Silesius—"I under God and God under me"—was lost in the twentieth century, and the scale sinks lower and lower under the weight of an ego that fancies itself more and more godlike. Paracelsus shared with Angelus Silesius his inner piety and the touching but dangerous simplicity of his relationship to God. But alongside this spirituality a countervailing chthonic spirit made itself felt to an almost frightening degree: there was no form of manticism and magic that Paracelsus did not practise himself or recommend to others. Dabbling in these arts—no matter how enlightened one thinks one is—is not without its psychological dangers. Magic always was and still is a source of fascination. At the time of Paracelsus, certainly, the world teemed with marvels: everyone was conscious of the immediate presence of the dark forces of nature. Astronomy and astrology were not yet separated. Kepler still cast horoscopes. Instead of

chemistry there was only alchemy. Amulets, talismans, spells for healing wounds and diseases were taken as a matter of course. A man so avid for knowledge as Paracelsus could not avoid a thorough investigation of all these things, only to discover that strange and remarkable effects resulted from their use. But so far as I know he never uttered a clear warning about the psychic dangers of magic for the adept.[19] He even scoffed at the doctors because they understood nothing of magic. But he does not mention that they kept away from it out of a quite justifiable fear. And yet we know from the testimony of Conrad Gessner, of Zurich, that the very doctors whom Paracelsus attacked shunned magic on religious grounds and accused him and his pupils of sorcery. Writing to Crato von Crafftheim[20] about Paracelsus's pupil Adam von Bodenstein, Gessner says: "I know that most people of this kind are Arians and deny the divinity of Christ . . . Oporin in Basel, once a pupil of Theophrastus and his private assistant [familiaris], reported strange tales concerning the latter's intercourse with demons. They are given to senseless astrology, geomancy, necromancy, and other forbidden arts. I myself suspect that they are the last of the Druids, those of the ancient Celts who were instructed for several years in underground places by demons. It is also certain that such things are done to this very day at Salamanca in Spain. From this school also arose the wandering scholars, as they are commonly called. The most famous of these was Faust, who died not so long ago." Elsewhere in the same letter Gessner writes: "Theophrastus has assuredly been an impious man and a sorcerer [magus], and has had intercourse with demons." [21]

155    Although this judgment is based in part on the unreliable testimony of Oporin and is essentially unfair or actually false, it nevertheless shows how unseemly, in the opinion of contemporary doctors of repute, was Paracelsus's preoccupation with magic. He himself, as we have said, had no such scruples. He drew magic, like everything else worth knowing, into his orbit and tried to exploit it medically for the benefit of the sick,

---

19 He did, however, once remark that he had found the stone which others sought "to their own hurt." But many other alchemists say the same.
20 [Personal physician to Ferdinand I. Cf. Jung, "Paracelsus the Physician," pars. 21f.—EDITORS.]
21 Epistolarum medicinalium Conradi Gessneri, fol. 1ᵛ.

unperturbed by what it might do to him personally or what the implications might be from the religious point of view. For him magic and the wisdom of nature had their place within the divinely ordained order as a *mysterium et magnale Dei,* and so it was not difficult for him to bridge the gulf into which half the world had plunged.[22] Instead of experiencing any conflict in himself, he found his arch-enemy outside in the great medical authorities of the past, as well as in the host of academic physicians against whom he let fly like the proper Swiss mercenary he was. He was infuriated beyond measure by the resistance of his opponents and he made enemies everywhere. His writings are as turbulent as his life and his wanderings. His style is violently rhetorical. He always seems to be speaking importunately into someone's ear—someone who listens unwillingly, or against whose thick skin even the best arguments rebound. His exposition of a subject is seldom systematic or even coherent; it is constantly interrupted by admonitions, addressed in a subtle or coarse vein to an invisible auditor afflicted with moral deafness. Paracelsus was a little too sure that he had his enemy in front of him, and did not notice that it was lodged in his own bosom. He consisted of two persons who never really confronted one another. He nowhere betrays the least suspicion that he might not be at one with himself. He felt himself to be undividedly one, and all the things that constantly thwarted him had of course to be his external enemies. He had to conquer them and prove to them that he was the "Monarcha," the sovereign ruler, which secretly and unknown to himself was the very thing he was not. He was so unconscious of the conflict within him that he never noticed there was a second ruler in his own house who worked against him and opposed everything he wanted. But every unconscious conflict works out like that: one obstructs and undermines oneself. Paracelsus did not see that the truth of the Church and the Christian standpoint could never get along with

22

> "I'm left to struggle still towards the light:
> Could I but break the spell, all magic spurning,
> And clear my path, all sorceries unlearning,
> Free then, in Nature's sight, from evil ban,
> I'd know at last the worth of being man."

(*Faust: Part Two,* trans. Wayne, pp. 263f.) Faust's belated insight never dawned on Paracelsus.

the thought implicit in all alchemy, "God under me." And when one unconsciously works against oneself, the result is impatience, irritability, and an impotent longing to get one's opponent down whatever the means. Generally certain symptoms appear, among them a peculiar use of language: one wants to speak forcefully in order to impress one's opponent, so one employs a special, "bombastic" style full of neologisms which might be described as "power-words." [23] This symptom is observable not only in the psychiatric clinic but also among certain modern philosophers, and, above all, whenever anything unworthy of belief has to be insisted on in the teeth of inner resistance: the language swells up, overreaches itself, sprouts grotesque words distinguished only by their needless complexity. The word is charged with the task of achieving what cannot be done by honest means. It is the old word magic, and sometimes it can degenerate into a regular disease. Paracelsus was afflicted with this malady to such a degree that even his closest pupils were obliged to compile "onomastica" (word-lists) and to publish commentaries. The unwary reader continually stumbles over these neologisms and is completely baffled at first, for Paracelsus never bothered to give any explanations even when, as often happens, the word was a *hapax legomenon* (one that occurs only once). Often it is only by comparing a number of passages that one can approximately make out the sense. There are, however, mitigating circumstances: doctors have always loved using magically incomprehensible jargon for even the most ordinary things. It is part of the medical persona. But it is odd indeed that Paracelsus, who prided himself on teaching and writing in German, should have been the very one to concoct the most intricate neologisms out of Latin, Greek, Italian, Hebrew, and possibly even Arabic.

156    Magic is insidious, and therein lies its danger. At one point, where Paracelsus is discussing witchcraft, he actually falls into using a magical witch-language without giving the least explanation. For instance, instead of "Zwirnfaden" (twine) he says "Swindafnerz," instead of "Nadel" (needle) "Dallen," instead of "Leiche" (corpse) "Chely," instead of

23 This expression was in fact used by an insane patient to describe her own neologisms. [See "The Psychology of Dementia Praecox," pars. 155, 208.—EDITORS.]

"Faden" (thread) "Daphne," and so on.[24] In magical rites the inversion of letters serves the diabolical purpose of turning the divine order into an infernal disorder. It is remarkable how casually and unthinkingly Paracelsus takes over these magically distorted words and simply leaves the reader to make what he can of them. This shows that Paracelsus must have been thoroughly steeped in the lowest folk beliefs and popular superstitions, and one looks in vain for any trace of disgust at such squalid things, though in his case its absence was certainly not due to lack of feeling but rather to a kind of natural innocence and naïveté. Thus he himself recommends the magical use of wax manikins in cases of sickness,[25] and seems to have designed and used amulets and seals.[26] He was convinced that physicians should have an understanding of the magic arts and should not eschew sorcery if this might help their patients. But this kind of folk magic is not Christian, it is demonstrably pagan—in a word, a "Pagoyum."

## B. ALCHEMY

157    Besides his manifold contacts with folk superstition there was another, more respectable source of "pagan" lore that had a great influence on Paracelsus. This was his knowledge of and intense preoccupation with alchemy, which he used not only in his pharmacology and pharmaceutics but also for "philosophical" purposes. Since earliest times alchemy contained, or actually was, a secret doctrine. With the triumph of Christianity under Constantine the old pagan ideas did not vanish but lived on in the strange arcane terminology of philosophical alchemy. Its chief figure was Hermes or Mercurius, in his dual significance as quicksilver and the world soul, with his companion figures Sol (= gold) and Luna (= silver). The alchemical operation consisted essentially in separating the prima materia, the so-called chaos, into the active principle, the soul, and the passive principle, the body, which were then reunited in personified form in

24 He calls this procedure likewise a "pagoyum." "De pestilitate," Tract. IV, ch. II (ed. Huser, I, p. 353).

25 For instance, the violent form of St. Vitus's Dance is cured by "a wax manikin into which oaths are stuck." "De morbis amentium," Tract. II, ch. III (ed. Huser, I, p. 501); also Paramirum, ch. V.

26 "Archidoxis magicae," ed. Huser, II, p. 546.

the *coniunctio* or "chymical marriage." In other words, the *coniunctio* was allegorized as the hierosgamos, the ritual cohabitation of Sol and Luna. From this union sprang the *filius sapientiae* or *filius philosophorum*, the transformed Mercurius, who was thought of as hermaphroditic in token of his rounded perfection. [Cf. fig. B2.]

158    The *opus alchymicum*, in spite of its chemical aspects, was always understood as a kind of rite after the manner of an *opus divinum*. For this reason Melchior Cibinensis, at the beginning of the sixteenth century, could still represent it in the form of a Mass,[27] since long before this the *filius* or *lapis philosophorum* had been regarded as an allegory of Christ.[28] Many things in Paracelsus that would otherwise remain incomprehensible must be understood in terms of this tradition. In it are to be found the origins of practically the whole of his philosophy in so far as it is not Cabalistic. It is evident from his writings that he had a considerable knowledge of Hermetic literature.[29] Like all medieval alchemists he seems not to have been aware of the true nature of alchemy, although the refusal of the Basel printer Conrad Waldkirch, at the end of the sixteenth century, to print the first part of *Aurora consurgens* (a treatise falsely ascribed to St. Thomas Aquinas) on account of its "blasphemous character" [30] shows that the dubious nature of alchemy was apparent even to a layman. To me it seems certain that Paracelsus was completely naïve in these matters and, intent only on the welfare of the sick, used alchemy primarily for its practical value regardless of its murky background. Consciously, alchemy for him meant a knowledge of the *materia medica* and a chemical procedure for preparing medicaments, above all the well-loved arcana, the secret remedies. He also believed that one could make gold and engender homunculi.[31] This aspect of it was so predominant that one is inclined to forget that alchemy meant very much more to him than that. We know this from a brief

27 *Theatrum chemicum*, III (1659), pp. 758ff. Cf. *Psychology and Alchemy*, pars. 480ff.; *Aurora Consurgens* (ed. von Franz), p. 43: "For [the science] is a gift and sacrament of God and a divine matter."
28 Cf. *Psychology and Alchemy*, Part III, ch. 5: "The Lapis-Christ Parallel."
29 He mentions Hermes, Archelaus, Morienus, Lully, Arnaldus, Albertus Magnus, Helia Artista, Rupescissa, and others.
30 *Artis auriferae* (1593), I, p. 185.
31 "De natura rerum," ed. Sudhoff, XI, p. 313.

remark in the *Paragranum,* where he says that the physician himself is "ripened" by the art.[32] This sounds as though the alchemical maturation should go hand in hand with the maturation of the physician. If we are not mistaken in this assumption, we must further conclude that Paracelsus not only was acquainted with the arcane teachings of alchemy but was convinced of their rightness. It is of course impossible to prove this without detailed investigation, for the esteem which he expressed for alchemy throughout his writings might in the end refer only to its chemical aspect. This special predilection of his made him a forerunner and inaugurator of modern chemical medicine. Even his belief in the transmutation of metals and in the *lapis philosophorum,* which he shared with many others, is no evidence of a deeper affinity with the mystic background of the *ars aurifera.* And yet such an affinity is very probable since his closest followers were found among the alchemical physicians.[33]

## C. THE ARCANE TEACHING

159    In the course of our inquiry we shall have to scrutinize more closely the arcane teaching of alchemy, which is so important for an understanding of the spiritual side of Paracelsus. I must ask the reader to forgive me in advance for putting his attention and patience to such a severe test. The subject is abstruse and wrapped in obscurity, but it constitutes an essential part of the Paracelsan spirit and exerted a profound influence on Goethe, so much so that the impressions he gained in his Leipzig days continued to engross him even in old age: indeed, they formed the matrix for *Faust.*

160    When one reads Paracelsus, it is chiefly the technical neologisms that seem to give out mysterious hints. But when one tries to establish their etymology and their meaning, as often as not one ends up in a blind alley. For instance, one can guess that

---

[32] *Das Buch Paragranum,* ed. Strunz, p. 13.

[33] His influence showed itself not so much in any essential modification of alchemical methods as in deepened philosophical speculation. The most important of these philosophical alchemists was the physician Gerard Dorn, of Frankfurt am Main. He wrote a detailed commentary on one of Paracelsus's rare Latin treatises, *De vita longa.* See infra, pars. 213ff.

"Iliaster" or "Yliastrum" is composed etymologically of ὕλη (matter) and ἀστήρ (star), and that it means about the same as the *spiritus vitae* of classical alchemy, or that "Cagastrum" is connected with κακός (bad) and ἀστήρ, or that "Anthos" and "Anthera" are embellishments of the alchemical *flores*. Even his philosophical concepts, such as the doctrine of the *astrum*, only lead us back to the known alchemical and astrological tradition, from which we can see that his doctrine of the *corpus astrale* was not a new discovery. We find this idea already in an old classic, the "Tractatus Aristotelis," where it is said that the "planets in man" have a more powerful influence than the heavenly bodies;[34] and when Paracelsus says that the medicine is found in the *astrum*, we read in the same treatise that "in man, who is made in the image of God, can be found the cause and the medicine."

161    But that other pivot of Paracelsus's teaching, his belief in the light of nature, allows us to surmise connections which illuminate the obscurities of his *religio medica*. The light hidden in nature and particularly in human nature likewise belongs to the stock of ancient alchemical ideas. Thus the "Tractatus Aristotelis" says: "See therefore that the light which is in thee be not darkness." The light of nature is indeed of great importance in alchemy. Just as, according to Paracelsus, it enlightens man as to the workings of nature and gives him an understanding of natural things "by cagastric magic" (*per magiam cagastricam*),[35] so it is the aim of alchemy to beget this light in the shape of the *filius philosophorum*. An equally ancient treatise of Arabic provenance attributed to Hermes,[36] the "Tractatus aureus," says (Mercurius is speaking): "My light excels all other lights, and my goods are higher than all other goods. I beget the light, but the darkness too is of my nature. Nothing better or more worthy of veneration can come to pass in the world than the union of

34 "Nam Planetae Sphaerae et elementa in homine per revolutionem sui Zodiaci verius et virtuosius operantur, quam aliena corpora seu signa superiora corporalia" (For the planets, spheres, and elements in man work more truly and powerfully through the revolution of their zodiac than foreign bodies or the higher bodily signs). *Theatr. chem.*, V (1660), p. 790.

35 "Liber Azoth," ed. Huser, II, p. 522. The *Cagastrum* is an inferior or "bad" form of the *Yliastrum*. That it is this "cagastric" magic which opens the understanding is worth noting.

36 Hermes is an authority often cited by Paracelsus.

myself with my son." [37] In the "Dicta Belini" (Belinus is a pseudo-Apollonius of Tyana) Mercurius says: "I enlighten all that is mine, and I make the light manifest on the journey from my father Saturn." [38] "I make the days of the world eternal, and I illumine all lights with my light." [39] Another author says of the "chymical marriage" from which arises the *filius philosophorum*: "They embrace and the new light is begotten of them, which is like no other light in the whole world." [40]

162      This idea of the light, with Paracelsus as with other alchemists, coincides with the concept of Sapientia and Scientia. We can safely call the light the central mystery of philosophical alchemy. Almost always it is personified as the *filius,* or is at least mentioned as one of his outstanding attributes. It is a δαιμόνιον pure and simple. Often the texts refer to the need for a familiar spirit who should help the adept at his work. The Magic Papyri do not hesitate to enlist the services even of the major gods. [41] The *filius* remains in the adept's power. Thus the treatise of Haly, king of Arabia, says: "And that son . . . shall serve thee in thy house in this world and in the next." [42] Long before Paracelsus, as I have said, this *filius* was equated with Christ. The parallel comes out very clearly in the sixteenth-century German alchemists who were influenced by Paracelsus. For instance, Heinrich Khunrath says: "This [the *filius philosophorum*], the Son of the Macrocosm, is God and creature . . .

---

[37] Quoted from the version in *Rosarium philosophorum,* vol. II of *De alchimia* (1550), p. 133. Reprinted in *Bibliotheca chemica curiosa,* II, pp. 87ff.

[38] The light arises from the darkness of Saturn.

[39] Quoted from the version of *Rosarium* in *Art. aurif.,* II, pp. 379 and 381. The original (1550) edition of the *Rosarium* is based on a text that dates back to about the middle of the 15th cent.

[40] Mylius, *Philosophia reformata,* p. 244. (Mylius was the greatest of the alchemical compilers and gave extracts from numerous ancient texts, mostly without naming the sources.) Significantly, the oldest of the Chinese alchemists, Wei-Po-yang, who lived about A.D. 140, was familiar with this idea. He says: "He who properly cultivates his innate nature will see the yellow light shine forth as it should." (Lu-ch'iang Wu and T. L. Davis, "An Ancient Chinese Treatise on Alchemy," p. 262.)

[41] Preisendanz, *Papyri Graecae Magicae,* I, p. 137, Pap. IV, line 2081, concerning the acquisition of a *paredros.*

[42] Quoted in *Rosarium* (*Art. aurif.,* II, p. 248). Cf. Preisendanz, II, pp. 45–46, line 48: "I know thee, Hermes, and thou knowest me. I am thou and thou art I, and thou shouldst serve me in all things."

that [Christ], is the son of God, the θεάνθρωπος, that is, God and man; the one conceived in the womb of the Macrocosm, the other in the womb of the Microcosm, and both of a virginal womb. . . . Without blasphemy I say: In the Book or Mirror of Nature, the Stone of the Philosophers, the Preserver of the Macrocosm, is the symbol of Christ Jesus Crucified, Saviour of the whole race of men, that is, of the Microcosm. From the stone you shall know in natural wise Christ, and from Christ the stone." [43]

163    To me it seems certain that Paracelsus was just as unconscious of the full implications of these teachings as Khunrath was, who also believed he was speaking "without blasphemy." But in spite of this unconsciousness they were of the essence of philosophical alchemy,[44] and anyone who practised it thought, lived, and acted in the atmosphere of these teachings, which perhaps had an all the more insidious effect the more naïvely and uncritically one succumbed to them. The "natural light of man" or the "star in man" sounds harmless enough, so that none of the authors had any notion of the possibilities of conflict that lurked within it. And yet that light or *filius philosophorum* was openly named the greatest and most victorious of all lights, and set alongside Christ as the Saviour and Preserver of the world! Whereas in Christ God himself became man, the *filius philosophorum* was extracted from matter by human art and, by means of the opus, made into a new light-bringer. In the former case the miracle of man's salvation is accomplished by God; in the latter, the salvation or transfiguration of the universe is brought about by the mind of man—"Deo concedente," as the authors never fail to add. In the one case man confesses "I under God," in the other he asserts "God under me." Man takes the place of the Creator. Medieval alchemy prepared the way for the greatest intervention in the divine world order that man has ever attempted: alchemy was the dawn of the scientific age, when the

---

[43] *Amphitheatrum sapientiae aeternae*, p. 197: "Hic, filius mundi maioris, Deus et creatura . . . ille (scl. Christus) filius Dei θεάνθρωπος, h. e. Deus et homo: Unus in utero mundi maioris; alter in utero mundi minoris, uterque Virgineo, conceptus. . . . Absque blasphemia dico: Christi crucifixi, salvatoris totius generis humani, i.e., mundi minoris, in Naturae libro, et ceu Speculo, typus est Lapis Philosophorum servator mundi maioris. Ex lapide Christum naturaliter cognoscito et ex Christo lapidem."

[44] Mylius (*Phil. ref.*, p. 97) says of the *filius ignis:* "Here lies all our philosophy."

daemon of the scientific spirit compelled the forces of nature to serve man to an extent that had never been known before. It was from the spirit of alchemy that Goethe wrought the figure of the "superman" Faust, and this superman led Nietzsche's Zarathustra to declare that God was dead and to proclaim the will to give birth to the superman, to "create a god for yourself out of your seven devils." [45] Here we find the true roots, the preparatory processes deep in the psyche, which unleashed the forces at work in the world today. Science and technology have indeed conquered the world, but whether the psyche has gained anything is another matter.

164     Paracelsus's preoccupation with alchemy exposed him to an influence that left its mark on his spiritual development. The inner driving-force behind the aspirations of alchemy was a presumption whose daemonic grandeur on the one hand and psychic danger[46] on the other should not be underestimated. Much of the overbearing pride and arrogant self-esteem, which contrasts so strangely with the truly Christian humility of Paracelsus, comes from this source. What erupted like a volcano in Agrippa von Nettesheim's "himself demon, hero, God" remained, with Paracelsus, hidden under the threshold of a Christian consciousness and expressed itself only indirectly in exaggerated claims and in his irritable self-assertiveness, which made him enemies wherever he went. We know from experience that such a symptom is due to unadmitted feelings of inferiority, i.e., to a real failing of which one is usually unconscious. In each of us there is a pitiless judge who makes us feel guilty even if we are not conscious of having done anything wrong. Although we do not know what it is, it is as though it were known somewhere. Paracelsus's desire to help the sick at all costs was doubtless quite

---

[45] *Thus Spake Zarathustra* (trans. Kaufmann), p. 176: "Lonely one, you are going the way to yourself. And your way leads past yourself and your seven devils. . . . You must consume yourself in your own flame; how could you wish to become new unless you had first become ashes! Lonely one, you are going the way of the creator: you would create a god for yourself out of your seven devils." Cf. "Consilium coniugii," *Ars chemica*, p. 237: "Our stone slays itself with its own dart"; and the role of the *incineratio* and the phoenix among the alchemists. The devil is the Saturnine form of the *anima mundi*.

[46] These were known to the alchemists since earliest times. Olympiodorus, for instance, says that in lead (Saturn) there is a shameless demon (the *spiritus mercurii*) who drives men mad. (Berthelot, *Alchimistes grecs*, II, iv, 43.)

pure and genuine. But the magical means he used, and in particular the secret content of alchemy, were diametrically opposed to the spirit of Christianity. And that remained so whether Paracelsus was aware of it or not. Subjectively, he was without blame; but that pitiless judge condemned him to feelings of inferiority that clouded his life.

### D. THE PRIMORDIAL MAN

165    This crucial point, namely the arcane doctrine of the marvellous son of the philosophers, is the subject of unfriendly but perspicacious criticism by Conrad Gessner. Apropos the works of a pupil of Paracelsus, Alexander à Suchten,[47] he writes to Crato: "But look who it is whom he reveals to us as the son of God, namely none other than the spirit of the world and of nature, and the same who dwells in our bodies (it is a wonder that he does not add the spirit of the ox and the ass!). This spirit can be separated from matter or from the body of the elements by the technical procedures of the Theophrastus school. If anyone were to take him at his word, he would say that he had merely voiced a principle of the philosophers, but not his own opinion. He repeats it, however, in order to express his agreement. And I know that other Theophrastians besmirch such things with their writings, from which it is easy to conclude that they deny the divinity of Christ. I myself am entirely convinced that Theophrastus has been an Arian. They endeavour to persuade us that Christ was a quite ordinary man, and that in him was no other spirit than in us."[48]

166    Gessner's charge against the Theophrastus school and against the Master himself applies to alchemy in general. The extraction of the world soul from matter was not a peculiarity of Paracelsan alchemy. But the charge of Arianism is unjustified. It was obviously prompted by the well-known parallel between the *filius philosophorum* and Christ, though so far as I know this nowhere occurs in Paracelsus's own writings. On the other hand, in a treatise called "Apokalypsis Hermetis," ascribed by Huser to Paracelsus, there is a complete alchemical confession of faith which lends Gessner's charge a certain weight. There Paracelsus

[47] Born in Danzig at the beginning of the 16th cent., studied in Basel.
[48] *Epistolarum medicinalium Conradi Gessneri*, Lib. I, fol. 2r.

says of the "spirit of the fifth essence": "This is the spirit of truth, whom the world cannot comprehend without the inspiration of the Holy Ghost, or without the instruction of those who know him." [49] "He is the soul of the world," moving all and preserving all. In his initial earthly form (that is, in his original Saturnine darkness) he is unclean, but he purifies himself progressively during the ascent through his watery, aerial, and fiery forms. Finally, in the fifth essence, he appears as the "clarified body." [50] "This spirit is the secret that has been hidden since the beginning of things."

167    Paracelsus is speaking here as a true alchemist. Like his pupils, he draws the Cabala, which had been made accessible to the world at large through Pico della Mirandola and Agrippa, into the scope of his alchemical speculations. "All you who are led by your religion to prophesy future events and to interpret the past and the present to people, you who see abroad and read hidden letters and sealed books, who seek in the earth and in walls for what is buried, you who learn great wisdom and art— bear in mind if you wish to apply all these things, that you take to yourselves the religion of the Gabal and walk in its light, for the Gabal is well-founded. Ask and it will be granted to you, knock, you will be heard and it will be opened unto you. From this granting and opening there will flow what you desire: you will see into the lowest depths of the earth, into the depths of hell, into the third heaven. You will gain more wisdom than Solomon, you will have greater communion with God than Moses and Aaron." [51]

168    Just as the wisdom of the Cabala coincided with the Sapientia of alchemy, so the figure of Adam Kadmon was identified with the *filius philosophorum*. Originally this figure may have been the ἄνθρωπος φωτεινός, the "man of light" who was imprisoned in Adam, and whom we encounter in Zosimos of Panopolis

---

[49] This is a recurrent formula in alchemical treatises.

[50] The *corpus glorificationis* of other authors.

[51] "De religione perpetua," ed. Sudhoff, Part 2, I, pp. 100f. An equally presumptuous view is expressed in "De podagricis" (ed. Huser, I, p. 565): "Thus man acquires his angelic qualities from heaven and is heavenly. He who knows the angels knows the *astra*, he who knows the *astra* and the *horoscopum* knows the whole world, and knows how to bring together man and the angels." [This and the above passage in the text are translated by Dr. R. T. Llewellyn.—TRANSLATOR.]

(third century).[52] But the man of light is an echo of the pre-Christian doctrine of the Primordial Man. Under the influence of Marsilio Ficino and Pico della Mirandola, these and other Neoplatonic ideas had already become popularized in the fifteenth century and were known to nearly every educated person. In alchemy they fell in with the remnants of classical tradition. Besides this there were the views of the Cabala, which had been philosophically assessed by Pico.[53] He and Agrippa[54] were probably the sources for Paracelsus's somewhat scanty knowledge of the Cabala. For Paracelsus the Primordial Man was identical with the "astral" man: "The true man is the star in us." [55] "The star desires to drive man towards great wisdom." [56] In his *Paragranum* he says: "For heaven is man and man is heaven, and all men are one heaven, and heaven is only one man." [57] Man stands in the relationship of a son to the inner heaven,[58] which is the Father, whom Paracelsus calls the *homo maximus*[59] or Adech,[60] an arcane name derived from Adam. Elsewhere he is called Archeus: "He is therefore similar to man and consists of the four elements and is an Archeus and is composed of four parts; say then, he is the great Cosmos." [61] Undoubtedly this is the Primordial Man, for Paracelsus says: "In the whole Ides there is but One Man, the same is extracted by the Iliastrum[62]

[52] In Zosimos the "man of light" ($\phi\dot{\omega}s$ = man, $\phi\tilde{\omega}s$ = light) is simply called $\phi\tilde{\omega}s$. He is the spiritual man who has clothed himself in Adam's body. Christ let Adam approach ($\pi\rho\sigma\tilde{\eta}\nu$) and accepted him into paradise (Berthelot, *Alch. grecs*, III, xlix, 5–10). Cf. *Psychology and Alchemy*, par. 456.

[53] "De arte cabalistica," *Opera omnia*, I.

[54] *Occulta philosophia.*

[55] *Astronomia magna*, ed. Sudhoff, XII, p. 55.

[56] Ibid., p. 62.

[57] Ed. Strunz, p. 56; also "Von der Astronomey," ed. Huser, I, p. 215.

[58] Strunz, p. 55.

[59] Pico della Mirandola also uses this term in *Heptaplus*, I, ch. VII (*Opera omnia*, I, p. 59).

[60] *De vita longa* (ed. Dorn), pp. 169ff. Adech is the "interior man," presumably identical with Aniadus and Edochinum (see infra). Concerning the *homo maximus* see *Paragranum*, pp. 45, 59. Dorn calls Adech the "invisibilem hominem maximum."

[61] "Von den dreyen ersten essentiis," ch. IX, ed. Huser, I, p. 325. The idea that the Primordial Man consists of four parts is found also in Gnosticism (Barbelo = "God is four").

[62] The Iliastrum (or Iliaster) is something like the *spiritus vitae* or *spiritus mercurialis* of the alchemists. This is the occult agent in quicksilver, which, ex-

and is the Protoplast." Ides or Ideus is "the gate through which all created things have proceeded," the "globule or materia" from which man was created.[63] Other secret names for the Primordial Man are Idechtrum[64] and Protothoma.[65] The number of names alone shows how preoccupied Paracelsus was with this idea. The ancient teachings about the Anthropos or Primordial Man assert that God, or the world-creating principle, was made manifest in the form of a "first-created" (*protoplastus*) man, usually of cosmic size. In India he is Prajāpati or Purusha, who is also "the size of a thumb" and dwells in the heart of every man, like the Iliaster of Paracelsus. In Persia he is Gayomart (*gayō-maretan*, 'mortal life'), a youth of dazzling whiteness, as is also said of the alchemical Mercurius. In the *Zohar* he is Metatron, who was created together with light. He is the celestial man whom we meet in the visions of Daniel, Ezra, Enoch, and also in Philo Judaeus. He is one of the principal figures in Gnosticism, where, as always, he is connected with the question of creation and redemption.[66] This is the case with Paracelsus.

---

tracted in the form of the *aqua permanens*, serves, in highly paradoxical fashion, to separate the occult agent, the anima (soul), from the body (or substance). The contradiction is due to the fact that Mercurius is a self-transforming being, represented as a dragon that devours itself from the tail (uroboros = tail-eater), or else as two dragons eating each other. The function of the Iliaster is just as paradoxical: it is itself a created thing, but it brings all creatures out of a potential state of existence in the world of ideas (which is probably the meaning of Paracelsus's Neoplatonic "Ides") into actual existence. [See also infra, pars. 170ff.]

[63] "De tartaro: Fragmenta anatomiae," ed. Sudhoff, III, p. 462.

[64] Ibid., p. 465: "He is the first man and the first tree and the first created of everything whatsoever."

[65] = "First Thomas," i.e., the first unbeliever and doubter.

[66] Bousset, *Hauptprobleme der Gnosis*, pp. 16ff.

## 2. "DE VITA LONGA":
## AN EXPOSITION OF THE SECRET DOCTRINE

169    The treatise *De vita longa*,[1] difficult as it is to understand in parts, gives us some information on this point, though we have to extricate it with an effort from the arcane terminology in which it is embedded. The treatise is one of the few that were written in Latin; the style is exceedingly strange, but all the same it contains so many significant hints that it is worth investigating more closely. Adam von Bodenstein, who edited it, says in a dedicatory letter[2] to Ludwig Wolfgang von Hapsberg, governor of Badenweiler, that it was "taken down from the mouth of Paracelsus and carefully revised." The obvious inference is that the treatise is based on notes of Paracelsus's lectures and is not an original text. As Bodenstein himself wrote fluent and easily understandable Latin, quite unlike that of the treatise, one must assume that he did not devote any particular attention to it and made no effort to put it into more intelligible form, otherwise much more of his own style would have crept in. Probably he left the lectures more or less in their original state, as is particularly apparent towards the end. It is also likely that he had no very clear understanding of what they were about, any more than had the supposed translator Oporin. This is not surprising, as the Master himself all too often lacks the necessary clarity when discussing these complicated matters. Under these circumstances it is difficult to say how much should be put down to incomprehension and how much to undisciplined thinking. Nor is the possibility of actual errors in transcription excluded.[3] In

1 Ed. Sudhoff, III.

2 Fol. d2r of the 1st edn. (1562).

3 To give but one example: one passage says that "there is nothing of mortality in the Scaiolae," while another speaks of the "death and life of the Scaiolae" (infra, pars. 207, 214). Not much reliance should therefore be placed on Bodenstein's "revision." As against my view that the *Vita longa* consists of lecture notes, one must consider the fact that there are original fragments written in

our interpretation, therefore, we are on uncertain ground from the start, and much must remain conjecture. But as Paracelsus, for all his originality, was strongly influenced by alchemical thinking, a knowledge of the earlier and contemporary alchemical treatises, and of the writings of his pupils and followers, is of considerable help in interpreting some of the concepts and in filling out certain gaps. An attempt to comment on and to interpret the treatise, therefore, is not entirely hopeless, despite the admitted difficulties.

## A. THE ILIASTER

170     The treatise is mainly concerned with the conditions under which longevity, which in Paracelsus's opinion extends up to a thousand years or more, can be attained. In what follows I shall give chiefly the passages that relate to the secret doctrine and are of help in explaining it.[4] Paracelsus starts by giving a definition of life, as follows: "Life, by Hercules, is nothing other than a certain embalsamed Mumia, which preserves the mortal body from the mortal worms and from corruption[5] by means of a mixed saline solution." Mumia was well known in the Middle Ages as a medicament, and it consisted of the pulverized parts of real Egyptian mummies, in which there was a flourishing trade. Paracelsus attributes incorruptibility to a special virtue or agent named "balsam." This was something like a natural elixir, by means of which the body was kept alive or, if dead, incorruptible.[6] By the same logic, a scorpion or venomous snake neces-

---

German (ed. Sudhoff, III, pp. 295ff.). These may be Paracelsus's drafts for a German version. The date of composition of the *Vita longa* is perhaps 1526. No original MSS. of Paracelsus have been preserved (ibid., pp. xxxiiff.).

[4] The following discussion makes no attempt to evaluate the treatise as a whole, for which reason I have not considered the *De vita libri tres* of Marsilio Ficino an important contribution in this respect.

[5] The word *aestphara* in the Latin may be of Arabic origin. Dorn translates it as *corruptio*. Another possible derivation is φάρω, 'to render invisible,' 'to kill,' and αἰστόω, 'to cleave,' 'to dismember.' Corruption or putrefaction involves decomposition and hence the disappearance of the previous form. "Nihil mehercle vita est aliud, nisi Mummia quaedam Balsamita, conservans mortale corpus a mortalibus vermibus et aestphara, cum impressa liquoris sallium commistura."

[6] Ruland, *A Lexicon of Alchemy*, p. 69 (s.v. *Balsamum s. Balsamus*): "It is the

sarily had in it an alexipharmic, i.e., an antidote, otherwise it would die of its own poison.

171 Paracelsus goes on to discuss a great many arcane remedies, since diseases shorten life and have above all to be cured. The chief among these remedies are gold and pearls, which latter can be transformed into the *quinta essentia*. A peculiar potency is attributed to *Cheyri*,[7] which fortifies the microcosmic body so much that it "must necessarily continue in its conservation through the universal anatomy of the four elements."[8] Therefore the physician should see to it that the "anatomy" (= structure) of the four elements "be contracted into the one anatomy of the microcosm, not out of the corporeal, but out of that which preserves the corporeal." This is the balsam, which stands even higher than the *quinta essentia*, the thing that ordinarily holds the four elements together. It "excels even nature herself" because it is produced by a "bodily operation."[9] The idea that the art can make something higher than nature is typically alchemical. The balsam is the life principle, the *spiritus mercurii*, and it more or less coincides with the Paracelsan concept of the Iliaster. The latter is higher than the four elements and determines the length of life. It is therefore roughly the same as the balsam, or one could say that the balsam is the pharmacological

---

liquor of an interior salt most carefully and naturally preserving its body from corruption. . . . In German the term [is] Baldzamen ['soon together'], i.e., quickly joined [*celeriter coniunctum:* hence a means of promoting the coniunctio, see infra]. External Balsam of the Elements is liquor of external Mercury . . . the firmamental essence of existences, the Quintessence." Hence *B. internus* is a *liquor Mercurii interni.*

7 *Cheyri* is the yellow wallflower [*Cheiranthus cheiri,* incorrectly given as] *Viola petraea lutea* [mountain pansy] in the *Herbal* of Tabernaemontanus; it is abortifacient and restorative. The plant bears four-petalled yellow blossoms. Galen (*De simplicium medicamentorum facultatibus,* Lib. VII) says it has a carminative and warming effect. In Ruland (*Lexicon,* p. 98), *Cheiri Paracelsicum,* as applied to minerals, is quicksilver; *Flos cheiri* is the white elixir of silver, also the essence of gold. "Others say it is potable gold," hence it is an arcanum subserving the philosophical aim of alchemy. Paracelsus himself alludes to its fourfold nature: ". . . and the Spagyric makes a temperate being out of the four [elements], as the flower Cheiri shows." "Fragmenta medica," ed. Sudhoff, III, p. 301.

8 "Quod per universam quatuor elementorum anatomiam perdurare in sua conservatione debet" (Lib. IV, ch. I). In the German fragments to the *Vita longa* Paracelsus says: "For Cheiri is more than Venus, Anthos more than Mars."

9 Probably by a process of extraction.

or chemical aspect of the Iliaster.[10] The Iliaster has three forms: *Iliaster sanctitus,*[11] *paratetus,*[12] and *magnus.* They are subordinate to man ("microcosmo subditi") and can be brought "into one gamonymus." Since Paracelsus attributes a special "vis ac potestas coniunctionis" to the Iliaster, this enigmatic "gamonymus" (γάμος = marriage, ὄνομα = name) must be interpreted as a kind of chymical wedding, in other words as an indissoluble, hermaphroditic union.[13] There are as many Iliastri as there are men; that is to say in every man there is an Iliaster that holds together each individual's peculiar combination of qualities.[14]

[10] [The following passage is a slight condensation of a note entitled "The Concept of Mercurius in Hermetic Philosophy," dated Einsiedeln, Oct. 11, 1942, discovered among Jung's posthumous papers:
"This concept—if one can call it such—not only has a wealth of meanings but appears in variant form as Iliastrum, Iliastes, Iliadus, Yleides, Yleidus, etc. Such an intensification of Paracelsus's etymological proclivities indicates that a special importance attaches to an idea so variously named. Sometimes the Iliaster is the *principium,* the *prima materia,* the *chaos,* the *prima compositio,* consisting of the three basic substances, Mercurius, sulphur, and salt; sometimes it is the *aer elementalis* or *coelum,* 'the true spirit in man, which pervades all his limbs'; sometimes the 'occult virtue of nature, by which all thing[s] increase, are nourished, multiply, and quicken,' as Ruland, a pupil of Paracelsus, defines it (*Lexicon,* p. 181); sometimes the *spiritus vitae,* which is none other than *vis Mercurii.* It is thus identical with the Mercurial spirit, which was the central concept of alchemy from the oldest times to its heyday in the seventeenth century. Like the *Mercurius philosophorum,* the Paracelsan Mercurius is a child of Sol and Luna, born with the help of sulphur and salt, the 'strange son of chaos,' as Goethe calls Mephistopheles. Paracelsus names it 'omne fumosum et humidum in quovis corpore,' the moist, breathlike or vaporous soul dwelling in all bodies. In its highest form the Iliaster signifies the passage of the mind or soul into another world, as took place with Enoch, Elias, and others. (Ruland, *Lexicon,* p. 181. Cf. Ezek. 1 : 13 and Luke 10 : 18.) Not only is it the life-giver, it is the psychopomp in the mystic transformation, leading the way to incorruptibility or immortality. The 'seed of the Iliastric soul' is the spirit of God himself, and on it is imprinted 'God's likeness.' "—EDITORS.]

[11] *Sanctitus* from *sancire,* 'to make unalterable or inviolable'; *sanctitus* = *affirmatus,* 'made firm.' Ruland (*Lexicon,* p. 181): "The first, or implanted [Iliaster] is the span of life."

[12] Probably derived from παραιτέομαι, 'to obtain by prayer,' 'to entreat.' Ruland: "The second Iliaster, prepared Iliaster."

[13] The product of Sol and Luna was represented as a hermaphrodite.

[14] *De vita longa,* Lib. IV, cap. IV: "Eius ultra mille sunt species . . . potius iuxta hoc, ut quilibet microcosmus peculiarem suam, atque adeo perfectam coniunctionem habeat, quilibet, inquam, utrinque perfectam suam ac propriam virtutem" (There are more than a thousand species thereof . . . so that each

It therefore seems to be a kind of universal formative principle and principle of individuation.

## B. THE AQUASTER

172    The Iliaster forms the starting point for the arcane preparation of longevity. "We will explain what is most needful in this process regarding the Iliaster. In the first place, the impure animate body must be purified through the separation of the elements, which is done by your meditating upon it; this consists in the confirmation of your mind beyond all bodily and mechanic work." [15] In this way a "new form is impressed" on the impure body.

173    I have translated *imaginatio* here by "meditating." In the Paracelsist tradition *imaginatio* is the active power of the *astrum* (star) or *corpus coeleste sive supracoeleste* (Ruland), that is, of the higher man within. Here we encounter the psychic factor in alchemy: the artifex accompanies his chemical work with a simultaneous mental operation which is performed by means of the imagination. Its purpose is to cleanse away the impure admixture and at the same time to bring about the "confirmation" of the mind. The Paracelsan neologism *confirmamentum* is probably not without reference to the "firmament." During this work man is "raised up in his mind, so that he is made equal to the Enochdiani" (those who enjoy an unusually long life, like Enoch).[16] Hence his "interior anatomy" must be heated to the

---

microcosm may have its own special and even perfect conjunction, each, I say, its own perfect and peculiar virtue).

[15] Lib. IV, cap. VI: "Quod maxime necessarium est in hoc processu erga iliastrum, describamus: Principio ut impurum animatum depuretur citra separationem elementorum, quod fit per tuam ipsius imaginationem, cum ea in animi tui confirmamento consistit, praeter omnem corporalem ac mechanicum laborem."

[16] Cf. Gen. 5 : 23–24: "And all the days of Enoch were three hundred sixty and five years. And Enoch walked with God: and he was not; for God took him." According to the chronologist Scaliger (*Animadversiones in chronologia Eusebii*) Enoch was responsible for the division of the year. Enoch was also considered a prefiguration of Christ, like Melchisedek. Cf. Pico della Mirandola ("De arte cabalistica," *Opera omnia*, I, p. 3020): "Denuo Simon ait, pater noster Adam, rursus ex Seth nepotem suscepit, memor eius Cabalae, quam sibi Raziel tradiderat, quod ex sua propagatione nasceretur homo futurus salvator. Quare vocatus est Enos, id est, homo." (Again Simon says that our father Adam received another grandchild from Seth, having in mind that Cabala which Raziel had

highest degree.[17] In this way the impurities are consumed and only the solid is left, "without rust." While the artifex heats the chemical substance in the furnace he himself is morally undergoing the same fiery torment and purification.[18] By projecting himself into the substance he has become unconsciously identical with it and suffers the same process. Paracelsus does not fail to point out to his reader that this fire is not the same as the fire in the furnace. This fire, he says, contains nothing more of the "Salamandrine Essence or Melusinian Ares," but is rather a *"retorta distillatio* from the midst of the centre, beyond all coal fire." Since Melusina is a watery creature, the "Melusinian Ares" [19] refers to the so-called "Aquaster," [20] which stands for the watery aspect of the Iliaster, i.e., the Iliaster which animates and preserves the liquids in the body. The Iliaster is without doubt a spiritual, invisible principle although it is also something like the prima materia, which, however, in alchemical usage by no means corresponds to what we understand by matter. For the alchemists the prima materia was the *humidum radicale* (radical moisture),[21] the water,[22] the *spiritus aquae*,[23] and *vapor terrae;* [24] it was also called the "soul" of the substances,[25] the *sperma mundi*,[26] Adam's tree of paradise with its

---

handed down to him, that of his seed should be born a man who would be a saviour. Wherefore he was called Enos, that is, Man.)

[17] Lib. IV, ch. VI: "Quare microcosmum in sua interiore anatomia reverberari oportet in supremam usque reverberationem" (Wherefore the microcosm in its interior anatomy must be reverberated up to the highest reverberation). This takes place in the *reverberatorium,* a calcining furnace. "Reverberation is ignition, reducing substances under the influence of a potent fire, and by means of reverberation and repercussion, into a fine calx" (Ruland, p. 276).

[18] The "Tractatus aureus" says (ch. IV): "Burn up the body of the air with very much fire, and it will imbue you with the grace you seek" (*Ars chemica,* p. 24).

[19] Ares is sometimes masculine, too.

[20] From *aqua* and *astrum* = 'water star.'

[21] Albertus Magnus, "De mineralibus et rebus metallicis" (Borgnet, vol. V, Tract. I, ch. 2).

[22] Rupescissa in Hoghelande, "De alchemiae difficultatibus," *Theatr. chem.,* I (1659), p. 172.

[23] Mylius, *Phil. ref.,* p. 16.

[24] Ibid.

[25] Dialogue between Synesios and Dioskoros in Berthelot, *Alch. grecs,* II, iii.

[26] *Turba Philosophorum* (ed. Ruska), Sermo XIII, p. 122; Hoghelande, in *Theatr. chem.,* I (1659), p. 150. A quotation from Senior.

many flowers, which grows on the sea,[27] the round body from the centre,[28] Adam and the accursed man,[29] the hermaphroditic monster,[30] the One and the root of itself,[31] the All,[32] and so on. The symbolical names of the prima materia all point to the *anima mundi,* Plato's Primordial Man, the Anthropos and mystic Adam, who is described as a sphere (= wholeness), consisting of four parts (uniting different aspects in itself), hermaphroditic (beyond division by sex), and damp (i.e., psychic). This paints a picture of the self, the indescribable totality of man.

174 The Aquaster, too, is a spiritual principle; for instance, it shows the adept the "way by which he can search out divine magic." The adept himself is an "aquastric magician." The "scayolic[33] Aquaster" shows him the "great cause" with the help of the *Trarames* (ghostly spirits). Christ took his body from the celestial Aquaster, and the body of Mary was "necrocomic"[34] and "aquastric." Mary "came from the iliastric Aquaster." There, Paracelsus emphasizes, she stood on the moon (the moon is always related to water). Christ was born in the celestial Aquaster. In the human skull there is an "aquastric fissure," in men on the forehead, in women at the back of the head. Through this fissure women are liable to be invaded in their "cagastric" Aquaster by a crowd of diabolical spirits; but men, through their fissure, give birth, "not cagastrically but necrocomically, to the necrocomic *Animam vel spiritum vitae microcosmi,* the iliastric spirit of life in the heart." In the "centre of the heart dwells the true soul, the breath of God."[35]

175 From these quotations it is easy to see what the Aquaster

27 Abu'l Qāsim, *Kitāb al-'ilm al-muktasab,* ed. Holmyard, p. 23.

28 Dorn, "Physica genesis," *Theatr. chem.,* I (1659), p. 349. Dorn says further: "Of the centre there is no end, and no pen can rightly describe its power and the infinite abyss of its mysteries."

29 Olympiodorus in Berthelot, *Alch. grecs,* II, iv, 32. The myth of the θεοκατάρακτος is to be found ibid., 52.

30 Hoghelande, "De alch. diff.," p. 159.

31 *Rosarium philosophorum,* in *Art. aurif.,* II, p. 369.

32 "Liber Platonis quartorum," *Theatr. chem.,* V (1660), p. 118.

33 Scaiolae are something like higher mental functions, comparable psychologically to the archetypes. See infra, pars. 206ff.

34 "Necrocomic" relating to the sphere of the *necrocomica,* i.e., telepathic phenomena or events indicative of the future. Ruland (*Lexicon,* p. 238) describes them as "signs falling from heaven upon earth."

35 "Liber Azoth," pp. 521ff.

means. Whereas the Iliaster seems to be a dynamic spiritual principle, capable of both good and evil, the Aquaster, because of its watery nature, is more a "psychic" principle with quasi-material attributes (since the bodies of Christ and Mary partook of it). But it functions psychically as a "necrocomic" (i.e., telepathic) agent related to the spiritual world, and as the birthplace of the *spiritus vitae*. Of all the Paracelsan concepts, therefore, the Aquaster comes closest to the modern concept of the unconscious. So we can see why Paracelsus personifies it as the homunculus and describes the soul as the celestial Aquaster. Like a true alchemist, he thought of the Aquaster and Iliaster as extending both upwards and downwards: they assume a spiritual or heavenly form as well as a quasi-material or earthly one. This is in keeping with the axiom from "Tabula smaragdina": "What is below is like what is above, that the miracle of the one thing may be accomplished." This one thing is the lapis or *filius philosophorum*.[36] As the definitions and names of the prima materia make abundantly plain, matter in alchemy is material and spiritual, and spirit spiritual and material. Only, in the first case matter is *cruda, confusa, grossa, crassa, densa,* and in the second it is *subtilis.* Such, too, is the opinion of Paracelsus.

### C. ARES

176    Rather superficially, Adam von Bodenstein conceives "Ares" to be the "prime nature of things, determining their form and species." [37] Ruland lumps it together with the Iliaster and Archeus. But whereas the Iliaster is the hypostasis of being in general ("generis generalissimi substantia"), Archeus is given the role of a "dispenser of nature" (*naturae dispensator*) and "initiator." Ares, however, is the "assigner, who extends the peculiar nature to each species, and gives individual form." [38] It can therefore be taken as the principle of individuation in the strict sense. It proceeds from the supracelestial bodies, for "such is the property and nature of supracelestial bodies that they straightway produce out of nothing a corporeal imagination [*imaginationem corporalem*], so as to be thought a solid body. Of this

36 Hortulanus, "Commentarius," *De alchemia,* pp. 363ff.
37 *Onomasticon,* pp. 18f.
38 Ruland, *Lexicon,* p. 38.

kind is Ares, so that when one thinks of a wolf, a wolf appears.[39] This world is like the creatures composed of the four elements. From the elements arise things which are in no way like their origins, but nonetheless Ares bears them all in himself." [40]

177      Ares, accordingly, is an intuitive concept for a preconscious, creative, and formative principle which is capable of giving life

[39] Ares = Mars. The reference to the wolf supports this interpretation, for the wolf is the animal of Mars. Johannes Braceschus of Brixen, a contemporary of Paracelsus, states in his "Lignum vitae" (*Bibl. chem.*, I, pp. 911ff.) that the principle of the life-prolonging medicine is Mars, to which he refers the saying of Rhazes: "Accipe petram post ingressum Solis in arietem" (Take the stone after the sun's entry into Aries). Braceschus continues: "This thing [Mars] is a man whose complexion is choleric. . . . This hot and bilious man is iron . . . it is called a man because it has soul, body, and spirit. . . . That metal, although it is begotten by the virtue of all the stars and planets, is nevertheless especially begotten in the earth by virtue of the most high and mighty Pole Star called the Great Bear." Mars is also called the Daemogorgon, "ancestor of all the gods of the Gentiles." "Surrounded on all sides by thick clouds and darkness, he walks in the midmost bowels of the earth, and is there hidden . . . not begotten of any, but eternal and the father of all things." He is a "shapeless chimaera." Daemogorgon is explained as the "god of the earth, or a terrible god, and iron." (For Paracelsus, as we saw, the body purified by the fire was associated with iron, in so far as the residue was "without rust.") "The ancients attributed to him eternity and chaos for companions: eternity and the prepared quicksilver, which is . . . the eternal liquor." He is the serpent, the *aqua mercurialis*. "The first son of Daemogorgon was Litigius, that is, the sulphur which is called Mars." "Chaos is that earthly salt called Saturn; for it is matter and in it everything is without form." All living and dead things are contained in it, or proceed from it. Daemogorgon, or Mars, thus corresponds to the Ares of Paracelsus. Pernety (*Dictionnaire mytho-hermétique*) defines "Daimorgon" as the "genius of the earth," "the fire which quickens nature, and in particular that innate and life-giving spirit of the earth of the sages, which acts throughout the whole course of the operations of the great work." Pernety also mentions "Demorgon" and a treatise of the same name by Raymund Lully. This treatise is not mentioned in Ferguson's *Bibliotheca chemica* (1906), but it might be a reference to the "Lignum vitae" of Braceschus, which is a dialogue between Lully and a pupil. Roscher (*Lexicon*, I, col. 987) defines Demogorgon as "an enigmatic god. Might be derived from δημιουργός." Astrologically, Mars characterizes the instinctual and affective nature of man. The subjugation and transformation of this nature seems to be the theme of the alchemical opus. It is worth noting that Colonna's *Hypnerotomachia* begins with the wolf as the initiating animal; he also has this significance in Canto I of Dante's *Inferno*, where he appears in a triad of animals. This lower triad corresponds to the upper Trinity; therefore we meet it again as the tricephalous Satan in Canto XXXIV.

[40] Bodenstein, *De vita longa*, Lib. I, ch. VII, p. 21.

to individual creatures. It is thus a more specific principle of individuation than the Iliaster, and as such it plays an important role in the purification of the natural man by fire and his transformation into an "Enochdianus." The fire he is heated with is, as we have seen, no ordinary fire, since it does not contain either the "Melusinian Ares" or the "Salamandrine Essence." The salamander symbolizes the fire of the alchemists. It is itself of the nature of fire, a fiery essence. According to Paracelsus, Salamandrini and Saldini are men or spirits of fire, fiery beings. It is an old tradition that, because they have proved their incorruptibility in the fire, such creatures enjoy a particularly long life. The salamander is also the "incombustible sulphur"—another name for the arcane substance from which the lapis or *filius* is produced. The fire for heating the artifex contains nothing more of the nature of the salamander, which is an immature, transitional form of the *filius,* that incorruptible being whose symbols indicate the self.

178    Paracelsus endows Ares with the attribute "Melusinian." Since Melusina undoubtedly belongs to the watery realm, the realm of the nymphs, this attribute imports a watery character into the concept of Ares, which in itself is spiritual. Ares is thus brought into relationship with the lower, denser region and is intimately connected with the body. As a result, Ares becomes so like the Aquaster that it is scarcely possible to distinguish them conceptually. It is characteristic of Paracelsan thinking, and of alchemy in general, that there are no clear-cut concepts, so that one concept can take the place of another *ad infinitum*. At the same time every concept behaves hypostatically, as though it were a substance that could not at the same time be another substance. This typical primitive phenomenon is found also in Indian philosophy, which swarms with hypostases. Examples of this are the myths of the gods, which, as in Greek and Egyptian mythology, make utterly contradictory statements about the same god. Despite their contradictions, however, the myths continue to exist side by side without disturbing one another.

### D. MELUSINA

179    As we shall meet with Melusina several times more in the course of our interpretation, we must examine more closely the

nature of this fabulous creature, and in particular the role she plays in Paracelsus. As we know, she belongs to the realm of the Aquaster, and is a water-nymph with the tail of a fish or snake. In the original old French legend she appears as "mère Lusine," the ancestress of the counts of Lusignan. When her husband once surprised her in her fish-tail, which she had to wear only on Saturdays, her secret was out and she was forced to disappear again into the watery realm. She reappeared only from time to time, as a presage of disaster.

180     Melusina comes into the same category as the nymphs and sirens who dwell in the "Nymphidida," the watery realm.[41] In the treatise "De sanguine," [42] the nymph is specified as a *Schröttli*, 'nightmare.' Melusines, on the other hand, dwell in the blood.[43] Paracelsus tells us in "De pygmaeis" [44] that Melusina was originally a nymph who was seduced by Beelzebub into practising witchcraft. She was descended from the whale in whose belly the prophet Jonah beheld great mysteries. This derivation is very important: the birthplace of Melusina is the womb of the mysteries, obviously what we today would call the unconscious. Melusines have no genitals,[45] a fact that characterizes them as paradisal beings, since Adam and Eve in paradise had no genitals either.[46] Moreover paradise was then beneath the water "and still is." [47] When the devil glided into the tree of paradise the tree was "saddened," and Eve was seduced by the "infernal basilisk." [48] Adam and Eve "fell for" the serpent and became "monstrous," that is, as a result of their slip-up with the snake they acquired genitals.[49] But the Melusines remained in the paradisal state as water creatures and went on living in the human blood. Since blood is a primitive symbol for the soul,[50] Melusina can be interpreted as a spirit, or at any rate as some

---

[41] "Das Buch Meteorum" (ed. Huser), p. 79. In the Book of Enoch 19 : 2 the wives of the fallen angels changed into sirens.
[42] P. 271.
[43] Ibid., p. 4; "Philosophia ad Athenienses," Lib. I, ch. XIII.
[44] Ed. Huser, II, p. 189.
[45] "Liber Azoth," p. 534.
[46] Ibid., pp. 523, 537.
[47] P. 542.
[48] P. 539.
[49] Pp. 539, 541.
[50] Crawley, *The Idea of the Soul*, pp. 19 and 237.

kind of psychic phenomenon. Gerard Dorn confirms this in his commentary on *De vita longa,* where he says that Melusina is a "vision appearing in the mind." [51] For anyone familiar with the subliminal processes of psychic transformation, Melusina is clearly an anima figure. She appears as a variant of the mercurial serpent, which was sometimes represented in the form of a snake-woman[52] by way of expressing the monstrous, double nature of Mercurius. The redemption of this monstrosity was depicted as the assumption and coronation of the Virgin Mary.[53]

[51] P. 178. See infra, par. 214.

[52] As in Reusner's *Pandora* (1588), Codex Germanicus Alchemicus Vadiensis (St. Gall, 16th cent.), and Codex Rhenoviensis (Zurich, 15th cent.). [Cf. Figs. B 3–5.]

[The following (undated) note on *Pandora* was found among Jung's posthumous papers:

"*Pandora* is one of the earliest synoptic accounts of alchemy, and it may be the first that was written in German. It was first published by Henric Petri in Basel, 1588. It is apparent from the foreword that the author was the physician Hieronymus Reusner, who, however, hides under the pseudonym Franciscus Epimetheus, by whom the book was allegedly 'made.' Reusner dedicates it to Dr. Ruland, the well-known compiler of the *Lexicon alchemiae sive Dictionarium alchemisticum* (Frankfurt a. M., 1612). The text of *Pandora* is a compilation in the manner of the *Rosarium philosophorum* (1550), which is copiously cited. But other sources are used besides this, for instance the 'Tractatus aureus Hermetis.' Reusner was a pupil of Paracelsus. His book, being written in German, is a contribution to the Germanization of medicine that was started by Paracelsus, and, as the foreword shows, to Paracelsus's revival of the spiritual trends of alchemy. The actual text remains uninfluenced by these innovations and runs along the traditional lines. It contains nothing that is not found in the earlier authors, though the long list of synonyms at the end deserves special mention. This contains a number of Arabic and quasi-Arabic terms which, it appears, multiplied greatly during the 16th century. But the chief value of *Pandora* lies in the series of eighteen symbolical pictures at the end of the volume. As usual, they do not explain the text, or only very indirectly, but they are of considerable interest as regards the secret content of alchemy. Some of the pictures date from the 15th century and are taken from the *Dreifaltigkeitsbuch* (Codex Germanicus 598, 1420, Staatsbibliothek, Munich), but most are from the 16th century. The chief source is probably the 'Alchymistisches Manuscript' in the Universitätsbibliothek, Basel. One of the pictures (the Echidna symbol of Mercurius) may come from a 16th-century MS. in St. Gall."—EDITORS.]

[53] See *Psychology and Alchemy,* Figs. 224 and 232.

## E. THE FILIUS REGIUS AS THE ARCANE SUBSTANCE
### (MICHAEL MAIER)

181   It is not my intention to enter more closely into the relations between the Paracelsan Melusines and the mercurial serpent. I only wish to point out the alchemical prototypes that may have had an influence on Paracelsus, and to suggest that the longing of Melusina for a soul and for redemption has a parallel in that kingly substance which is hidden in the sea and cries out for deliverance. Of this *filius regius* Michael Maier says:[54] "He lives and calls from the depths:[55] Who shall deliver me from the waters and lead me to dry land? Even though this cry be heard of many, yet none takes it upon himself, moved by pity, to seek the king. For who, they say, will plunge into the waters? Who will imperil his life by taking away the peril of another? Only a few believe his lament, and think rather that they hear the crashing and roaring of Scylla and Charybdis. Therefore they remain sitting indolently at home, and give no thought to the kingly treasure, nor to their own salvation."

182   We know that Maier can have had no access to the *Philosophumena* of Hippolytus, long believed lost, and yet it might well have served him as a model for the king's lament. Treating of the mysteries of the Naassenes, Hippolytus says: "But what that form is which comes down from above, from the Uncharacterized [ἀχαρακτηρίστου], no man knows. It is found in earthly clay, and yet none recognize it. But that is the god who dwells in the great flood.[56] In the Psalter he calls and cries out from many waters.[57] The many waters, they say, are the multitude of mortal men, whence he calls and cries aloud to the uncharacterized Man:[58] Save mine Only-Begotten[59] from the lions." [60]

---

54 *Symbola aureae mensae,* p. 380.

55 Psalm 129 : 1 (DV): "Out of the depth I have cried to thee, O Lord."

56 Psalm 29 : 10 (AV): "The Lord sitteth upon the flood: yea, the Lord sitteth King for ever."

57 Psalm 28 : 3 (DV): "The voice of the Lord is upon the waters; the God of majesty hath thundered; the Lord is upon many waters."

58 In the sense of θεὸς ἄνθρωπος.

59 τὴν μονογενῆ μου. This feminine "only-begotten" seems to refer to a daughter, or to the soul, as Psalm 34 : 17 (DV) affirms: "Rescue thou my soul from their malice: my only one from the lions."

60 Psalm 21 : 22 (DV): "Save me from the lion's mouth. . . ."

And he receives the reply [Isaiah 43 : 1ff.]: "And now thus saith the Lord that created thee, O Jacob, and formed thee, O Israel: Fear not, for I have redeemed thee, and called thee by thy name. Thou art mine. When thou shalt pass through the waters, I will be with thee, and the rivers shall not cover thee. When thou shalt walk through the fire, thou shalt not be burnt, and the flames shall not burn in thee." Hippolytus goes on to quote Psalm 23 : 7ff., (DV), referring it to the ascent (ἄνοδος) or regeneration (ἀναγέννησις) of Adam: "Lift up your gates, O ye princes, and be ye lifted up, O eternal gates, and the King of Glory shall enter in. Who is this King of Glory? The Lord who is strong and mighty, the Lord mighty in battle. . . . But who, say the Naassenes, is this King of Glory? A worm and no man, the reproach of men and the outcast of the people." [61]

183    It is not difficult to see what Michael Maier means. For him the *filius regius* or *Rex marinus,* as is evident from a passage in the text not quoted here, means antimony,[62] though in his usage it has only the name in common with the chemical element. In reality it is the secret transformative substance, which fell from the highest place into the darkest depths of matter where it awaits deliverance. But no one will plunge into these depths in order, by his own transformation in the darkness and by the torment of fire, to rescue his king. They cannot hear the voice of the king and think it is the chaotic roar of destruction. The sea (*mare nostrum*) of the alchemists is their own darkness, the unconscious. In his way, Epiphanius[63] correctly interpreted the "mire of the deep" (*limus profundi*) as "matter born of the mind, smutty reflections and muddy thoughts of sin." Therefore David in his affliction had said (Psalm 68 : 3, DV): "I stick fast

[61] Hippolytus, *Elenchos,* V, 8. The extreme lowliness of the redeemer's origin is expressed even more strongly in alchemy: the stone is "cast on the dunghill," "found in filth," etc. The "Tractatus Aristotelis" says (*Theatr. chem.,* V, 1660, p. 787): "Lapidem animalem esse, qui tanquam serpens ex corruptione perfectissimae naturae humanae de industria inter duos montes emissus gignitur, scinditur et prolabitur, et in fossa cavernae clauditur" (The living stone which is industriously brought forth as a serpent between the two mountains from the corruption of the most perfect human nature, is torn away and slips forth, and is shut up in a hollow cave). σκώληξ in conjunction with ἐξουδένημα, 'outcast,' might therefore be interpreted as an intestinal worm.

[62] From ἀνθεμώνιον, the efflorescence of metallic salts. Cf. Lippmann, *Entstehung und Ausbreitung der Alchemie,* II, p. 40.

[63] *Panarium* (ed. Holl), Haer. 36, cap. 4 (II, pp. 47ff).

in the mire of the deep." For the Church Father these dark
depths could only be evil itself, and if a king got stuck in them it
was on account of his own sinfulness. The alchemists took a
more optimistic view: the dark background of the soul contains
not only evil but a king in need of, and capable of, redemption,
of whom the *Rosarium* says: "At the end of the work the king
will go forth for thee,.crowned with his diadem, radiant as the
sun, shining like the carbuncle . . . constant in the fire." [64]
And of the worthless prima materia they say: "Despise not the
ash, for it is the diadem of thy heart, and the ash of things that
endure." [65]

184    These quotations give one an idea of the mystic aura that
surrounded the figure of the *filius regius,* and I do not think it
superfluous to have drawn attention to that distant period when
the central ideas of philosophical alchemy were being freely discussed by the Gnostics. Hippolytus gives us perhaps the most
complete insight into their analogical thinking, which is akin to
that of the alchemists. Anyone who came into contact with alchemy during the first half of the sixteenth century could not
fail to feel the fascination of these Gnostic ideas. Although
Maier lived and wrote more than seventy years after Paracelsus,
and we have no reason to suppose that Paracelsus was acquainted with the heresiologists, his knowledge of the alchemical treatises, and particularly of Hermes [Fig. B6] which he
so often quotes, would have sufficed to impress upon him the
figure of the *filius regius* and also that of the much lauded Mater
Natura—a figure not entirely in accord with the views of Christianity. Thus the "Tractatus aureus Hermetis" says: "O mightiest nature of the natures, who containest and separatest the midmost of the natures, who comest with the light and art born with
the light, who hast given birth to the misty darkness, who art the
mother of all beings!" [66] This invocation echoes the classical
feeling for nature, and its style is reminiscent of the oldest alchemical treatises, such as those of pseudo-Democritus, and of

---

64 *Art. aurif.,* II, p. 329, quotation from Lilius. Cf. The vision of the "man coming up from the midst of the sea" (II Esdras 13 : 25 and 51).
65 *Rosarium philosophorum (De alchimia,* 1550), fol. L3ᵛ.
66 *Ars chemica,* p. 21. The "Tractatus aureus" is of Arabic origin, but its content
dates back to much older sources. It may have been transmitted by the Harranite school.

the Greek Magic Papyri. In this same treatise we encounter the *Rex coronatus* and *filius noster rex genitus*, of whom it is said: "For the son is a blessing and possesses wisdom. Come hither, ye sons of the wise, and let us be glad and rejoice, for death is overcome, and the son reigns; he is clothed with the red garment, and the purple [*chermes*] is put on." He lives from "our fire," and nature "nourishes him who shall endure for ever" with a "small fire." When the son is brought to life by the opus, he becomes a "warrior fire" or a "fighter of fire." [67]

## F. THE PRODUCTION OF THE ONE, OR CENTRE, BY DISTILLATION

185      After this discussion of some of the basic concepts of alchemy, let us come back to the Paracelsan process of transforming the Iliaster. Paracelsus calls this process a *retorta distillatio*. The purpose of distillation in alchemy was to extract the volatile substance, or spirit, from the impure body. This process was a psychic as well as a physical experience. The *retorta distillatio* is not a known technical term, but presumably it meant a distillation that was in some way turned back upon itself. It might have taken place in the vessel called the Pelican [Fig. B7], where the distillate runs back into the belly of the retort. This was the "circulatory distillation," much favoured by the alchemists. By means of the "thousandfold distillation" they hoped to achieve a particularly "refined" result.[68] It is not unlikely that Paracelsus had something like this in mind, for his aim was to purify the human body to such a degree that it would finally unite with the *maior homo*, the inner spiritual man, and partake of his longevity. As we have remarked, this was not an ordinary chemical operation, it was essentially a psychological procedure. The fire to be used was a symbolical fire, and the distillation had to start "from the midst of the centre" (*ex medio centri*).

186      The accentuation of the centre is again a fundamental idea in alchemy. According to Michael Maier, the centre contains the "indivisible point," which is simple, indestructible, and eternal.

[67] *Bellator ignis* is ambiguous. *Chermes* = arab. *kermes* = 'purple,' L. *carmesinus* = Ital. *chermisi*, whence F. *cramoisi*, E. carmine, crimson. Cf. Du Cange, *Glossarium*, s.v. "carmesinus."

[68] Rupescissa, *La Vertu et propriété de la quinte essence de toutes choses*, p. 26.

Its physical counterpart is gold, which is therefore a symbol of eternity.[69] In Christianos the centre is compared to paradise and its four rivers. These symbolize the philosophical fluids (ὑγρά), which are emanations from the centre.[70] "In the centre of the earth the seven planets took root, and left their virtues there, wherefore in the earth is a germinating water," says *Aurora consurgens*.[71] Benedictus Figulus[72] writes:

> Visit the centre of the earth,
> There you will find the global fire.
> Rectify it of all dirt,
> Drive it out with love and ire. . . .

He calls this centre the "house of fire" or "Enoch," obviously borrowing the latter term from Paracelsus. Dorn says that nothing is more like God than the centre, for it occupies no space, and cannot be grasped, seen, or measured. Such, too, is the nature of God and the spirits. Therefore the centre is "an infinite abyss of mysteries." [73] The fire that originates in the centre carries everything upward, but when it cools everything falls back again to the centre. "The physiochemists call this move-

---

69 *De circulo physico quadrato*, pp. 27ff.

70 Berthelot, *Alch. grecs*, VI, i, 2.

71 Ed. von Franz, p. 125.

72 *Rosarium novum olympicum*, Pars. I, p. 71. Enoch is the "son of man" (Book of Enoch, in Charles, *Apocrypha and Pseudepigrapha*, II, p. 237).

73 "Nam ut ipsa [Divinitas] incomprehensibilis, invisibilis, non mensurabilis, infinita, indeterminata, et siquid ultra dici potest, omnia similiter in centro quadrare convenireque certum est. Hoc enim quia locum nullum occupat ob quantitatis carentiam, comprehendi non potest, videri nec mensurari. Tum etiam cum ea de causa infinitum sit, et absque terminis, locum non occupat, nec depingi potest, vel imitatione fingi. Nihilominus omnia quae locum etiam non implent ob carentiam corpulentiae, ut sunt spiritus omnes, centro comprehendi possunt, quod utraque sint incomprehensibilia." (For it is certain that it [the Divinity] is incomprehensible, invisible, immeasurable, infinite, indeterminable, and if aught more may be said, that it squares and brings all things together in a centre. For this, because it occupies no space, since it lacks quantity, cannot be comprehended, seen, or measured. Also because for that reason it is infinite and has no bounds, it occupies no space, nor can it be depicted, nor can any likeness of it be made. Nevertheless all things which likewise fill no place because they lack body, as is the case with all spirits, can be comprehended in the centre, for both are incomprehensible. As therefore there is no end of the centre, no pen can rightly describe its power and the infinite abyss of its mysteries.) ("Physica genesis," *Theatr. chem.*, I, 1659, pp. 339f.)

ment circular, and they imitate it in their operations." At the moment of culmination, just before the descent, the elements "conceive the male seeds of the stars," which enter into the elemental matrices (i.e., the non-sublimated elements) during the descent. Thus all created things have four fathers and four mothers. The conception of the seeds results from the "influxum et impressionem" of Sol and Luna, who thus function as nature gods, though Dorn does not say this quite as clearly.[74]

187    The creation of the elements and their ascent to heaven through the force of the fire serve as a model for the spagyric process. The lower waters, cleansed of their darkness, must be separated from the celestial waters by a carefully regulated fire. "In the end it will come to pass that this earthly, spagyric foetus clothes itself with heavenly nature by its ascent, and then by its descent visibly puts on the nature of the centre of the earth, but nonetheless the nature of the heavenly centre which it acquired by the ascent is secretly preserved." [75] The spagyric birth (*spagirica foetura*) is nothing other than the *filius philosophorum*, the inner, eternal man in the shell of the outer, mortal man. The *filius* is not only a panacea for all bodily defects, it also conquers the "subtle and spiritual sickness in the human mind." "For in the One," says Dorn,[76] "is the One and yet not the One; it is simple and consists of the number four. When this is purified by the fire in the sun,[77] the pure water[78] comes forth, and,

[74] Ibid., p. 349. In "Physica Trismegisti" (ibid., p. 375) Dorn says: "[Sol] primus post Deum pater ac parens omnium vocatus est, cum in eo quorumvis seminaria virtus atque formalis delitescit." (The Sun is called after God the father and parent of all things, since in him lies hidden the seminal and formal virtue of everything whatever.) P. 376: "Lunam esse matrem et uxorem solis, quae foetum spagiricum a sole conceptum in sua matrice uteroque, vento gestat in aere." (The moon is the mother and wife of the sun, who bears in her aerial womb the spagyric foetus conceived from the sun.) From this it is evident that the *filius* is begotten of nature gods in a very unchristian manner.
[75] Ibid., p. 363.
[76] "Physica Trithemii," *Theatr. chem.*, I (1659), p. 391.
[77] The sun is the birthplace of the "spiritual fire," mentioned above. Light-symbols always refer psychologically to consciousness or to a content that is becoming conscious.
[78] The *aqua pura* is the *aqua permanens* of the Latin and Arabic alchemists and the ὕδωρ θεῖον of the Greeks. It is the *spiritus mercurialis* in water form, which in turn serves to extract the "soul" of the substance. The *spiritus mercurialis* corresponds to the spiritual fire, hence *aqua = ignis*. Although these terms are used

having returned to simplicity,[79] it [the quaternity as unity] will show the adept the fulfilment of the mysteries. This is the centre of the natural wisdom, whose circumference, closed in itself, forms a circle: an immeasurable order reaching to infinity." "Here is the number four, within whose bounds the number three, together with the number two combined into One, fulfils all things, which it does in miraculous wise." In these relations between four, three, two, and one is found, says Dorn, the "culmination of all knowledge and of the mystic art, and the infallible midpoint of the centre (*infallibile medii centrum*)." [80] The One is the midpoint of the circle, the centre of the triad, and it is also the "novenary foetus" (*foetus novenarius*), i.e., it is as the number nine to the ogdoad, or as the quintessence to the quaternity.[81]

188    The midpoint of the centre is fire. On it is modelled the simplest and most perfect form, which is the circle. The point is most akin to the nature of light,[82] and light is a *simulacrum Dei*.[83] Just as the firmament was created in the midst of the waters above and below the heavens, so in man there is a shining body, the radical moisture, which comes from the sphere of the heavenly waters.[84] This body is the "sidereal balsam," which maintains the animal heat. The spirit of the supracelestial wa-

indiscriminately, they are not the same, since fire is active, spiritual, emotional, close to consciousness, whereas water is passive, material, cool, and of the nature of the unconscious. Both are necessary to the alchemical process since this is concerned with the union of opposites. Cf. *Psychology and Alchemy*, Fig. 4.

79 Khunrath (*Von hylealischen Chaos*, p. 203) says that the *ternarius*, purified "by the Circumrotation or Circular Philosophical revolving of the Quaternarius . . . is brought back to the highest and most pure Simplicity . . . of the plus-quamperfect Catholic Monad. . . . The impure, crude One becomes an exceeding pure and subtle One, through the manifestation of the occult and the occultation of the manifest."

80 "Physica Trithemii," p. 391.

81 Dorn, "Duellum animi cum corpore," *Theatr. chem.*, I (1659), p. 482. This number symbolism refers to the axiom of Maria: "One becomes Two, Two becomes Three, and out of the Third comes One as the Fourth" (Berthelot, *Alch. grecs*, VI, v, 6). This axiom runs through the whole of alchemy, and is not unconnected with Christian speculations regarding the Trinity. Cf. my "Psychology and Religion," p. 60, and "A Psychological Approach to the Dogma of the Trinity," pp. 164ff.

82 Steeb, *Coelum Sephiroticum*, p. 19.

83 Ibid., p. 38.

84 P. 42.

ters has its seat in the brain, where it controls the sense organs. In the microcosm the balsam dwells in the heart,[85] like the sun in the macrocosm. The shining body is the *corpus astrale,* the "firmament" or "star" in man. Like the sun in the heavens, the balsam in the heart is a fiery, radiant centre. We meet this solar point in the *Turba,*[86] where it signifies the "germ of the egg, which is in the yolk, and that germ is set in motion by the hen's warmth." The "Consilium coniugii" says that in the egg are the four elements and the "red sun-point in the centre, and this is the young chick." [87] Mylius interprets this chick as the bird of Hermes,[88] which is another synonym for the mercurial serpent.

189    From this context we can see that the *retorta distillatio ex medio centri* results in the activation and development of a psychic centre, a concept that coincides psychologically with that of the self.

### G. THE CONIUNCTIO IN THE SPRING

190    At the end of the process, says Paracelsus, a "physical lightning" will appear, the "lightning of Saturn" will separate from the lightning of Sol, and what appears in this lightning pertains "to longevity, to that undoubtedly great Iliaster." [89] This process does not take anything away from the body's weight but only from its "turbulence," and that "by virtue of the translucent colours." [90] "Tranquillity of mind" [91] as a goal of the opus is stressed also by other alchemists. Paracelsus has nothing good to say about the body. It is "bad and putrid." When it is alive, it lives only from the "Mumia." Its "continual endeavour" is to rot and turn back into filth. By means of the Mumia the

---

85 P. 117.

86 Ed. Ruska, p. 94. Cf. Codex Berolinensis 532, fol. 154ᵛ: ". . . the sun-point, that is the germ of the egg, which is in the yolk."

87 *Ars chemica.* The "Consilium coniugii" may date from the 13th cent.

88 *Phil. ref.,* p. 131.

89 There is only *one* flash of lightning, which changes the darkness of Saturn into the brightness of Jupiter. Ruland (*Lexicon,* p. 153) states: "Metallic fulmination is, with the higher metals, a process of purging. . . . Fulmination is a metallic gradation, with excoction, educing the pure part, the perfection thereof being indicated by an irradiating splendour."

90 The colours refer to the *cauda pavonis,* which appears just before the completion of the opus.                    91 Cf. infra, pars. 201f.

A fish meal, with accompanying statue of the hermaphrodite. Though the picture is undoubtedly secular, it contains echoes of early Christian motifs. The significance of the hermaphrodite in this context is unknown to me. British Museum, MS. Add. 15268 (13th cent.)

The *filius* or *rex* in the form of a hermaphrodite. The axiom of
Maria is represented by 1 + 3 snakes: the *filius,* as mediator, unites
the one with the three. Characteristically, he has bat's wings. To the
right is the Pelican, symbol of the *distillatio circulatoria;* to the left,
the *arbor philosophica* with golden flowers; underneath, the chthonic
triad as a three-headed serpent. From *Rosarium philosophorum*
(1550), fol. X, iiiv

The Rebis: from "Book of the Holy Trinity and Description of the Secret of the Transmutation of Metals" (1420), in the Codex Germanicus 598 (Staatsbibliothek, Munich), fol. 105$^v$. The illustration may have served as a model for the hermaphrodite in the *Rosarium* (pl. B2)

B3

Melusina as the *aqua permanens,* opening the side of the *filius* (an allegory of Christ) with the lance of Longinus. The figure in the middle is Eve (earth), who is reunited with Adam (Christ) in the coniunctio. From their union is born the hermaphrodite, the incarnate Primordial Man. To the right is the athanor (furnace) with the vessel in the centre, from which the lapis (hermaphrodite) will arise. The vessels on either side contain Sol and Luna. Woodcut from Reusner's *Pandora: Das ist, die edelst Gab Gottes, oder der werde und heilsame Stein der Weysen* (Basel, 1588), p. 249

The anima as Melusina, embracing a man rising out of the sea (= unconscious):
a *coniunctio animae cum corpore*. The gnomes are the planetary spirits in the
form of *paredroi* (familiars). British Museum, MS. Sloane 5025, a variant of the
Ripley *Scrowle* (1588)

The King's Son (*filius regis*) and the mystagogue Hermes on a mountain, an obvious allusion to the Temptation (Luke, ch. 4). The accompanying text says: "Another mountain of India lies in the vessel, which the Spirit and Soul, as son and guide, have together ascended." The two are called spirit and soul because they represent volatile substances which rise up during the heating of the prima materia. From Lambspringk, "De lapide philosophico," fig. XII, in *Musaeum hermeticum* (Frankfurt a. M., 1678), p. 365

**Sed** fi fimplicium partes fpirituofæ effentiæ craffa-
mentis, & terrenis fæcibus immerfæ, ut tenuiores, &
puriores evadant, & craffis illis, & impuris exonercn-
tur, & in fecibus relinquant, velut medicis ufibus inc-
ptæ, oportet multiplicatis viribus, in fe ipfas refolvan-
tur, & reducantur, ut affiduo motu circumgyratæ nobi-
liorem vim, & magis egregiam fortiantur. Vas excogi-
tatum eft, quod Pelicanū vocant, quod ad avis Pelicani
figuram adumbratum eft, in quo fimplicium partes magis tenues per collum eductæ, & per roftrum in apertū
pectus infixum quafi in ventum fuper feces regeran-
tur, iterumque per collum fublatæ indefatigabili motu aquofitatem, craffitiem recipientem paulatim ex-
hauriant, & fimplicia affidua rotatione non folum de-
purentur: fed etiam altius virtutes exaltentur. Vas, E,
litera infignitur.

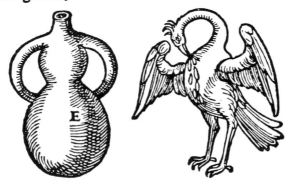

Alii verò alio modo effingunt. Duo vafa capiunt,
quod alteri alter innectatur & quod unum recipit alteri
reddit, utrumque alterius altero alvo roftro infigitur.
H

Picture of the Pelican, the vessel in which the circulatory distillation
takes place. Page from Rhenanus, *Solis e puteo emergentis sive dissertationis chymotechnicae libri tres* (Frankfurt a. M., 1613)

"peregrinus microcosmus" (wandering microcosm) controls the physical body, and for this the arcana are needed.[92] Here Paracelsus lays particular stress on Thereniabin[93] and Nostoch[94] (as before on Cheyri) and on the "tremendous powers" of Melissa. Melissa is singled out for special honour because in ancient medicine it was considered to be a means of inducing happiness, and was used as a remedy for melancholia and for purging the body of "black, burnt-out blood." [95] It unites in itself the powers of the "supracelestial coniunctio," and that is "Iloch, which comes from the true Aniadus." As Paracelsus had spoken just before of Nostoch, the Iliaster has changed under his eyes into Iloch. The Aniadus that now makes its appearance constitutes the essence of Iloch, i.e., of the coniunctio. But to what does the coniunctio refer? Before this Paracelsus had been speaking of a separation of Saturn and Sol. Saturn is the cold, dark, heavy, impure element, Sol is the opposite. When this separation is completed and the body has been purified by Melissa and freed from Saturnine melancholy, then the coniunctio can take place with the long-living inner, or astral, man,[96] and from this conjunction arises the "Enochdianus." Iloch or Aniadus appears to be something like the virtue or power of the everlasting man. This "Magnale" comes about by the "exaltation of both worlds," and "in the true May, when the exaltations of Aniada begin, these should be gathered." Here again Paracelsus outdoes

---

[92] "For from mortal man can nothing be called forth which produces longevity, for longevity is outside the body." "Fragmenta medica," ed. Sudhoff, III, p. 291.

[93] *Thereniabin* is a favourite arcanum of Paracelsus. It is *pinguedo mannae* (the fat or oil of manna), popularly known as honeydew—a sticky, resinous coating on leaves, with a sweetish taste. This honey, Paracelsus says, falls from the air. Being a heavenly food, it assists sublimation. He also calls it "maydew." [For a possible connection between ergot-based honeydew and Coleridge's image in "Kubla Khan," see Todd, "Coleridge and Paracelsus, Honeydew and LSD."—EDITORS.]

[94] *Nostoch* is not, as Bodenstein supposes, a species of fire, but a gelatinous alga that appears after continuous rain. These algae are still known as Nostocs in modern botany. It was earlier supposed that Nostocs fell from the air, or from the stars. (They are also called star jelly and witches'-butter.) Ruland (*Lexicon*, p. 240) defines it as "a ray or radiation of a certain star, or its offscouring, superfluity, etc. cast on earth." Hence, like *thereniabin*, it is a sublimating arcanum, because it comes from heaven.

[95] Tabernaemontanus, *Herbal*, s.v. "Melissa."

[96] For this reason the coniunctio is depicted as the embrace of two winged beings, as in the *Rosarium*. Cf. *Psychology and Alchemy*, Fig. 268.

himself in obscurity, but this much at least is evident, that Aniadus denotes a springtime condition, the "efficacity of things," as Dorn defines it.

191    We meet this motif in one of the earliest Greek texts, entitled the "Instruction of Cleopatra by the Archpriest Komarios," [97] where Ostanes[98] and his companions say to Cleopatra:

Make known to us how the highest descends to the lowest, and the lowest ascends to the highest, and the midmost draws near to the lowest and the highest, so that they are made one with it;[99] how the blessed waters come down from above to awaken the dead, who lie round about in the midst of Hades, chained in the darkness; how the elixir of life comes to them and awakens them, rousing them out of their sleep. . . .

192    Cleopatra answers:

When the waters come in, they awaken the bodies and the spirits, which are imprisoned and powerless. . . . Gradually they bestir themselves, rise up, and clothe themselves in bright colours,[100] glorious as the flowers in spring. The spring is glad and rejoices in the blossoming ripeness they have put on.

193    Ruland defines Aniada[101] as "fruits and powers of paradise and heaven; they are also the Christian Sacraments . . . those things which by thought, judgment, and imagination promote longevity in us." [102] They seem therefore to be powers that confer everlasting life, an even more potent φάρμακον ἀθανασίας than Cheyri, Thereniabin, Nostoch, and Melissa. They correspond to the blessed waters of Komarios and also, apparently, to the Communion substances. In the spring all the forces of life are in a state of festive exaltation, and the *opus alchymicum* should also begin in the spring[103] (already in the month of Aries, whose ruler is Mars). At that time the Aniada should be "gathered,"

[97] The text is assigned to the 1st cent. A.D. Berthelot, *Alch. grecs*, IV, xx, 8.

[98] An already legendary (Persian) alchemist of perhaps the 4th cent. B.C.

[99] I insert in Berthelot's text the reading of MS. Paris 2250 (καὶ κατώτατον ὥστε), which makes better sense.

[100] The *cauda pavonis* of the Latin alchemists.

[101] The nominative plural corresponding to *aniadorum* is presumably *aniada* rather than *aniadi*.                    [102] *Lexicon,* p. 30.

[103] A derivation that would come closest in meaning to the term *Aniadus* would be from ἀνύειν, 'to perfect, complete.' The form *Anyadei*, defined by Ruland (*Lexicon,* p. 32) as "eternal spring, the new world, the Paradise to come," argues in favour of this.

as though they were healing herbs. There is an ambiguity here: it could also mean the gathering together of all the psychic powers for the great transformation. The hierosgamos of Poliphilo likewise takes place in the month of May,[104] that is, the union with the soul, the latter embodying the world of the gods. At this marriage the human and the divine are made one; it is an "exaltation of both worlds," as Paracelsus says. He adds significantly: "And the exaltations of the nettles burn too, and the colour of the little flame[105] sparkles and shines." Nettles were used for medicinal purposes (the preparation of nettle water), and were collected in May because they sting most strongly when they are young. The nettle was therefore a symbol of youth, which is "most prone to the flames of lust." [106] The allusion to the stinging nettle and the *flammula* is a discreet reminder that not only Mary but Venus, too, reigns in May. In the next sentence Paracelsus remarks that this power can be "changed into something else." There are exaltations, he says, far more powerful than the nettle, namely the Aniada, and these are found not in the matrices, that is, in the physical elements, but in the heavenly ones. The Ideus would be nothing if it had not brought forth greater things. For it had made another May, when heavenly flowers bloomed. At this time Anachmus[107] must be extracted and preserved, even as "musk rests in the pomander[108] and the virtue of gold in laudanum." [109] One can

104 Taurus, the zodiacal sign of May, is the House of Venus. In the Greek-Egyptian zodiac the bull carries the sun-disk, which rests in the sickle moon (the ship of Venus), an image of the coniunctio. (Cf. Budge, *Amulets and Superstitions,* p. 410.) The Taurus sign is composed of the sun-disk with the moon's horns: ♉. Cf. the alchemical parallel in Dee, "Monas hieroglyphica," *Theatr. chem.,* II (1659), pp. 200ff.

105 I have given a literal translation of "nitetque ac splendet flammulae color." But since Paracelsus was familiar with Agrippa's *De occulta philosophia,* he may have been referring to, or quoting, a passage from this work. In Book I, ch. XXVII, we read of trees and plants that "are armed with sharp thorns, or burn, prick, or cut the skin by their contact, such as the thistle, nettle, and little flame *(flammula)."* Here *flammula* is the name for various kinds of crowfoot *(ranunculus),* which was used as a corrosive and vesicant and is mentioned as such in Dioscorides *(Medica materia,* p. 295).

106 Picinellus, *Mundus symbolicus,* s.v. "urtica."

107 Anachmus is mentioned along with the Scaiolae; see infra, par. 207.

108 Pomander = *pomambra* = *pomum ambrae. Ambra* is a bezoar of the pot-fish or sperm-whale, prized on account of its perfume (ambergris). These and other aromatics were used as "plague balls" to drive away the fetid vapours of sick-

enjoy longevity only when one has gathered the powers of An-achmus. To my knowledge, there is no way of distinguishing Anachmus from Aniadus.

---

rooms. *Muscus* is mentioned as an aromatic in Dioscorides (*Medica materia,* p. 42). In Agrippa (*Occult. phil.,* I, p. xxxiv) the aromatics subordinated to Venus include "ladanum, ambra muscus." In our text "muscus in pomambra" is immediately followed by "laudanum." According to Dioscorides (*Med. mat.,* p. 106), *ladanum* is the juice of an exotic plant whose leaves "acquire in the spring a certain fattiness . . . out of which is made what is called ladanum." Tabernaemontanus says this juice is aromatic.

109 *Laudanum* is the arcane remedy of Paracelsus. It has nothing to do with opium, though it may be derived from the above-mentioned *ladanum.* Adam von Bodenstein (*De vita longa,* p. 98) mentions two *laudanum* recipes of Paracelsus.

## 3. THE NATURAL TRANSFORMATION MYSTERY

194    Aniadus (or Aniadum), interpreted by Bodenstein and Dorn as the "efficacity of things," is defined by Ruland as "the regenerated spiritual man in us, the heavenly body implanted in us Christians by the Holy Ghost through the most Holy Sacraments." This interpretation does full justice to the role which Aniadus plays in the writings of Paracelsus. Though it is clearly related to the sacraments and to the Communion in particular, it is equally clear that there was no question of arousing or implanting the inner man in the Christian sense, but of a "scientific" union of the natural with the spiritual man with the aid of arcane techniques of a medical nature. Paracelsus carefully avoids the ecclesiastical terminology and uses instead an esoteric language which is extremely difficult to decipher, for the obvious purpose of segregating the "natural" transformation mystery from the religious one and effectively concealing it from prying eyes. Otherwise the welter of esoteric terms in this treatise would have no explanation. Nor can one escape the impression that this mystery was in some sense opposed to the religious mystery: as the "nettle" and the *flammula* show, the ambiguities of Eros were also included in it.[1] It had far more to do with pagan antiquity, as is evidenced by the *Hypnerotomachia Poliphili*, than with the Christian mystery. Nor is there any reason to suppose that Paracelsus was sniffing out nasty secrets; a more cogent motive was his experience as a physician who had to deal with man as he is and not as he should be and biologically speaking never can be. Many questions are put to a doctor which he cannot honestly answer with "should" but only from his knowledge and experience of nature. In these fragments of a nature

[1] Confirmation of this may be found in the work of the alchemist and mystic John Pordage (1607–1681), "Ein Philosophisches Send-Schreiben vom Stein der Weissheit," printed in Roth-Scholtz, *Deutsches Theatrum chemicum*, I, pp. 557–596. For text, see my "Psychology of the Transference," pars. 507ff.

mystery there is nothing to suggest a misplaced curiosity or perverse interest on Paracelsus's part; they bear witness rather to the strenuous efforts of a physician to find satisfactory answers to psychological questions which the ecclesiastical casuist is inclined to twist in his own favour.

195     This nature mystery was indeed so much at odds with the Church—despite the superficial analogies—that the Hungarian alchemist Nicolaus Melchior Szebeny,[2] court astrologer to Ladislaus II (1471–1516), made the bold attempt to present the *opus alchymicum* in the form of a Mass.[3] It is difficult to prove whether and to what extent the alchemists were aware that they were in conflict with the Church. Mostly they showed no insight into what they were doing. This is true also of Paracelsus—except for a few hints about the "Pagoyum." It is the more understandable that no real self-criticism could come about, since they genuinely believed that they were performing a work wellpleasing to God on the principle "quod natura relinquit imperfectum, ars perficit" (what nature left imperfect, the art perfects). Paracelsus himself was wholly filled with the godliness of his profession as a doctor, and nothing disquieted or disturbed his Christian faith. He took it for granted that his work supplemented the hand of God and that he was the faithful steward of the talent that had been entrusted to him. And as a matter of fact he was right, for the human soul is not something cut off from nature. It is a natural phenomenon like any other, and its problems are just as important as the questions and riddles which are presented by the diseases of the body. Moreover there is scarcely a disease of the body in which psychic factors do not play a part, just as physical ones have to be considered in many psychogenic disturbances. Paracelsus was fully alive to this. In his own peculiar way he took the psychic phenomena into account as perhaps none of the great physicians ever did before or after him. Although his homunculi, *Trarames, Durdales,* nymphs, Melusines, etc., are the grossest superstitions for us socalled moderns, for a man of Paracelsus's time they were nothing

[2] Condemned to death under Ferdinand I, and executed in Prague, May 2, 1531. See *Psychology and Alchemy,* par. 480 and n.

[3] "Addam et processum sub forma missae, a Nicolao Cibinensi, Transilvano, ad Ladislaum Ungariae et Bohemiae regem olim missum," *Theatr. chem.,* III (1659), pp. 758ff.

of the sort. In those days these figures were living and effective forces. They were projections, of course; but of that, too, Paracelsus seems to have had an inkling, since it is clear from numerous passages in his writings that he was aware that homunculi and suchlike beings were creatures of the imagination. His more primitive cast of mind attributed a reality to these projections, and this reality did far greater justice to their psychological effect than does our rationalistic assumption of the absolute unreality of projected contents. Whatever their reality may be, functionally at all events they behave just like realities. We should not let ourselves be so blinded by the modern rationalistic fear of superstition that we lose sight completely of those little-known psychic phenomena which surpass our present scientific understanding. Although Paracelsus had no notion of psychology, he nevertheless affords—precisely because of his "benighted superstition"—deep insights into psychic events which the most up-to-date psychology is only now struggling to investigate again. Even though mythology may not be "true" in the sense that a mathematical law or a physical experiment is true, it is still a serious subject for research and contains quite as many truths as a natural science; only, they lie on a different plane. One can be perfectly scientific about mythology, for it is just as good a natural product as plants, animals or chemical elements.

196 Even if the psyche were a product of the will, it would still not be outside nature. No doubt it would have been a greater achievement if Paracelsus had developed his natural philosophy in an age when the psyche had been discredited as an object of scientific study. As it was, he merely included in the scope of his investigations something that was already present, without being obliged to prove its existence anew. Even so his achievement is sufficiently great, despite the fact that we moderns still find it difficult to estimate correctly the full psychological implications of his views. For what, in the end, do we know about the causes and motives that prompted man, for more than a thousand years, to believe in that "absurdity" the transmutation of metals and the simultaneous psychic transformation of the artifex? We have never seriously considered the fact that for the medieval investigator the redemption of the world by God's son and the transubstantiation of the Eucharistic elements were not the last word, or rather, not the last answer to the manifold enigmas of

man and his soul. If the *opus alchymicum* claimed equality with the *opus divinum* of the Mass, the reason for this was not grotesque presumption but the fact that a vast, unknown Nature, disregarded by the eternal verities of the Church, was imperiously demanding recognition and acceptance. Paracelsus knew, in advance of modern times, that this Nature was not only chemical and physical but also psychic. Even though his Trarames and whatnot cannot be demonstrated in a test tube, they nevertheless had their place in his world. And even if, like all the rest of them, he never produced any gold, he was yet on the track of a process of psychic transformation that is incomparably more important for the happiness of the individual than the possession of the red tincture.

## A. THE LIGHT OF THE DARKNESS

197    So when we try to elucidate the riddles of the *Vita longa* we are following the traces of a psychological process that is the vital secret of all seekers after truth. Not all are vouchsafed the grace of a faith that anticipates all solutions, nor is it given to all to rest content with the sun of revealed truth. The light that is lighted in the heart by the grace of the Holy Spirit, that same light of nature, however feeble it may be, is more important to them than the great light which shines in the darkness and which the darkness comprehended not. They discover that in the very darkness of nature a light is hidden, a little spark without which the darkness would not be darkness.[4] Paracelsus was one of these. He was a well-intentioned, humble Christian. His ethics and his professed faith were Christian, but his most secret, deepest passion, his whole creative yearning, belonged to the *lumen naturae,* the divine spark buried in the darkness, whose sleep of death could not be vanquished even by the revelation of God's son. The light from above made the darkness still darker; but the *lumen naturae* is the light of the darkness itself, which illuminates its own darkness, and this light the darkness comprehends. Therefore it turns blackness into brightness, burns away "all superfluities," and leaves behind nothing but "faecem

[4] "Pharmaco ignito spolianda densi est corporis umbra" (The drug being ignited, the shadow of the dense body is to be stripped away). Maier, *Symbola aureae mensae,* p. 91.

et scoriam et terram damnatam" (dross and scoriae and the rejected earth).

198    Paracelsus, like all the philosophical alchemists, was seeking
for something that would give him a hold on the dark, body-
bound nature of man, on the soul which, intangibly interwoven
with the world and with matter, appeared before itself in the
terrifying form of strange, demoniacal figures and seemed to be
the secret source of life-shortening diseases. The Church might
exorcise demons and banish them, but that only alienated man
from his own nature, which, unconscious of itself, had clothed
itself in these spectral forms. Not separation of the natures but
union of the natures was the goal of alchemy. From the time of
Democritus its *leitmotiv* had been: "Nature rejoices in nature,
nature conquers nature, nature rules over nature." [5] This principle is pagan in feeling and an expression of nature worship.
Nature not only contains a process of transformation—it is itself
transformation. It strives not for isolation but for union, for the
wedding feast followed by death and rebirth. Paracelsus's "exaltation in May" is this marriage, the "gamonymus" or hierosgamos of light and darkness in the shape of Sol and Luna. Here
the opposites unite what the light from above had sternly divided. This is not so much a reversion to antiquity as a continuation of that religious feeling for nature, so alien to Christianity, which is expressed most beautifully in the "Secret Inscription" in the Great Magic Papyrus of Paris: [6]

Greetings, entire edifice of the Spirit of the air, greetings, Spirit that
penetratest from heaven to earth, and from earth, which abideth in
the midst of the universe, to the uttermost bounds of the abyss,
greetings, Spirit that penetratest into me, and shakest me, and depart-
est from me in goodness according to God's will; greetings, beginning
and end of irremovable Nature, greetings, thou who revolvest the
elements which untiringly render service, greetings, brightly shining
sun, whose radiance ministereth to the world, greetings, moon shining by night with disc of fickle brilliance, greetings, all ye spirits of
the demons of the air, greetings, ye for whom the greeting is offered
in praise, brothers and sisters, devout men and women! O great,
greatest, incomprehensible fabric of the world, formed in a circle!

---

5 Ἡ φύσις τῇ φύσει τέρπεται, καὶ ἡ φύσις τὴν φύσιν νικᾷ, καὶ ἡ φύσις τὴν φύσιν κρατεῖ.
Berthelot, *Alch. grecs*, II, i, 3.

6 Preisendanz, *Papyri Graecae Magicae*, I. p. 111.

Heavenly One, dwelling in the heavens, aetherial spirit, dwelling in the aether, having the form of water, of earth, of fire, of wind, of light, of darkness, star-glittering, damp-fiery-cold Spirit! I praise thee, God of gods, who hast fashioned the world, who hast established the depths upon the invisible support of their firm foundation, who hast separated heaven and earth, and hast encompassed the heavens with golden, eternal wings, and founded the earth upon eternal bases, who hast hung the aether high above the earth, who hast scattered the air with the self-moving wind, who hast laid the waters round about, who callest forth the tempests, the thunder, the lightning, the rain: Destroyer, Begetter of living things, God of the Aeons, great art thou, Lord, God, Ruler of All!

199    Just as this prayer has come down to us embedded in a mass of magical recipes, so does the *lumen naturae* rise up from a world of kobolds and other creatures of darkness, veiled in magical spells and almost extinguished in a morass of mystification. Nature is certainly equivocal, and one can blame neither Paracelsus nor the alchemists if, anxiously aware of their responsibilities, they cautiously expressed themselves in parables. This procedure is indeed the more appropriate one in the circumstances. What takes place between light and darkness, what unites the opposites, has a share in both sides and can be judged just as well from the left as from the right, without our becoming any the wiser: indeed, we can only open up the opposition again. Here only the symbol helps, for, in accordance with its paradoxical nature, it represents the "tertium" that in logic does not exist, but which in reality is the living truth. So we should not begrudge Paracelsus and the alchemists their secret language: deeper insight into the problems of psychic development soon teaches us how much better it is to reserve judgment instead of prematurely announcing to all and sundry what's what. Of course we all have an understandable desire for crystal clarity, but we are apt to forget that in psychic matters we are dealing with processes of experience, that is, with transformations which should never be given hard and fast names if their living movement is not to petrify into something static. The protean mythologem and the shimmering symbol express the processes of the psyche far more trenchantly and, in the end, far more clearly than the clearest concept; for the symbol not only conveys a visualization of the process but—and this is perhaps just as impor-

tant—it also brings a re-experiencing of it, of that twilight which we can learn to understand only through inoffensive empathy, but which too much clarity only dispels. Thus the symbolic hints of marriage and exaltation in the "true May," when the heavenly flowers bloom and the secret of the inner man is made manifest, by the very choice and sound of the words convey a vision and experience of a climax whose significance could be amplified only by the finest flights of the poets. But the clear and unambiguous concept would find not the smallest place where it would fit. And yet something deeply significant has been said, for as Paracelsus rightly remarks: "When the heavenly marriage is accomplished, who will deny its superexcellent virtue?"

### B. THE UNION OF MAN'S TWO NATURES

200     Paracelsus is concerned here with something of great importance, and in recognition of this I have put in an apologia for the symbol, which unites what is divided. But he too felt the need of some explanation. Thus he says in the second chapter of Book V that man has two life forces: one of them natural, the other "aerial, wherein is nothing of the body." (We would say that life has a physiological and a psychic aspect.) He therefore ends *De vita longa* with a discussion of incorporeal things. "Miserable in this respect are mortals to whom Nature has denied her first and best treasure, which the monarchy of Nature contains, namely, the *lumen naturae!*" [7] he exclaims, leaving us in no doubt what the *lumen naturae* meant to him. He says that he will now go beyond Nature and consider Aniadus. Let no one take exception to what he will now set forth concerning the power of the Guarini, Saldini, Salamandrini, and Melusina. If any should be astonished at his words, he should not let that detain him, but should rather read to the end, when he will understand all.

201     Those live longest, says Paracelsus, who have lived "the aerial life" (*vitam aeream*). Their life lasts anything from six hundred to a thousand or eleven hundred years, and this is because they have lived in accordance with the "rule of the Magnalia,

---

[7] "Miseros hoc loco mortales, quibus primum ac optimum thesaurum (quam naturae monarchia in se claudit) natura recusavit, puta, naturae lumen." *De vita longa,* ed. Bodenstein, p. 88.

which are easily understood." One should therefore imitate Ani-adus, "and that by means of the air alone"—that is, by psychic means—"whose power is so great that the end of life has nothing in common with it. Further, if the said air be wanting, that which lies hidden in the capsule will burst forth." By the "capsule" Paracelsus probably means the heart. The soul or *anima iliastri* dwells in the fire of the heart. It is *impassibilis* (non-sentient, incapable of suffering), whereas the cagastric soul, which is *passibilis,* "floats" on the water of the capsule.[8] The heart is also the seat of the imagination, and is the "sun in the Microcosm." [9] Hence the *anima iliastri* can burst forth from the heart when it lacks "air"; that is to say, if psychic remedies are not applied, death occurs prematurely.[10] Paracelsus continues: "But if this [i.e., the *anima iliastri*] should be wholly filled with that [air] which renews itself again, and is then moved into the centre, that is, outside that under which it lay hidden before and still lies hid [i.e., in the heart capsule], then as a tranquil thing it is not heard at all by anything corporeal, and resounds only as Aniadus, Adech, and Edochinum. Whence comes the birth of that great Aquaster, which is born beyond Nature" (i.e., supernaturally).[11]

[8] "Liber Azoth," p. 534.

[9] "De pestilitate," Tract. I, ed. Huser, I, p. 334.

[10] "Nihil enim aliud mors est, nisi dissolutio quaedam, quae ubi accidit, tum demum moritur corpus. . . . Huic corpori Deus adiunxit aliud quoddam, puta coeleste, id quod in corpore vitae existit. Hoc opus, hic labor est, ne in dissolutionem, quae mortalium est et huic soli adiuncta, erumpat." (For death is nothing but a kind of dissolution which takes place when the body dies. . . . To this body God has added a certain other thing of a heavenly nature, that of the life which exists in the body. This is the task, this the toil: that it burst not forth at the dissolution which is the lot of mortals, but is joined to this [body] alone.) "Fragmenta," ed. Sudhoff, III, p. 292.

[11] "Sequuntur ergo qui vitam aeream vixerunt, quorum alii a 600 annis ad 1000 et 1100 annum pervenerunt, id quod iuxta praescriptum magnalium quae facile deprehenduntur, ad hunc modum accipe: Compara aniadum, idque per solum aera, cuius vis tanta est, ut nihil cum illo commune habeat terminus vitae. Porro si abest iam dictus aer, erumpit extrinsecus id, quod in capsula delitescit. Jam si idem ab illo, quod denuo renovatur fuerit refertum, ac denuo in medium perlatum, scilicet extra id sub quo prius delitescebat, imo adhuc delitescit, iam ut res tranquilla prorsus non audiatur a re corporali, et ut solum aniadum adech, denique et edochinum resonet." Lib. V, cap. III.

Dorn (*De vita longa,* p. 167) comments on this passage as follows:

a) The *imitation of Aniadus* is effected under the influence of "imaginationis,

202     The meaning of this laborious explanation seems to be that by psychic means the soul is not only prevented from escaping but is also brought back into the centre, the heart region. But this time it is not enclosed in the *capsula cordis,* where it lay hidden and as it were imprisoned till then; it is now outside its previous habitation. This indicates a certain degree of freedom from bondage to the body, hence the "tranquillity" of the soul, which, when it dwelt inside the heart, was too much exposed to the power of imagination, to Ares and the formative principle. The heart, for all its virtues, is a restless and emotional thing, all too easily swayed by the turbulence of the body. In it dwells that lower, earthbound, "cagastric" soul which has to be separated from the higher, more spiritual Iliaster. In this liberated and more tranquil sphere the soul, unheard by the body, can re-echo those higher entities, Aniadus, Adech, and Edochinum, who form the upper triad.

203     We have seen already that Adech stands for the inner *homo maximus.* He is the astral man, the manifestation of the macrocosm in the microcosm. Since he is named along with Aniadus and Edochinum, they are probably parallel designations. Ania-

---

aestimationis vel phantasiae," which is equivalent to "air" = spirit. By this is obviously meant the kind of active imagination that takes place in yoga or in the spiritual exercises of Ignatius Loyola, who employs the terms *consideratio, contemplatio, meditatio, ponderatio,* and *imaginatio per sensus* for the "realization" of the imagined content. (Cf. *The Spiritual Exercises of St. Ignatius Loyola,* trans. Rickaby, in particular pp. 40ff., the meditation on Hell.) The realization of Aniadus has about the same purpose as the contemplation of the life of Jesus in these exercises, with the difference that in the former case it is the unknown Primordial Man who is assimilated through individual experience, whereas in the later it is the known, historical personality of the Son of Man.

    b) The *lack of air* is explained by Dorn as due to the fact that it was "exhausted" by the efforts required for the realization.

    c) That which *bursts forth from the heart* is evil, which dwells in the heart. Dorn continues: "Indeed it is constrained under the vehicle under which it still lies hid." His conjecture of evil and constraint is not supported by the text. On the contrary, Dorn overlooks the preceding *depuratio* as a result of which the operation takes place in an already purified ("calcined") body. The *reverberatio* and the subsequent subliming processes have already removed the denser elements, including the *nigredo* and evil.

    d) As a result of his conjecture Dorn is obliged to read "intranquilla" for "tranquilla."

    e) Dorn here defines Adech as the "imaginary inner man" and Edochinum as Enochdianum.

dus certainly has this meaning, as mentioned earlier. Edochinum seems to be a variant of Enochdianus: Enoch belonged to the race of protoplasts related to the Original Man, who "tasted not death," or at any rate lived for several hundred years. The three different names are probably only amplifications of the same conception—that of the deathless Original Man, to whom the mortal man can be approximated by means of the alchemical opus. As a result of this approximation the powers and attributes of the *homo maximus* flow like a helpful and healing stream into the earthly nature of the microcosmic mortal man. Paracelsus's conception of the *homo maximus* does much to elucidate the psychological motives of the alchemical opus in general, since it shows how the main product of the work, the *aurum non vulgi* or *lapis philosophorum,* came to have such a variety of names and definitions: elixir, panacea, tincture, quintessence, light, east, morning, Aries, living fount, fruit-tree, animal, Adam, man, *homo altus,* form of man, brother, son, father, *pater mirabilis,* king, hermaphrodite, *deus terrenus, salvator, servator, filius macrocosmi,* and so on.[12] In comparison with the "mille nomina" of the alchemists, Paracelsus used only about ten names for this entity, which exercised the speculative fantasy of the alchemists for more than sixteen hundred years.

204      Dorn's commentary lays particular emphasis on the significance of this passage. According to him, these three—Aniadus, Adech, and Edochinum—form the one "pure and well-tempered element" (*elementum purum temperatum*) as contrasted with the four, impure, gross, and worldly elements, which are far removed from longevity. From these three comes the "mental vision" of that great Aquaster, which is born supernaturally. That is to say, from the Aniadic mother, with the aid of Adech and through the power of the imagination, comes the great vision, which impregnates the supernatural matrix so that it gives birth to the invisible foetus of longevity, that is created or begotten by the invisible or extrinsic Iliaster. Dorn's insistence on three as opposed to four is based on his polemical attitude to the axiom of Maria and to the relation of the quaternity to the Trinity, which I have discussed elsewhere.[13] Characteristically, Dorn

12 "Lapidis philosophorum nomina," MS. 2263–64, Ste. Geneviève, Paris, vol. II, fol. 129, and Pernety, *Fables égyptiennes et grecques,* I, pp. 136ff.
13 "Psychology and Religion," p. 60.

overlooks the fact that the fourth is in this case the microcosmic mortal man, who complements the upper triad.[14]

205     Union with the *homo maximus* produces a new life, which Paracelsus calls "vita cosmographica." In this life "time appears as well as the body Jesahach" (*cum locus tum corpus Jesahach*).[15] *Locus* can mean "time" as well as "space," and since, as we shall see, Paracelsus is here concerned with a sort of Golden Age, I have translated it as "time." The *corpus Jesahach* may thus be the *corpus glorificationis,* the resurrected body of the alchemists, and would coincide with the *corpus astrale.*

### C. THE QUATERNITY OF THE HOMO MAXIMUS

206     In this last chapter Paracelsus makes almost untranslatable allusions to the four Scaiolae, and it is not at all clear what could be meant. Ruland, who had a wide knowledge of the contemporary Paracelsist literature, defines them as "spiritual powers of the mind" (*spirituales mentis vires*), qualities and faculties which are fourfold, to correspond with the four elements. They are the four wheels of the fiery chariot that swept Elijah up to heaven. The Scaiolae, he says, originate in the mind of man, "from whom they depart and to whom they are turned back" (*a quo recedunt, et ad quem reflectuntur*).

207     Like the four seasons and the four quarters of heaven, the four elements are a quaternary system of orientation which always expresses a totality. In this case it is obviously the totality of the mind (*animus*), which here would be better translated as "consciousness" (including its contents). The orienting system of consciousness has four aspects, which correspond to four empirical functions: thinking, feeling, sensation (sense-perception), intuition. This quaternity is an archetypal arrangement.[16] As an archetype, it can be interpreted in any number of ways, as Ruland shows: he interprets the four first of all psychologically, as *phantasia,*[17] *imaginatio,*[18] *speculatio,*[19] and *agnata fides* (in-

---

14 Cf. "A Psychological Approach to the Dogma of the Trinity," pp. 164ff.

15 Lib. V, cap. V. Jesahach is not a known Hebrew word.

16 Concerning the logical aspect of this arrangement see Schopenhauer, "On the Fourfold Root of the Principle of Sufficient Reason."

17 Even at that time *phantasia* meant a subjective figment of the mind without objective validity.          18, 19 See p. 168.

born faith). This interpretation is of value only so far as it alludes unmistakably to certain psychic functions. Since every archetype is psychologically a *fascinosum,* i.e., exerts an influence that excites and grips the imagination, it is liable to clothe itself in religious ideas (which are themselves of an archetypal nature). Accordingly Ruland says that the four Scaiolae also stand for the four main articles[20] of the Christian faith: baptism, belief in Jesus Christ, the sacrament of the Last Supper, and love of one's neighbour.[21] In Paracelsus, Scaio*li* are lovers of wisdom. He says: "Ye pious filii Scaiolae et Anachmi." [22] The Anachmus (= Aniadus) is therefore closely connected with the four Scaiolae. So it would not be overbold to conclude that the four Scaiolae correspond to the traditional quadripartite man and express his all-encompassing wholeness. The quadripartite nature of the *homo maximus* is the basis and cause of all division into four: four elements, seasons, directions, etc.[23] In this last chapter, says Paracelsus, the Scaiolae caused him the greatest difficulties,[24] "for in them is nothing of mortality." But, he assures us, whoever lives "by reason of the Scaiolae" is immortal, and he proves this by the example of the Enochdiani and their

---

[18] An image-making, form-giving, creative activity of the mind. For Paracelsus it was the *corpus astrale,* or the creative power of the astral man.

[19] By this is meant "philosophical" thinking.

[20] Ruland was a Protestant.

[21] "Whereby we attain not merely prolonged but eternal life," adds Ruland. Dorn (*De vita longa,* pp. 176f.) agrees with Ruland's psychological interpretation.

[22] [Sudhoff, XIV, p. 644. This could be translated either as "Ye pious sons, Scaiolae and Anachmi" (nom. pl.) or as "Ye pious sons of Scaiola (gen. fem. sing.) and Anachmus" (gen. masc. sing.). Scaio*lae* must be fem. and therefore can hardly be in apposition to "filii." The quotation has been located and checked, and begins: "Now mark well in this my philosophy: I have written a special treatise on the nymphis, pygmaeis, silvestribus, gnomis for the love and delectation of the true Scaiolis (*den waren Scaiolis zuliebe und gefallen*). Therefore, ye pious filii Scaiolae et Anachmi . . ." This may be Jung's source for the statement that the "Scaioli are lovers of wisdom." (If Scaiolis is taken as masc. in this context, the nom. sing. would be Scaiolus and the nom. pl. Scaioli.) Cf. *Psychology and Alchemy,* par. 422, n. 50: "Scayolus . . . means the adept." Neither Scaiolus nor Scaioli can be traced from the *Registerband* to the Sudhoff edn., compiled by Martin Müller (Einsiedeln, 1960).—TRANSLATOR.]

[23] For this reason it is said that the lapis or *filius* contains the four elements or is their quintessence, which can be extracted from them, like Aniadus.

[24] "In quo me plurimum offendunt Scaiolae" (Dorn, p. 174).

descendants. Dorn explains the difficulty of the Scaiolae by saying that the mind must exercise itself with extraordinary labours (*mentem exercere miris laboribus*), and, as there is in the Scaiolae nothing of mortality, this work exceeds our mortal endeavours.[25]

208     Although Dorn, like Ruland, emphasizes the psychic nature of the Scaiolae ("mental powers and virtues, properties of the arts of the mind"), so that actually they are attributes of the natural man and must therefore be mortal, and although Paracelsus himself says in other writings that even the *lumen naturae* is mortal, it is nevertheless asserted here that the natural powers of the mind are immortal and belong to the *Archa*—the principle that existed before the world. We hear nothing more about the "mortality" of the *lumen naturae*, but rather of eternal principles, of the *invisibilis homo maximus* (Dorn) and his four Scaiolae, which appear to be interpreted as mental powers and psychological functions. This contradiction is resolved when we bear in mind that these concepts of Paracelsus were the result not of rational reflection but of intuitive introspection, which was able to grasp the quaternary structure of consciousness and its archetypal nature. The one is mortal, the other immortal.

209     Dorn's explanation as to why the Scaiolae are "difficult" might also be extended to Adech (= Adam, Anthropos),[26] who is the ruler of the Scaiolae and/or their quintessence. Paracelsus

---

25 Ibid., p. 177.

26 The following passages from Pico della Mirandola (*Opera omnia*, I, p. 3018), on the Cabalistic interpretation of Adam, may have been known to Paracelsus: "Dixit namque Deus: Ecce Adam sicut unus ex nobis, non ex vobis inquit, sed unus ex nobis. Nam in vobis angelis, numerus est et alteritas. In nobis, id est, Deo, unitas infinita, aeterna, simplicissima et absolutissima. . . . Hinc sane coniicimus alterum quendam esse Adam coelestem, angelis in coelo demonstratum, unum ex Deo, quem verbo fecerat, et alterum esse Adam terrenum. . . . Iste, unus est cum Deo, hic non modo alter est, verumetiam alius et aliud a Deo. . . . Quod Onkelus . . . sic interpretatur. . . . Ecce Adam fuit unigenitus meus." (And God said, Lo, Adam is as one of us—he said not "of you," but "of us." For in you angels there is number and difference; but in us, that is, in God, there is unity, infinite, eternal, simple, and absolute. . . . Hence we clearly conjecture that there is a certain other heavenly Adam, shown to the angels in heaven, the one from God, whom he made by his word, and the other, earthly Adam. . . . The former is one with God, the latter not only second, but other and separate from God. . . . Which Onkelos thus interprets: Lo, Adam was my only begotten son.)

actually calls him "that difficult Adech." Also, it is "that great Adech" who hinders our intentions.[27] The difficulties of the art play no small role in alchemy. Generally they are explained as technical difficulties, but often enough, in the Greek texts as well as in the later Latin ones, there are remarks about the psychic nature of the dangers and obstacles that complicate the work. Partly they are demonic influences, partly psychic disturbances such as melancholia. These difficulties find expression also in the names and definitions of the prima materia, which, as the raw material of the opus, provides ample occasion for wearisome trials of patience. The prima materia is, as one can so aptly say in English, "tantalizing": it is cheap as dirt and can be had everywhere, only nobody knows it; it is as vague and evasive as the lapis that is to be produced from it; it has a "thousand names." And the worst thing is that without it the work cannot even be begun. The task of the alchemist is obviously like shooting an arrow through a thread hung up in a cloud, as Spitteler says. The prima materia is "saturnine," and the malefic Saturn is the abode of the devil, or again it is the most despised and rejected thing, "thrown out into the street," "cast on the dunghill," "found in filth." These epithets reflect not only the perplexity of the investigator but also his psychic background, which animates the darkness lying before him, so that he discovers in the projection the qualities of the unconscious. This easily demonstrable fact helps to elucidate the darkness that shrouds his spiritual endeavours and the *labor Sophiae:* it is a process of coming to terms with the unconscious, which always sets in when a man is confronted with its darkness. This confrontation forced itself on the alchemist as soon as he made a serious effort to find the prima materia.

### D. THE RAPPROCHEMENT WITH THE UNCONSCIOUS

210    I do not know how many or how few people today can imagine what "coming to terms with the unconscious" means. I fear they are only too few. But perhaps it will be conceded that the second part of Goethe's *Faust* presents only incidentally and in

27 See next note and par. 214.

doubtful degree an aesthetic problem, but primarily and in far greater degree a human one. It was a preoccupation that accompanied the poet right into old age, an alchemical encounter with the unconscious, comparable to the *labor Sophiae* of Paracelsus. It is on the one hand an endeavour to understand the archetypal world of the psyche, on the other hand a struggle against the sanity-threatening danger of fascination by the measureless heights and depths and paradoxes of psychic truth. The denser, concretistic, daytime mind here reaches its limits; for the "Cedurini" (Paracelsus), the "men of crasser temperament" (Dorn), there is no way into "the untrodden, the untreadable regions"—"and in this place," says Paracelsus, "the Aquaster does not break in" (the damp soul that is akin to matter). Here the human mind is confronted with its origins, the archetypes; the finite consciousness with its archaic foundations; the mortal ego with the immortal self, Anthropos, purusha, atman, or whatever else be the names that human speculation has given to that collective preconscious state from which the individual ego arose. Kinsman and stranger at once, it recognizes and yet does not recognize that unknown brother who steps towards it, intangible yet real. The more it is bound by time and space, the more it will feel the other as "that difficult Adech" who crosses its purpose at every misguided step, who gives fate an unexpected twist, and sets it as a task the very thing it feared. Here we must feel our way with Paracelsus into a question that was never openly asked before in our culture, and was never clearly put, partly from sheer unconsciousness, partly from holy dread. Moreover, the secret doctrine of the Anthropos was dangerous because it had nothing to do with the teachings of the Church, since from that point of view Christ was a reflection—and only a reflection—of the inner Anthropos. Hence there were a hundred good reasons for disguising this figure in indecipherable secret names.

211    That being so, we may perhaps be able to understand another dark passage from the concluding chapter, which runs: "If, therefore, I should count myself among the Scaiolae [or: Scaioli, 'lovers of wisdom'] in the manner of the Necrolii [= adepts], that would be something which in my view should be undertaken, but it is hindered by that great Adech, who deflects

our purpose but not the procedure. I leave this to you theoreticians to discuss." [28]

212    One gets the impression that Adech is almost hostile to the adept, or at least intent on frustrating him in some way. From our above reflections, which are based on practical experience, we have seen how problematical is the relation of the ego to the self. We have only to make the further assumption that this is what Paracelsus meant. And this does indeed seem to be the case: he "counts himself" among the Scaioli, the philosophers, or "implants himself" in the Scaiolae, the quaternity of the Original Man—which seems to me a quite possible conception since another synonym for the quaternity is Paradise with its four rivers, or the eternal city, the Metropolis, with its four gates[29] (the alchemical equivalent is the *domus sapientiae* and the squared circle). He would thus find himself in the immediate vicinity of Adech and would be a citizen of the eternal city—another echo of Christian ideas. The fact that Adech does not deflect the work (*modus* here presumably means method, procedure, as contrasted with *propositum,* purpose, intention) is understandable since Paracelsus is no doubt speaking of the alchemical opus, which always remains the same as a general procedure though its goal may vary: sometimes it is the production of gold (*chrysopoea*), sometimes the elixir, sometimes the *aurum potabile* or, finally, the mysterious *filius unicus.* Also, the artifex can have a selfish or an idealistic attitude towards the work.

[28] "Porro si pro ratione Necroliorum Scaiolis insereret, esset quod excipiendum ducerem, id quod maximus ille Adech antevertit et propositum nostrum, at non modum deducit: Quod vobis Theoricis discutiendum relinquo" (*De vita longa,* ed. Dorn, pp. 174f.). *Necrolii* are the adepts ("Liber Azoth," p. 524). *Necrolia* or *necrolica* means "medicine conserving life" (*De vita longa,* p. 173).

[29] The Monogenes (*filius unigenitus*) is identical with the city, and his limbs with its gates. Cf. Baynes, *A Coptic Gnostic Treatise,* pp. 58 and 89; also *Psychology and Alchemy,* pars. 138f.

# 4. THE COMMENTARY OF GERARD DORN

<sup></sup>²¹³ We now come to the end of the treatise *De vita longa*. Paracelsus here sums up the whole operation in an extremely condensed way which makes interpretation even more hazardous than usual. As with so many other passages in the *Vita longa,* we must ask ourselves: Is the author being intentionally obscure, or can't he help it? Or should we ascribe the confusion to his editor, Adam von Bodenstein? The obscurities of this last chapter have no parallel in all Paracelsus's writings. One would be inclined to let the whole treatise go hang did it not contain things which seem to belong to the most modern psychological insights.

²¹⁴ I now give the original text of Paracelsus together with Dorn's commentary for the benefit of readers who wish to form their own judgment:

Paracelsus: *De vita longa* (1562), Lib. V, cap. V, pp. 94f.

Atque ad hunc modum abiit e nymphididica natura intervenientibus Scaiolis in aliam transmutationem permansura Melosyne, si difficilis ille Adech annuisset, qui utrunque existit, cum mors tum vita Scaiolarum. Annuit praeterea prima tempora, sed ad finem seipsum immutat. Ex quibus colligo supermonica[1] figmenta in cyphantis aperire fenestram. Sed ut ea figantur, recusant gesta Melosynes, quae cuiusmodi sunt, missa facimus. Sed ad naturam nymphididicam. Ea ut in animis nostris concipiatur, atque ita ad annum

And in this manner, through the intervention of the Scaiolae, Melusina departs from her nymphididic nature, to remain in another transmutation if that difficult Adech permit, who rules over both the death and life of the Scaiolae. Moreover, he permits the first times, but at the end he changes himself. From which I conclude that the supermonic[1] figments in the Cyphanta open a window. But in order to become fixed, they have to oppose the acts of Melusina, which, of whatever kind they may be, we dismiss to the nymphididic

[1] From *super* = 'above,' and *monere* = 'inspire,' hence 'inspired from above.'

aniadin[2] immortales perveniamus arripimus characteres Veneris, quos et si vos una cum aliis cognoscitis, minime tamen usurpatis. Idipsum autem absolvimus eo quod in prioribus capitibus indicavimus, ut hanc vitam secure tandem adsequamur, in qua aniadus dominatur ac regnat, et cum eo, cui sine fine assistimus, permanet. Haec atque alia arcana, nulla re prorsus indigent.[3] Et in hunc modum vitam longam conclusam relinquimus.

realm. But in order that [she] may be conceived in our minds, and we arrive immortal at the year Aniadin,[2] we take the characters of Venus, which, even if you know yourselves one with others, you have nevertheless put to little use. With this we conclude what we treated of in the earlier chapters, that we may safely attain that life over which Aniadus dominates and reigns, and which endures for ever with him, in whom we are present without end. This and other mysteries are in need of nothing whatever.[3] And herewith we end our discourse on longevity.

### Dorn: *De vita longa* (1583), p. 178

[Paracelsus] ait Melosinam, i.e. apparentem in mente visionem . . . e nymphididica natura, in aliam transmutationem abire, in qua permansura[m] esse, si modo difficilis ille Adech, interior homo vdl. annuerit, hoc est, faveret: qui quidem utrunque efficit, videlicet mortem, et vitam Scaiolarum, i.e. mentalium operationum. Harum tempora prima, i.e. initia annuit, i.e. admittit, sed ad finem seipsum immutat, intellige propter intervenientes ac impedientes distractiones, quo minus consequantur effectum inchoatae, scl. operationes. Ex quibus [Paracelsus] colligit supermonica[1] figmenta, hoc est, speculationes aenigmaticas, in cyphantis [vas stillatorium], i.e.

[Paracelsus] says that Melusina, i.e., the vision appearing in the mind, departs from her nymphididic nature into another transmutation, in which she will remain if only that difficult Adech, that is, the inner man, permit, that is, approve: who brings about both, that is, death and life, of the Scaiolae, that is, the mental operations. The first times, that is, the beginnings, of these he permits, that is, favours; but at the end he changes himself, namely because of the distractions that intervene and impede, so that the things begun, that is, the operations, do not obtain their effect. From which [Paracelsus] concludes that the supermonic[1] figments, that is,

[2] Not found anywhere else. May be interpreted as the "time of perfection."

[3] A favourite saying of the alchemists, applied to the lapis.

[1] See above.

separationum vel praeparationum operationibus, aperire fenestram, hoc est, intellectum, sed ut figantur, i.e. ad finem perducantur, recusant gesta Melosines, hoc est, visionum varietates, et observationes, quae cuius modi sunt (ait) missa facimus. Ad naturam nymphididicam rediens, ut in animis nostris concipiatur, inquit atque hac via ad annum aniadin[2] perveniamus, hoc est, ad vitam longam per imaginationem, arripimus characteres Veneris, i.e. amoris scutum et loricam ad viriliter adversis resistendum obstaculis: amor enim omnem difficultatem superat: quos et si vos una cum aliis cognoscitis, putato characteres, minime tamen usurpatis. Absolvit itaque iam Paracelsus ea, quae prioribus capitibus indicavit in vitam hanc secure consequendam, in qua dominatur et regnat aniadus, i.e. rerum efficicia et cum ea is, cui sine fine assistimus, permanet, aniadus nempe coelestis: Haec atque alia arcana nulla re prorsus indigent.[3]

enigmatical speculations, in the Cyphanta [distilling vessel], open a window, that is, the understanding, by means of the operations of separation or preparation; but in order to become fixed, that is, brought to an end, they have to oppose the acts of Melusina, that is, divers visions and observations, which of whatever kind they may be, he says, we dismiss. Returning to the nymphididic realm, in order that [she] may be conceived in our minds, and that in this way we may attain to the year Aniadin,[2] that is, to a long life by imagination, we take the characters of Venus, that is, the shield and buckler of love, to resist manfully the obstacles that confront us, for love overcomes all difficulties; which characters, even if you know yourselves one with others, you have nevertheless put to little use. And thus Paracelsus brings to an end those things which he treated of in the earlier chapters, that we may safely obtain that life over which Aniadus, that is, the efficacity of things, dominates and reigns, and which endures for ever with him, namely the heavenly Aniadus, in whom we are present without end: this and other mysteries are in need of nothing whatever.[3]

2, 3 See above.

175

## A. MELUSINA AND THE PROCESS OF INDIVIDUATION

215    The text certainly needs a commentary! The Scaiolae, as the four parts, limbs, or emanations of the Anthropos,[4] are the organs with which he actively intervenes in the world of appearances or by which he is connected with it, just as the invisible *quinta essentia,* or aether, appears in this world as the four elements or, conversely, is composed out of them. Since the Scaiolae, as we have seen, are also psychic functions, these must be understood as manifestations or effluences of the One, the invisible Anthropos. As functions of consciousness, and particularly as *imaginatio, speculatio, phantasia,* and *fides,* they "intervene" and stimulate Melusina, the water-nixie, to change herself into human form. Dorn thinks of this as a "vision appearing in the mind" and not as a projection on a real woman. So far as our biographical knowledge extends, this latter possibility does not seem to have occurred to Paracelsus either. In Colonna's *Hypnerotomachia Poliphili* the Lady Polia attains a high degree of reality (far more so than Dante's ethereal Beatrice but still not as much as Helen in *Faust II*), yet even she dissolves into a lovely dream as the sun rises on the first day of May:

> . . . tears shone in her eyes like clear crystals, like round pearls, like the dew which Aurora strews on the clouds of dawn. Sighing like a heavenly image, like incense of musk and amber rising to give delight to the spirits of heaven, she dissolved into thin air, leaving nought behind her but a breath of heavenly fragrance. So, with my happy dream, she vanished from my sight, saying as she went: Poliphilo, most dear beloved, farewell! [5]

216    Polia dissolves just before the long-desired union with her lover. Helen, on the other hand, vanishes only with the dissolution of her son Euphorion. Though Paracelsus gives clear indications of the nuptial mood with his "exaltation" in May and his allusion to the stinging nettle and the little flame, he disregards entirely the projection on a real person or a concretely visualized, personified image, but chooses instead the legendary figure of Melusina. Now this figure is certainly not an allegorical chimera or a mere metaphor: she has her particular psychic reality

4 For a parallel, cf. Enoch 40 : 2, where God has four faces and is surrounded by the four angels of the Face.

5 *The Dream of Poliphilo* (ed. Fierz-David), p. 210.

in the sense that she is a glamorous apparition who, by her very nature, is on one side a psychic vision but also, on account of the psyche's capacity for imaginative realization (which Paracelsus calls Ares), is a distinct objective entity, like a dream which temporarily becomes reality. The figure of Melusina is eminently suited to this purpose. The anima belongs to those borderline phenomena which chiefly occur in special psychic situations. They are characterized by the more or less sudden collapse of a form or style of life which till then seemed the indispensable foundation of the individual's whole career. When such a catastrophe occurs, not only are all bridges back into the past broken, but there seems to be no way forward into the future. One is confronted with a hopeless and impenetrable darkness, an abysmal void that is now suddenly filled with an alluring vision, the palpably real presence of a strange yet helpful being, in the same way that, when one lives for a long time in great solitude, the silence or the darkness becomes visibly, audibly, and tangibly alive, and the unknown in oneself steps up in an unknown guise.

217    This peculiarity of the anima is found also in the Melusina legend: Emmerich, Count of Poitiers, had adopted Raymond, the son of a poor kinsman. The relation between adoptive father and son was harmonious. But once, on the hunt, when pursuing a wild boar, they got separated from the rest and went astray in the forest. Night fell and they lit a fire to warm themselves. Suddenly the Count was attacked by the boar, and Raymond struck at it with his sword. But by an unlucky accident the blade rebounded and dealt the Count a mortal blow. Raymond was inconsolable, and in despair mounted his horse to flee he knew not where. After a time he came to a meadow with a bubbling spring. There he found three beautiful women. One of them was Melusina, who by her clever counsel saved him from dishonour and a homeless fate.

218    According to the legend, Raymond found himself in the catastrophic situation we have described, when his whole way of life had collapsed and he faced ruin. That is the moment when the harbinger of fate, the anima, an archetype of the collective unconscious, appears. In the legend Melusina sometimes has the tail of a fish and sometimes that of a snake; she is half human, half animal. Occasionally she appears only in snake form. The

legend apparently has Celtic roots,[6] but the motif is found practically everywhere. It was not only extraordinarily popular in Europe during the Middle Ages, but occurs also in India, in the legend of Urvashi and Pururavas, which is mentioned in the Shatapatha-Brāhmana.[7] It also occurs among the North American Indians.[8] The motif of half-man, half-fish is universally disseminated. Special mention should be made of Conrad Vecerius,[9] according to whom Melusina, or Melyssina, comes from an island in the sea where nine sirens dwell, who can change into any shape they want. This is of particular interest as Paracelsus mentions Melusina along with "Syrena." [10] The tradition probably goes back to Pomponius Mela,[11] who calls the island "Sena" and the beings who dwell there "Senae." They cause storms, can change their shape, cure incurable diseases, and know the future.[12] Since the mercurial serpent of the alchemists is not infrequently called *virgo* and, even before Paracelsus, was represented in the form of a Melusina, the latter's capacity to change her shape and to cure diseases is of importance in that these peculiarities were also predicated of Mercurius, and with special emphasis. On the other hand, Mercurius was also depicted as the grey-bearded Mercurius *senex* or Hermes Trismegistus, from which it is evident that two empirically very common archetypes, namely the anima and the Wise Old Man,[13] flow together in the symbolic phenomenology of Mercurius. Both are daemons of revelation and, in the form of Mercurius, represent the panacea. Again and again Mercurius is called *versatilis, versipellis, mutabilis, servus* or *cervus fugitivus*, Proteus, etc.

219    The alchemists, and Paracelsus too, were no doubt confronted often enough with the dark abyss of not-knowing, and, unable to go forward, were on their own admission dependent on revelation or illumination or a helpful dream. For this rea-

6 Grimm, *Teutonic Mythology*, I, p. 434.

7 Sacred Books of the East, XXVI, p. 91.

8 Baring-Gould, *Curious Myths of the Middle Ages*, pp. 502ff.

9 "De rebus gestis Imperatoris Henrici VII," *Germaniae Historicorum* (ed. Urstisius), II, pp. 63f.

10 *Paragranum*, p. 105. [Cf. "Paracelsus the Physician," par. 24.]

11 Fl. 1st cent. A.D.    12 *Chronographia*, ed. Frick, p. 67.

13 Cf. my "Archetypes of the Collective Unconscious" and "Concerning the Archetypes, with Special Reference to the Anima Concept."

son they needed a "ministering spirit," a familiar or πάρεδρος, to whose invocation the Greek Magic Papyri bear witness. The snake form of the god of revelation, and of spirits in general, is a universal type.

220 Paracelsus seems to have known nothing of any psychological premises. He attributes the appearance and transformation of Melusina to the effect of the "intervening" Scaiolae, the driving spiritual forces emanating from the *homo maximus*. The opus was subordinated to them, for its aim was to raise man to the sphere of the Anthropos. There is no doubt that the goal of the philosophical alchemist was higher self-development, or the production of what Paracelsus calls the *homo maior,* or what I would call individuation. This goal confronts the alchemist at the start with the loneliness which all of them feared, when one has "only" oneself for company. The alchemist, on principle, worked alone. He formed no school. This rigorous solitude, together with his preoccupation with the endless obscurities of the work, was sufficient to activate the unconscious and, through the power of imagination, to bring into being things that apparently were not there before. Under these circumstances "enigmatical speculations" arise in which the unconscious is visually experienced as a "vision appearing in the mind." Melusina emerges from the watery realm and assumes human form—sometimes quite concretely, as in *Faust I,* where Faust's hopelessness leads him straight into the arms of Gretchen, in which form Melusina would doubtless remain were it not for the catastrophe which drives Faust still deeper into magic: Melusina changes into Helen. But she does not remain even there, for all attempts at concretization are shattered like the retort of the homunculus against the throne of Galatea. Another power takes over, "that difficult Adech," who "at the end changes himself." The greater man "hinders our purpose," for Faust has to change himself at death into a boy, the *puer aeternus,* to whom the true world will be shown only after all desirousness has fallen away from him. "Miserable mortals, to whom Nature has denied her first and best treasure, the *lumen naturae!*"

221 It is Adech, the inner man, who with his Scaiolae guides the purpose of the adept and causes him to behold fantasy images from which he will draw false conclusions, devising out of them situations of whose provisional and fragile nature he is unaware.

Nor is he aware that by knocking on the door of the unknown he is obeying the law of the inner, future man, and that he is disobedient to this law whenever he seeks to secure a permanent advantage or possession from his work. Not his ego, that fragment of a personality, is meant; it is rather that a wholeness, of which he is a part, wants to be transformed from a latent state of unconsciousness into an approximate consciousness of itself.

222   The "acts of Melusina" are deceptive phantasms compounded of supreme sense and the most pernicious nonsense, a veritable veil of Maya which lures and leads every mortal astray. From these phantasms the wise man will extract the "supermonic" elements, that is, the higher inspirations; he extracts everything meaningful and valuable as in a process of distillation,[14] and catches the precious drops of the *liquor Sophiae* in the ready beaker of his soul, where they "open a window" for his understanding. Paracelsus is here alluding to a discriminative process of critical judgment which separates the chaff from the wheat—an indispensable part of any rapprochement with the unconscious. It requires no art to become stupid; the whole art lies in extracting wisdom from stupidity. Stupidity is the mother of the wise, but cleverness never. The "fixation" refers alchemically to the lapis but psychologically to the consolidation of feeling. The distillate must be fixed and held fast, must become a firm conviction and a permanent content.

### B. THE HIEROSGAMOS OF THE EVERLASTING MAN

223   Melusina, the deceptive Shakti, must return to the watery realm if the work is to reach its goal. She should no longer dance before the adept with alluring gestures, but must become what she was from the beginning: a part of his wholeness.[15] As such she must be "conceived in the mind." This leads to a union of conscious and unconscious that was always present uncon-

---

14 "And so this spirit is extracted and separated from the other spirit, and then the Spagyric has the wine of health." ("Fragmenta," ed. Sudhoff, III, p. 305.)

15 The apparent contradiction between the rejection of the *gesta Melosines* and the assimilation of the anima is due to the fact that the *gesta* occur in a state of anima possession, for which reason they must be prevented. The anima is thereby forced into the inner world, where she functions as the medium between the ego and the unconscious, as does the persona between the ego and the environment.

sciously but was always denied by the one-sidedness of the conscious attitude. From this union arises that wholeness which the introspective philosophy of all times and climes has characterized with an inexhaustible variety of symbols, names, and concepts. The "mille nomina" disguise the fact that this coniunctio is not concerned with anything tangible or discursively apprehensible; it is an experience that simply cannot be reproduced in words, but whose very nature carries with it an unassailable feeling of eternity or timelessness.

224     I will not repeat here what I have said elsewhere on this subject. It makes no difference anyway what one says about it. Paracelsus does, however, give one more hint which I cannot pass over in silence: this concerns the "characters of Venus." [16]

[16] This recalls the "signs and characters of the planets" in Agrippa, which are imprinted on man at birth as on everything else. But man has, conversely, the faculty of re-approximating himself to the stars: "Potest enim animus noster per imaginationem vel rationem quandam imitatione, ita alicui stellae conformari, ut subito cuiusdam stellae muneribus impleatur. . . . Debemus igitur in quovis opere et rerum applicatione vehementer affectare, imaginari, sperare firmissimeque credere, id enim plurimum erit adiumento . . . animum humanum quando per suas passiones et effectus ad opus aliquod attentissimus fuerit, coniungi ipsum cum stellarum animis, etiam cum intelligentiis: et ita quoque coniunctum causam esse ut mirabilis quaedam virtus operibus ac rebus nostris infundatur, cum quia est in eo rerum omnium apprehensio et potestas, tum quia omnes res habent naturalem obedientiam ad ipsum, et de necessitate efficaciam et movent ad id quod desiderat nimis forti desiderio. Et secundum hoc verificatur artificium characterum, imaginum, incantationum et sermonum, etc. . . . Animus enim noster quando fertur in aliquem magnum excessum alicuius passionis vel virtutis, arripit saepissime ex se ipso horam vel opportunitatem fortiorem, etc. . . . hic est modus per quem invenitur efficacia [operationum]." (For through a certain mental faculty our spirit can thus by imitation be made like to some star, so that it is suddenly filled with the functions of a star. . . . We ought therefore in every work and application of things eagerly to aspire, imagine, hope, and most firmly believe, for that will be a very great help. . . . [De occult. phil., Lib. I, cap. 66.] The human spirit, when through its passions and operations it is highly intent upon any work, should join itself with the spirits of the stars, yea, with their intelligences; and when thus conjoined, be the cause that a certain wonderful virtue is infused into our works and affairs, both because there is in it a grasping of and power over all things, and because all things have a natural and necessarily efficacious obedience to it, and move towards what it desires with an extremely strong desire. And according to this is verified the work of the characters, images, incantations, and words, etc. . . . For when our spirit is moved to any great excess of any passion or virtue, it very often snatches for itself a more effective hour or opportunity, etc. . . . This is the way by which the efficacy [of the operations] is found.) (Lib. I, cap. 67.)

225    Melusina, being a water-nixie, is closely connected with Morgana, the "sea-born," whose classical counterpart is Aphrodite, the "foam-born." Union with the feminine personification of the unconscious is, as we have seen, a well-nigh eschatological experience, a reflection of which is to be found in the Apocalyptic Marriage of the Lamb, the Christian form of the hierosgamos. The passage runs (Revelation 19 : 6–10):

> And I heard as it were the voice of a great multitude, and as the voice of many waters, and as the voice of mighty thunderings, saying, Alleluia; for the Lord God omnipotent reigneth.
> Let us be glad and rejoice, and give honour to him: for the marriage of the Lamb is come, and his wife hath made herself ready.
> And to her was granted that she should be arrayed in fine linen, clean and white: for the fine linen is the righteousness of saints.
> And he saith unto me: Write, Blessed are they which are called unto the marriage supper of the Lamb. And he saith unto me, These are the true sayings of God.
> And I fell at his feet to worship him. And he said unto me, See thou do it not: I am thy fellowservant, and of thy brethren . . .

226    The "he" of the text is the angel that speaks to John; in the language of Paracelsus, he is the *homo maior,* Adech. I need hardly point out that Venus is closely related to the love-goddess Astarte, whose sacred marriage-festivals were known to everyone. The experience of union underlying these festivals is, psychologically, the embrace and coming together again of two souls in the exaltation of spring, in the "true May"; it is the successful reuniting of an apparently hopelessly divided duality in the wholeness of a single being. This unity embraces the multiplicity of all beings. Hence Paracelsus says: "If you know yourselves one with others." Adech is not *my* self, he is also that of my brothers: "I am thy fellowservant, and of thy brethren." That is the specific definition of this experience of the coniunctio: the self which includes me includes many others also, for the unconscious that is "conceived in our mind" does not belong to me and is not peculiar to me, but is everywhere. It is the quintessence of the individual and at the same time the collective.

227    The participants in the marriage of the Lamb enter into eternal blessedness; they are "virgins, which were not defiled with women" and are "redeemed from among men" (Rev.

182

14 : 4). In Paracelsus the goal of redemption is "the year Ania-din," or time of perfection, when the One Man reigns for ever.

### C. SPIRIT AND NATURE

228    Why did Paracelsus not avail himself of the Christian imag-ery, when it expresses the same thought so very clearly? Why does Venus appear in the place of Melusina, and why is it not the marriage of the Lamb, but a hierosgamos of Venus and Mars, as the text itself hints? The reason is probably the same as that which compelled Francesco Colonna to make Poliphilo seek his beloved Polia not with the Mother of God but with Venus. For the same reason the boy in Christian Rosencreutz's *Chymi-cal Wedding*[17] led the hero down to an underground chamber, on the door of which was a secret inscription graven in copper characters. Copper (*cuprum*) is correlated with the Cyprian (Aphrodite, Venus). In the chamber they found a three-cor-nered tomb containing a copper cauldron, and in it was an angel holding a tree that dripped continually into the cauldron. The tomb was supported by three animals: an eagle, an ox, and a lion.[18] The boy explained that in this tomb Venus lay buried, who had destroyed many an upright man. Continuing their de-scent, they came to the bedchamber of Venus and found the goddess asleep on a couch. Indiscreetly, the boy twitched the coverlet away and revealed her in all her naked beauty.[19]

[17] Trans. Foxcroft, pp. 126ff.

[18] The lower triad, corresponding to the upper Trinity, and consisting of the theriomorphic symbols of the three evangelists. The angel as the fourth symbol occupies a special position, which in the Trinity is assigned to the devil. Re-versal of moral values: what is evil above is good below, and vice versa.

[19] In the *Golden Ass* of Apuleius the process of redemption begins at the moment when the hero, who has been changed into an ass because of his dissolute life, succeeds in snatching a bunch of roses from the hand of the priest of Isis, and eating them. Roses are the flowers of Venus. The hero is then initiated into the mysteries of Isis, who, as a mother goddess, corresponds to the Mater Gloriosa in *Faust II*. It is of interest to note the analogies between the prayer to the Mater Gloriosa at the end of *Faust* and the prayer to Isis at the end of the *Golden Ass:*

| (*Faust II*, trans. Wayne, p. 288) | (*Golden Ass*) |
|---|---|
| O contrite hearts, seek with your eyes | You are indeed the holy preserver of humankind, |

229    The ancient world contained a large slice of nature and a number of questionable things which Christianity was bound to overlook if the security of a spiritual standpoint was not to be hopelessly compromised. No penal code and no moral code, not even the sublimest casuistry, will ever be able to codify and pronounce just judgment upon the confusions, the conflicts of duty, and the invisible tragedies of the natural man in collision with the exigencies of culture. "Spirit" is one aspect, "Nature" another. "You may pitch Nature out with a fork, yet she'll always come back again," says the poet.[20] Nature *must not* win the game, but she *cannot* lose. And whenever the conscious mind clings to hard and fast concepts and gets caught in its own rules and regulations—as is unavoidable and of the essence of civilized consciousness—nature pops up with her inescapable demands. Nature is not matter only, she is also spirit. Were that not so, the only source of spirit would be human reason. It is the great achievement of Paracelsus to have elevated the "light of nature" to a principle and to have emphasized it in a far more fundamental way than his predecessor Agrippa. The *lumen naturae* is the natural spirit, whose strange and significant workings we can observe in the manifestations of the unconscious now that psy-

| | |
|---|---|
| The visage of salvation; | Offering amid the evil chances of the unfortunate the kindly protection of a mother, |
| Blissful in that gaze, arise | And no smallest moment that passes is devoid of your favours, |
| Through glad regeneration. | But both by land and by sea you care for men, driving off life's storms and stretching out to them your saving hand; wherewith you unravel the most tangled webs of fate, and calm the tempests of fortune, and control the varied wanderings of the stars. |
| Now may every pulse of good Seek to serve before thy face; | Wherefore, poor though I am, I will do what I may, as a devotee, |
| Virgin, Queen of Motherhood, Keep us, Goddess, in thy grace. | To keep ever hidden in my heart the vision of your divine face and most holy godhead. |

20 Horace, *Epist.* I. x. 24.

chological research has come to realize that the unconscious is not just a "subconscious" appendage or the dustbin of consciousness, but is a largely autonomous psychic system for compensating the biases and aberrations of the conscious attitude, for the most part functionally, though it sometimes corrects them by force. Consciousness can, as we know, be led astray by naturalness as easily as by spirituality, this being the logical consequence of its freedom of choice. The unconscious is not limited only to the instinctual and reflex processes of the cortical centres; it also extends beyond consciousness and, with its symbols, anticipates future conscious processes. It is therefore quite as much a "supraconsciousness."

230    Convictions and moral values would have no meaning if they were not believed and did not possess exclusive validity. And yet they are man-made and time-conditioned assertions or explanations which we know very well are capable of all sorts of modifications, as has happened in the past and will happen again in the future. All that has happened during the last two thousand years shows that they are reliable signposts for certain stretches of the way, then comes a painful upheaval, which is felt as subversive and immoral, until a new conviction takes root. So far as the essential traits of human nature remain the same, certain moral values enjoy permanent validity. The most meticulous observance of the Ten Commandments, however, is no obstacle to the more refined forms of turpitude, and the far loftier principle of Christian love of one's neighbour can lead to such tangled conflicts of duty that sometimes the Gordian knot can only be cut with a very unchristian sword.

### D. THE ECCLESIASTICAL SACRAMENT
### AND THE OPUS ALCHYMICUM

231    Paracelsus, like many others, was unable to make use of the Christian symbolism because the Christian formula inevitably suggested the Christian solution and would thus have conduced to the very thing that had to be avoided. It was nature and her particular "light" that had to be acknowledged and lived with in the face of an attitude that assiduously overlooked them. This could only be done under the protective aegis of the arcanum. But one should not imagine Paracelsus or any other alchemist

settling down to invent an arcane terminology that would make the new doctrine a kind of private code. Such an undertaking would presuppose the existence of definite views and clearly defined concepts. But there is no question of that: none of the alchemists ever had any clear idea of what his philosophy was really about. The best proof of this is the fact that everyone with any originality at all coined his own terminology, with the result that no one fully understood anybody else. For one alchemist, Lully was an obscurantist and a charlatan and Geber the great authority; while for another, Geber was a Sphinx and Lully the source of all enlightenment. So with Paracelsus: we have no reason to suppose that behind his neologisms there was a clear, consciously disguised concept. It is on the contrary probable that he was trying to grasp the ungraspable with his countless esotericisms, and snatched at any symbolic hint that the unconscious offered. The new world of scientific knowledge was still in a nascent dreamstate, a mist heavy with the future, in which shadowy figures groped about for the right words. Paracelsus was not reaching back into the past; rather, for lack of anything suitable in the present, he was using the old remnants to give new form to a renewed archetypal experience. Had the alchemists felt any serious need to revive the past, their erudition would have enabled them to draw on the inexhaustible storehouse of the heresiologists. But except for the "Aquarium sapientum," [21] which likewise treats of heresies, I have found only one alchemist (of the sixteenth century) who shudderingly admits to having read the *Panarium* of Epiphanius. Nor are any secret traces of Gnostic usages to be found, despite the fact that the texts swarm with unconscious parallels.

232    To return to our text: it is clear that it describes a procedure for attaining nothing less than immortality ("that we may arrive immortal at the year Aniadin"). There is, however, only one way to this goal, and that is through the sacraments of the Church. These are here replaced by the "sacrament" of the *opus alchymicum*, less by word than by deed, and without the least sign of any conflict with the orthodox Christian standpoint.

233    Which way did Paracelsus hold to be the true one? Or were

[21] *Musaeum hermeticum*, pp. 73ff. [This sentence has been altered in accordance with the correction given in *Psychology and Alchemy*, 2nd edn., par. 431, n. 11.—TRANSLATOR.]

both of them true for him? Presumably the latter, and the rest
he "leaves to the theoreticians to discuss."

234 　　What is meant by the "characters of Venus" remains obscure. The "sapphire" [22] which Paracelsus prized so much, the
*cheyri, ladanum, muscus,* and *ambra* belong, according to
Agrippa,[23] to Venus. The goddess undoubtedly appears in our
text on a higher level, in keeping with her classical cognomens:
*docta, sublimis, magistra rerum humanarum divinarumque,*
etc.[24] One of her characters is certainly love in the widest sense,
so Dorn is not wrong when he interprets them as the "shield and
buckler of love." Shield and buckler are martial attributes, but
there is also a *Venus armata.*[25] Mythologically, the personified
Amor is a son of Venus and Mars, whose cohabitation in alchemy is a typical coniunctio.[26] Dorn, despite being a Paracelsist, had a decidedly polemical attitude towards certain fundamental tenets of alchemy,[27] so that a Christian love of one's
neighbour, well armed against evil, suited him very well. But so
far as Paracelsus is concerned this interpretation is doubtful.
The word Venus points in quite another direction, and since the
Christian gifts of grace were included in his Catholic faith he
had in any case no need of a christianized Amor. On the contrary, a Venus Magistra or Aphrodite Urania, or even a Sophia,
would have seemed to him more appropriate to the mystery
of the *lumen naturae.* The words "minime tamen usurpatis"
might also be a hint at discretion.[28] Hence the Venus episode in
the *Chymical Wedding* may have more bearing on the interpretation of this cryptic passage than Dorn's well-meant circumlo-
cution.

235 　　The concluding reference to a "life without end" under

---

22 "For before the sapphire existed, there was no arcanum" (*Paragranum,* p. 77).
*De vita longa,* ed. Dorn, p. 72: "They are to be referred to the cheyri and the sapphirine flower, i.e., to those two precious stones of the philosophers." Bodenstein
(*Onomasticon,* p. 64): "The sapphirine material: that liquid in which there is no
harmful matter."
23 *Occult. phil.,* I, cap. 28, p. xxxiv.
24 Carter, *Epitheta Deorum,* s.v. "Venus."
25 Ibid.
26 The hermaphroditic Venus was regarded as typifying the coniunctio of Sulphur
and Mercurius. Cf. Pernety, *Fables égyptiennes et grecques,* II, p. 119.
27 Cf. "Psychology and Religion," p. 60.
28 It could be translated as "you have mentioned not at all."

the dominion of Aniadus is very reminiscent of Rev. 20 : 4: ". . . and they lived and reigned with Christ a thousand years." The year Aniadin would thus correspond to the thousand-year reign in the Apocalypse.

236    In conclusion I would remark that the survey of the secret doctrine which I have attempted to sketch here makes it seem likely that besides the physician and Christian in Paracelsus there was also an alchemical philosopher at work who, pushing every analogy to the very limit, strove to penetrate the divine mysteries. The parallel with the mysteries of the Christian faith, which we can only feel as a most dangerous conflict, was no Gnostic heresy for him, despite the most disconcerting resemblances; for him as for every other alchemist, man had been entrusted with the task of bringing to perfection the divine will implanted in nature, and this was a truly sacramental work. To the question "Are you, as it would seem, an Hermetic?" he could have replied with Lazarello: "I am a Christian, O King, and it is no disgrace to be that and an Hermetic at the same time." [29]

[29] Lazarello, *Crater Hermetis* (1505), fol. 32r-v. (As in Reitzenstein, *Poimandres,* p. 320.)

# 5. EPILOGUE

237    I had long been aware that alchemy is not only the mother of chemistry, but is also the forerunner of our modern psychology of the unconscious. Thus Paracelsus appears as a pioneer not only of chemical medicine but of empirical psychology and psychotherapy.

238    It may seem that I have said too little about Paracelsus the self-sacrificing physician and Christian, and too much about his dark shadow, that other Paracelsus, whose soul was intermingled with a strange spiritual current which, issuing from immemorial sources, flowed beyond him into a distant future. But—*ex tenebris lux*—it was precisely because he was so fascinated by magic that he was able to open the door to the realities of nature for the benefit of succeeding centuries. The Christian and the primitive pagan lived together in him in a strange and marvellous way to form a conflicting whole, as in other great Renaissance figures. Although he had to endure the conflict, he was spared that agonizing split between knowledge and faith that has riven the later epochs. As a man he had one father, but as a spirit he had two mothers. His spirit was heroic, because creative, and as such was doomed to Promethean guilt. The secular conflict that broke out at the turn of the sixteenth century, and whose living image stands before our eyes in the figure of Paracelsus, is a prerequisite for higher consciousness; for analysis is always followed by synthesis, and what was divided on a lower level will reappear, united, on a higher one.

# IV

## THE SPIRIT MERCURIUS

[Given as two lectures at the Eranos Conference, Ascona, Switzerland, in 1942, the theme of which was "The Hermetic Principle in Mythology, Gnosis, and Alchemy." Published as "Der Geist Mercurius," *Eranos-Jahrbuch 1942* (Zurich, 1943); revised and expanded in *Symbolik des Geistes: Studien über psychische Phänomenologie* . . . (Psychologische Abhandlungen, VI; Zurich, 1948). An English translation by Gladys Phelan and Hildegard Nagel, titled *The Spirit Mercury,* was published as a book by the Analytical Psychology Club of New York, Inc., in 1953, and forms the basis of the present translation. Some brief chapters have been combined.— EDITORS.]

Ἑρμῆ κοσμοκράτωρ, ἐνκάρδιε, κύκλε σελήνης,
στρογγύλε καὶ τετράγωνε, λόγων ἀρχηγέτα γλώσσης,
πειθοδικαιόσυνε, χλαμυδηφόρε, πτηνοπέδιλε,
παμφώνου γλώσσης μεδέων, θνητοῖσι προφῆτα . . .

(Hermes, ruler of the world, dweller in the heart, circle of the moon,
Round and square, inventor of the words of the tongue,
Obedient to justice, wearer of the chlamys, shod in winged sandals,
Guardian of the many-sounding tongue, prophet to mortals.)

—A Magic Papyrus (Preisendanz, II, p. 139)

## Part I

### 1. THE SPIRIT IN THE BOTTLE

239     In my contribution[1] to the symposium on Hermes I will try to show that this many-hued and wily god did not by any means die with the decline of the classical era, but on the contrary has gone on living in strange guises through the centuries, even into recent times, and has kept the mind of man busy with his deceptive arts and healing gifts. Children are still told Grimm's fairytale of "The Spirit in the Bottle," which is ever-living like all fairytales, and moreover contains the quintessence and deepest meaning of the Hermetic mystery as it has come down to us today:

Once upon a time there was a poor woodcutter. He had an only son, whom he wished to send to a high school. However, since he could give him only a little money to take with him, it was used up long before the time for the examinations. So the son went home and helped his father with the work in the forest. Once, during the midday rest, he roamed the woods and came to an immense old oak. There he heard a voice calling from the ground, "Let me out, let me out!" He dug down among the roots of the tree and found a well-sealed glass bottle from which, clearly, the voice had come. He opened it and instantly a spirit rushed out and soon became half as high as the tree. The spirit cried in an awful voice: "I have had my punishment and I will be revenged! I am the great and mighty spirit Mercurius, and now you shall have your reward. Whoso releases me, him I must strangle." This made the boy uneasy and, quickly thinking up a trick, he said, "First, I must be sure that you are the same spirit that was shut up in that little bottle." To prove this, the spirit crept back into the bottle. Then the boy made haste to seal it and the spirit was caught again. But now the spirit promised to reward him richly if the boy would let

[1] I give only a general survey of the Mercurius concept in alchemy and by no means an exhaustive exposition of it. The illustrative material cited should therefore be taken only as examples and makes no claim to completeness. [For the "symposium on Hermes" see the editorial note on p. 191.—EDITORS.]

him out. So he let him out and received as a reward a small piece of rag. Quoth the spirit: "If you spread one end of this over a wound it will heal, and if you rub steel or iron with the other end it will turn into silver." Thereupon the boy rubbed his damaged axe with the rag, and the axe turned to silver and he was able to sell it for four hundred thaler. Thus father and son were freed from all worries. The young man could return to his studies, and later, thanks to his rag, he became a famous doctor.[2]

240    Now, what insight can we gain from this fairytale? As you know, we can treat fairytales as fantasy products, like dreams, conceiving them to be spontaneous statements of the unconscious about itself.

241    As at the beginning of many dreams something is said about the scene of the dream action, so the fairytale mentions the forest as the place of the magic happening. The forest, dark and impenetrable to the eye, like deep water and the sea, is the container of the unknown and the mysterious. It is an appropriate synonym for the unconscious. Among the many trees—the living elements that make up the forest—one tree is especially conspicuous for its great size. Trees, like fishes in the water, represent the living contents of the unconscious. Among these contents one of special significance is characterized as an "oak." Trees have individuality. A tree, therefore, is often a symbol of personality.[3] Ludwig II of Bavaria is said to have honoured certain particularly impressive trees in his park by having them saluted. The mighty old oak is proverbially the king of the forest. Hence it represents a central figure among the contents of the unconscious, possessing personality in the most marked degree. It is the prototype of the *self*, a symbol of the source and goal of the individuation process. The oak stands for the still unconscious core of the personality, the plant symbolism indicating a state of deep unconsciousness. From this it may be concluded that the hero of the fairytale is profoundly unconscious of himself. He is one of the "sleepers," the "blind" or "blindfolded," whom we

---

2 [Author's paraphrase. Cf. "The Spirit in the Bottle," *Grimm's Fairy Tales* (trans. Hunt, rev. Stern), pp. 458–62.—EDITORS.]
3 Concerning personification of trees, see Frazer, *The Magic Art*, II, ch. 9. Trees are also the dwelling places of spirits of the dead or are identical with the life of the newborn child (ibid., I, p. 184).

encounter in the illustrations of certain alchemical treatises.[4] They are the unawakened who are still unconscious of themselves, who have not yet integrated their future, more extensive personality, their "wholeness," or, in the language of the mystics, the ones who are not yet "enlightened." For our hero, therefore, the tree conceals a great secret.[5]

242    The secret is hidden not in the top but in the roots of the tree;[6] and since it is,· or has, a personality it also possesses the most striking marks of personality—voice, speech, and conscious purpose, and it demands to be set free by the hero. It is caught and imprisoned against its will, down there in the earth among the roots of the tree. The roots extend into the inorganic realm, into the mineral kingdom. In psychological terms, this would mean that the self has its roots in the body, indeed in the body's chemical elements. Whatever this remarkable statement of the fairytale may mean in itself, it is in no way stranger than the miracle of the living plant rooted in the inanimate earth. The alchemists described their four elements as *radices*, corresponding to the Empedoclean *rhizomata*, and in them they saw the constituents of the most significant and central symbol of alchemy, the *lapis philosophorum*, which represents the goal of the individuation process.

243    The secret hidden in the roots is a spirit sealed inside a bottle. Naturally it was not hidden away among the roots to start with, but was first confined in a bottle, which was then hidden. Presumably a magician, that is, an alchemist, caught and imprisoned it. As we shall see later, this spirit is something like the numen of the tree, its *spiritus vegetativus*, which is one

4 Cf. the title-page of *Mutus liber*, showing an angel waking the sleeper with a trumpet ("The Psychology of the Transference," Fig. 11). Also the illustration in Michelspacher's *Cabala, speculum artis et naturae* (*Psychology and Alchemy*, Fig. 93). In the foreground, before a mountain upon which is a temple of the initiates, stands a blindfolded man, while further back another man runs after a fox which is disappearing into a hole in the mountain. The "helpful animal" shows the way to the temple. The fox or hare is itself the "evasive" Mercurius as guide (ὁδηγός).
5 For additional material on the tree symbol, see infra, "The Philosophical Tree," Part II.
6 This motif was used in the same sense by the Gnostics. Cf. Hippolytus, *Elenchos*, V, 9, 15, where the many-named and thousand-eyed "Word of God" is "hidden in the root of All."

definition of Mercurius. As the life principle of the tree, it is a sort of spiritual quintessence abstracted from it, and could also be described as the *principium individuationis*. The tree would then be the outward and visible sign of the realization of the self. The alchemists appear to have held a similar view. Thus the "Aurelia occulta" says: "The philosophers have sought most eagerly for the centre of the tree which stands in the midst of the earthly paradise." [7] According to the same source, Christ himself is this tree.[8] The tree comparison occurs as early as Eulogius of Alexandria (*c.* A.D. 600), who says: "Behold in the Father the root, in the Son the branch, and in the Spirit the fruit: for the substance [οὐσία] in the three is one." [9] Mercurius, too, is *trinus et unus.*

244     So if we translate it into psychological language, the fairytale tells us that the mercurial essence, the *principium individuationis,* would have developed freely under natural conditions, but was robbed of its freedom by deliberate intervention from outside, and was artfully confined and banished like an evil spirit. (Only evil spirits have to be confined, and the wickedness of this spirit was shown by its murderous intent.) Supposing the fairytale is right and the spirit was really as wicked as it relates, we would have to conclude that the Master who imprisoned the *principium individuationis* had a good end in view. But who is this well-intentioned Master who has the power to banish the principle of man's individuation? Such power is given only to a ruler of souls in the spiritual realm. The idea that the principle of individuation is the source of all evil is found in Schopenhauer and still more in Buddhism. In Christianity, too, human nature is tainted with original sin and is redeemed from this stain by Christ's self-sacrifice. Man in his "natural" condition is neither good nor pure, and if he should develop in the natural way the result would be a product not essentially different from an animal. Sheer instinctuality and naïve unconsciousness untroubled by a sense of guilt would prevail if the Master had not interrupted the free development of the natural being by introducing a distinction between good and evil and outlawing the evil. Since without guilt there is no moral consciousness and

---

[7] *Theatrum chemicum,* IV (1659), p. 500.

[8] Ibid., p. 478: "(Christ), who is the tree of life both spiritual and bodily."

[9] Krueger, *Das Dogma von der Dreieinigkeit und Gottmenschheit,* p. 207.

without awareness of differences no consciousness at all, we must concede that the strange intervention of the master of souls was absolutely necessary for the development of any kind of consciousness and in this sense was for the good. According to our religious beliefs, God himself is this Master—and the alchemist, in his small way, competes with the Creator in so far as he strives to do work analogous to the work of creation, and therefore he likens his microcosmic opus to the work of the world creator.[10]

245     In our fairytale the natural evil is banished to the "roots," that is, to the earth, in other words the body. This statement agrees with the historical fact that Christian thought in general has held the body in contempt, without bothering much about the finer doctrinal distinctions.[11] For, according to doctrine, neither the body nor nature in general is evil *per se:* as the work of God, or as the actual form in which he manifests himself, nature cannot be identical with evil. Correspondingly, the evil spirit in the fairytale is not simply banished to the earth and allowed to roam about at will, but is only hidden there in a safe and special container, so that he cannot call attention to himself anywhere except right under the oak. The bottle is an artificial human product and thus signifies the intellectual purposefulness and artificiality of the procedure, whose obvious aim is to isolate the spirit from the surrounding medium. As the *vas Hermeticum* of alchemy, it was "hermetically" sealed (i.e., sealed with the sign of Hermes);[12] it had to be made of glass, and had also to be as round as possible, since it was meant to represent the cosmos in which the earth was created.[13] Transparent glass is something like solidified water or air, both of which are synonyms for spirit. The alchemical retort is therefore equivalent to the *anima mundi,* which according to an old alchemical conception surrounds the cosmos. Caesarius of Heisterbach (thirteenth century) mentions a vision in which the soul appeared as a

---

10 In the "Dicta Belini" Mercurius even says: "Out of me is made the bread from which comes the whole world, and the world is formed from my mercy, and it fails not, because it is the gift of God" (Distinctio XXVIII, in *Theatr. chem.,* V, 1660, p. 87).

11 Cf. the doctrine of the *status iustitiae originalis* and *status naturae integrae.*

12 Cf. Rev. 20 : 3: "and set a seal upon him."

13 "The Fift is of Concord and of Love, / Betweene your Warkes and the Spheare above."—Norton's "Ordinall of Alchimy," *Theatrum chemicum Britannicum,* ch. 6, p. 92.

spherical glass vessel.[14] Likewise the "spiritual" or "ethereal" (*aethereus*) philosophers' stone is a precious *vitrum* (sometimes described as *malleabile*) which was often equated with the gold glass (*aurum vitreum*) of the heavenly Jerusalem (Rev. 21 : 21).

246     It is worth noting that the German fairytale calls the spirit confined in the bottle by the name of the pagan god, Mercurius, who was considered identical with the German national god, Wotan. The mention of Mercurius stamps the fairytale as an alchemical folk legend, closely related on the one hand to the allegorical tales used in teaching alchemy, and on the other to the well-known group of folktales that cluster round the motif of the "spellbound spirit." Our fairytale thus interprets the evil spirit as a pagan god, forced under the influence of Christianity to descend into the dark underworld and be morally disqualified. Hermes becomes the demon of the mysteries celebrated by all *tenebriones* (obscurantists), and Wotan the demon of forest and storm; Mercurius becomes the soul of the metals, the metallic man (*homunculus*), the dragon (*serpens mercurialis*), the roaring fiery lion, the night raven (*nycticorax*), and the black eagle—the last four being synonyms for the devil. In fact the spirit in the bottle behaves just as the devil does in many other fairytales: he bestows wealth by changing base metal into gold; and like the devil, he also gets tricked.

14 *Dialogus miraculorum,* trans. by Scott and Bland, I, pp. 42, 236.

## 2. THE CONNECTION BETWEEN
## SPIRIT AND TREE

247    Before continuing our discussion of the spirit Mercurius, I should like to point out a not unimportant fact. The place where he lies confined is not just any place but a very essential one—namely, under the oak, the king of the forest. In psychological terms, this means that the evil spirit is imprisoned in the roots of the self, as the secret hidden in the principle of individuation. He is not identical with the tree, nor with its roots, but has been put there by artificial means. The fairytale gives us no reason to think that the oak, which represents the self, has grown out of the spirit in the bottle; we may rather conjecture that the oak presented a suitable place for concealing a secret. A treasure, for instance, is preferably buried near some kind of landmark, or else such a mark is put up afterwards. The tree of paradise serves as a prototype for this and similar tales: it, too, is not identical with the voice of the serpent which issued from it.[1] However, it must not be forgotten that these mythical motifs have a significant connection with certain psychological phenomena observed among primitive peoples. In all such cases there is a notable analogy with primitive animism: certain trees are animated by souls—have the character of personality, we would say—and possess a voice that gives commands to human beings. Amaury Talbot[2] reports one such case from Nigeria, where a native soldier heard an *oji* tree calling to him, and tried desperately to break out of the barracks and hasten to the tree. Under cross-examination he alleged that all those who bore the name of the tree now and then heard its voice. Here the voice is undoubtedly identical with the tree. These psychic phenomena

---

[1] Mercurius, in the form of Lilith or Melusina, appears in the tree in the Ripley *Scrowle*. To this context belongs also the hamadryad as an interpretation of the so-called "Aenigma Bononiense." Cf. *Mysterium Coniunctionis*, pp. 68f.
[2] *In the Shadow of the Bush*, pp. 31f.

suggest that originally the tree and the daemon were one and the same, and that their separation is a secondary phenomenon corresponding to a higher level of culture and consciousness. The original phenomenon was nothing less than a nature deity, a *tremendum* pure and simple, which is morally neutral. But the secondary phenomenon implies an act of discrimination which splits man off from nature and thus testifies to the existence of a more highly differentiated consciousness. To this is added, as a tertiary phenomenon testifying to a still higher level, the moral qualification which declares the voice to be an evil spirit under a ban. It goes without saying that this third level is marked by a belief in a "higher" and "good" God who, though he has not finally disposed of his adversary, has nevertheless rendered him harmless for some time to come by imprisonment (Rev. 20 : 1–3).

248    Since at the present level of consciousness we cannot suppose that tree daemons exist, we are forced to assert that the primitive suffers from hallucinations, that he hears his own unconscious which has projected itself into the tree. If this theory is correct— and I do not know how we could formulate it otherwise today— then the second level of consciousness has effected a differentiation between the object "tree" and the unconscious content projected into it, thereby achieving an act of enlightenment. The third level rises still higher and attributes "evil" to the psychic content which has been separated from the object. Finally a fourth level, the level reached by our consciousness today, carries the enlightenment a stage further by denying the objective existence of the "spirit" and declaring that the primitive has heard nothing at all, but merely had an auditory hallucination. Consequently the whole phenomenon vanishes into thin air— with the great advantage that the evil spirit becomes obviously non-existent and sinks into ridiculous insignificance. A fifth level, however, which is bound to take a quintessential view of the matter, wonders about this conjuring trick that turns what began as a miracle into a senseless self-deception—only to come full circle. Like the boy who told his father a made-up story about sixty stags in the forest, it asks: "But what, then, was all the rustling in the woods?" The fifth level is of the opinion that something did happen after all: even though the psychic content was not the tree, nor a spirit in the tree, nor indeed any spirit at

all, it was nevertheless a phenomenon thrusting up from the unconscious, the existence of which cannot be denied if one is minded to grant the psyche any kind of reality. If one did not do that, one would have to extend God's *creatio ex nihilo*—which seems so obnoxious to the modern intellect—very much further to include steam engines, automobiles, radios, and every library on earth, all of which would presumably have arisen from unimaginably fortuitous conglomerations of atoms. The only thing that would have happened is that the Creator would have been renamed Conglomeratio.

249 The fifth level assumes that the unconscious exists and has a reality just like any other existent. However odious it may be, this means that the "spirit" is also a reality, and the "evil" spirit at that. What is even worse, the distinction between "good" and "evil" is suddenly no longer obsolete, but highly topical and necessary. The crucial point is that so long as the evil spirit cannot be proved to be a subjective psychic experience, then even trees and other suitable objects would have, once again, to be seriously considered as its lodging places.

## 3. THE PROBLEM OF FREEING MERCURIUS

250    We will not pursue the paradoxical reality of the unconscious any further now, but will return to the fairytale of the spirit in the bottle. As we have seen, the spirit Mercurius bears some resemblance to the "cheated devil." The analogy, however, is only a superficial one, since, unlike the gifts of the devil, the gold of Mercurius does not turn to horse droppings but remains good metal, and the magic rag does not turn to ashes by morning but retains its healing power. Nor is Mercurius tricked out of a soul that he wanted to steal. He is only tricked into his own better nature, one might say, in that the boy succeeds in bottling him up again in order to cure his bad mood and make him tractable. Mercurius becomes polite, gives the young fellow a useful ransom and is accordingly set free. We now hear about the student's good fortune and how he became a wonder-working doctor, but—strangely enough—nothing about the doings of the liberated spirit, though these might be of some interest in view of the web of meanings in which Mercurius, with his many-sided associations, entangles us. What happens when this pagan god, Hermes-Mercurius-Wotan, is let loose again? Being a god of magicians, a *spiritus vegetativus,* and a storm daemon, he will hardly have returned to captivity, and the fairytale gives us no reason to suppose that the episode of imprisonment has finally changed his nature to the pink of perfection. The bird of Hermes has escaped from the glass cage, and in consequence something has happened which the experienced alchemist wished at all costs to avoid. That is why he always sealed the stopper of his bottle with magic signs and set it for a very long time over the lowest fire, so that "he who is within may not fly out." For if he escapes, the whole laborious opus comes to nothing and has to be started all over again. Our lad was a Sunday's child and possibly one of the poor in spirit, on whom was bestowed a bit of the Kingdom of Heaven in the shape of the self-

202

renewing tincture, with reference to which it was said that the opus needed to be performed only once.[1] But if he had lost the magic rag he would certainly never have been able to produce it a second time, by himself. It looks as though some Master had succeeded in capturing the mercurial spirit and then hid him in a safe place, like a treasure—perhaps putting him aside for some future use. He may even have planned to tame the wild Mercurius to serve him as a willing "familiar," like Mephisto—such trains of thought are not strange to alchemy. Perhaps he was disagreeably surprised when he returned to the oak tree and found that his bird had flown. At any rate, it might have been better not to have left the fate of the bottle to chance.

251    Be that as it may, the behaviour of the boy—successfully as it worked out for him—must be described as alchemically incorrect. Apart from the fact that he may have infringed upon the legitimate claims of an unknown Master by setting Mercurius free, he was also totally unconscious of what might follow if this turbulent spirit were let loose upon the world. The golden age of alchemy was the sixteenth and the first half of the seventeenth century. At that time a storm bird did indeed escape from a spiritual vessel which the daemons must have felt was a prison. As I have said, the alchemists were all for not letting Mercurius escape. They wanted to keep him in the bottle in order to transform him: for they believed, like Petasios, that lead (another arcane substance) was "so bedevilled and shameless that all who wish to investigate it fall into madness through ignorance."[2] The same was said of the elusive Mercurius who evades every grasp—a real trickster who drove the alchemists to despair.[3]

[1] "For he that shall end it once for certeyne, / Shall never have neede to begin againe."—Norton's "Ordinall of Alchimy," *Theatr. chem. Brit.*, ch. 4, p. 48.

[2] Olympiodorus in Berthelot, *Alchimistes grecs*, II, iv, 43.

[3] Cf. the entertaining "Dialogus Mercurii alchymistae et naturae," in *Theatr. chem.*, IV (1659), pp. 449ff.

## 1. INTRODUCTORY

252  The interested reader will want, as I do, to find out more about this spirit—especially what our forefathers believed and said about him. I will therefore try with the aid of text citations to draw a picture of this versatile and shimmering god as he appeared to the masters of the royal art. For this purpose we must consult the abstruse literature of alchemy, which has not yet been properly understood. Naturally, in later times, the history of alchemy was mainly of interest to the chemist. The fact that it recorded the discovery of many chemical substances and drugs could not, however, reconcile him to the pitiful meagreness, so it seemed to him, of its scientific content. He was not in the position of the older authors, such as Schmieder, who could look on the possibility of goldmaking with hopeful esteem and sympathy; instead he was irritated by the futility of the recipes and the fraudulence of alchemical speculation in general. To him alchemy was bound to seem a gigantic aberration that lasted for more than two thousand years. Had he only asked himself whether the chemistry of alchemy was authentic or not, that is, whether the alchemists were really chemists or merely spoke a chemical jargon, then the texts themselves would have suggested a line of observation other than the purely chemical. The scientific equipment of the chemist does not, however, fit him to pursue this other line, since it leads straight into the history of religion. Thus it was a philologist, Reitzenstein, whom we have to thank for preliminary researches of the greatest value in this field. It was he who recognized the mythological and Gnostic ideas embedded in alchemy, thereby opening up the whole subject from an angle which promises to be most fruitful. For alchemy, as the earliest Greek and Chinese texts show, originally formed part of Gnostic philosophical speculations which also included a detailed knowledge of the techniques of the goldsmith and ironsmith, the faker of precious stones, the druggist and

apothecary. In East and West alike, alchemy contains as its core the Gnostic doctrine of the Anthropos and by its very nature has the character of a peculiar doctrine of redemption. This fact necessarily escaped the chemist, although it is expressed clearly enough in the Greek and Latin texts as well as in the Chinese of about the same period.

253    To begin with, of course, it is almost impossible for our scientifically trained minds to feel their way back into that primitive state of *participation mystique* in which subject and object are identical. Here the findings of modern psychology stood me in very good stead. Practical experience shows us again and again that any prolonged preoccupation with an unknown object acts as an almost irresistible bait for the unconscious to project itself into the unknown nature of the object and to accept the resultant perception, and the interpretation deduced from it, as objective. This phenomenon, a daily occurrence in practical psychology and more especially in psychotherapy, is without doubt a vestige of primitivity. On the primitive level, the whole of life is governed by animistic assumptions, that is, by projections of subjective contents into objective situations. For example, Karl von den Steinen says that the Bororos think of themselves as red cockatoos, although they readily admit that they have no feathers.[1] On this level, the alchemists' assumption that a certain substance possesses secret powers, or that there is a *prima materia* somewhere which works miracles, is self-evident. This is, however, not a fact that can be understood or even thought of in chemical terms, it is a psychological phenomenon. Psychology, therefore, can make an important contribution towards elucidating the alchemists' mentality. What to the chemist seem to be the absurd fantasies of alchemy can be recognized by the psychologist without too much difficulty as psychic material contaminated with chemical substances. This material stems from the collective unconscious and is therefore identical with fantasy products that can still be found today among both sick and healthy people who have never heard of alchemy. On account of the primitive character of its projections, alchemy, so barren a field for the chemist, is for the psychologist a veritable gold-mine of materials which throw an exceedingly valuable light on the structure of the unconscious.

[1] Von den Steinen, *Unter den Naturvölkern Zentral-Brasiliens*, pp. 352f., 512.

254    Since in what follows I shall often refer to the original texts, it might be as well to say a few words about this literature, some of which is not easily accessible. I shall leave out of account the few Chinese texts that have been translated, and shall only mention that *The Secret of the Golden Flower,* published by Richard Wilhelm and myself, is representative of its class. Nor can I consider the Indian "Quicksilver System." [2] The Western literature I have used falls into four groups:

1. *Texts by ancient authors.* This group comprises mainly Greek texts, which have been edited by Berthelot, and those transmitted by the Arabs, likewise edited by him. They date from the period between the first and eighth centuries.

2. *Texts by the early Latinists.* The most important of these are translations from the Arabic (or Hebrew?). Recent research shows that most of these texts derive from the Harranite school, which flourished until about 1050, and was also, probably, the source of the *Corpus Hermeticum.* To this group belong certain texts whose Arabic origin is doubtful but which at least show Arabic influence—for instance, the "Summa perfectionis" of Geber and the Aristotle and Avicenna treatises. This period extends from the ninth to the thirteenth century.

3. *Texts by the later Latinists.* These comprise the principal group and range from the fourteenth to the seventeenth century.

4. *Texts in modern European languages.* Sixteenth to seventeenth century. After that, alchemy fell into decline, which is why I have only occasionally used eighteenth-century texts.

[2] Cf. Deussen, *Allgemeine Geschichte der Philosophie,* I, Part 3, pp. 336ff. This undoubtedly alchemical philosophy belongs to the fairly late (medieval) *Upa-Puranas,* more particularly to the *Maheshvarapurana,* hence to a doctrine principally concerned with Shiva. "Pāra-da" (bestowing the Other Shore) signifies quicksilver.

## 2. MERCURIUS AS QUICKSILVER AND/OR WATER

<sup>255</sup> Mercurius was first understood pretty well everywhere as *hydrargyrum*[1] (Hg), quicksilver or *argentum vivum* (Fr. *vif-argent* or *argent vive*). As such, it was called *vulgaris* (common) and *crudus*. As a rule, *mercurius philosophicus* was specifically distinguished from this, as an avowedly arcane substance that was sometimes conceived to be present in *mercurius crudus,* and then, again, to differ from it completely. It was the true object of the alchemical procedure. Quicksilver, because of its fluidity and volatility, was also defined as water. A popular saying is: "Aqua manus non madefaciens" (the water that does not make the hands wet).[2] Other designations are *aqua vitae,*[3] *aqua alba,*[4] *aqua sicca.*[5] The last designation, dry water, is paradoxical, for which reason I should like to call special attention to it as characterizing the nature of the object described. *Aqua septies distillata* (seven times distilled water) and *aqueum subtile*[6] point to the sublimated ("spiritual") nature of the philosophic Mercurius. Many treatises simply speak of Mercurius as water.[7] The doctrine of the *humidum radicale* (root-moisture or radical moisture) underlies such designations as *humidum album,*[8] *humiditas maxime permanens incombustibilis et unctuosa,*[9] and *humiditas radicalis.*[10] Mercurius is also said to arise from the moisture like a vapour[11] (which again points to his spiritual

---

[1] From ὕδωρ, 'water,' and ἄργυρος, 'silver.'

[2] E.g., Hoghelande, "De alchemiae difficultatibus," *Theatr. chem.,* I (1659), p. 161.

[3] "Aquarium sapientum," *Musaeum hermeticum,* pp. 84, 93.

[4] Ibid., p. 84. Hence also *lac virginis, nivis, terra alba foliata, magnesia,* etc.

[5] Hoghelande, p. 161.

[6] Mylius, *Philosophia reformata,* p. 176.

[7] "Novum lumen," *Mus. herm.,* p. 581; "Tractatus aureus," ibid., p. 34; "Gloria mundi," ibid., p. 250; Khunrath, *Von hylealischen Chaos,* p. 214.

[8] *Rosarium philosophorum,* in *Artis auriferae,* II, p. 376.

[9] "Tractatus aureus," *Mus. herm.,* p. 39.

[10] Mylius, *Phil. ref.,* p. 31.

[11] "Gloria mundi," p. 244.

nature), or to rule the water.[12] The "divine water" ($\H{v}\delta\omega\rho$ $\vartheta\epsilon\tilde{\iota}o\nu$) so often mentioned in the Greek texts is quicksilver.[13] Mercurius as the arcane substance and golden tincture is indicated by the designation *aqua aurea*[14] and by the description of the water as *Mercurii caduceus*.[15]

[12] *Aurora consurgens* II, in *Art. aurif.*, I, p. 189. This text remarks that the water is fire (p. 212).
[13] Berthelot, *Alch. grecs*, IV, vii, 2.
[14] Basilius Valentinus, "Practica," *Mus. herm.*, p. 404.
[15] Philaletha, "Metallorum metamorphosis," ibid., p. 771, and "Introitus apertus," ibid., p. 654.

## 3. MERCURIUS AS FIRE

256     Many treatises define Mercurius simply as fire.[1] He is *ignis elementaris*,[2] *noster naturalis ignis certissimus*,[3] which again indicates his "philosophic" nature. The *aqua mercurialis* is even a divine fire.[4] This fire is "highly vaporous" (*vaporosus*).[5] Indeed, Mercurius is really the only fire in the whole procedure.[6] He is an "invisible fire, working in secret."[7] One text says that the "heart" of Mercurius is at the North Pole and that he is like a fire (northern lights).[8] He is, in fact, as another text says, "the universal and scintillating fire of the light of nature, which carries the heavenly spirit within it."[9] This passage is particularly important as it relates Mercurius to the *lumen naturae*, the source of mystical knowledge second only to the holy revelation of the Scriptures. Once more we catch a glimpse of the ancient role of Hermes as the god of revelation. Although the *lumen naturae*, as originally bestowed by God upon his creatures, is not by nature ungodly, its essence was nevertheless felt to be abysmal, since the *ignis mercurialis* was also connected with the fires of hell. It seems, however, that the alchemists did not understand hell, or its fire, as absolutely outside of God or opposed to him, but rather as an internal component of the deity, which must indeed be so if God is held to be a *coincidentia opposi-*

[1] *Aurora consurgens* II, in *Art. aurif.*, I, p. 212; Dorn, "Congeries Paracelsicae," *Theatr. chem.*, I (1659), p. 502; Mylius, *Phil. ref.*, p. 245.

[2] "Via veritatis," *Mus. herm.*, p. 200.

[3] "Tractatus aureus," ibid., p. 39.

[4] "Aquarium sapientum," ibid., p. 91.

[5] Ibid., p. 90.

[6] "There is no fire in all the work save Mercurius" ("Fons chymicae veritatis," ibid., p. 803).

[7] "Metall. metamorph.," ibid., p. 766.

[8] "At the Pole is the heart of Mercurius, which is the true fire, in which is the resting place of his Lord, sailing through this great sea" ("Introit. apert.," *Mus. herm.*, p. 655). A somewhat obscure symbolism!

[9] "Aquarium sap.," ibid., p. 84.

*torum.* The concept of an all-encompassing God must necessarily include his opposite. The *coincidentia,* of course, must not be too radical or too extreme, otherwise God would cancel himself out.[10] The principle of the coincidence of opposites must therefore be completed by that of absolute opposition in order to attain full paradoxicality and hence psychological validity.

257    The mercurial fire is found in the "centre of the earth," or dragon's belly, in fluid form. Benedictus Figulus writes: "Visit the centre of the earth, there you will find the global fire." [11] Another treatise says that this fire is the "secret, infernal fire, the wonder of the world, the system of the higher powers in the lower." [12] Mercurius, the revelatory light of nature, is also hell-fire, which in some miraculous way is none other than a rearrangement of the heavenly, spiritual powers in the lower, chthonic world of matter, thought already in St. Paul's time to be ruled by the devil. Hell-fire, the true energic principle of evil, appears here as the manifest counterpart of the spiritual and the good, and as essentially identical with it in substance. After that, it can surely cause no offence when another treatise says that the mercurial fire is the "fire in which God himself burns in divine love." [13] We are not deceiving ourselves if we feel in scattered remarks of this kind the breath of true mysticism.

258    Since Mercurius is himself of fiery nature, fire does not harm him: he remains unchanged within it, rejoicing like the salamander.[14] It is unnecessary to point out that quicksilver does not behave like this but vaporizes under heat, as the alchemists themselves knew from very early times.

[10] This is a purely psychological explanation having to do with human conceptions and statements and not with the unfathomable Being.

[11] Figulus, *Rosarium novum olympicum,* Pars I, p. 71. This is the "domus ignis idem Enoch." Cf. "Paracelsus as a Spiritual Phenomenon," supra, par. 186.

[12] "Ignis infernalis secretus . . . mundi miraculum, virtutum superiorum in inferioribus systema" ("Introit. apert.," p. 654).

[13] "Ignis in quo Deus ipse ardet amore divino" ("Gloria mundi," p. 246).

[14] "For it is he who overcomes the fire, and is himself not overcome by the fire, but rests in it as a friend, rejoicing in it" (Geber, "Summa perfectionis," *De alchemia,* cap. LXIII, p. 139).

## 4. MERCURIUS AS SPIRIT AND SOUL

259    If Mercurius had been understood simply as quicksilver, there would obviously have been no need for any of the appellations I have listed. The fact that this need arose points to the conclusion that one simple and unmistakable term in no way sufficed to designate what the alchemists had in mind when they spoke of Mercurius. It was certainly quicksilver, but a very special quicksilver, "our" Mercurius, the essence, moisture, or principle behind or within the quicksilver—that indefinable, fascinating, irritating, and elusive thing which attracts an unconscious projection. The "philosophic" Mercurius, this *servus fugitivus* or *cervus fugitivus* (fugitive slave or stag), is a highly important unconscious content which, as may be gathered from the few hints we have given, threatens to ramify into a set of far-reaching psychological problems. The concept swells dangerously and we begin to perceive that the end is nowhere in sight. Therefore we would rather not tie this concept prematurely to any special meaning, but shall content ourselves with stating that the philosophic Mercurius, so dear to the alchemist as the transformative substance, is obviously a projection of the unconscious, such as always takes place when the inquiring mind lacks the necessary self-criticism in investigating an unknown quantity.

260    As has already been indicated, the psychic nature of the arcane substance did not escape the alchemists; indeed, they actually defined it as "spirit" and "soul." But since these concepts—especially in earlier times—were always ambiguous, we must approach them with caution if we want to gain a moderately clear idea of what the terms *spiritus* and *anima* meant in alchemical usage.

## A. MERCURIUS AS AN AERIAL SPIRIT

261    Hermes, originally a wind god, and his counterpart the
Egyptian Thoth, who "makes the souls to breathe," [1] are the
forerunners of the alchemical Mercurius in his aerial aspect.
The texts often use the terms *pneuma* and *spiritus* in the original concrete sense of "air in motion." So when Mercurius is described in the *Rosarium philosophorum* (fifteenth century) as
*aereus* and *volans*[2] (winged), and in Hoghelande (sixteenth
century) as *totus aereus et spiritualis*,[3] what is meant is nothing more than a gaseous state of aggregation. Something similar
is meant by the poetic expression *serenitas aerea* in the Ripley
*Scrowle*,[4] and by the same author's statement that Mercurius is
changed into wind.[5] He is the *lapis elevatus cum vento* (the
stone uplifted by the wind).[6] The expressions *spirituale corpus*[7] and *spiritus visibilis, tamen impalpabilis*[8] (visible yet im-
palpable spirit) might also mean little more than "air" if one
recalls the aforementioned vapour-like nature of Mercurius, and
the same is probably true even of the *spiritus prae cunctis valde
purus*[9] (pre-eminently pure spirit). The designation *incom-
bustibilis*[10] is more doubtful, since this was often synonymous
with *incorruptibilis* and then meant "eternal," as we shall see
later. Penotus (sixteenth century), a pupil of Paracelsus, stresses
the corporeal aspect when he says that Mercurius is "nothing
other than the spirit of the world become body within the
earth." [11] This expression shows better than anything else the
contamination—inconceivable to the modern mind—of two separate realms, spirit and matter; for to people in the Middle Ages

---

[1] This characteristic of Mercurius is stressed in *Aurora consurgens* II, in *Art.
aurif.*, I, pp. 146 and 190: "He makes the nostrils [of the foetus] in the fifth
month."

[2] *Rosarium*, pp. 252, 271.

[3] *Theatrum chemicum*, I (1659), p. 169.

[4] 16th cent. British Museum, MS. Add. 10302.

[5] Ripley, *Opera*, p. 35.

[6] "Tractatus aureus," *Mus. herm.*, p. 39.

[7] *Rosarium*, p. 282.

[8] Basilius Valentinus, "Practica," *Mus. herm.*, p. 404.

[9] "Introit. apert.," ibid., p. 654.

[10] *Rosarium*, p. 252.

[11] *Theatr. chem.*, I (1659), p. 600.

the *spiritus mundi* was also the spirit which rules nature, and not just a pervasive gas. We find ourselves in the same dilemma when another author, Mylius, in his *Philosophia reformata*,[12] describes Mercurius as an "intermediate substance" (*media substantia*), which is evidently synonymous with his concept of the *anima media natura*[13] (soul as intermediate nature), for to him Mercurius was the "spirit and soul of the bodies." [14]

### B. MERCURIUS AS SOUL

262    "Soul" represents a higher concept than "spirit" in the sense of air or gas. As the "subtle body" or "breath-soul" it means something non-material and finer than mere air. Its essential characteristic is to animate and be animated; it therefore represents the life principle. Mercurius is often designated as *anima* (hence, as a feminine being, he is also called *foemina* or *virgo*), or as *nostra anima*.[15] The *nostra* here does not mean "our own" soul but, as in *aqua nostra, Mercurius noster, corpus nostrum*, refers to the arcane substance.

263    However, *anima* often appears to be connected with *spiritus*, or is equated with it.[16] For the spirit shares the living quality of the soul, and for this reason Mercurius is often called the *spiritus vegetativus*[17] (spirit of life) or *spiritus seminalis*.[18] A peculiar appellation is found in that seventeenth-century forgery which purports to be the secret book of Abraham le Juif, mentioned by Nicolas Flamel (fourteenth century). The epithet is *spiritus Phytonis* (from φύω, 'to procreate,' φυτόν, 'creature,' φύτωρ, 'procreator,' and *Python*, the Delphic serpent), and is accompanied by the serpent sign: ♌.[19] Very much more material is the definition of Mercurius as a "life-giving power like a

12 P. 183.
13 P. 19.
14 P. 308.
15 "Tractatus aureus," *Mus. herm.*, p. 39.
16 Mylius, *Phil. ref.*, p. 308: "(Mercurius est) spiritus et anima corporis." The same in Ventura, *Theatr. chem.*, II (1659), p. 282, and in "Tractatus Micreris," ibid., V (1660), p. 92.
17 Aegidius de Vadis, ibid., II (1659), p. 106.
18 Philaletha, "Metall. metamorph.," *Mus. herm.*, p. 766.
19 Abraham Eleazar, *Uraltes Chymisches Werck*, pp. 29ff. "Phyton is the life of all things," p. 34.

glue, holding the world together and standing in the middle between body and spirit." [20] This concept corresponds to Mylius' definition of Mercurius as the *anima media natura*. From here it is but a step to the identification of Mercurius with the *anima mundi*,[21] which is how Avicenna had defined him very much earlier (twelfth to thirteenth century). "He is the spirit of the Lord which fills the whole world and in the beginning swam upon the waters. They call him also the spirit of Truth, which is hidden from the world." [22] Another text says that Mercurius is the "supracelestial spirit which is conjoined with the light, and rightly could be called the *anima mundi*." [23] It is clear from a number of texts that the alchemists related their concept of the *anima mundi* on the one hand to the world soul in Plato's *Timaeus* and on the other to the Holy Spirit, who was present at the Creation and played the role of procreator ($\phi\acute{v}\tau\omega\rho$), impregnating the waters with the seed of life just as, later, he played a similar role in the *obumbratio* (overshadowing) of Mary.[24] Elsewhere we read that a "life-force dwells in *Mercurius non vulgaris*, who flies like solid white snow. This is a spirit of the macrocosmic as of the microcosmic world, upon whom, after the *anima rationalis*, the motion and fluidity of human nature itself depends." [25] The snow represents the purified Mercurius in the state of *albedo* (= spirituality); here again matter and spirit are identical. Worth noting is the duality of soul caused by the presence of Mercurius: on the one hand the immortal *anima rationalis* given by God to man, which distinguishes him from animals; on the other hand the mercurial life-soul, which to all appearances is connected with the *inflatio* or *inspiratio* of the Holy Spirit. This fundamental duality forms the psychological basis of the two sources of illumination.

[20] Happelius, "Aphorismi Basiliani," *Theatr. chem.*, IV (1659), p. 327.
[21] *Verus Hermes* (1620).
[22] "Aquarium sap.," *Mus. herm.*, p. 85.
[23] Steeb, *Coelum Sephiroticum*, p. 33.
[24] Ibid., p. 39.
[25] Happelius, loc. cit.

## C. MERCURIUS AS SPIRIT IN THE
### INCORPOREAL, METAPHYSICAL SENSE

264    In many of the passages it remains doubtful whether *spiritus* means spirit in an abstract sense.[26] It is moderately certain that this is so in Dorn, for he says that "Mercurius possesses the quality of an incorruptible spirit, which is like the soul, and because of its incorruptibility is called intellectual"[27]—i.e., pertaining to the *mundus intelligibilis*. One text expressly calls him "spiritual and hyperphysical,"[28] and another says that the spirit of Mercurius comes from heaven.[29] Laurentius Ventura (sixteenth century) may well have been associating himself with the "Platonis liber quartorum" and hence with the neo-Platonist ideas of the Harranite school when he defined the spirit of Mercurius as "completely and entirely like itself" (*sibi omnino similis*) and *simplex*,[30] for this Harranite text defines the arcane substance as the *res simplex* and equates it with God.[31]

265    The oldest reference to the mercurial *pneuma* occurs in an Ostanes quotation of considerable antiquity (possibly pre-Christian), which says: "Go to the streamings of the Nile, and there you will find a stone that has a spirit."[32] In Zosimos Mercurius is characterized as incorporeal (ἀσώματον),[33] and by another author as ethereal (αἰθερῶδες πνεῦμα) and as having become rational or wise (σώφρων γενομένη).[34] In the very old treatise "Isis to Horus" (first century) the divine water is brought by an angel and is clearly of celestial or possibly daemonic origin, since according to the text the angel Amnael who brings it is not a morally irreproachable figure.[35] For the alchemists, as we know not only from the ancient but also from the later writers,

---

26 For instance, Djābir in Berthelot, *Chimie au moyen âge*, III, p. 169; *Rosarium*, in *Art. aurif.*, II, p. 339; Hoghelande, *Theatr. chem.*, I (1602), pp. 153, 183.

27 *Theatr. chem.*, I (1659), p. 419. The same in Ripley, "Axiomata," ibid., II (1659), p. 123.

28 "Tractatus aureus," *Mus. herm.*, p. 11. Here cited from Valentinus.

29 Steeb, *Coelum Sephiroticum*, p. 137.

30 *Theatr. chem.*, II (1659), p. 231.

31 Ibid., V (1660), p. 129.

32 Berthelot, *Alch. grecs*, III, vi, 5.

33 Ibid., III, xxviii, 5.

34 Ibid., IV, vii, 2.

35 Ibid., I, xiii, 3. [Cf. supra, "The Visions of Zosimos," pars. 97ff.]

Mercurius as the arcane substance had a more or less secret connection with the goddess of love. In the "Book of Krates," which was transmitted by the Arabs and is possibly of Alexandrian origin, Aphrodite appears with a vessel from the mouth of which pours a ceaseless stream of quicksilver,[36] and in the *Chymical Wedding* of Christian Rosencreutz the central mystery is his visit to the secret chamber of the sleeping Venus.

266    The fact that Mercurius is interpreted as spirit and soul, in spite of the spirit-body dilemma which this involves, indicates that the alchemists themselves conceived of their arcane substance as something that we today would call a psychic phenomenon. Indeed, whatever else spirit and soul may be, from the phenomenological point of view they are psychic structures. The alchemists never tired of drawing attention to the psychic nature of Mercurius. So far we have concerned ourselves with, statistically, the commonest synonyms such as water and fire, spirit and soul, and it is now possible for us to conclude that these exemplify a psychological state of affairs best characterized by (or, indeed, actually demanding) an antinomian nomenclature. Water and fire are classic opposites and can be valid definitions of one and the same thing only if this thing unites in itself the contrary qualities of water and fire. The psychologem "Mercurius" must therefore possess an essentially antinomian dual nature.

[36] Berthelot, *Moyen âge*, III, p 63.

## 5. THE DUAL NATURE OF MERCURIUS

Mercurius, following the tradition of Hermes, is many-sided, changeable, and deceitful. Dorn speaks of "that inconstant Mercurius,"[1] and another calls him *versipellis* (changing his skin, shifty).[2] He is *duplex*[3] and his main characteristic is duplicity. It is said of him that he "runs round the earth and enjoys equally the company of the good and the wicked."[4] He is "two dragons,"[5] the "twin,"[6] made of "two natures"[7] or "two substances."[8] He is the "giant of twofold substance," in explanation of which the text[9] cites the twenty-sixth chapter of Matthew, where the sacrament of the Last Supper is instituted. The Christ analogy is thus made plain. The two substances of Mercurius are thought of as dissimilar, sometimes opposed; as the dragon he is "winged and wingless."[10] A parable says: "On this mountain lies an ever-waking dragon, who is called Pantophthalmos, for he is covered with eyes on both sides of his body, before and behind, and he sleeps with some open and some closed."[11] There is the "common and the philosophic" Mercurius;[12] he consists of "the dry and earthy, the moist and viscous."[13] Two of his elements are passive, earth and water, and two active, air

1 *Theatr. chem.*, I (1659), p. 470.
2 Aegidius de Vadis, ibid., II (1659), p. 105.
3 "Aquarium sap.," *Mus. herm.*, p. 84; Trevisanus, in *Theatr. chem.*, I (1659), p. 695; Mylius, *Phil. ref.*, p. 176.
4 "Aurelia occulta," *Theatr. chem.*, IV (1659), p. 506.
5 "Brevis manuductio," *Mus. herm.*, p. 788.
6 Valentinus, "Practica," ibid., p. 425.
7 Mylius, *Phil. ref.*, p. 18; "Exercitationes in Turbam," *Art. aurif.*, I, pp. 159, 161.
8 Dorn, in *Theatr. chem.*, I (1659), p. 420.
9 "Aquarium sap.," *Mus. herm.*, p. 111. [Cf. infra, par. 384. n. 5.]
10 "Summarium philosophicum," ibid., pp. 172f.
11 Cf. the snake vision of Ignatius Loyola and the polyophthalmia motif discussed in "On the Nature of the Psyche," pp. 198f.
12 "Tractatus aureus," *Mus. herm.*, p. 25.
13 "Consilium coniugii," *Ars chemica* (1566), p. 59.

and fire.[14] He is both good and evil.[15] The "Aurelia occulta" gives a graphic description of him:[16]

I am the poison-dripping dragon, who is everywhere and can be cheaply had. That upon which I rest, and that which rests upon me, will be found within me by those who pursue their investigations in accordance with the rules of the Art. My water and fire destroy and put together; from my body you may extract the green lion and the red. But if you do not have exact knowledge of me, you will destroy your five senses with my fire. From my snout there comes a spreading poison that has brought death to many. Therefore you should skilfully separate the coarse from the fine, if you do not wish to suffer utter poverty. I bestow on you the powers of the male and the female, and also those of heaven and of earth. The mysteries of my art must be handled with courage and greatness of mind if you would conquer me by the power[17] of fire, for already very many have come to grief, their riches and labour lost. I am the egg of nature, known only to the wise, who in piety and modesty bring forth from me the microcosm, which was prepared for mankind by Almighty God, but given only to the few, while the many long for it in vain, that they may do good to the poor with my treasure and not fasten their souls to the perishable gold. By the philosophers I am named Mercurius; my spouse is the [philosophic] gold; I am the old dragon, found everywhere on the globe of the earth, father and mother, young and old, very strong and very weak, death and resurrection, visible and invisible, hard and soft; I descend into the earth and ascend to the heavens, I am the highest and the lowest, the lightest and the heaviest; often the order of nature is reversed in me, as regards colour, number, weight, and measure; I contain the light of nature; I am dark and light; I come forth from heaven and earth; I am known and yet do not exist at all;[18] by virtue of the sun's rays all colours shine in me, and all metals. I am the carbuncle of the sun, the most noble purified earth, through which you may change copper, iron, tin, and lead into gold.

268    Because of his united double nature Mercurius is described as hermaphroditic. Sometimes his body is said to be masculine and his soul feminine, sometimes the reverse. The *Rosarium*

14 *Rosarium*, in *Art. aurif.*, II, p. 208.
15 Khunrath, *Hyl. Chaos*, p. 218.
16 *Theatr. chem.*, IV (1659), pp. 501ff.
17 I read *vi* instead of *vim*.
18 This paradox recalls the Indian *asat* (non-existing). Cf. Chhāndogya Upanishad, VI, ii, 1 (Sacred Books of the East, II, p. 93).

*philosophorum,* for example, has both versions.[19] As *vulgaris* he
is the dead masculine body, but as "our" Mercurius he is feminine, spiritual, alive and life-giving.[20] He is also called husband
and wife,[21] bridegroom and bride, or lover and beloved.[22] His
contrary natures are often called *Mercurius sensu strictiori* and
sulphur, the former being feminine, earth, and Eve, and the latter masculine, water, and Adam.[23] In Dorn he is the "true hermaphroditic Adam," [24] and in Khunrath he is "begotten of the
hermaphroditic seed of the Macrocosm" as "an immaculate birth
from the hermaphroditic matter" (i.e., the *prima materia*).[25]
Mylius calls him the "hermaphroditic monster." [26] As Adam
he is also the microcosm, or even "the heart of the microcosm," [27] or he has the microcosm "in himself, where are als
the four elements and the *quinta essentia* which they call
Heaven." [28] The term *coelum* for Mercurius does not, as one
might think, derive from the *firmamentum* of Paracelsus, but
occurs earlier in Johannes de Rupescissa (fourteenth century).[29]
The term *homo* is used as a synonym for "microcosm," as when
Mercurius is named the "Philosophic ambisexual Man." [30] In
the very old "Dicta Belini" (Belinus or Balinus is a corruption
of Apollonius of Tyana), he is the "man rising from the river," [31]
probably a reference to the vision of Ezra.[32] In Trismosin's
*Splendor solis* (sixteenth century) there is an illustration of
this.[33] The idea itself may go back to the Babylonian teacher
of wisdom, Oannes. The designation of Mercurius as the "high

19 *Art. aurif.,* II, pp. 239, 249.
20 "Introit. apert.," *Mus. herm.,* p. 653.
21 "Gloria mundi," ibid., p. 250.
22 *Aurora consurgens* I, Parable VII.
23 Ruland, *Lexicon alchemiae,* p. 47.
24 *Theatr. chem.,* I (1659), p. 510.
25 *Hyl. Chaos,* p. 62.
26 *Phil. ref.,* p. 19.
27 Happelius in *Theatr. chem.,* IV (1659), p. 327.
28 *Phil. ref.,* p. 5.
29 *La Vertu et propriété de la quinte essence,* p. 15. The "metal of the philosophers" will become like "heaven," says the "Tractatus Micreris," *Theatr. chem.,*
V (1660), p. 100.
30 Khunrath, *Hyl. Chaos,* p. 195.
31 Manget, *Bibliotheca chemica,* I, p. 478b.
32 IV Ezra 13 : 25–53. Cf. Charles, *Apocrypha and Pseudepigrapha,* II, pp. 618f.
33 In *Aureum vellus* (1598), Tract 3: *Splendor Solis* (1920 facsimile), p. 23, Pl. VIII.

man" [34] does not fit in badly with such a pedigree. The terms Adam and microcosm occur frequently in the texts,[35] but the Abraham le Juif forgery unblushingly calls Mercurius Adam Kadmon.[36] As I have discussed this unmistakable continuation of the Gnostic doctrine of the Anthropos elsewhere,[37] there is no need for me to go more closely now into this aspect of Mercurius.[38] Nevertheless, I would like to emphasize once again that the Anthropos idea coincides with the psychological concept of the self. The atman and purusha doctrine as well as alchemy give clear proofs of this.

269    Another aspect of the dual nature of Mercurius is his characterization as *senex*[39] and *puer*.[40] The figure of Hermes as an old man, attested by archaeology, brings him into direct relation with Saturn—a relationship which plays a considerable role in alchemy (see infra, pars. 274ff.). Mercurius truly consists of the most extreme opposites; on the one hand he is undoubtedly akin to the godhead, on the other he is found in sewers. Rosinus (Zosimos) even calls him the *terminus ani*.[41] In the Bundahish,[42] the anus of Garotman is "like hell on earth."

[34] Ruland, *Lexicon alchemiae*, p. 47.

[35] John Dee in *Theatr. chem.*, II (1659), p. 195; *Rosarium*, in *Art. aurif.*, II, p. 309.

[36] Eleazar, *Uraltes Chymisches Werck*, p. 51. Adam Kadmon is the Primordial Man; cf. *Mysterium Coniunctionis*, ch. V.

[37] "Paracelsus as a Spiritual Phenomenon," supra, pars. 165ff., and *Psychology and Alchemy*, index, s.v.

[38] Gayomart also is a kind of vegetation numen like Mercurius, and like him fertilizes his mother, the earth. At the place where his life came to an end the earth turned to gold, and where his limbs disintegrated various metals appeared. Cf. Christensen, *Les Types du premier homme et du premier roi dans l'histoire légendaire des Iraniens*, pp. 26, 29.

[39] *Senex draco* in Valentinus, "Practica," *Mus. herm.*, p. 425. In *Verus Hermes* (1620), pp. 15, 16, Mercurius is also designated with the Gnostic name "Father-Mother."

[40] "De arte chimica," *Art. aurif.*, I, p. 581. *Regius puellus* in "Introit. apert.," *Mus. herm.*, pp. 678, 655.

[41] *Art. aurif.*, I, p. 310. Here it is the stone identical with Mercurius that is so called. The context disallows the reading "anni." The passage which follows soon after, "nascitur in duobus montibus," refers to the "Tractatus Aristotelis" (*Theatr. chem.*, V, 1660, pp. 787ff.), where the act of defecation is described. (Cf. supra, "Paracelsus as a Spiritual Phenomenon," par. 182, n. 61.) Corresponding illustrations for *Aurora consurgens* may be found in the Codex Rhenoviensis. [42] Ch. XXVIII. Cf. Reitzenstein and Schaeder, *Studien zum antiken Synkretismus aus Iran und Griechenland*, p. 119.

# 6. THE UNITY AND TRINITY OF MERCURIUS

270    In spite of his obvious duality the unity of Mercurius is also emphasized, especially in his form as the lapis. "In all the world he is One." [1] The unity of Mercurius is at the same time a trinity, with clear reference to the Holy Trinity, although his triadic nature does not derive from Christian dogma but is of earlier date. Triads occur as early as the treatise of Zosimos, περὶ ἀρετῆς (Concerning the Art).[2] Martial calls Hermes *omnia solus et ter unus* (All and Thrice One).[3] In Monakris (Arcadia), a three-headed Hermes was worshipped, and in Gaul there was a three-headed Mercurius.[4] This Gallic god was also a psychopomp. The triadic character is an attribute of the gods of the under-world, as for instance the three-bodied Typhon, three-bodied and three-faced Hecate,[5] and the "ancestors" (τριτοπάτορες) with their serpent bodies. According to Cicero,[6] these latter are the three sons of Zeus the King, the *rex antiquissimus*.[7] They are called the "forefathers" and are wind-gods;[8] obviously by the same logic the Hopi Indians believe that snakes are at the same time flashes of lightning auguring rain. Khunrath calls Mer-curius *triunus*[9] and *ternarius*.[10] Mylius represents him as a three-

---

1 *Rosarium,* in *Art. aurif.,* II, p. 253.

2 Berthelot, *Alch. grecs,* III, vi, 18: "The unity of the composition [produces] the indivisible triad, and thus an undivided triad composed of separate elements creates the cosmos, through the forethought [προνοίᾳ] of the First Author, the cause and demiurge of creation; wherefore he is called Trismegistos, having be-held triadically that which is created and that which creates."

3 *Epigrammata,* V, 24.

4 Reinach, *Cultes, mythes et religions,* III, pp. 160f.

5 Schweitzer, *Herakles,* pp. 84ff.

6 *De natura deorum,* 3, 21, 53.

7 There is also a *Zeus triops.*

8 Roscher, *Lexicon,* V, col. 1208.

9 *Hyl. Chaos,* pp. 6 and 199.

10 Ibid., p. 203.

headed snake.[11] The "Aquarium sapientum" says that he is a "triune, universal essence which is named Jehova.[12] He is divine and at the same time human." [13]

271    From all this one must conclude that Mercurius corresponds not only to Christ, but to the triune divinity in general. The "Aurelia occulta" calls him "Azoth," and explains the term as follows: "For he is the A and O that is everywhere present. The philosophers have adorned [him] with the name Azoth, which is compounded of the A and Z of the Latins, the alpha and omega of the Greeks, and the aleph and tau of the Hebrews:

$$A \left\{ \begin{array}{c} Z \\ \omega \\ \hbar \end{array} \right\} \text{Azoth."} \;^{14}$$

The parallel with the Trinity could not be more clearly indicated. The anonymous commentator of the "Tractatus aureus" puts the parallel with Christ as Logos just as unmistakably. All things proceed from the "philosophic heaven adorned with an infinite multitude of stars," [15] from the creative Word incarnate, the Johannine Logos, without which "was not any thing made that was made." The commentator says: "Thus the Word of renewal is invisibly inherent in all things, but it is not evident in elementary solid bodies unless they have been brought back to the fifth, or heavenly and astral essence. Hence this Word of renewal is the seed of promise, or the philosophic heaven refulgent with the infinite lights of the stars." [16] Mercurius is the Logos become world. The description given here may point to his basic identity with the collective unconscious, for as I tried to show in my essay "On the Nature of the Psyche," [17] the image of the starry heaven seems to be a visualization of the peculiar nature of the unconscious. Since Mercurius is often called *filius,* his sonship is beyond question.[18] He is therefore like a

11 *Phil. ref.,* p. 96.
12 This peculiar designation refers to the demiurge, the saturnine Ialdabaoth, who was connected with the "God of the Jews."
13 *Mus. herm.,* p. 112.
14 *Theatr. chem.,* IV (1659), p. 507.
15 Ibid., p. 614.
16 Ibid., p. 615.
17 Pp. 198f.
18 Cf. *Rosarium,* in *Art. aurif.,* II, p. 248: "filius . . . coloris coelici" (cited from

brother to Christ and a second son of God, though in point of time he must be accounted the elder and the first-born. This idea goes back to the conceptions of the Euchites reported in Michael Psellus,[19] who believed that God's first son was Satanaël [20] and that Christ was the second.[21] However, Mercurius is not only the counterpart of Christ in so far as he is the "son"; he is also the counterpart of the Trinity as a whole in so far as he is conceived to be a chthonic triad. According to this view he would be equal to one half of the Christian Godhead. He is indeed the dark chthonic half, but he is not simply evil as such, for he is called "good *and* evil," or a "system of the higher powers in the lower." He calls to mind that double figure which seems to stand behind both Christ and the devil—that enigmatic Lucifer whose attributes are shared by both. In Rev. 22 : 16 Christ says of himself: "I am the root and the offspring of David, the bright and the morning star."

272        One peculiarity of Mercurius which undoubtedly relates him to the Godhead and to the primitive creator god is his ability to beget himself. In the "Allegoriae super librum Turbae" he says: "The mother bore me and is herself begotten of me." [22] As the uroboros dragon, he impregnates, begets, bears, devours, and slays himself, and "himself lifts himself on high," as the *Rosarium* says,[23] so paraphrasing the mystery of God's sacrificial death. Here, as in many similar instances, it would be rash to assume that the alchemists were as conscious of their reasoning processes as perhaps we are. But man, and through him the un-

---

Haly's "Secretum"); Khunrath, *Hyl. Chaos,* passim: "filius macrocosmi," p. 59: "unigenitus"; Penotus in *Theatr. chem.,* I (1659), p. 601: "filius hominis, fructus virginis."

19 *De daemonibus* (trans. Marsilio Ficino), fol. N. V[v].

20 Cf. the report on the Bogomils in Euthymios Zigabenos, "Panoplia dogmatica" (Migne, *P.G.,* vol. 130, cols. 129ff.).

21 The duality of the sonship appears to date back to the Ebionites in Epiphanius: "Two, they assert, were raised up by God, the one (is) Christ, the other the devil" (*Panarium,* XXX, 16, 2).

22 *Art. aurif.,* I, p. 151. The same is said of God in the *Contes del Graal* of Chrétien de Troyes:

"Ce doint icil glorïeus pere
Qui de sa fille fist sa mere."

(Hilka, *Der Percevalroman,* p. 372.)

23 *Art. aurif.,* II, p. 339.

conscious, expresses a great deal that is not necessarily conscious in all its implications. Nevertheless I should like to avoid giving the impression that the alchemists were absolutely unconscious of their thought-processes. How little this was so is proved by the above quotations. But although Mercurius, in many texts, is stated to be *trinus et unus,* this does not prevent him from sharing very strongly the *quaternity* of the lapis, with which he is essentially identical. He thus exemplifies that strange dilemma which is posed by the problem of three and four—the well-known axiom of Maria Prophetissa. There is a classical *Hermes tetracephalus* as well as the *Hermes tricephalus.*[24] The ground-plan of the Sabaean temple of Mercurius was a triangle inside a square.[25] In the scholia to the "Tractatus aureus" the sign for Mercurius is a square inside a triangle surrounded by a circle (symbol of totality).[26]

[24] Schweitzer, *Herakles,* p. 84.
[25] Chwolsohn, *Die Ssabier und der Ssabismus,* II, p. 367.
[26] *Bibl. chem.,* I, p. 409.

## 7. THE RELATION OF MERCURIUS TO ASTROLOGY AND THE DOCTRINE OF THE ARCHONS

273 One of the roots of the peculiar philosophy relating to Mercurius lies in ancient astrology and in the Gnostic doctrine of the archons and aeons, which is derived from it. Between Mercurius and the planet there is a relation of mystical identity due either to contamination or to an actual spiritual identity. In the first case quicksilver is simply the planet Mercury as it appears in the earth (just as gold is simply the sun in the earth);[1] in the second, the "spirit" of quicksilver is identical with the planetary spirit. Both spirits individually, or the two as one spirit, were personified and called upon for aid or magically conjured into service as a *paredros* or "familiar." Within the alchemical tradition we find directions for such procedures in the Harranite treatise "Clavis maioris sapientiae" of Artefius,[2] which agree with descriptions of the invocations mentioned by Dozy and de Goeje.[3] There are also references to procedures of this kind in the "Liber Platonis quartorum."[4] Parallel with this is the account according to which Democritus received the secret of the hieroglyphs from the genius of the planet Mercury.[5] The spirit Mercurius appears here in the role of a mystagogue, as in the *Corpus Hermeticum* or the visions of Zosimos. He plays the same role in the remarkable dream-vision recorded in "Aurelia occulta," where he appears as the Anthropos with a crown of stars.[6] As the little star near the sun, he is the child of sun and

1 Maier, *Circulus physicus quadratus*, pp. 15ff.

2 *Theatr. chem.*, IV (1659), pp. 198ff.

3 "Nouveaux documents pour l'étude de la religion des Harraniens," p. 341.

4 *Theatr. chem.*, V (1660), pp. 101ff.

5 Berthelot, *Alch. grecs*, Introduction, p. 236.

6 *Theatr. chem.*, IV (1659), p. 510. [Supra, par. 106.] He corresponds to the *stella semptemplex* which appears at the end of the work. ". . . cook, until the sevenfold star appears, running about through the sphere" (ibid., p. 508). Cf. the early

moon.[7] But contrariwise he is also the begetter of his parents;[8] or, as the treatise of Wei Po-yang (c. A.D. 142) remarks, the gold (sun) gets its qualities from Mercurius.[9] (Owing to the contamination, the astrological myth is always thought of in chemical terms as well.) Because of his half-feminine nature, Mercurius is often identified with the moon[10] and Venus.[11] As his own divine consort he easily turns into the goddess of love, just as in his role of Hermes he is ithyphallic. But he is also called the "most chaste virgin." [12] The relation of quicksilver to the moon (silver) is obvious enough. Mercurius as the shining and shimmering planet, appearing like Venus close to the sun in the morning or evening sky, is like her a Lucifer, a light-bringer (φωσφόρος). He heralds, as the morning star does, only much more directly, the coming of the light.

274    But the most important of all for an interpretation of Mercurius is his relation to Saturn. Mercurius senex is identical with Saturn, and to the earlier alchemists especially, it is not quicksilver, but the lead associated with Saturn, which usually repre-

---

Christian idea of Christ as the leader of the "round dance" of the stars. ("Transformation Symbolism in the Mass," pp. 273ff.)

7 "Tabula smaragdina," Rosarium, in Art. aurif., II, p. 253, and Mylius, Phil. ref., p. 101.

8 "Allegoriae super librum Turbae," Art. aurif., I, p. 155: "origo Solis"; Ventura, Theatr. chem., II (1659), p. 296: "The sun rises together with the moon in the belly of Mercurius."

9 Wei Po-yang, "An Ancient Chinese Treatise," p. 241.

10 "Epistola ad Hermannum," Theatr. chem., V (1660), p. 800; "Gloria mundi," Mus. herm., pp. 224, 244. As the arcane substance magnesia he is called the "full moon" (Rosarium, in Art. aurif., II, p. 231) and succus lunariae (p. 211). He has fallen down from the moon (Berthelot, Alch. grecs, III, vi, 9). The sign for Mercurius is ☽ in the "Book of Krates" (Berthelot, Moyen âge, III, p. 48). In the Greek Magic Papyri, Hermes is invoked as "circle of the moon" (Preisendanz, Papyri Graecae Magicae, I, p. 195).

11 Vision of Krates in Berthelot, Moyen âge, III, p. 63. As Adam with Venus in the bath, Valentinus, "Practica," Mus. herm., p. 425 (cf. Mysterium Coniunctionis, pp. 303, 383). As Sal Veneris, green and red lion (= Venus), Khunrath, Hyl. Chaos, pp. 91, 104. The substance of Mercurius consists of Venus (Mylius, Phil. ref., p. 17). Since his mother Venus is the matrix corrupta, Mercurius as her son is the puer leprosus ("Rosinus ad Sarratantam," Art. aurif., I, p. 318). In the Magic Papyri, the day of Aphrodite is associated with Hermes (Preisendanz, Pap. Graec. Mag., II, p. 120). In Al-'Irāqī the attributes of Venus are identical with those of Mercurius: sister, bride, air, green, green lion, phoenix (Holmyard, p. 420).

12 "Aurelia occulta," Theatr. chem., IV (1659), p. 480.

sents the prima materia. In the Arabic text of the *Turba*[13] quicksilver is identical with the "water of the moon and of Saturn." In the "Dicta Belini" Saturn says: "My spirit is the water that loosens the rigid limbs of my brothers."[14] This refers to the "eternal water" which is just what Mercurius is. Raymund Lully remarks that "a certain oil of a golden colour is extracted from the philosophic lead."[15] In Khunrath Mercurius is the "salt of Saturn,"[16] or Saturn is simply Mercurius. Saturn "draws the eternal water."[17] Like Mercurius, Saturn is hermaphroditic.[18] Saturn is "an old man on a mountain, and in him the natures are bound with their complement [i.e., the four elements], and all this is in Saturn."[19] The same is said of Mercurius. Saturn is the father and origin of Mercurius, therefore the latter is called "Saturn's child."[20] Quicksilver comes "from the heart of Saturn or is Saturn,"[21] and a "bright water" is extracted from the plant Saturnia, "the most perfect water and flower in the world."[22] This statement of Sir George Ripley, Canon of Bridlington, is a most remarkable parallel to the Gnostic teaching that Kronos (Saturn) is a "power of the colour of water" (ὑδατόχρους) which destroys everything, since "water is destruction."[23]

275    Like the planetary spirit of Mercurius, the spirit of Saturn is "very suited to this work."[24] One of the manifestations of Mercurius in the alchemical process of transformation is the lion, now green and now red. Khunrath calls this transformation "luring the lion out of Saturn's mountain cave." From ancient times the lion was associated with Saturn.[25] Khunrath calls him

13 Ed. Ruska, p. 204.

14 *Art. aurif.*, II, p. 379. The same in Dorn, *Theatr. chem.*, I (1659), pp. 56of.

15 Cited in Mylius, *Phil. ref.*, p. 302.

16 *Hyl. Chaos*, p. 197.

17 "Aenigma philosophorum," *Theatr. chem.*, IV (1659), pp. 458ff.

18 *Hyl. Chaos*, p. 195.

19 "Rhasis Epist." in Maier, *Symb. aur. mens.*, p. 211. Like Saturn, Mercurius combines all metals in himself (ibid., p. 531).

20 Mylius, *Phil. ref.*, p. 305. "Saturn's Chyld" in Ripley's "Medulla" (*Theatr. chem. Brit.*, p. 391).

21 Pantheus, *Ars transmut. metall.*, fol. 9ʳ.

22 Ripley, *Opera*, p. 317.

23 Hippolytus, *Elenchos*, V, 16, 2.

24 "Liber Platonis quartorum," *Theatr. chem.*, V (1660), pp. 127, 136.

25 Preller, *Griechische Mythologie*, I, p. 43.

"the lion of the Catholic tribe," [26] paraphrasing the "lion of the tribe of Judah"—an allegory of Christ.[27] He calls Saturn "the lion green and red." [28] In Gnosticism Saturn is the highest archon, the lion-headed Ialdabaoth,[29] meaning "child of chaos." But in alchemy the child of chaos is Mercurius.[30]

276    The relation to and identity with Saturn is important because Saturn is not only a *maleficus* but actually the dwelling-place of the devil himself. Even as the highest archon and demiurge his Gnostic reputation was not the best. According to one Cabalistic source, Beelzebub was associated with him.[31] Mylius says that if Mercurius were to be purified, then Lucifer would fall from heaven.[32] A contemporary marginal note in a seventeenth-century treatise in my possession explains the term sulphur, the masculine principle of Mercurius,[33] as *diabolus*. If Mercurius is not exactly the Evil One himself, he at least contains him—that is, he is morally neutral, good and evil, or as Khunrath says: "Good with the good, evil with the evil." [34] His nature is more exactly defined, however, if one conceives him as a *process* that begins with evil and ends with good. A rather deplorable but picturesque poem in *Verus Hermes* (1620) summarizes the process as follows:

> A weakling babe, a greybeard old,
> Surnamed the Dragon: me they hold
> In darkest dungeon languishing
> That I may be reborn a king.
>
> A fiery sword makes me to smart,
> Death gnaws my flesh and bones apart.

[26] *Hyl. Chaos*, p. 93.

[27] Cf. Christ as lion in the *Ancoratus* of Epiphanius and as lion cub in St. Gregory, *In Septem Psalm. Penit.*, Ps. 5 : 10 (Migne, *P.L.*, vol. 79, col. 609).

[28] *Hyl. Chaos*, p. 195.

[29] Bousset, *Hauptprobleme der Gnosis*, pp. 10, 321, 352.

[30] For Saturn's day as the last day of creation, see infra, par. 301.

[31] Codex Parisiensis 2419, fol. 277ʳ. Cited in Reitzenstein, *Poimandres*, p. 75.

[32] *Phil. ref.*, p. 18.

[33] Sulphur is the "fire hidden in Mercurius" (Trevisanus in *Theatr. chem.*, I, 1659, p. 700). He is identical with Mercurius: "Sulphur is mercurial and Mercurius is sulphureal" ("Brevis manuductio," *Mus. herm.*, p. 788).

[34] *Hyl. Chaos*, p. 186. Therefore, he says, we should pray to God for the spirit of discretion, that it may teach us the distinction between good and evil.

> My soul and spirit fast are sinking,
> And leave a poison, black and stinking.
>
> To a black crow am I akin,
> Such be the wages of all sin.
> In deepest dust I lie alone,
> O that the Three would make the One!
>
> O soul, O spirit with me stay,
> That I may greet the light of day.
> Hero of peace, come forth from me,
> Whom the whole world would like to see!

277    In this poem Mercurius is describing his own transformation, which at the same time signifies the mystic transformation of the artifex; for not only Mercurius but also what happens to him is a projection of the collective unconscious. This, as can easily be seen from what has gone before, is the projection of the individuation process, which, being a natural psychic occurrence, goes on even without the participation of consciousness. But if consciousness participates with some measure of understanding, then the process is accompanied by all the emotions of a religious experience or revelation. As a result of this, Mercurius was identified with Sapientia and the Holy Ghost. It is therefore very probable that those heresies which began with the Euchites, Paulicians, Bogomils, and Cathars, and which developed the concept of the Paraclete very much in the spirit of the founder of Christianity, were continued in alchemy, partly unconsciously and partly under a deliberate disguise.[35]

---

[35] It is conceivable that the curious name for the alchemists in Rupescissa's *La Vertu et propriété de la quinte essence,* "les poures hommes evangelisans," goes back to the Cathar *perfecti* and *pauperes Christi.* Rupescissa (Jean de Roquetaillade) lived about the middle of the 14th cent. He was a critic of the Church and the clergy (Ferguson, *Bibliotheca chemica,* II, p. 305). The Cathar trials lasted into the middle of the 14th cent.

## 8. MERCURIUS AND HERMES

278     We have already met with a number of alchemical statements which show plainly that the character of the classical Hermes was faithfully reproduced later in the figure of Mercurius. This is in part an unconscious repetition, in part a spontaneous re-experience, and finally also a conscious reference to the pagan god. There can be no doubt that Michael Maier was consciously alluding to Hermes as pointer of the way (ὁδηγός) when he said that he found on his mystic peregrination a statue of Mercurius pointing the way to paradise,[1] and that he was referring to Hermes the mystagogue when he made the Erythraean Sibyl say of Mercurius: "He will make you a witness of the mysteries of God and the secrets of nature." [2] Again, as the *divinus terna-rius*, Mercurius is the revealer of divine secrets,[3] or in the form of gold is conceived to be the soul of the arcane substance (magnesia),[4] or the fructifier of the philosophical tree.[5] In the "Epigramma Mercurio philosophico dicatum" [6] he is called the messenger of the gods, the hermeneut (interpreter), and the Egyptian "Theutius" (Thoth). Maier even goes so far as to relate him to Hermes Kyllenios when he calls him "this faithless and all too elusive Arcadian youth," [7] for in Arcadia was the sanctuary of Kyllenios, the ithyphallic Hermes. In the scholia to the "Tractatus aureus" Mercurius is named outright the "Kyllenian hero." [8] Maier's words might also be a reference to Eros. And in fact, in Rosencreutz's *Chymical Wedding*, Mer-

[1] *Symb. aur. mens.*, p. 592. [Cf. *Mysterium Coniunctionis*, pars. 276ff.]
[2] Ibid., p. 600.
[3] Dorn, in *Theatr. chem.*, I (1659), p. 547.
[4] Khunrath, *Hyl. Chaos*, p. 233.
[5] Ripley, in *Theatr. chem.*, II (1659), p. 113.
[6] *Mus. herm.*, p. 738.
[7] *Symb. aur. mens.*, p. 386.
[8] *Theatr. chem.*, IV (1659), p. 673.

curius does appear in the form of Cupid,[9] and punishes the adept for his curiosity in visiting the Lady Venus by wounding him in the hand with an arrow. The arrow is the "dart of passion" (*telum passionis*), which is also an attribute of Mercurius.[10] He is an "archer," and indeed one who "shoots without a bowstring" and is "nowhere to be found on earth," [11] so is obviously a daemon. In the Table of Symbols in Penotus[12] he is associated with nymphs, which reminds one of the pastoral god, Pan. His lasciviousness is borne out by an illustration in the *Tripus chimicus* of Sendivogius,[13] where he appears on a triumphal chariot drawn by a cock and a hen, and behind him is a naked pair of embracing lovers. In this connection may also be mentioned the numerous somewhat obscene pictures of the coniunctio in old prints, often preserved merely as pornographica. Pictures in old manuscripts of excretory acts, including vomiting, likewise belong to this sphere of the "underworldly Hermes." [14] Again, Mercurius represents the "continuous cohabitation" [15] which is found in unalloyed form in the Tantric Shiva-Shakti concept. Connections between Greek and Arabic alchemy and India are not unlikely. Reitzenstein[16] reports the story of Padmanaba from a Turkish book of folklore[17] about the forty viziers, which may date back to the time of the Moguls. Already in the first centuries of our era, Indian religious influences were at work in southern Mesopotamia, and in the second century B.C. there were Buddhist monasteries in Persia. In the royal temple of Padmanabhapura in Travancore (c. fifteenth century) I found two reliefs representing an entirely non-Indian *senex ithyphallicus* with wings. In one of them he stands up to his waist in the bowl of the moon. One is reminded of the winged ithyphal-

---

9 Also in the form of the boy showing the way and the "age-old son of the mother."

10 Ripley, *Opera,* pp. 421ff.

11 "Introit. apert.," *Mus. herm.,* p. 653.

12 *Theatr. chem.,* II (1659), facing p. 109.

13 P. 67.

14 E.g., Codex Rhenoviensis, Zurich, and Codex Vossianus, Leyden.

15 For this motif see *Symbols of Transformation,* pp. 209f.

16 *Alchemische Lehrschriften und Märchen bei den Arabern,* pp. 77f.

17 Belletête, trans., *Contes turcs.*

lic old man who pursues the "blue" or "doglike" [18] woman in Hippolytus. Kyllenios does in fact appear in Hippolytus[19] as identical on the one hand with the Logos and on the other with the wicked Korybas, the phallus, and the demiurgic principle in general.[20] Another aspect of this dark Mercurius is the mother-son incest, which may be traceable to Mandaean influences: there Nabu (Mercurius) and Istar (Astarte) form a syzygy. Astarte is the mother and love goddess throughout the whole Near East, where she is also tainted with the incest motif. Nabu is the "Messiah of the Lie," who because of his malice is punished and kept in prison by the sun.[21] The texts remind us again and again that Mercurius is "found in the dung-heaps," but they add ironically that "many have grubbed in the dung-heaps, but extracted nothing thereby." [22]

279     This dark Mercurius must once again be understood as representing the initial *nigredo* state, the lowest being a symbol of the highest and vice versa:

> Anfang und Ende
> Reichen sich die Hände.[23]

He is the uroboros, the One and All, the union of opposites accomplished during the alchemical process, of which Penotus says:[24]

Mercurius is begotten by nature as the son of nature and the fruit of the liquid element. But even as the Son of Man is begotten by the philosopher and created as the fruit of the Virgin, so must he [Mercurius] be raised from the earth and cleansed of all earthiness, then he ascends entire into the air, and is changed into spirit. Thus

---

[18] κυανοειδῆ or κυνοειδῆ. Hippolytus, *Elenchos*, V, 20, 6 and 7 (ed. Wendland) has the latter reading. The alchemical equivalents of this strange mythologem support both possibilities: Dog as Logos, psychopomp, and *filius canis coelici coloris* (puppy of celestial hue), all referring to Mercurius. [Cf. *Mysterium Coniunctionis*, pars. 174ff.]

[19] *Elenchos*, V, 7, 29.

[20] The duality of the Mercurius concept has a parallel in the syncretist views of the Naassenes, who sought to grasp and express the psychological experience of the paradoxical First Cause. But I must be content with this hint.

[21] Bousset, *Hauptprobleme der Gnosis*, pp. 43, 55, 142.

[22] *Rosarium*, in *Art. aurif.*, II, p. 243.

[23] "Beginnings and ends/Touch hands."

[24] *Theatr. chem.*, I (1659), p. 601.

is fulfilled the word of the philosopher: He ascends from earth to heaven and receives the power of Above and Below, and puts off his earthy and impure nature and clothes himself in the heavenly nature.

280    Since Penotus is here referring to the "Tabula smaragdina," it must be emphasized that he departs from the spirit of the "Tabula" in one essential point. In the version of Penotus, the ascent of Mercurius is in entire accord with the Christian transformation of the hylic into the pneumatic man. The "Tabula," on the other hand, says: "He ascends from earth to heaven and descends again to earth, and receives the power of Above and Below. His power is complete when he has returned to earth." So it is not a question of a one-way ascent to heaven, but, in contrast to the route followed by the Christian Redeemer, who comes from above to below and from there returns to the above, the *filius macrocosmi* starts from below, ascends on high, and, with the powers of Above and Below united in himself, returns to earth again. He carries out the reverse movement and thereby manifests a nature contrary to that of Christ and the Gnostic Redeemers, while on the other hand he displays a certain affinity with the Basilidian concept of the third sonship. Mercurius has the circular nature of the uroboros, hence he is symbolized by the *circulus simplex* of which he is at the same time the centre.[25] He can therefore say of himself: "I am One and at the same time Many in myself."[26] This same treatise says that the centre of the circle in man is the earth, and calls it the "salt" to which Christ referred when he said: "Ye are the salt of the earth."[27]

281    Hermes is a god of thieves and cheats, but also a god of revelation who gave his name to a whole philosophy. Seen in historical retrospect, it was a moment of the utmost significance when the humanist Patrizi proposed to Pope Gregory XIV that Hermetic philosophy should take the place of Aristotle in ecclesiastical doctrine. At that moment two worlds came into contact, which—after heaven knows what happenings!—must yet be

25 "Tractatus aureus cum scholiis," ibid., IV, p. 608.
26 "Aurelia occulta," ibid., p. 507.
27 Ibid., p. 489.

united in the future. At that time it was obviously impossible. A psychological differentiation of religious as well as scientific views is still needed before a union can begin to be brought about.[28]

[28] [This paragraph originally ended the monograph.—EDITORS.]

# 9. MERCURIUS AS THE ARCANE SUBSTANCE

282     Mercurius, it is generally affirmed, is the arcanum,[1] the prima materia,[2] the "father of all metals,"[3] the primeval chaos, the earth of paradise, the "material upon which nature worked a little, but nevertheless left imperfect."[4] He is also the ultima materia, the goal of his own transformation, the stone,[5] the tincture, the philosophic gold, the carbuncle, the philosophic man, the second Adam, the analogue of Christ, the king, the light of lights, the *deus terrestris,* indeed the divinity itself or its perfect counterpart. Since I have already discussed the synonyms and meanings of the stone elsewhere there is no need for me to go into further details now.

283     Besides being the prima materia of the lowly beginning as well as the lapis as the highest goal, Mercurius is also the process which lies between, and the means by which it is effected. He is the "beginning, middle, and end of the work."[6] Therefore he is called the Mediator,[7] Servator, and Salvator. He is a mediator like Hermes. As the *medicina catholica* and *alexipharmakon* he is the "preserver [*servator*] of the world." He is the "healer [*salvator*] of all imperfect bodies"[8] and the "image of Christ's incarnation,"[9] the *unigenitus* "consubstantial with the paren-

1 "Tract. aur. cum scholiis," *Theatr. chem.,* IV (1659), p. 608.
2 Mylius, *Phil. ref.,* p. 179; "Tract. aureus," *Mus. herm.,* p. 25; Trevisanus in *Theatr. chem.,* I (1659), p. 695.
3 "Exercit. in Turb.," *Art. aurif.,* I, p. 154.
4 *Rosarium,* ibid., II, p. 231.
5 Ventura, in *Theatr. chem.,* II (1659), p. 232: "lapis benedictus"; Dorn, in *Theatr. chem.,* I (1659), p. 510: "fiery and perfect Mercurius"; p. 520: "The Adamic stone is made out of the Adamic Mercurius in the woman Eve"; Lully, *Codicillus,* pp. 880f.: "The good that is sought is our stone and Mercurius."
6 "Tract. aur. cum scholiis," *Theatr. chem.,* IV (1659), p. 608.
7 "Exercit. in Turb.," *Art. aurif.,* I, p. 170; Ripley, *Chymische Schrifften,* p. 31; "Tract. aur. cum scholiis," p. 610: "A mediator making peace between enemies."
8 "Aquarium sap.," *Mus. herm.,* p. 111.
9 Ibid., p. 118.

235

tal hermaphrodite." [10] Altogether, in the macrocosm of nature he occupies the position which Christ holds in the *mundus rationalis* of divine revelation. But as the saying "My light surpasses all other lights" [11] shows, the claim of Mercurius goes even further, which is why the alchemists endowed him with the attributes of the Trinity[12] in order to make clear his complete correspondence to God. In Dante, Satan is three-headed and therefore three-in-one. He is the counterpart of God in the sense that he is God's antithesis. The alchemists did not hold this view of Mercurius; on the contrary, they saw him as a divine emanation harmonious with God's own being. The stress they laid on his capacity for self-generation, self-transformation, self-reproduction, and self-destruction contradicts the idea that he is a created being. It is therefore only logical when Paracelsus and Dorn state that the prima materia is an "increatum" and a principle coeternal with God. This denial of *creatio ex nihilo* is supported by the fact that in the beginning God found the Tehom already in existence, that same maternal world of Tiamat whose son we encounter in Mercurius.[13]

[10] Khunrath, *Hyl. Chaos,* p. 59.

[11] "Septem Tract. hermet.," *Ars chemica,* p. 22. *Rosarium,* p. 381: "I illumine the air with my light and warm the earth with my heat, I bring forth and nourish the things of nature, plants and stones, and with my power I take away the darkness of night, and cause day to endure in the world, and I lighten all lights with my light, even those in which there is no splendour nor greatness. For all these are of my work, when I put upon me my garments; and those who seek me, let them make peace between me and my bride." This is cited from the "Dicta Belini" (printed in Manget's *Bibl. chem.,* I, p. 478). There are variations in the text. I have quoted the passage in full because of its psychological interest.

[12] "For in the Stone are body, soul, and spirit, and yet it is one stone" ("Exercit. in Turb.," *Art. aurif.,* I, p. 170).

[13] Cf. *Psychology and Alchemy,* par. 26.

<sup>284</sup> The multiple aspects of Mercurius may be summarized as follows:

(1) Mercurius consists of all conceivable opposites. He is thus quite obviously a duality, but is named a unity in spite of the fact that his innumerable inner contradictions can dramatically fly apart into an equal number of disparate and apparently independent figures.

(2) He is both material and spiritual.

(3) He is the process by which the lower and material is transformed into the higher and spiritual, and vice versa.

(4) He is the devil, a redeeming psychopomp, an evasive trickster, and God's reflection in physical nature.

(5) He is also the reflection of a mystical experience of the artifex that coincides with the *opus alchymicum*.

(6) As such, he represents on the one hand the self and on the other the individuation process and, because of the limitless number of his names, also the collective unconscious.[1]

* * *

<sup>285</sup> Certainly goldmaking, as also chemical research in general, was of great concern to alchemy. But a still greater, more impassioned concern appears to have been—one cannot very well say the "investigation"—but rather the *experience* of the unconscious. That this side of alchemy—the μυστικά—was for so long misunderstood is due solely to the fact that nothing was known of psychology, let alone of the suprapersonal, collective unconscious. So long as one knows nothing of psychic actuality, it will be projected, if it appears at all. Thus the first knowledge of psychic law and order was found in the stars, and was later extended by projections into unknown matter. These two realms of experience branched off into sciences: astrology became astron-

---

[1] Hence the designation of Mercurius as *mare nostrum*.

omy, and alchemy chemistry. On the other hand, the peculiar connection between character and the astronomical determination of time has only very recently begun to turn into something approaching an empirical science. The really important psychic facts can neither be measured, weighed, nor seen in a test tube or under a microscope. They are therefore supposedly indeterminable, in other words they must be left to people who have an inner sense for them, just as colours must be shown to the seeing and not to the blind.

286    The store of projections found in alchemy is, if possible, even less known, and there is a further drawback which makes closer investigation extremely difficult. For, unlike the astrological constituents of character which, if negative, are at most unpleasant for the individual, though amusing to his neighbour, the alchemical projections represent collective contents that stand in painful contrast—or rather, in compensatory relation—to our highest rational convictions and values. They give the strange answers of the natural psyche to the ultimate questions which reason has left untouched. Contrary to all progress and belief in a future that will deliver us from the sorrowful present, they point back to something primeval, to the apparently hopelessly static, eternal sway of matter that makes our fondly believed-in world look like a phantasmagoria of shifting scenes. They show us, as the redemptive goal of our active, desirous life, a symbol of the inorganic—the stone—something that does not live but merely exists or "becomes," the passive subject of a limitless and unfathomable play of opposites. "Soul," that bodiless abstraction of the rational intellect, and "spirit," that two-dimensional metaphor of dry-as-dust philosophical dialectic, appear in alchemical projection in almost physical, plastic form, like tangible breath-bodies, and refuse to function as component parts of our rational consciousness. The hope for a psychology without the soul is brought to nothing, and the illusion that the unconscious has only just been discovered vanishes: in a somewhat peculiar form, admittedly, it has been known for close on two thousand years. Let us, however, not delude ourselves: no more than we can separate the constituents of character from the astronomical determinants of time are we able to separate that unruly and evasive Mercurius from the autonomy of matter. Something of the projection-carrier always clings to the projec-

tion, and even if we succeed to some degree in integrating into our consciousness the part we recognize as psychic, we shall integrate along with it something of the cosmos and its materiality; or rather, since the cosmos is infinitely greater than we are, we shall have been assimilated by the inorganic. "Transform yourselves into living philosophical stones!" cries an alchemist, but he did not know how infinitely slowly the stone "becomes." Anyone who gives serious thought to the "natural light" that emanates from the projections of alchemy will certainly agree with the Master who spoke of the "wearisomeness of the interminable meditation" demanded by the work. In these projections we encounter the phenomenology of an "objective" spirit, a true matrix of psychic experience, the most appropriate symbol for which is matter. Nowhere and never has man controlled matter without closely observing its behaviour and paying heed to its laws, and only to the extent that he did so could he control it. The same is true of that objective spirit which today we call the unconscious: it is refractory like matter, mysterious and elusive, and obeys laws which are so non-human or suprahuman that they seem to us like a *crimen laesae majestatis humanae.* If a man puts his hand to the opus, he repeats, as the alchemists say, God's work of creation. The struggle with the unformed, with the chaos of Tiamat, is in truth a primordial experience.

287     Since the psyche, when directly experienced, confronts us in the "living" substance it has animated and appears to be one with it, Mercurius is called *argentum vivum.* Conscious discrimination, or consciousness itself, effects that world-shattering intervention which separates body from soul and divides the spirit Mercurius from the *hydrargyrum,* as if drawing off the spirit into the bottle, to speak in terms of our fairytale. But since body and soul, in spite of the artificial separation, are united in the mystery of life, the mercurial spirit, though imprisoned in the bottle, is yet found in the roots of the tree, as its quintessence and living numen. In the language of the Upanishads, he is the personal atman of the tree. Isolated in the bottle, he corresponds to the ego and the principle of individuation, which in the Indian view leads to the illusion of individual existence. Freed from his prison, Mercurius assumes the character of the suprapersonal atman. He becomes the *one* animating principle of all

239

created things, the *hiranyagarbha* (golden germ),[2] the supra-personal self, represented by the *filius macrocosmi,* the *one* stone of the wise. "Rosinus ad Sarratantam" cites a saying of "Malus Philosophus"[3] which attempts to formulate the psychological relation of the lapis to consciousness: "This stone is below thee, as to obedience; above thee, as to dominion; therefore from thee, as to knowledge; about thee, as to equals."[4] Applied to the self, this would mean: "The self is subordinate to you, yet on the other hand rules you. It is dependent on your own efforts and your knowledge, but transcends you and embraces all those who are of like mind." This refers to the collective nature of the self, since the self epitomizes the wholeness of the personality. By definition, wholeness includes the collective unconscious, which as experience seems to show is everywhere identical.

288    The encounter of the poor student with the spirit in the bottle portrays the spiritual adventure of a blind and unawakened human being. The same motif underlies the tale of the swine-herd who climbed the world-tree,[5] and also forms the *leitmotiv* of alchemy. For what it signifies is the individuation process as it prepares itself in the unconscious and gradually enters consciousness. The commonest alchemical symbol for this is the tree, the *arbor philosophica,* which derives from the paradisal tree of knowledge. Here, as in our fairytale, a daemonic serpent, an evil spirit, prods and persuades to knowledge. In view of the Biblical precedent, it is not surprising that the spirit Mercurius has, to say the least, a great many connections with the dark side. One of his aspects is the female serpent-daemon, Lilith or Melusina, who lives in the philosophical tree. At the same time, he not only partakes of the Holy Spirit but, according to alchemy, is actually identical with it. We have no choice but to accept this shocking paradox after all we have learnt about the ambivalence of the spirit archetype. Our ambiguous Mercurius simply con-

[2] Cf. Maitrayana-Brāhmana Upanishad, V, 8 (Sacred Books of the East, vol. 15, p. 311). He occurs as the *spiritus vegetativus* and collective soul in the Vedanta-Sutras (ibid., vol. 34, p. 173, and vol. 48, p. 578).

[3] The treatise of Rosinus (Zosimos) is probably of Arabic origin. "Malus" might be a corruption of "Magus." The *Fihrist* of Ibn al-Nadim (A.D. 987) lists, along with writings of Rimas (Zosimos), two works by Magus one of which is entitled "The Book of the Wise Magus (?) on the Art" (Ruska, *Turba,* p. 272).

[4] *Art. aurif.,* I, p. 310.

[5] Cf. "The Phenomenology of the Spirit in Fairytales," pp. 231ff.

firms the rule. In any case, the paradox is no worse than the Creator's whimsical notion of enlivening his peaceful, innocent paradise with the presence of an obviously rather dangerous tree-snake, "accidentally" located on the very same tree as the forbidden apples.

²⁸⁹     It must be admitted that the fairytale and alchemy both show Mercurius in a predominantly unfavourable light, which is all the more striking because his positive aspect relates him not only to the Holy Spirit, but, in the form of the lapis, also to Christ and, as a triad, even to the Trinity. It looks as if it were precisely these relationships which led the alchemists to put particular stress on the dark and dubious quality of Mercurius, and this militates strongly against the assumption that by their lapis they really meant Christ. If this had been their meaning, why should they have renamed Christ the *lapis philosophorum?* The lapis is at most a counterpart or analogy of Christ in the physical world. Its symbolism, like that of Mercurius who constitutes its substance, points, psychologically speaking, to the self, as also does the symbolic figure of Christ.[6] In comparison with the purity and unity of the Christ symbol, Mercurius-lapis is ambiguous, dark, paradoxical, and thoroughly pagan. It therefore represents a part of the psyche which was certainly not moulded by Christianity and can on no account be expressed by the symbol "Christ." On the contrary, as we have seen, in many ways it points to the devil, who is known at times to disguise himself as an angel of light. The lapis formulates an aspect of the self which stands apart, bound to nature and at odds with the Christian spirit. It represents all those things which have been eliminated from the Christian model. But since they possess living reality, they cannot express themselves otherwise than in dark Hermetic symbols. The paradoxical nature of Mercurius reflects an important aspect of the self—the fact, namely, that it is essentially a *complexio oppositorum,* and indeed can be nothing else if it is to represent any kind of totality. Mercurius as *deus terrestris* has something of that *deus absconditus* (hidden god) which is an essential element of the psychological self, and the self cannot be distinguished from a God-image (except by incontestable and unprovable faith). Although I have stressed that the lapis is

6 [Cf. *Psychology and Alchemy,* ch. 5, "The Lapis-Christ Parallel," and *Aion,* ch. 5, "Christ, a Symbol of the Self."—EDITORS.]

a symbol embracing the opposites, it should not be thought of as a—so to speak—more complete symbol of the self. That would be decidedly incorrect, for actually it is an image whose form and content are largely determined by the unconscious. For this reason it is never found in the texts in finished and well-defined form; we have to combine all the scattered references to the various arcane substances, to Mercurius, to the transformation process and the end product. Although the lapis in one aspect or another is almost always the subject discussed, there is no real consensus of opinion in regard to its actual form. Almost every author has his own special allegories, synonyms, and metaphors. This makes it clear that the stone, though indeed an object of general experiment, was to an even greater extent an outcropping of the unconscious, which only sporadically crossed the borderline of subjectivity and gave rise to the vague general concept of the *lapis philosophorum*.

290     Opposed to this figure veiled in the twilight of more or less secret doctrines there stands, sharply outlined by dogma, the Son of Man and Salvator Mundi, Christ the Sol Novus, before whom the lesser stars pale. He is the affirmation of the daylight of consciousness in trinitarian form. So clear and definite is the Christ figure that whatever differs from him must appear not only inferior but perverse and vile. This is not the result of Christ's own teaching, but rather of what is taught about him, and especially of the crystal purity which dogma has bestowed upon his figure. As a result, a tension of opposites such as had never occurred before in the whole history of Christianity beginning with the Creation arose between Christ and the Antichrist, as Satan or the fallen angel. At the time of Job, Satan is still found among the sons of God. "Now there was a day," it says in Job 1 : 6, "when the sons of God came to present themselves before the Lord, and Satan came also among them." This picture of a celestial family reunion gives no hint of the New Testament "Get thee hence, Satan" (Matthew 4 : 10), nor yet of the dragon chained in the underworld for a thousand years (Rev. 20 : 2). It looks as if the superabundance of light on one side had produced an all the blacker darkness on the other. One can also see that the uncommonly great diffusion of black substance makes a sinless being almost impossible. A loving belief in such a being naturally involves cleansing one's own house of black filth. But the

filth must be dumped somewhere, and no matter where the dump lies it will plague even the best of all possible worlds with a bad smell.

291    The balance of the primordial world is upset. What I have said is not intended as a criticism, for I am deeply convinced not only of the relentless logic but of the expediency of this development. The emphatic differentiation of opposites is synonymous with sharper discrimination, and that is the *sine qua non* for any broadening or heightening of consciousness. The progressive differentiation of consciousness is the most important task of human biology and accordingly meets with the highest rewards— vastly increased chances of survival and the development of power technology. From the phylogenetic point of view, the effects of consciousness are as far-reaching as those of lung-breathing and warm-bloodedness. But clarification of consciousness necessarily entails an obscuration of those dimmer elements of the psyche which are less capable of becoming conscious, so that sooner or later a split occurs in the psychic system. Since it is not recognized as such it is projected, and appears in the form of a metaphysical split between the powers of light and the powers of darkness. The possibility of this projection is guaranteed by the presence of numerous archaic vestiges of the original daemons of light and darkness in any age. It seems likely, therefore, that the tension of opposites in Christianity is derived to a still unclarified degree from the dualism of ancient Persia, though the two are not identical.

292    There can be no doubt that the moral consequences of the Christian development represent a very considerable advance compared with the ancient Israelite religion of law. The Christianity of the synoptic gospels signifies little more than a coming to terms with issues inside Judaism, which may fairly be compared with the much earlier Buddhist reformation inside Hindu polytheism. Psychologically, both reformations resulted in a tremendous strengthening of consciousness. This is particularly evident in the maieutic method employed by Shakyamuni. But the sayings of Jesus manifest the same tendency, even if we discard as apocryphal the clearest formulation of this kind, the logion in Codex Bezae to Luke 6 : 4: "Man, if thou knowest what thou doest, thou art blessed. If thou knowest it not, thou art accursed and a transgressor of the law." At all events, the para-

ble of the unjust steward (Luke 16) has not found its way into the Apocrypha, where it would have fitted so well.

293 The rift in the metaphysical world has slowly risen into consciousness as a split in the human psyche, and the struggle between light and darkness moves to the battleground within. This shift of scene is not entirely self-evident, for which reason St. Ignatius Loyola considered it necessary to open our eyes to the conflict and impress it on our feelings by means of the most drastic spiritual exercises.[7] These efforts, for obvious reasons, had only a very limited range of application. And so, strangely enough, it was the medical men who, at the turn of the nineteenth century, were forced to intervene and get the obstructed process of conscious realization going again. Approaching the problem from a scientific angle, and innocent of any religious aim, Freud uncovered the abysmal darkness of human nature which a would-be enlightened optimism had striven to conceal. Since then psychotherapy, in one form or another, has persistently explored the extensive area of darkness which I have called the shadow. This attempt of modern science opened the eyes of only a few. However, the historic events of our time have painted a picture of man's psychic reality in indelible colours of blood and fire, and given him an object lesson which he will never be able to forget if—and this is the great question—he has today acquired enough consciousness to keep up with the furious pace of the devil within him. The only other hope is that he may learn to curb a creativity which is wasting itself in the exploitation of material power. Unfortunately, all attempts in that direction look like bloodless Utopias.

294 The figure of Christ the Logos has raised the *anima rationalis* in man to a level of importance which remains unobjectionable so long as it knows itself to be below and subject to the κύριος, the Lord of Spirits. Reason, however, has set itself free and proclaimed itself the ruler. It has sat enthroned in Notre Dame as Déesse Raison and heralded events that were to come. Our consciousness is no longer confined within a sacred temenos of otherworldly, eschatological images. It was helped to break free by a force that did not stream down from above—like the *lumen de lumine*—but came up with tremendous pressure from below and increased in strength as consciousness detached itself from the

7 *The Spiritual Exercises* (trans. Rickaby), pp. 75ff.

darkness and climbed into the light. In accordance with the principle of compensation which runs through the whole of nature, every psychic development, whether individual or collective, possesses an optimum which, when exceeded, produces an enantiodromia, that is, turns into its opposite. Compensatory tendencies emanating from the unconscious may be noted even during the approach to the critical turning-point, though if consciousness persists in its course they are completely repressed. The stirrings in the darkness necessarily seem like a devilish betrayal of the ideal of spiritual development. Reason cannot help condemning as unreasonable everything that contradicts it or deviates from its laws, in spite of all evidence to the contrary. Morality can permit itself no capacity for change, for whatever it does not agree with is inevitably immoral and has therefore to be repressed. It is not difficult to imagine the multitude of energies which must flow off into the unconscious under such conscious domination.

295    Hesitantly, as in a dream, the introspective brooding of the centuries gradually put together the figure of Mercurius and created a symbol which, according to all the psychological rules, stands in a compensatory relation to Christ. It is not meant to take his place, nor is it identical with him, for then indeed it could replace him. It owes its existence to the law of compensation, and its object is to throw a bridge across the abyss separating the two psychological worlds by presenting a subtle compensatory counterpoint to the Christ image. The fact that in *Faust* the compensatory figure is not, as one might almost have expected from the author's classical predilections, the wily messenger of the gods, but, as the name "Mephistopheles" [8] shows, a *familiaris* risen from the cesspits of medieval magic, proves, if anything, the ingrained Christian character of Goethe's consciousness. To the Christian mentality, the dark antagonist is always the devil. As I have shown, Mercurius escapes this prejudice by only a hair's breadth. But he escapes it, thanks to the fact that he scorns to carry on opposition at all costs. The magic of his name enables him, in spite of his ambiguity and duplicity, to keep outside the split, for as an ancient pagan god he possesses a natural undividedness which is impervious to logical and moral contradictions. This gives him invulnerability and incorrupti-

8 [From L. *mephitis*, a noxious exhalation from the earth.—TRANSLATOR.]

bility, the very qualities we so urgently need to heal the split in ourselves.

296     If one makes a synopsis of all the descriptions and alchemical pictures of Mercurius, they form a striking parallel to the symbols of the self derived from other sources. One can hardly escape the conclusion that Mercurius as the lapis is a symbolic expression for the psychological complex which I have defined as the self. Similarly, the Christ figure must be viewed as a self symbol, and for the same reasons. But this leads to an apparently insoluble contradiction, for it is not at first clear how the unconscious can shape two such different images from one and the same content, which moreover possesses the character of totality. Certainly the centuries have done their spiritual work upon these two figures, and one is inclined to assume that both have been in large measure anthropomorphized during the process of assimilation. For those who hold that both figures are inventions of the intellect, the contradiction is quickly resolved. It then merely reflects the subjective psychic situation: the two figures would stand for man and his shadow.

297     This very simple and obvious solution is, unfortunately, founded on premises that do not stand up to criticism. The figures of Christ and the devil are both based on archetypal patterns, and were never invented but rather *experienced*. Their existence preceded all cognition of them,[9] and the intellect had no hand in the matter, except to assimilate them and if possible give them a place in its philosophy. Only the most superficial intellectualism can overlook this fundamental fact. We are actually confronted with two different images of the self, which in all likelihood presented a duality even in their original form. This duality was not invented, but is an autonomous phenomenon.

298     Since we naturally think from the standpoint of consciousness, we inevitably come to the conclusion that the split between consciousness and the unconscious is the sole cause of this duality. But experience has demonstrated the existence of a preconscious psychic functioning and of corresponding autonomous factors, the archetypes. Once we can accept the fact that the voices and delusions of the insane and the phobias and obsessions of the neurotic are beyond rational control, and that the ego cannot voluntarily fabricate dreams but simply dreams what

[9] Evidence for this is the widespread motif of the two hostile brothers.

it has to, then we can also understand that the gods came first and theology later. Indeed, we must go a step further and assume that in the beginning there were two figures, one bright and one shadowy, and only afterwards did the light of consciousness detach itself from the night and the uncertain shimmer of its stars.

299    So if Christ and the dark nature-deity are autonomous images that can be directly experienced, we are obliged to reverse our rationalistic causal sequence, and instead of deriving these figures from our psychic conditions, must derive our psychic conditions from these figures. This is expecting a good deal of the modern intellect but does not alter the logic of our hypothesis. From this standpoint Christ appears as the archetype of consciousness and Mercurius as the archetype of the unconscious. As Cupid and Kyllenios, he tempts us out into the world of sense; he is the *benedicta viriditas* and the *multi flores* of early spring, a god of illusion and delusion of whom it is rightly said: "Invenitur in vena / Sanguine plena" (He is found in the vein swollen with blood). He is at the same time a Hermes Chthonios and an Eros, yet it is from him that there issues the "light surpassing all lights," the *lux moderna,* for the lapis is none other than the figure of light veiled in matter.[10] It is in this sense that St. Augustine quotes I Thessalonians 5 : 5, "Ye are all the children of light, and the children of the day: we are not of the night, nor of darkness," and distinguishes two forms of knowledge, a *cognitio vespertina* and a *cognitio matutina,* the first corresponding to the *scientia creaturae* and the second to the *scientia Creatoris.*[11] If we equate *cognitio* with consciousness, then Augustine's thought would suggest that the merely human and natural consciousness gradually darkens, as at nightfall. But just as evening gives birth to morning, so from the darkness arises a new light, the *stella matutina,* which is at once the evening and the morning star—Lucifer, the light-bringer.

300    Mercurius is by no means the Christian devil—the latter

10 Cf. the saying of Ostanes concerning the stone that has a spirit.
11 "For the knowledge of the creature, in comparison with the knowledge of the Creator, is but a twilight; and so it dawns and breaks into morning when the creature is drawn to the love and praise of the Creator. Nor is it ever darkened, save when the Creator is abandoned by the love of the creature."—*The City of God,* XI, vii.

could rather be said to be a "diabolization" of Lucifer or of Mercurius. Mercurius is an adumbration of the primordial light-bringer, who is never himself the light, but a φωσφόρος who brings the light of nature, the light of the moon and the stars which fades before the new morning light. Of this light St. Augustine says that it will never turn to darkness unless the Creator is abandoned by the love of his creatures. But this, too, belongs to the rhythm of day and night. As Hölderlin says in "Patmos";

> and shamefully
> A power wrests away the heart from us;
> For the Heavenly each demand sacrifice,
> But if it should be withheld,
> Never has that led to good.

301    When all visible lights are extinguished one finds, according to the words of the wise Yajñavalkya, the light of the self. "What then is the light of man? Self is his light. It is by the light of the self that a man rests, goes forth, does his work and returns." [12] Thus, with Augustine, the first day of creation begins with self-knowledge, *cognitio sui ipsius*,[13] by which is meant a knowledge not of the ego but of the self, that objective phenomenon of which the ego is the subject.[14] Then, following the order of the days of creation in Genesis, comes knowledge of the firmament, of the earth, the sea, the plants, the stars, the animals of the water and air, and finally, on the sixth day, knowledge of the land animals and of *ipsius hominis,* of man himself. The *cognitio matutina* is self-knowledge, but the *cognitio vespertina* is knowledge of man.[15] As Augustine describes it, the *cognitio*

[12] Brihadāranyaka Upanishad, IV, 3, 6 (cf. Hume, *The Thirteen Principal Upanishads*, p. 133).

[13] "And when it [the creature's knowledge] comes to the knowledge of itself, that is one day" (Et hoc cum facit in cognitione sui ipsius, dies unus est).—*The City of God*, XI, vii. This may be the source for the strange designation of the lapis as "filius unius diei." [Cf. *Mysterium Coniunctionis*, pp. 335, 504.]

[14] "Since no knowledge is better than that by which man knows himself, let us examine our thoughts, words, and deeds. For what does it avail us if we are to investigate carefully and understand rightly the nature of all things, yet do not understand ourselves?"—*Liber de Spiritu et Anima*, LI (Migne, *P.L.*, vol. 40, cols. 816–17). This book is a very much later treatise falsely attributed to Augustine.

[15] "Wherefore the knowledge of the creature, which is in itself evening knowledge, was in God morning knowledge; for the creature is more plainly seen in

*matutina* gradually grows old as it loses itself in the "ten thousand things" and finally comes to man, although one would expect this to have happened already with the onset of self-knowledge. But if this were true, Augustine's parable would have lost its meaning by contradicting itself. Such an obvious lapse cannot be ascribed to so gifted a man. His real meaning is that self-knowledge is the *scientia Creatoris*,[16] a morning light revealed after a night during which consciousness slumbered, wrapped in the darkness of the unconscious. But the knowledge arising with this first light finally and inevitably becomes the *scientia hominis,* the knowledge of man, who asks himself: "Who is it that knows and understands everything? Why, it is myself." That marks the coming of darkness,[17] out of which arises the seventh day, the day of rest: "But the rest of God signifies the rest of those who rest in God." [18] The Sabbath is therefore the day on which man returns to God and receives anew the light of the *cognitio matutina*. And this day has no evening.[19] From the symbological standpoint it may not be without significance that Augustine had in mind the pagan names of the days of the week. The growing darkness reaches its greatest intensity on the day of Venus (Friday), and changes into Lucifer on Sat-

---

God than it is seen in itself."—*Dialogus Quaestionum LXV,* Quaest. XXVI (Migne, *P.L.,* vol. 40, col. 741).

[16] The *Liber de Spiritu et Anima* attributes very great importance to self-knowledge, as being an essential condition for union with God. "There are some who seek God through outward things, forsaking that which is in them, and in them is God. Let us therefore return to ourselves, that we may ascend to ourselves. . . . At first we ascend to ourselves from these outward and inferior things. Secondly, we ascend to the high heart. . . . In the third ascent we ascend to God" (chs. LI–LII; Migne, *P.L.,* vol. 40, col. 817). The "high heart" (*cor altum;* also "deep heart") is the mandala divided into four, the *imago Dei,* or self. The *Liber de Spiritu et Anima* is in the mainstream of Augustinian tradition. Augustine himself says (*De vera religione LXXII,* Migne, *P.L.,* vol. 34, col. 154): "Go not outside, return into yourself; truth dwells in the inner man. And if you find that you are by nature changeable, transcend yourself. But remember that when you transcend yourself, you must transcend yourself as a reasoning soul."

[17] "Evening descends when the sun sets. Now the sun has set for man, that is to say, that light of justice which is the presence of God."—*Enarrationes in Ps. XXIX,* II, 16 (trans. Hobgin and Corrigan, I, p. 308). These words refer to Ps. 30 : 5 (A.V.): "Weeping may tarry for the night but joy cometh in the morning."

[18] *The City of God,* XI, viii. Cf. also *Dialog. Quaest. LXV,* Quaest. XXVI.

[19] *Confessions* (trans. Sheed), p. 289.

urn's day. Saturday heralds the light which appears in full strength on Sun-day. As I have shown, Mercurius is closely related not only to Venus but more especially to Saturn. As Mercurius he is *juvenis,* as Saturn *senex.*

302    It seems to me that Augustine apprehended a great truth, namely that every spiritual truth gradually turns into something material, becoming no more than a tool in the hand of man. In consequence, man can hardly avoid seeing himself as a knower, yes, even as a creator, with boundless possibilities at his command. The alchemist was basically this sort of person, but much less so than modern man. An alchemist could still pray: "Purge the horrible darknesses of our mind," but modern man is already so darkened that nothing beyond the light of his own intellect illuminates his world. "Occasus Christi, passio Christi." [20] That surely is why such strange things are happening to our much lauded civilization, more like a *Götterdämmerung* than any normal twilight.

303    Mercurius, that two-faced god, comes as the *lumen naturae,* the Servator and Salvator, only to those whose reason strives towards the highest light ever received by man, and who do not trust exclusively to the *cognitio vespertina.* For those who are unmindful of this light, the *lumen naturae* turns into a perilous *ignis fatuus,* and the psychopomp into a diabolical seducer. Lucifer, who could have brought light, becomes the father of lies whose voice in our time, supported by press and radio, revels in orgies of propaganda and leads untold millions to ruin.

20 *Enarrationes in Ps. CIII,* Sermo III, 21 (Migne, *P.L.,* vol. 37, col. 1374).

# V

# THE PHILOSOPHICAL TREE

[Originally written for a Festschrift planned to mark the 70th birthday of Gustav Senn, professor of botany at the University of Basel. Owing to the untimely death of Professor Senn, the Festschrift did not appear, and Jung's essay, entitled "Der philosophische Baum," was published in the *Verhandlungen der Naturforschenden Gesellschaft Basel,* LVI (1945): 2, 411–23. A revised and expanded version appeared in *Von den Wurzeln des Bewusstseins: Studien über den Archetypus* (Psychologische Abhandlungen, Vol. IX; Zurich, 1954), from which the present translation is made.—Editors.]

All theory, my friend, is grey,
But green life's golden tree.
*Faust I*

# INDIVIDUAL REPRESENTATIONS
# OF THE TREE SYMBOL

304     An image which frequently appears among the archetypal configurations of the unconscious is that of the tree or the wonder-working plant. When these fantasy products are drawn or painted, they very often fall into symmetrical patterns that take the form of a mandala. If a mandala may be described as a symbol of the self seen in cross section, then the tree would represent a profile view of it: the self depicted as a process of growth. I shall not discuss here the conditions under which these pictures are produced, for I have already said all that is necessary in my essays "A Study in the Process of Individuation" and "Concerning Mandala Symbolism." The examples I now propose to give all come from a series of pictures in which my patients tried to express their inner experiences.

305     In spite of the diversity of the tree symbol, a number of basic features may be established. In the first part of my essay I shall comment on the pictures that have been reproduced and then, in the second part, give an account of the philosophical tree in alchemy and its historical background. My case material has not been influenced in any way, for none of the patients had any previous knowledge of alchemy or of shamanism. The pictures were spontaneous products of creative fantasy, and their only conscious purpose was to express what happens when unconscious contents are taken over into consciousness in such a way that it is not overwhelmed by them and the unconscious not subjected to any distortion. Most of the pictures were done by patients who were under treatment, but some by persons who

were not, or were no longer, under any therapeutic influence. I must emphasize that I carefully avoided saying anything in advance that might have had a suggestive effect. Nineteen of the thirty-two pictures were done at a time when I myself knew nothing of alchemy, and the rest before my book *Psychology and Alchemy* was published.

### Figure 1

306    The tree stands by itself on an island in the sea. Its great size is indicated by the fact that the upper part of it is cut off by the edge of the picture. The buds and the little white flowers suggest the coming of spring, when the great tree, whose age far exceeds the span of human existence, will awaken to new life. The solitariness of the tree and its axial position in the centre of the picture bring to mind the world-tree and the world-axis—attributes with which the tree symbol is almost universally endowed. These traits give expression to the inner process at work in the painter, and show that it has nothing to do with his personal psychology. Here the tree represents a symbol that is universal and alien to the personal consciousness. It is possible, however, that the painter was making conscious use of the Christmas tree in order to illustrate his inner state.

### Figure 2

307    The abstract stylization and the position of the tree on the globe of the earth illustrate the feeling of spiritual isolation. To make up for this, the perfect symmetry of the crown points to a union of opposites. This is the motivating force and the goal of the individuation process. If the painter of such a picture neither identifies with the tree nor is assimilated by it,[1] he will not succumb to the danger of an auto-erotic isolation, but will only be intensely aware that his ego personality is confronted with a symbolical process he must come to terms with because it is just as real and undeniable as his ego. One can deny and nullify this process in all sorts of ways, but in doing so all the values represented by the symbol are lost. A naïvely curious mind will naturally cast round for a rational explanation, and if it does not

[1] Cf. *Aion*, pp. 24ff.

find one at once it either makes do with a facile and completely inadequate hypothesis or else turns away in disappointment. It seems to be very hard for people to live with riddles or to let them live, although one would think that life is so full of riddles as it is that a few more things we cannot answer would make no difference. But perhaps it is just this that is so unendurable, that there are irrational things in our own psyche which upset the conscious mind in its illusory certainties by confronting it with the riddle of its existence.

### Figure 3

308    The picture shows a tree of light that is at the same time a candelabrum. The abstract form of the tree points to its spiritual nature. The ends of the branches are lighted candles illuminating the darkness of an enclosed space, perhaps a cave or vault. The secret and hidden nature of the process is thus emphasized and its function made clear: the illumination of consciousness.

### Figure 4

309    Although cut out of gold-foil, the tree is realistic. It is still in the wintry, leafless state of sleep. It rises up against a cosmic background and bears in its branches a large golden ball, probably the sun. The gold indicates that though the painter does not yet have a living, conscious relation to this content, she nevertheless has an emotional intuition of its great value.

### Figure 5

310    The tree is leafless but bears little red flowers, harbingers of spring. The branches are tipped with flames, and fire leaps up from the water out of which the tree is growing. So the tree is also something like the jet of a fountain. The symbol of the fountain, the *fontina,* is known in alchemy; in the alchemical pictures it is often shown as a medieval town fountain,[2] and the upright part in the middle would correspond to the tree. The union of fire and water expresses the union of opposites. The picture bears out the alchemical saying: "Our water is fire."

2 [Cf. "The Psychology of the Transference," Fig. 1.]

### Figure 6

311     The tree is red and looks like a branch of coral. It is not reflected in the water, but grows simultaneously downwards and upwards. The four mountains in the lower half of the picture are not reflections either, for their opposites are five mountains. This suggests that the lower world is not a mere reflection of the upper world, but that each is a world in itself. The tree stands in the middle between two walls of rock, representing the opposites. The four mountains also appear in Figure 24.

### Figure 7

312     The tree has broken with irresistible force through the earth's crust, heaving up mountainous boulders on either side. The painter is expressing an analogous process in himself, which runs its course of necessity and cannot be checked by any amount of resistance. Since the boulders are snow-capped mountains, the tree has the cosmic character of the world-tree.

### Figure 8

313     The tree is leafless, but its branches end in little flames like a Christmas tree. Instead of growing from the earth or water, it grows out of the body of a woman. The painter was a Protestant and was not familiar with the medieval symbolism of Mary as earth and *stella maris*.

### Figure 9

314     The tree is old and huge and stands on a tangle of roots which is strongly emphasized. Two dragons are approaching from left and right. In the tree there is a boy who has climbed up to watch the dragons. We are reminded of the dragons that guard the tree of the Hesperides, and of the snakes that guard the hoard. The conscious side of the boy is in a rather precarious situation because the modicum of security it has just acquired is liable to be devoured again by the unconscious. The turmoil of the unconscious is indicated by the tangled roots as well as by the evidently enormous dragons and the tininess of the child.

The tree itself is not threatened inasmuch as its growth is independent of human consciousness. It is a natural process, and it is even dangerous to risk disturbing it since it is guarded by dragons. But because this is a natural and ever-present process it can give man protection provided that he summons up courage enough to climb into the tree despite its guardians.

### Figure 10

315 Once again we meet the two dragons, but in the form of crocodiles. The tree is abstract and doubled, and is loaded with fruit. For all its duality it gives the impression of being a single tree. This, besides the ring that unites the two trees, points to the union of opposites which are also represented by the two crocodiles. In alchemy, Mercurius is symbolized by the tree as well as by the dragon. He is notoriously "duplex," is both masculine and feminine, and is made one in the hierosgamos of the chymical wedding. The synthesis of Mercurius forms an important part of the alchemical procedure.

### Figure 11

316 Although tree and snake are both symbols of Mercurius, they stand for two different aspects on account of the latter's dual nature. The tree corresponds to the passive, vegetative principle, the snake to the active, animal principle. The tree symbolizes earthbound corporeality, the snake emotionality and the possession of a soul. Without the soul the body is dead, and without the body the soul is unreal. The union of the two, which is plainly imminent in this picture, would mean the animation of the body and the materialization of the soul. Similarly, the tree of paradise is an earnest of the real life which awaits the first parents when they emerge from their initial childlike (i.e., pleromatic) state.

### Figure 12

317 Tree and snake are united. The tree bears leaves, and the sun rises in its midst. The roots are snakelike.

### Figure 13

318     The stylized tree has in its trunk a locked door leading to a hidden recess. The middle branch is decidedly snakelike and bears a luminous body like a sun. The simple-minded bird, representing the painter, weeps because it has forgotten the key to the door. It obviously suspects that there is something valuable inside the tree.

### Figure 14

319     The same painter did a number of variations on the treasure motif. Here and in the next picture it takes the form of a hero myth: the hero discovers a sealed coffer in a hidden vault, with a wonderful tree growing out of it. The little green dragon that follows the hero like a dog corresponds to the familiar spirit of the alchemists, the mercurial serpent or *draco viridis*. Mythlike fantasies of this kind are not infrequent, and are more or less the equivalent of alchemical parables or didactic tales.

### Figure 15

320     The tree does not want to yield up the treasure and clasps the coffer all the tighter. When the hero touches the tree, a flame springs out at him. It is a fire-tree, like that of the alchemists, and like the world-tree of Simon Magus.

### Figure 16

321     Many birds are sitting on the leafless tree, a motif found also in alchemy. The tree of wisdom (Sapientia) is surrounded by numerous birds, as in Reusner's *Pandora* (1588), or else the birds fly round the figure of Hermes Trismegistus, as in *De chemia* (1566).[3] The tree is shown guarding a treasure. The precious stone hidden in its roots recalls Grimm's fairytale of the bottle hidden in the roots of the oak tree, which contained the spirit Mercurius. The stone is a dark blue sapphire, but its connection with the sapphire stone in Ezekiel, which played a great role in ecclesiastical allegory, was not known to the painter. The

---

3 [Cf. *Psychology and Alchemy*, Figs. 231 (the *Pandora* picture) and 128 (the Hermes picture). *De chemia* is the work by Zadith Senior.—Editors.]

special virtue of the sapphire is that it endows its wearer with chastity, piety, and constancy. It was used as a medicament for "comforting the heart." [4] The lapis was called the "sapphirine flower." [5] Birds, as winged beings, have always symbolized spirit or thoughts. So the many birds in our picture mean that the thoughts of the painter are circling round the secret of the tree, the treasure hidden in its roots. This symbolism underlies the parables of the treasure in the field, the pearl of great price, and the grain of mustard seed. Only, the alchemists were not referring to the Kingdom of Heaven, but to the "admirandum Mundi Maioris Mysterium" (the wondrous mystery of the macrocosm), and it looks as though the sapphire in the picture has a similar meaning.

### Figure 17

322    This was done by the same painter, but at a much later stage, when the same idea reappeared in differentiated form. Her technical ability has also improved. The birds have been replaced by heart-shaped blossoms, for the tree has now come alive. Its four branches correspond to the square-cut sapphire, whose "constancy" is emphasized by the little uroboros encircling it. In Horapollo the uroboros is the hieroglyph of eternity.[5a] For the alchemists the self-devouring dragon was hermaphroditic because it begot and gave birth to itself. They therefore called the sapphirine flower (i.e., the lapis) "Hermaphroditi flos saphyricus." Constancy and permanence are expressed not only in the age of the tree but also in its fruit, the lapis. Like a fruit, the lapis is at the same time a seed, and although the alchemists constantly stressed that the "seed of corn" dies in the earth, the lapis despite its seedlike nature is incorruptible. It represents, just as man does, a being that is forever dying yet eternal.

### Figure 18

323    The picture shows an initial state in which the tree is unable to raise itself from the earth in spite of its cosmic nature. It is a

4 Ruland, *A Lexicon of Alchemy*, p. 286.
5 "Epistola ad Hermannum," *Theatrum chemicum*, V (1660), p. 804.
5a [But cf. *The Hieroglyphics of Horapollo*, tr. Boas, p. 57.]

case of regressive development, probably due to the fact that while the tree has a natural tendency to grow away from the earth into a cosmic space filled with strange astronomical and meteorological phenomena, this would mean reaching up into an eerie unearthly world and making contact with otherworldly things which are terrifying to the earthbound rationality of the natural man. The upward growth of the tree would not only endanger the supposed security of his earthly existence but would be a threat to his moral and spiritual inertia, because it would carry him into a new time and a new dimension where he could not get along without making considerable efforts at re-adaptation. The patient in these cases is held back not by mere cowardice, but by a largely justifiable fear that warns him of the exacting demands of the future, without his being aware of what these demands are or knowing the dangers of not fulfilling them. His anxious resistance and aversion seem quite ground-less, and it is only too easy for him to rationalize them away and, with a little assistance, brush them aside like a troublesome in-sect. The result is just the psychic situation shown by our pic-ture: an inturned growth which throws the supposedly solid earth into increasing turmoil. Secondary fantasies then arise which, according to the patient's disposition, revolve round sex-uality or the power drive or both. This leads sooner or later to the formation of neurotic symptoms and to the almost unavoid-able temptation for both patient and analyst to take these fan-tasies seriously as causative factors and thus to overlook the real task.

*Figure 19*

324    This picture, done by a different patient, shows that Figure 18 is not unique. It is, however, no longer a case of unconscious regression, but of one that is becoming conscious, which is why the tree has a human head. We cannot tell from the picture whether the witchlike tree nymph is clutching at the earth or rising unwillingly from it. This is in complete accord with the divided state of the patient's consciousness. But the upright trees standing around show that within or outside herself she has per-ceived living examples of the way trees ought to grow. She has

interpreted the tree as a witch and the regressive growth as the cause of magical effects of a sinister nature.

### Figure 20

325    The tree stands in isolation dominating the top of a mountain. It is thick with leaves and has in its trunk a doll swathed in multicoloured wrappings. The painter was reminded of the harlequin motif. The fool's motley shows that she felt she was dealing with something crazy and irrational. She was conscious of having thought of Picasso, whose style was apparently suggested by the harlequin's dress. The association probably has a deeper meaning and is not just a superficial combination of ideas. It was this same impression of irrationality that led to the regressive development in the two previous pictures. All three cases are concerned with a process which the modern mind finds extremely disturbing, and not a few of my patients have openly confessed their fear of any such autonomous development of their psychic contents. In these cases it is of the greatest therapeutic value if one can demonstrate to them the historicity of their apparently unique and unassimilable experiences. When a patient begins to feel the inescapable nature of his inner development, he may easily be overcome by a panic fear that he is slipping helplessly into some kind of madness he can no longer understand. More than once I have had to reach for a book on my shelves, bring down an old alchemist, and show my patient his terrifying fantasy in the form in which it appeared four hundred years ago. This has a calming effect, because the patient then sees that he is not alone in a strange world which nobody understands, but is part of the great stream of human history, which has experienced countless times the very things that he regards as a pathological proof of his craziness.

### Figure 21

326    The doll in the previous picture contained a sleeping human figure undergoing metamorphosis like the larva of an insect. Here as well the tree acts as a mother to the human figure hidden in its trunk. This accords with the traditional maternal significance of the tree.

*Figure 22*

327    The development has gone a stage further. The sleeping figure awakes, half emerges from the tree and makes contact with
the animal world. The "tree-born" is thus characterized not
only as a child of nature but as an autochthonous primordial
being growing treelike out of the earth. The tree nymph is an
Eve who, instead of being taken from Adam's side, has come into
existence independently. This symbol is evidently intended to
compensate not merely the one-sidedness and unnaturalness of
the ultra-civilized man but also, and in particular, the biblical
myth of the secondary creation of Eve.

*Figure 23*

328    The tree nymph carries the sun and is a figure composed of
light. The wavy band in the background is red, and consists of
living blood that flows round the grove of transformation. This
indicates that the transformation is not just an airy fantasy, but
is a process that reaches down into the somatic sphere or even
arises from it.

*Figure 24*

329    This drawing combines various motifs from the preceding
pictures but lays particular stress on the light- or sun-symbol,
which is represented as a quaternity. It is watered by four rivers
each done in a different colour. They flow down from what the
patient called four heavenly or "metaphysical" mountains. We
met the four mountains earlier in Figure 6. They also appear in
the drawing of a male patient which I mentioned in *Psychology
and Alchemy*,[6] where the four rivers are reproduced in Figs. 62
and 109. In all these cases I am as little responsible for the number four as I am for all the other alchemical, Gnostic, and mythological quaternities. My critics seem to have the funny idea that
I have a special liking for the number four and therefore find it
everywhere. Just for once, they should look into an alchemical
treatise—but that is evidently too much of an effort. Since "sci-

6 Par. 217.

entific" criticism is ninety per cent prejudice, it invariably takes a very long time for the facts to be recognized.

330    The number four, like the squaring of the circle, is not accidental, which is why—to take an example known even to my critics—there are not three or, for that matter, five directions, but precisely four. I will only mention in passing that, besides this, the number four possesses special mathematical properties. The quaternary elements in our picture, as well as accentuating the light-symbol, amplify it in such a way that it is not difficult to see what is meant: an acceptance of wholeness by the little female figure, an intuitive apprehension of the self.

## Figure 25

331    A still later stage is shown here. The female figure is no longer just the recipient or bearer of the light-symbol but has been drawn into it. The personality is more powerfully affected than in the previous picture. This increases the danger of identification with the self—a danger not to be taken lightly. Anyone who has passed through such a development will feel tempted to see the goal of his experiences and efforts in union with the self. Indeed, there are suggestive precedents for this, and in the present case it is altogether possible. But there are certain factors in the picture which enable the painter to distinguish her ego from the self. She was an American woman who was influenced by the mythology of the Pueblo Indians: the corn-cobs characterize the female figure as a goddess. She is fastened to the tree by a snake, and thus forms an analogy to the crucified Christ, who, as the self, was sacrificed for earthly humanity, just as Prometheus was chained to the rock. Man's efforts to achieve wholeness correspond, as the divine myth shows, to a voluntary sacrifice of the self to the bondage of earthly existence. Here I will only point out this correspondence without going into it further.

332    In this picture, then, there are so many elements of the divine myth that unless the patient's consciousness were utterly blinded (and there are no signs of this) she could easily discriminate between ego and self. At this stage it is important not to succumb to an inflation, such as would inevitably supervene with all its very unpleasant consequences if, at the moment when the self became recognizable, she identified with it and

thus blinded herself to the insight she had attained. If the natural impulse to identify with the self is recognized, one then has a good chance of freeing oneself from a state of unconsciousness. But if this opportunity is overlooked or not used, the situation does not remain the same as before but gives rise to a repression coupled with dissociation of the personality. The development of consciousness which the realization of the self might have led to turns into a regression. I must emphasize that this realization is not just an intellectual act but is primarily a moral one, in comparison with which intellectual understanding is of secondary importance. For this reason, the symptoms I have described can also be observed in patients who, from inferior motives which they will not admit, refuse a task that has been laid upon them by fate.

333    I would like to draw attention to a further peculiarity: the tree has no leaves, and its branches could just as well be roots. All its vitality is concentrated in the centre, in the human figure that represents its flower and fruit. A person whose roots are above as well as below is thus like a tree growing simultaneously downwards and upwards. The goal is neither height nor depth, but the centre.

## Figure 26

334    The idea developed in the previous picture reappears here in slightly variant form. This idea may truly be said to be in the process of delineating itself, for the conscious mind of the patient follows only a vague feeling which gradually takes shape in the act of drawing. She would have been quite unable to formulate beforehand, in a clear concept, what she wanted to express. The structure of the picture is a mandala divided into four, with the midpoint displaced downwards, beneath the feet of the figure. The figure stands in the upper section and thus belongs to the realm of light. This mandala is an inversion of the traditional Christian cross, whose long upright is below the cross-beam. We must conclude from the picture that the self was realized first of all as an ideal figure of light which nonetheless takes the form of an inverted Christian cross. Whereas the latter's point of intersection is near the top, so that the goal of unconscious striving towards the centre is displaced upwards, the

downward glance of the figure shows that her goal should lie below. The short upright beam of the cross of light rests on the black earth, and the figure holds in her left hand a black fish drawn from the dark sphere. The *mudrā*-like,[7] hesitant gesture of the right hand, directed towards the fish coming from the left (i.e., from the unconscious), is characteristic of the patient, who had studied theosophy and was therefore under Indian influence. The fish has a soteriological significance whether conceived in Christian or in Indian terms (as the fish of Manu and as an avatar of Vishnu). There is reason to conjecture (see Figure 29) that the patient was acquainted with the Bhagavadgītā, which says (X, 31): "Among fishes I am Makara." Makara is a dolphin or a species of Leviathan, and is one of the symbols of the *svādhisthāna-chakra* in Tantric yoga. This centre is localized in the bladder and is characterized as the water region by the fish and moon symbols. As the *chakras* are presumably equivalent to earlier localizations of consciousness (the *anāhata-chakra*, for instance, corresponding to the φρένες of the Greeks),[8] *svādhisthāna* is probably the earliest localization of all. From this region comes the fish symbol with its age-old numen. We are reminded of the "days of Creation," of the time when consciousness arose, when the primordial unity of being was barely disturbed by the twilight of reflection,[9] and man swam like a fish in the ocean of the unconscious. In this sense the fish signifies a restoration of the pleromatic paradisal state or, in the language of Tibetan Tantrism, of the Bardo.[10]

335    The plants at the foot of the figure are really rooted in the air. Tree, tree nymph, and plants are all lifted up from the earth or, more probably, are on the point of coming down to it. This is also suggested by the fish as emissary of the deep. The situation is in my experience an unusual one and may be due to theosophical influences. Filling the conscious mind with ideal conceptions is a characteristic feature of Western theosophy, but not the confrontation with the shadow and the world of darkness. One does not become enlightened by imagining figures of light,

7 *Mudrā* (Skt.) is a ritual or magical gesture.
8 For the *chakra* theory see Avalon, *The Serpent Power*, and concerning φρένες see Onians, *The Origins of Thought*, pp. 14ff.
9 [Cf. supra, par. 301.]
10 Cf. Evans-Wentz, *The Tibetan Book of the Dead*, pp. 101ff.

but by making the darkness conscious. The latter procedure, however, is disagreeable and therefore not popular.

### Figure 27

336     Unlike the prèvious picture, this one is thoroughly Western, although it comes into the archetypal category of the god's birth from the tree or lotus blossom. The archaic plant world of the carboniferous era illustrates the mood the painter was in when she intuitively apprehended the birth of the self. The human figure growing out of the archaic plant represents the union and quintessence of the four heads at its base, in agreement with the alchemical view that the lapis is composed of four elements. Awareness of the archetype imbues the experience with a primeval character. The division of the plant into six segments, like so much else in the realm of fantasy, may be purely accidental. Nevertheless, it should not be forgotten that the number six (the *senarius*) was considered in ancient times "aptissimus generationi" (most fit for generation).[11]

### Figure 28

337     Drawn by the same patient as Figure 26. The female figure wearing a tree-crown is in a sitting position—again a displacement downwards. The black earth that was previously far below her feet is now in her body as a black ball, in the region of the *manipūra-chakra,* which coincides with the solar plexus. (The alchemical parallel to this is the "black sun.")[12] This means that the dark principle, or shadow, has been integrated and is now felt as a kind of centre in the body. Possibly this integration is connected with the eucharistic significance of the fish: eating the fish brings about a *participation mystique* with God.[13]

338     Numerous birds are flying round the tree. As birds represent winged thoughts, we must conclude that the female figure progressively detached itself from the world of thought as the centre

---

11 Philo, "De opificio mundi" [see Colson/Whitaker trans., I, p. 13].
12 Synonymous with the *caput corvi* and *nigredo.* Cf. Mylius, *Philosophia reformata,* p. 19, who says that in the *nigredo* the *anima media natura* holds sway. This is roughly the equivalent of what I call the collective unconscious.
13 Cf. *Aion,* pp. 113ff.

was displaced downwards, and that the thoughts have consequently returned to their natural element. She and her thoughts were identical before, with the result that she was raised above the earth as though she were an aerial being, while her thoughts lost their freedom of flight, since they had to support the whole weight of a human being in the air.

*Figure 29*

339    The process of separation from the world of thought continues. A masculine daemon,[14] who has obviously woken up all of a sudden, reveals himself with an air of triumph: he is the animus, the personification of masculine thinking in a woman (and of her masculine side in general). The patient's previous state of suspension turns out to have been an animus possession, which is now sloughed off. Differentiation between her feminine consciousness and her animus means liberation for both. The sentence "I am the Game of the gambler" probably refers to Bhagavadgītā X, 36: "I am the game of dice."[15] Krishna says this of himself. The section in which it occurs begins with the words (X, 20–21): "I am the self, O Gudākesha! seated in the hearts of all beings. I am the beginning and the middle and the end also of all beings. I am Vishnu among the Ādityas;[16] the beaming sun among the shining bodies."

340    Like Krishna, Agni is the game of dice in the Shatapatha-Brāhmana of the Yajur-Veda: "He (the Adhvaryu)[17] throws down the dice, with 'Hallowed by Svāhā,[18] strive ye with Surya's[19] rays for the middlemost place among brethren!' For that gaming ground is the same as 'ample Agni,' and those dice are his coals, thus it is him (Agni) he thereby pleases."[20]

14 By which I mean the Greek δαίμων and not the Christian devil.
15 Sacred Books of the East, VIII, p. 91. Unfortunately I was unable to ask the patient about the source of this saying, but I know she was acquainted with the Bhagavadgītā.
16 Solar gods.
17 The priest who recites the prayers of the Yajur-Veda.
18 *Svāhā* is one of the holy syllables. It is uttered at the recitation of the Veda during thunderstorms (Apastamba, in SBE, II, p. 45) and at sacrifices to the gods (ibid., p. 48).
19 Surya = sun.
20 SBE, XLI, p. 112.

341    Both texts relate light, sun, and fire, as well as the god, to the game of dice. Similarly the Atharva-Veda speaks of the "brilliancy that is in the chariot, in the dice, in the strength of the bull, in the wind, Parjanya,[21] and in the fire of Varuna." [22] The "brilliancy" corresponds to what is known in primitive psychology as "mana," and in the psychology of the unconscious as "libido investment" or "emotional value" or "feeling tone." In point of emotional intensity, which is a factor of decisive importance for the primitive consciousness, the most heterogeneous things—rain, storm, fire, the strength of the bull, and the passionate game of dice—can be identical. In emotional intensity, game and gambler coincide.

342    This train of thought may help to explain the mood of the picture, which expresses liberation and relief. The patient evidently felt this moment as a breath of the divine numen. As the Bhagavadgītā text makes clear, Krishna is the self, with which the patient's animus identifies. This identification is a regular occurrence when the shadow, the dark side, has not been sufficiently realized. Like every archetype, the animus has a Janus face, and besides this the limitation of being a merely masculine principle. He is therefore quite unfitted to represent totality, whether of God or the self. He must be content with an intermediate position. The generalizations characteristic of Indian theosophy, however, induced the patient, by a kind of psychological short-circuit, to identify the animus at least provisionally with wholeness, and to put him in the place of the self.

*Figure 30*

343    The same motif as in Figure 29 is shown here in differentiated form by the painter of Figure 2. The stylization of the leafless tree is highly abstract, and so is the gnomelike figure in a monkish robe. The outstretched arms express balance and the cross motif. The ambiguity of the figure is emphasized on the one hand by the bird coming down from above,[23] painted like a fantastic flower, and on the other by the obviously phallic arrow rising up from the roots below. The daemon thus represents an

21 Rain-god.
22 SBE, XLII, p. 116. [Varuna = sky-god.]
23 Cf. the stork on the tree, infra, pars. 415ff.

equilibrium of left and right as well as a union of intellect and sexuality, just as the alchemical Mercurius duplex, in the form of the lapis, is a quaternity composed of the four elements. The striped band running down the globe recalls the mercurial band which I discussed in "A Study in the Process of Individuation." [24] There the patient herself took it to be quicksilver.

344    The concept of the alchemical Mercurius derives exclusively from masculine psychology and symbolizes the typical opposition in a man between Nous and sex, owing to the absence of the feminine Eros which would unite them. The animus figure in the picture is a piece of purely masculine psychology that has crystallized out of a woman's psyche during the process of individuation.

## *Figure 31*

345    Embroidery by the same patient as before. The tree has turned into a blossoming lotus plant, with the gnomelike figure sitting in the flower, reminding us that the lotus is the birthplace of the gods. Eastern influences are evident in these two figures, but of a different kind from those we met in Figures 28 and 29. It is not a matter of Indian theosophy learnt and imitated in the West, for the present patient was born in the East without, however, consciously absorbing its theosophy. But inwardly she was permeated by it so thoroughly that it had a very disturbing effect on her psychic balance.

346    In this figure the daemon has visibly taken a back place, but the crown of the tree has undergone a rich development: leaves and blossoms appear, forming a wreath, a corona, round a flowerlike centre. The alchemists used the term *corona* or *diadema cordis tui* (diadem of thy heart), meaning by it a symbol of perfection. The crown appears in the figure as the crowning point or culmination of the developmental process symbolized by the tree. It has taken the form of a mandala, the "golden flower" of Chinese and the "sapphirine flower" of Western alchemy. The animus no longer usurps the place of the self, but has been transcended by it.

[24] P. 292, Picture 3.

## Figure 32

347    I reproduce this picture with some hesitation because, unlike the others, its material is not "pure" in the sense of being uninfluenced by what the patient read or picked up by hearsay. It is nevertheless "authentic" in so far as it was produced spontaneously and expresses an inner experience in the same way as all the others, only much more clearly and graphically because the patient was able to avail herself of ideas that fitted her theme better. Consequently, it combines a great deal of material which I do not want to comment on here, as its essential components have already been discussed or will be found in the relevant literature. The actual composition of the tree is at any rate original. I reproduce the picture only to show what kind of influence a knowledge of the symbolism can have on such configurations.

348    I will bring my picture series to a close with a literary example of spontaneous tree symbolism. In his poem "Soleil Noir" (1952), Noël Pierre, a modern French poet who is personally unknown to me, has described an authentic experience of the unconscious:

> J'arrivais de la sorte sur une crape
> D'où bâillait un aven embué.
> Une foule compacte s'y pressait
> Des quatre directions. Je m'y mêlais.
> Je remarquais que nous roulions en spirale,
> Un tourbillon dans l'entonnoir nous aspirait.
> Dans l'axe, un catalpa gigantesque
> Où pendaient les cœurs des morts,
> A chaque fourche avait élu résidence
> Un petit sage qui m'observait en clignotant.
>
> . . . . . . . . . . . . . . . . . .
>
> Jusqu'au fond, où s'étalent les lagunes.
> Quelle quiétude, au Nœud des Choses!
> Sous l'Arbre de ma Vie, le Dernier Fleuve
> Entoure une Ile où s'érige
> Dans les brumes un cube de roche grise,
> Une Forteresse, la Capitale des Mondes.[25]

25 [From verses XXVI–XXVII; with kind permission of Editions Pierre Seghers. "And then I came upon an outcropping of rock From which yawned a mist-covered pit.

349    The main characteristics of this description are: (1) Universal midpoint of mankind. (2) Spiral rotation.[26] (3) Tree of life and death. (4) The heart as the centre of man's vitality in conjunction with the tree.[27] (5) Natural wisdom in the form of a dwarf. (6) The island as seat of the tree of life. (7) Cube = philosophers' stone = treasure guarded by the tree.

> A dense crowd was hastening thither
> From the four quarters. I mingled among them.
> I noticed that we were turning in a spiral.
> A vortex in the funnel sucked us in.
> In the centre, a colossal catalpa
> On which hung the hearts of the dead.
> At each fork had chosen to settle
> A little sage who winked as he saw me.
>
> . . . . . . . . . . . . . . . . . . .
>
> At the very bottom, where the lagoons spread out,
> What quietness, at the hub of things!
> Beneath the tree of my life, the last river
> Surrounds an island where there rises
> In the mists a cube of grey rock,
> A Fortress, the Capital of the Worlds."]

26 Often represented by a snake.
27 Cf. the heart-shaped leaves and flowers in Figs. 14, 15, 17.

## II

## ON THE HISTORY AND INTERPRETATION
## OF THE TREE SYMBOL

### 1. THE TREE AS AN ARCHETYPAL IMAGE

350     After having given some examples of spontaneously produced, modern tree symbols in the first part of this essay, I should
like, in the second part, to say something about the historical
background of the tree symbol in order to justify my title "The
Philosophical Tree." Although it will be obvious to anyone acquainted with the material that my examples are nothing more
than special instances of a widely disseminated tree symbolism,
it is nevertheless of importance, in interpreting the individual
symbols, to know something about their historical antecedents.
Like all archetypal symbols, the symbol of the tree has undergone a development of meaning in the course of the centuries. It
is far removed from the original meaning of the shamanistic
tree, even though certain basic features prove to be unalterable.
The psychoid form underlying any archetypal image retains its
character at all stages of development, though empirically it is
capable of endless variations. The outward form of the tree may
change in the course of time, but the richness and vitality of a
symbol are expressed more in its change of meaning. The aspect
of meaning is therefore essential to the phenomenology of the
tree symbol. Taken on average, the commonest associations to
its meaning are growth, life, unfolding of form in a physical and
spiritual sense, development, growth from below upwards and
from above downwards, the maternal aspect (protection, shade,
shelter, nourishing fruits, source of life, solidity, permanence,
firm-rootedness, but also being "rooted to the spot"), old age,
personality,[1] and finally death and rebirth.

[1] In the dream of Nebuchadnezzar the king himself is a tree. There is a very

The tree bears buds and white blossoms. It stands on an island. In the background is the sea

Fig. 1

The tree stands on the globe, and reminded the painter of the baobab whose roots burst the planetoid on which St. Exupéry's *Little Prince* dwelt. It also recalls the world-tree of Pherekydes, the shamanic tree, and the world-axis

Fig. 2

Abstract tree represented as seven-branched candelabrum or Christmas tree. The lights symbolize the illumination and expansion of consciousness

Fig. 3

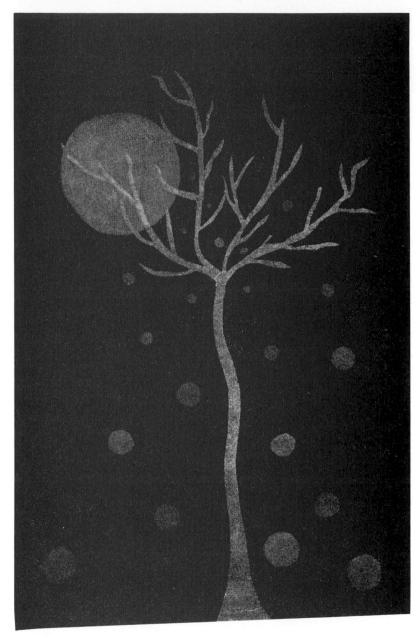

Montage in gold-foil, analogous to the alchemical *arbor aurea* and cosmic tree.
The golden globes are heavenly bodies

Fig. 4

The tree grows in water. It bears red flowers, but it consists also of fire licking up from the water, and the branches are tipped with flame

Fig. 5

The tree is painted bright red, and grows in the water simultaneously upwards
and downwards

Fig. 6

The tree thrusts up from below and breaks through the earth's surface

Fig. 7

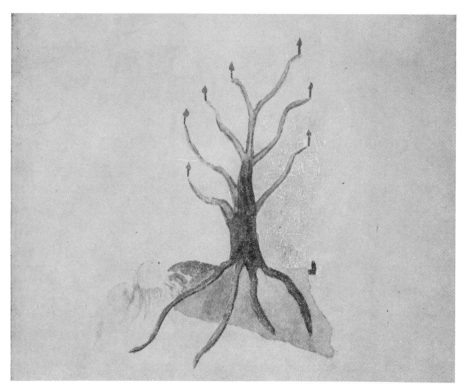

Its branches tipped with flame, the tree grows out of the body of a woman. She is synonymous with earth and water, an embodiment of the idea that the tree is a process originating in the unconscious. Cf. the Mexican world-tree which grows in the belly of the earth goddess (Lewis Spence, *The Gods of Mexico,* p. 58)

Fig. 8

Drawing by an eleven-year-old boy

Fig. 9

Union of opposites represented by two trees growing into one another and joined by a ring. The crocodiles in the water are the separated opposites, which are therefore dangerous

Fig. 10

The vertical growth of the tree contrasts with the horizontal movement of the snake. The snake is about to take up its abode in the tree of knowledge

Fig. 11

Corresponding to the sun in the branches, the snake in the roots of the tree
wears a halo, an indication of the successful union of tree and snake

Fig. 12

The tree has 4 + 1 branches. The central branch bears the sun, the other four bear stars. The tree is hollow inside and is shut by a door. The bird weeps "because it has forgotten the key"

Fig. 13

This and the following picture come from a series depicting the hero myth. The hero is accompanied by a familiar in the form of a small, green, crowned dragon. The tree grows out of a coffer containing the secret treasure

Fig. 14

The tree clasps the coffer in its roots, and a flame springs out of a leaf as the hero
touches it

Fig. 15

Done by the same patient at an earlier stage. In the roots of the tree a sapphire
lies hidden

Fig. 16

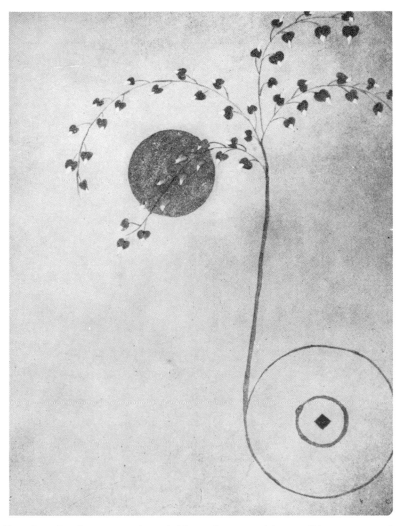

Done later by the same patient. A blossoming tree with sun disk grows out of a magic circle enclosing the uroboros with the sapphire at the centre

Fig. 17

The cosmic tree is caught by the earth and cannot grow upwards

Fig. 18

The same regressive state (depicted by a different painter), but coupled with greater consciousness

Fig. 19

The tree has a cosmic character, with a multicoloured doll hidden in its trunk

Fig. 20

The same motif done by a different patient. The sleeping figure is now visible

Fig. 21

The hidden figure awakens and half emerges from the tree. The snake whispers in her
ear; bird, lion, lamb, and pig complete the paradisal scene

Fig. 22

The tree itself assumes human form and carries the sun. In the background is a
wavy band of blood, surging rhythmically round the island

Fig. 23

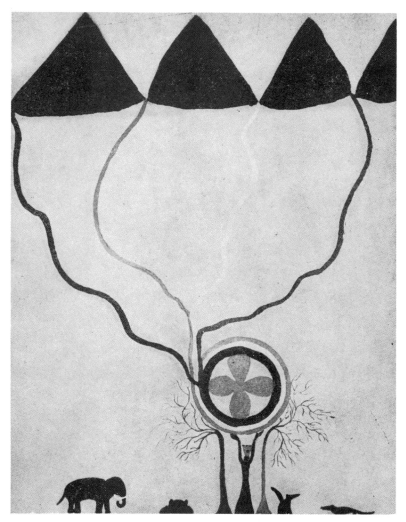

Done by the same painter as Figures 13–17. A female figure has taken the place of the tree. The sun disk is now a symbol of individuation, and is characterized as such by the quaternity fed by four different-coloured rivers flowing down from four mountains, and flanked by four animals. The scene is paradisal

Fig. 24

The tree is a female figure encircled by a snake and holding two globes of light.
The cardinal points are marked by corn-cobs and four animals: bird, tortoise, lion,
and grasshopper

Fig. 25

Most of the tree has been replaced by a female figure, the lower part taking the
form of a cross. Below is the earth, in the sky a rainbow

Fig. 26

The tree stands in a forest of prehistoric mare's-tails. It grows like the pistil of a flower (in six stages) from a calyx bearing four human heads. A woman's head rises out of the petals

Fig. 27

Drawn by the same patient as Figure 26. The foliage growing out of the woman's head is surrounded by flying birds

Fig. 28

Drawn by the same patient, but here the tree grows out of a man's head rising
above the rainbow

Fig. 29

Painted by the same patient as Figure 2. A stylized world-tree surmounting a globe with a multicoloured band running down it. The trunk is a daemonic masculine figure with a bird coming down from above and a phallic symbol rising up from below

Fig. 30

Made by the same patient. The tree has turned into a lotus with a gnomelike figure inside. His head is encircled by a mandala with a flowerlike centre, surrounded by a wreath or corona

Fig. 31

Here again the tree is painted like a flower, and symbolizes the union of a number of opposites. Below, a swan and a catlike creature; then Adam and Eve, hiding their faces in shame; then a kingfisher with fish and a three-headed snake; in the centre, the four cherubim of Ezekiel, flanked by sun and moon; then the flower of light with a crowned boy inside; at the top, a bird with a shining egg and a crowned serpent, and two hands pouring water out of a jug

Fig. 32

351     This characterization is the deposit of many years of research into the statements of individual patients. Even the layman reading this essay will be struck by the amount of material from fairytale, myth, and poetry that appears in the illustrations. In this connection it is astonishing how relatively seldom the persons I interrogated were conscious of sources of this kind. The main reasons for this are: (1) In general, people think little, if at all, about the origins of dream images, and still less about myth motifs. (2) The sources have been forgotten. (3) The sources were never in any sense conscious; that is to say, the images are new, archetypal creations.

352     The third possibility is much less rare than one might suppose. On the contrary, it occurs so frequently that comparative research into symbols becomes unavoidable in elucidating the spontaneous products of the unconscious. The widely held view that mythologems or myth motifs[2] are always connected with a tradition proves untenable, since they may reappear anywhere, at any time, and in any individual regardless of tradition. An image can be considered archetypal when it can be shown to exist in the records of human history, in identical form and with the same meaning. Two extremes must be distinguished here: (1) The image is clearly defined and is consciously connected with a tradition. (2) The image is without doubt autochthonous, there being no possibility let alone probability of a tradition.[3] Every degree of mutual contamination may be found between these two extremes.

353     In consequence of the collective nature of the image it is often impossible to establish its full range of meaning from the associative material of a single individual. But since it is of importance to do this for practical therapeutic purposes, the necessity of comparative research into symbols for medical psychology becomes evident on these grounds also.[4] For this purpose the

---

ancient, indeed primitive idea that the tree actually represents the life of a man; for instance, a tree is planted at the birth of a child, and its and the child's fates are identical. "Therefore the tree is the image and mirror of our condition" (Alciati, *Emblemata cum commentariis,* p. 888b).

2 Including figures of speech.

3 It is not always easy to prove this, because the tradition is often unconscious yet is recalled cryptomnesically.

4 The relation is similar to that between comparative anatomy and human

investigator must turn back to those periods in human history when symbol formation still went on unimpeded, that is, when there was still no epistemological criticism of the formation of images, and when, in consequence, facts that in themselves were unknown could be expressed in definite visual form. The period of this kind closest to us is that of medieval natural philosophy, which reached its zenith in the seventeenth century, and in the eighteenth century gradually left the field to science. It attained its most significant development in alchemy and Hermetic philosophy. Here, as in a reservoir, were collected the most enduring and the most important mythologems of the ancient world. It is significant that Hermetic philosophy was, in the main, practised by physicians.[5]

## 2. THE TREE IN THE TREATISE OF JODOCUS GREVERUS

354    I would now like to show how the phenomenology of the tree is reflected in the medium of the epoch immediately preceding the one just mentioned. Holmberg,[1] who wrote a comprehensive study of the tree of life, says that it is "mankind's most magnificent legend," thus confirming that the tree occupies a central position in mythology and is so widespread that its ramifications are to be found everywhere. The tree appears frequently in the medieval alchemical texts and in general represents the growth of the arcane substance and its transformation into the philosophical gold (or whatever the name of the goal may be). We read in the treatise of Pelagios that Zosimos had said the transformation process was like "a well-tended tree, a watered plant, which, beginning to ferment because of the plentiful water, and sprouting in the humidity and warmth of the air, puts forth blossoms and fruits by virtue of the great sweetness and special quality ($\pi o \iota \acute{o} \tau \eta \tau \iota$) of nature." [2]

---

anatomy, with the difference that in psychology the comparative findings have a practical as well as a theoretical importance.

5 We can say this not only because very many well-known alchemists were physicians, but also because chemistry in those days was essentially a pharmacopeia. The object of the quest was not merely the *aurum philosophicum seu potabile,* but the *medicina catholica,* the panacea and alexipharmic.

1 Holmberg, *Der Baum des Lebens,* p. 9.

2 Berthelot, *Collection des anciens alchimistes grecs,* IV, i, 12.

355    A typical example of this process is to be found in the treatise
of Jodocus Greverus, which was first printed in Leiden, 1588.[3]
The whole opus is depicted as the sowing and nurturing of the
tree in a well-tended garden, into which nothing extraneous
might enter. The soil consists of purified Mercurius; Saturn,
Jupiter, Mars, and Venus form the trunk (or trunks)[4] of the tree,
and the sun and moon supply their seeds. These planetary names
refer partly to the corresponding metals, but we can see what
they meant from the author's qualifying remark: "For there
enters into this work not the common gold, nor the common
Mercurius, nor the common silver, nor anything else that is
common, but [the metals] of the Philosophers." [5] The ingredients of the work might therefore be anything. At any rate they
are imaginary ones, even though they were expressed outwardly
by chemical substances. The planetary names refer ultimately
not only to metals but, as every alchemist knew, to the (astrological) temperaments, that is, to psychic factors. These consist
of instinctive dispositions which give rise to specific fantasies and
desires and so reveal their character. Avarice as one of the original motives of the royal art is still apparent in the term *aurum
non vulgi,* though it is just here that we discern the change of
motivation and the displacement of the goal to another plane. In
the parable that comes at the end of the treatise the wise old man
says to the adept: "Son, lay aside the snares of worldly appe-
tites." [6] Even when, as is often undoubtedly the case, the procedure given by an author has no other aim than the production
of the common gold, the psychic meaning of the opus nevertheless comes through in the symbolic nomenclature he employs in
spite of his conscious attitude. In the treatise of Greverus this
stage has been overcome and it is openly admitted that the goal

3 "Secretum nobilissimum et verissimum Venerabilis Viri Domini Iodoci Greveri
Presbyteri," as reprinted in *Theatrum chemicum,* III (1659), pp. 699–722.
4 The text has: "Saturnus, Jupiter, etc. sunt trunci," which might mean that
there are several trunks, or that the trunk consists of the four. Evidently Michael
Maier, who cites Greverus (*Symbola aureae mensae,* p. 269), was not clear about
this either, for he ascribes to Greverus the view that Mercurius is the root, Saturn, Jupiter, Mars, and Venus are the trunk and branches, sun and moon the
leaves and flowers of the tree. In my opinion he correctly understands the four
as the classical tetrasomia (see infra).
5 "Secretum," p. 700.
6 P. 720.

of the opus is "not of this world." Accordingly, at the conclusion of his treatise on the "universal process of our work," [7] the author avows that it is a "gift of God, containing the secret of the undivided oneness of the Holy Trinity. O most excellent science, theatre of all nature and its anatomy, earthly astrology,[8] proof of God's omnipotence, testimony to the resurrection of the dead, example of the remission of sins, infallible proof of the judgment to come and mirror of eternal blessedness." [9]

356    A modern reader of this hymnlike paean of praise cannot help feeling that it is exaggerated and out of key, for one cannot imagine how the science of alchemy could, for instance, contain the Holy Trinity. Such enthusiastic comparisons with the mysteries of religion had already caused offence in the Middle Ages.[10] Far from being rarities, they even became a *leitmotiv* of certain treatises in the seventeenth century, which however had their precursors in the thirteenth and fourteenth centuries. In my view they should not always be taken as spurious mystification, for the authors had something definite in mind. They obviously saw a parallel between the alchemical process and religious ideas—a parallel which is certainly not immediately perceptible to us. A bridge between two such very different realms of thought can be constructed only when we take into account the factor common to both: the *tertium comparationis* is the psychological element. Naturally an alchemist would have defended himself just as indignantly against the charge that his ideas about chemical substances were fantasies as would a metaphysician today, who still thinks that his statements amount to more than anthropomorphisms. Just as the alchemist was unable to distinguish between things as they are and the notions he had about them, so the modern metaphysician still believes that his views give valid expression to their metaphysical object. It

[7] P. 721.
[8] "Anatomia" and "astrologia terrestris" are specifically Paracelsan concepts. Accordingly the *terminus a quo* for the treatise is the second half of the 16th cent. "Astrologia terrestris" might also be translated as the "earthly firmament" of Paracelsus.
[9] ". . . argumentum omnipotentiae Dei, testimonium resurrectionis mortuorum, exemplum remissionis peccatorum, infallibile futuri iudicii experimentum et speculum aeternae beatitudinis." "Secretum," p. 721.
[10] Cf. the refusal of the Basel printer, Conrad Waldkirch, to include *Aurora consurgens* I in *Artis auriferae*. See *Psychology and Alchemy,* par. 464.

obviously never occurred to either of them that a great diversity of views concerning their respective objects has been held since earliest times. But unlike metaphysicians, and unlike theologians in particular, the alchemists displayed no polemical tendencies; at most they lamented the obscurity of the authors whom they could not understand.

357 It is clear to every reasonable person that in both cases we are concerned primarily with ideas born of fantasy—which is not to say that their unknown object does not exist. No matter what the ideas refer to, they are always organized by the same psychic laws, that is, by the archetypes. In their way the alchemists realized this when they insisted on the parallelism between their ideas and religious ones, as when Greverus compares his synthetic process with the Trinity. The common archetype in this case is the number three. As a Paracelsist, he must have been acquainted with the Paracelsan triad of sulphur, salt, and Mercurius. Sulphur belongs to the sun or represents it, and salt stands in the same relation to the moon. However, he says nothing about a synthesis of this kind.[11] Sun and moon supply the seeds that are planted in the earth (= Mercurius), and presumably the four other planets form the trunk of the tree. The four that are to be united into one refer to the tetrasomia of Greek alchemy, where, corresponding to the planets, they stand for lead, tin, iron, and copper.[12] Hence in his process of *henosis* (unification or synthesis), as Michael Maier correctly understood it,[13] what Greverus had in mind was not the three basic Paracelsan substances but the ancient tetrasomia, which at the end of his treatise he compares with the "union of persons in the Holy Trinity." For him the triad of sun, moon, and Mercurius was the starting point, the initial material as it were, in so far as it signified the seed of the tree and the earth in which it was sown. This is the so-called *coniunctio triptativa*. But here he is concerned with the *coniunctio tetraptiva*,[14] whereby the four

11 He does mention, however, gold, silver, and mercury as initial ingredients which have to be prepared and purified first, so that "common substances" (*vulgaria*) may become "physical ones" (*physica*) (p. 702). Here "physical" means *non vulgi*, i.e., symbolic.

12 Berthelot, *Les Origines de l'alchimie*, p. 59.

13 Supra, par. 355, n. 4.

14 "Triptativa coniunctio: id est, Trinitatis unio fit ex corpore, spiritu et anima. . . . Sic ista Trinitas in essentia est unitas: quia coaeternae simul sunt et

are joined in the "union of persons." This is a characteristic example of the dilemma of three and four, which plays a great role in alchemy as the well-known axiom of Maria Prophetissa.[15]

### 3. THE TETRASOMIA

358    The aim of the tetrasomia is the reduction (or synthesis) of a quaternio of opposites to unity. The names of the planets themselves indicate two dyads, one benevolent (Jupiter and Venus), the other malefic (Saturn and Mars), and such dyads often constitute an alchemical quaternity.[1] Zosimos gives the following description of the transformation process that is needed for the preparation of the tincture:

> You have need of an earth formed from two bodies and a water formed from two natures to water it. When the water has been mingled with the earth . . . the sun must act on this clay and transform it into stone. This stone must be burnt, and that burning will bring out the secret of this matter, that is to say its spirit, which is the tincture[2] sought by the philosophers.[3]

As the text shows, the synthesis depends on the unification of a double dyad. This is expressed particularly clearly in another archetypal form of the same idea: in the structure of the royal marriage, which follows that of the cross-cousin marriage.[4]

359    As a rule, the lapis is synthesized from the quaternity of the elements or from the ogdoad of elements plus qualities (cold/warm, moist/dry). Similarly Mercurius, known from ancient times as *quadratus*, is the arcane substance through whose

---

coaequales. Tetraptiva coniunctio dicitur principiorum correctio." (The threefold coniunctio: that is, the union of the Trinity is composed of body, spirit, and soul. . . . Thus the Trinity is in its essence a unity for they are coeternal and coequal. The fourfold coniunctio is called the correction of the principles.)— "Scala philosophorum," *Art. aurif.*, II, p. 138. The *coniunctio tetraptiva* is called the "noblest coniunctio" because it produces the lapis by uniting the four elements.

15 *Psychology and Alchemy,* pars. 26, 209.

1 "And in our opus there are two earths and two waters."—"Scala phil.," *Art. aurif.*, II, p. 137.

2 According to the "Book of Krates," the tincture is a "fiery and gaseous poison."— Berthelot, *La Chimie au moyen âge*, III, p. 67.

3 Ibid., p. 82.

4 Cf. "The Psychology of the Transference," ch. 2.

transformation the lapis, or goal of the opus, is produced. Thus in the love-magic of Astrampsychos the invocation to Hermes says:

Your names . . . are in the four corners of the heavens. I know also your forms, which are: in the East you have the form of an ibis, in the West you have the form of a dog-headed baboon, in the North you have the form of a serpent, but in the South you have the form of a wolf. Your plant is the grape,[5] which in that place is the olive.[6] I know also your wood: it is ebony, etc.[7]

360    The fourfold Mercurius is also the tree or its *spiritus vegeta-tivus*. The Hellenistic Hermes is on the one hand an all-encompassing deity, as the above attributes show, but on the other hand, as Hermes Trismegistus, he is the arch-authority of the alchemists. The four forms of Hermes in Egyptian Hellenism are clearly derived from the four sons of Horus. A god with four faces is mentioned as early as the Pyramid Texts of the fourth and fifth dynasties.[8] The faces obviously refer to the four quarters of heaven—that is, the god is all-seeing. Budge points out that in chapter CXII of the Egyptian Book of the Dead the same god appears as the ram of Mendes with four heads.[9] The original Horus, who represented the face of heaven, had long hair hanging down over his face, and these strands of hair were associated with the four pillars of Shu, the air god, which supported the four-cornered plate of the sky. Later the four pillars became associated with the four sons of Horus, who replaced the old gods of the four quarters of heaven. Hapi corresponded to

---

[5] *Vitis* was the name given to the philosophical tree in late antiquity, and the opus was called the "vintage" (*vindemia*). An Ostanes quotation in Zosimos (Berthelot, *Alch. grecs*, III, vi, 5) says: "Press the grape." Cf. Hoghelande in *Theatr. chem.*, I (1659), p. 180: "Man's blood and the red juice of the grape is our fire." *Uvae Hermetis* = "philosophical water" (Ruland, *Lexicon*, p. 325). Concerning the "true vine" see the interpretation in *Aurora consurgens* II (*Art. aurif.*, I, p. 186). *Vinum* is a frequent synonym for the *aqua permanens*. Cf. "Hermes the vintager" in Berthelot, *Alch. grecs*, VI, v. 3.

[6] The olive is the equivalent of the grape inasmuch as both are pressed and yield a precious juice.

[7] Preisendanz, *Papyri Graecae Magicae*, II, pp. 45f.

[8] Pyramid Text of Pepi I: "Homage to thee, O thou who hast four faces which rest and look in turn upon what is in Kenset. . . ." (Budge, *The Gods of the Egyptians*, I, p. 85). Kenset was the first nome (district) of ancient Egypt, the region of the first cataract (ibid., II, p. 42).

[9] Ibid., I, p. 496. For illustration, see ibid., II, p. 311.

the North, Tuamutef to the East, Amset to the South, and Qebhsennuf to the West. They played a large role in the cult of the dead, watching over the life of the dead man in the underworld. His two arms corresponded to Hapi and Tuamutef, his legs to Amset and Qebhsennuf. The Egyptian quaternity consisted of two dyads, as is evident from the text of the Book of the Dead: "Then said Horus to Re, Give me two divine brethren in the city of Pe and two divine brethren in the city of Nekhen, who [have sprung] from my body." [10] The quaternity is in fact a *leitmotiv* in the ritual for the dead: four men carry the coffin with the four Canopic jars, there are four sacrificial animals, all instruments and vessels are fourfold. Formulas and prayers are repeated four times, etc.[11] It is evident from this that the quaternity was of special importance for the dead man: the four sons of Horus had to see to it that the four parts (i.e., the wholeness) of the body were preserved. Horus begot his sons with his mother Isis. The incest motif, which was continued in Christian tradition and extended into late medieval alchemy, thus begins far back in Egyptian antiquity. The four sons of Horus are often shown standing on a lotus before their grandfather Osiris, Mestha[12] having a human head, Hapi the head of an ape, Tuamutef the head of a jackal, and Qebhsennuf the head of a hawk.

361    The analogy with the vision of Ezekiel (chapters 1 and 10) is at once apparent. There the four cherubim had "the likeness of a man." Each of them had four faces, a man's, a lion's, an ox's, and an eagle's, so that, as with the four sons of Horus, one quarter was human and three quarters animal. In the love-magic of Astrampsychos, on the other hand, all four forms are animal, probably because of the magic purport of the incantation.[13]

362    In keeping with the Egyptian predilection for multiples of four, there are 4 x 4 faces in the vision of Ezekiel.[14] Moreover

[10] Ibid., I, p. 497; cf. p. 210.
[11] I, p. 491.
[12] A later form of Amset.
[13] The one human head would indicate consciousness of an aspect or function of the individual psyche. Horus as the rising sun is the enlightener, just as the vision of Ezekiel signifies enlightenment. On the other hand magic, if it is to be effective, always presupposes unconsciousness. This would explain the absence of the human face.
[14] Cf. the symbolism of the self, whose totality is characterized by four quaternions: *Aion*, pp. 242ff.

each of the cherubim has a wheel. In later commentaries the four wheels were interpreted as Merkabah, the chariot.[15] Corresponding to the four pillars of Shu and the four sons of Horus as gods of the four quarters, who bear up the floor of the sky, there was "a firmament as the colour of terrible crystal, stretched forth over the heads" of the cherubim. On it stood the throne of him who had "the appearance of a man," the counterpart of Osiris, who with the help of the older Horus and of Set had climbed up to heaven.

363    The four wings of the cherubim recall the winged female genies who protect the coffin of Pharaoh. Each of the Horus sons had a female counterpart who fulfilled this same tutelary function. The cherubim, too, were protective genies, as is apparent from Ezekiel 28 : 14 and 16.[16] The apotropaic significance of the quaternity is borne out by Ezekiel 9 : 4, where the prophet, at the behest of the Lord, sets a cross[17] on the foreheads of the righteous to protect them from punishment. It is evidently the sign of God, who himself has the attribute of quaternity. The cross is the mark of his protégés. As attributes of God and also symbols in their own right, the quaternity and the cross signify wholeness. Thus Paulinus of Nola says:

Extended on the four arms of the wood of the cross, he reached out to the four quarters of the world, that he might draw together unto life the peoples from every shore; and because Christ our God by the death of the cross shows himself all things to all men, that life may come into being and evil be destroyed, A and Ω stand beside the cross, each letter by its three strokes displaying a different figure in threefold wise, a single meaning perfected in triple form.[18]

---

[15] The old pagodas in India are actually stone chariots on which the gods are enthroned. In Daniel 7 : 9, the Ancient of Days sits on a throne.

[16] "A cherub stretched out and protecting," "covering cherub."

[17] ["Mark" in DV, AV, RSV, and Hebrew Bible. Vulgate: "signa Thau." Cf. *La Sainte Bible, traduit en français sous la direction de l'Ecole Biblique de Jérusalem* (Paris, 1956), where the word is translated as "croix," with a note: "literally Tav, as Vulgate translates. This letter had, in the ancient alphabet, exactly the shape of a cross."—TRANSLATOR.]

[18] *Carmina*, XIX, verse 640 (Migne, *P.L.*, vol. 61, cols. 546f.):
    "Qui cruce dispensa per quattuor extima ligni
    Quattuor attingit dimensum partibus orbem
    Ut trahat ad vitam populos ex omnibus oris
    Et quia morte crucis cunctis deus omnia Christus

364    In the spontaneous symbolism of the unconscious the cross as quaternity refers to the self, to man's wholeness.[19] The sign of the cross is thus an indication of the healing effect of wholeness, or of becoming whole.

365    Four animals also appear in the vision of Daniel. The first was like a lion and was "made stand upon the feet as a man, and a man's heart was given to it." The second was like a bear, the third like a leopard, and the fourth was a beast "dreadful and terrible," with "great iron teeth" and "ten horns." [20] Only the special treatment of the lion in any way recalls the human quarter of the tetramorph. All four of them are beasts of prey or, in psychological terms, functions that have succumbed to desire, lost their angelic character, and become daemonic in the worst sense. They represent the negative and destructive aspect of the four angels of God who, as the Book of Enoch shows, form his inner court. This regression has nothing to do with magic (see n. 13) but rather expresses the daemonization of man, or of certain powerful individuals. Accordingly Daniel interprets the four beasts as four kings which shall arise out of the earth (7 : 17, A.V.). The interpretation continues (7 : 18): "But the saints of the most High shall take the kingdom, and possess the kingdom for ever, even for ever and ever." Like the lion with the human heart, this surprising interpretation is based on the positive aspect of the quaternity and refers to a blessed, protected state of things when four guardian angels reign in heaven and four just kings on earth, and the saints possess the kingdom. But this happy state is about to disappear, for the fourth beast in the quaternity has assumed monstrous form, has ten horns and represents "the fourth kingdom upon earth, which shall be diverse from all kingdoms, and shall devour the whole earth" (7 : 23). In other words, a monstrous lust for power will make the human quarter unconscious again. This is a psychological process which can be observed only too often both individually and collectively. It has recurred countless times in the history of mankind.

---

Extat in exortum vitae finemque malorum,
Alpha crucem circumstat et Ω, tribus utraque virgis
Littera diversam trina ratione figuram
Perficiens, quia perfectum est mens una, triplex vis."

19 Cf. "Concerning Mandala Symbolism."

20 Daniel 7 : 4ff.

366    Via Daniel and Enoch, the quaternity of God's sons penetrated very early into Christian ideology. There are the three
synoptic gospels and the one gospel of St. John, to which were
assigned as emblems the symbols of the cherubim. The four gospels are as it were the pillars of Christ's throne, and in the Middle Ages the tetramorph became the riding animal of the
Church. But it was Gnostic speculation in particular that appro-
priated the quaternity. This theme is so far-reaching that it
cannot be dealt with more closely here. I would only draw attention to the synonymity of Christ, Logos, and Hermes,[21] and
the derivation of Jesus from the so-called "second tetrad" [22]
among the Valentinians. "Thus our Lord in his fourfoldness
preserves the form of the tetraktys and is composed of (1) the
spiritual, which comes from Achamoth, (2) the psychic, which
comes from the world-creator, (3) the body prepared with in-
effable art, and (4) the divine, the saviour." [23]

367    The alchemical tetrasomia and its reduction to unity therefore have a long prehistory which reaches back far beyond the
Pythagorean tetraktys into Egyptian antiquity. From all this we
can see without difficulty that we are confronted with the archetype of a *totality image divided into four*. The resultant conceptions are always of a central nature, characterize divine figures,
and carry over those qualities to the arcane substances of alchemy.

368    It is not the task of empirical psychology to speculate about
the possible metaphysical significance of this archetype. We can
only point out that in spontaneous psychic products such as
dreams and fantasies the same archetype is at work and in principle produces over and over again the same figures, meanings,
and values *autochthonously*. Anyone who studies impartially
the above series of dream pictures will be able to convince himself of the validity of my conclusions.

### 4. THE IMAGE OF WHOLENESS

369    After this excursus into the history of the Hermetic quaternity, let us turn back to the image of wholeness in alchemy.

[21] [And Adamas: cf. *Aion*, pp. 208f.—EDITORS.] Hippolytus, *Elenchos*, V, 7, 29ff.
[22] *Elenchos*, VI, 51, 1.
[23] Usener, *Das Weihnachtsfest*, p. 149.

370    One of the commonest and most important of the arcana is
the *aqua permanens,* the ὕδωρ θεῖον of the Greeks. This, according
to the unanimous testimony of both the ancient and the later
alchemists, is an aspect of Mercurius, and of this divine water
Zosimos says in his fragment περὶ τοῦ θείου ὕδατος:

This is the great and divine mystery which is sought, for it is the
whole [τοῦτο γάρ ἐστι τὸ πᾶν]. And from it is the whole and through
the same is the whole. Two natures, one substance [οὐσία]. But the
one [substance] attracts the one, and the one rules the one. This is
the silver water, male and female, which forever flees. . . . For it is
not to be ruled. It is the whole in all things. And it has life and spirit
and is destructive [ἀναιρετικόν].[1]

371    With regard to the central significance of the *aqua permanens*
I must refer the reader to my earlier writings.[2] The "water" is
just as much the arcanum of alchemy as are Mercurius, the
lapis, the *filius philosophorum,* etc. Like them it is a totality
image, and as the above Zosimos quotation shows, this was so
even in the Greek alchemy of the third century A.D. The text
leaves no doubt in this respect: the water is wholeness. It is the
"silver water" (= *hydrargyrum*), but not the ὕδωρ ἀεικίνητον, 'ever-
moving water,' i.e., ordinary quicksilver which in Latin alchemy
was called *Mercurius crudus* as distinct from *Mercurius non
vulgi.* In Zosimos the quicksilver is a πνεῦμα (spirit).[3]

372    Zosimos's "whole" is a microcosm, a reflection of the universe
in the smallest particle of matter, and is therefore found in
everything organic and inorganic. Because the microcosm is
identical with the macrocosm, it attracts the latter and thus
brings about a kind of apocatastasis, a restoration of all in-
dividua to the original wholeness. Thus "every grain becomes
wheat, and all metal gold," as Meister Eckhart says; and the
little, single individual becomes the "great man," the *homo
maximus* or Anthropos, i.e., the self. The moral equivalent of
the physical transmutation into gold is *self-knowledge,* which is
a re-remembering of the *homo totus.*[4] Olympiodorus, citing
Zosimos's exhortation to Theosebeia, says:

1 Berthelot, *Alch. grecs,* III, ix. Cf. the poisonous tincture, supra, par. 358, n. 2.
2 *Psychology and Alchemy,* pars. 336f.
3 Berthelot, *Alch. grecs,* III, vi, 5. Cf. supra, "The Spirit Mercurius," pars. 264f.
4 Cf. *Aion,* pp. 162ff.

If thou wilt calmly humble thyself in relation to thy body, thou wilt calm thyself also in relation to the passions, and by acting thus, thou wilt summon the divine to thyself, and in truth the divine, which is everywhere,[5] will come to thee. But when thou knowest thyself, thou knowest also the God who is truly one.[6]

Hippolytus bears this out in his account of the Christian doctrine:

But thou shalt speak with God and be joint heir with Christ. . . . For thou wilt have become God [γέγονας γὰρ θεός]. For whatever sufferings thou didst undergo as a man, thou hast shown that thou art a man; but whatever is appurtenant to a God, that God has promised to bestow, because thou hast been made divine [θεοποιηθῆς], since thou hast been begotten immortal [γεννηθείς]. That is the "Know thyself," the knowing of the God who made thee. For to him who knoweth himself it is given to be known of Him by whom he is called.[7]

373    The foregoing account of the associative background of the tree, prompted by the treatise of Jodocus Greverus, seemed to me a necessary prelude to a discussion of the significance of the tree in alchemy. A general survey of this kind may help the reader not to lose sight of the whole amid the unavoidable confusion of alchemical opinions and fantasies. Unfortunately my exposition will not be rendered any easier by my having to give numerous parallels from other fields of study. These, however, cannot be dispensed with, because the views of the alchemists were derived to a large extent from unconscious archetypal assumptions which also underlie other domains of human thought.

[5] The immediately preceding passage remarks that God "is everywhere" and "not in the smallest place, like the daemon" ( οὐκ ἐν τόπῳ ἐλαχίστῳ ὡς τὸ δαιμόνιον ). Thus one of God's attributes is infinity, whereas the distinguishing mark of the daemon is limitation in space. Man as microcosm would then be included in the concept of the daemonic, and psychologically this would mean that the ego, separated and split off from God, is likely to become daemonic as soon as it accentuates its independence of God by its egocentricity. The divine dynamism of the self, which is identical with the dynamism of the cosmos, is then placed at the service of the ego, and the latter is daemonized. This would account for the magically effective personality of those historical figures whom Burckhardt called the "great despoilers." Exempla sunt odiosa.

[6] Berthelot, Alch. grecs, II, iv, 26.

[7] Elenchos, X, 34, 4 (cf. Legge, Philosophumena, II, p. 178).

5. THE NATURE AND ORIGIN OF THE PHILOSOPHICAL TREE

374    In my book *Psychology and Alchemy* I devoted a special chapter[1] to the projection of psychic contents (hallucinations, visions, etc.) and therefore need not dwell here on the spontaneous production of the tree symbol among the alchemists. Suffice to say that the adept saw branches and twigs[2] in the retort, where his tree grew and blossomed.[3] He was advised to contemplate its growth, that is, to reinforce it with active imagination. The vision was the thing to be sought (*res quaerenda*).[4] The tree was "prepared" in the same way as salt.[5] And just as the tree grew in the water, so also it was putrefied in it, "burnt" or "cooled" with the water.[6] It was called oak,[7] vine,[8] myrtle.[9] Djābir ibn Hayyān says of the myrtle: "Know that the myrtle is the leaf and the twig; it is a root yet no root. It is both a root and a branch. As a root, it is unquestionably a root if it be set over against the leaves and the fruits. It is separate from the trunk and forms part of the deep roots." The myrtle, he says, is "what Maria[10] calls the golden rungs, what Democritus calls the green bird. . . . It has been so called because of its green colour and because it is like the myrtle, in that it keeps its green colour for a

1 Pars. 342ff.
2 "When the body is dissolved, there will sometimes appear two branches, sometimes three, sometimes more. . . ." (*Theatr. chem.*, I, 1659, pp. 147f.).
3 ". . . that it may grow within the glass like a tree," "it made it grow upward in its glass with discoloured flowers" (Ripley, *Opera*, p. 86). "The philosophical tree flourished with its branches" ("Introitus apertus," *Musaeum hermeticum*, p. 694).
4 "Senior, the author of *Lilium*, says that the sight of it [the vessel] is more to be desired than the scripture" (Hoghelande, *Theatr. chem.*, I, 1659, p. 177). Cf. also *Psychology and Alchemy*, par. 360.
5 "The salt and the tree can be made in any moist and convenient place" ("Gloria mundi," *Mus. herm.*, p. 216).
6 Ripley, *Opera*, pp. 39, 46; cf. "Tractatus aureus de lapide," *Mus. herm.*, p. 39.
7 Ripley, *Opera*, p. 46.
8 *Vitis arborea* in Ripley's *Scrowle* (British Museum, MS. Sloane 5025). "Do you not know that all holy Scripture is written in parables? For Christ the Son of God followed this method, and said, I am the true vine." (*Aurora consurgens* II, *Art. aurif.*, I, p. 186.) *Vitis sapientum* (ibid., p. 193, and "Hermetis Trismegisti Tractatus aureus," *Theatr. chem.*, IV, 1659, p. 613).
9 Djābir ibn Hayyān, "Le Livre du Mercure oriental, occidental, et du feu de la pierre," in Berthelot, *Moyen âge*, III, pp. 214f.
10 Maria Prophetissa.

long time despite the alternations of heat and cold." [11] It has
seven branches.[12]

375    Gerard Dorn says of the tree:

After nature has planted the root of the metallic tree in the midst
of her womb, viz., the stone which shall bring forth the metals, the
gem, the salt, the alum, the vitriol, the salty spring, sweet, cold, or
warm, the tree of coral or the Marcasita,[13] and has set its trunk in
the earth, this trunk is divided into different branches, whose substance is a liquid, not after the manner of water, nor of oil, nor of
clay,[14] nor of slime, but is not to be thought of otherwise than as the
wood born of the earth, which is not earth although growing from
it. The branches spread in such a way that the one is separated from
the other by a space of two or three climates and as many regions:
from Germany even as far as Hungary and beyond. In this way the
branches of different trees spread through the whole globe of the
earth, as in the human body the veins spread through the different
limbs, which are separated from one another.

The fruits of this tree drop off, and the tree itself dies and vanishes in the earth. "Afterwards, in accordance with natural conditions, another new [tree] is there." [15]

376    In this text Dorn draws an impressive picture of the growth,
expansion, death, and rebirth of the philosophical tree. Its
branches are veins running through the earth, and although
they spread to the most distant points of the earth's surface they
all belong to the same immense tree, which apparently renews
itself. The tree is obviously thought of as a system of blood vessels. It consists of a liquid like blood, and when this comes out
it coagulates into the fruit of the tree.[16] Strangely enough, in

---

[11] Referring to the *viriditas benedicta* of Latin alchemy, here an allusion to the
incorruptibility of the fruit of the tree.

[12] "Galen speaks of the Philosophical tree, which has seven branches" (*Art.
aurif.*, I, p. 222).

[13] "Marcasita = an imperfect metallic substance" (Ruland, *Lexicon*, p. 217). In
chemistry, a collective name for various pyrites (Lippmann, *Entstehung und
Ausbreitung der Alchemie*, indices).

[14] *Lutum* is gypsum or clay; mixed with hair, it was used for sealing the lids of
vessels (Lippmann, I, p. 663).

[15] "De genealogia mineralium," *Theatr. chem.*, I (1659), p. 574.

[16] "Their [the fruits'] coagulation takes place instantaneously." The fruits are
"sent forth at the extremities of the *locustae*." *Locustae* are the tips of the
branches (Ruland, p. 209: "tops or young shoots of trees"). The form *lucusta* in

ancient Persian tradition the metals are connected with the blood of Gayomart: his blood, soaking into the earth, turned into the seven metals.

377 Dorn appends to his description of the tree a brief observation which I would not like to withhold from the reader since it affords an important insight into what is in its way the classic mode of alchemical thinking. He says:

> This and suchlike things proceed from the true physics and from the springs of the true philosophy, from which, by meditative contemplation of the wondrous works of God, the true knowledge of the supreme author and of his powers dawns upon the spiritual eyes of the philosophers, even as to the fleshly eyes the light is made visible. To those eyes the hidden is revealed. But that Greek Satan has implanted in the philosophic field of the true wisdom the tares[17] and their false seeds, namely Aristotle, Albertus, Avicenna,[18] Rasis,[19] and men of that kidney, who are inimical to the light of God and the light of nature, and have perverted the whole physical truth from the time when they turned the name Sophia into Philosophia.[20]

378 Dorn was a Platonist and a fanatical opponent of Aristotle and, quite obviously, of the scientific empiricists as well. His attitude was essentially the same as that of Robert Fludd in respect of John Kepler.[21] Basically, it was the old controversy about universals, the opposition between realism and nominalism, which in our scientific age has been decided in favour of a nominalistic tendency. Whereas the scientific attitude seeks, on the basis of careful empiricism, to explain nature in her own terms, Hermetic philosophy had for its goal an explanation that included the psyche in a total description of nature. The empiricist tries, more or less successfully, to forget his archetypal ex-

MS. seems to derive from *lucus*, 'grove' (Walde, *Lateinisches Etymologisches Wörterbuch*, I, p. 818).

[17] In text, *Lolium temulentum* L.
[18] Ibn Sina (980–1037), a physician and opponent of alchemy.
[19] abu-Bakr Muhammad ibn-Zakārīya' al-Rāzī (d. 925), also named Rasis or Rhazes, physician and alchemist. Known in the West by his "Excerpta ex libro luminis luminum" in Lacinius, *Pretiosa margarita novella*, pp. 167ff.
[20] *Theatr. chem.*, I (1659), p. 574.
[21] Pauli, "The Influence of Archetypal Ideas on the Scientific Theories of Kepler," in Jung and Pauli, *Interpretation of Nature and the Psyche*.

planatory principles, that is, the psychic premises that are a *sine qua non* of the cognitive process, or to repress them in the interests of "scientific objectivity." The Hermetic philosopher regarded these psychic premises, the archetypes, as inalienable components of the empirical world-picture. He was not yet so dominated by the object that he could ignore the palpable presence of psychic premises in the form of eternal ideas which he felt to be real. The empirical nominalist, on the other hand, already had the modern attitude towards the psyche, namely, that it had to be eliminated as something "subjective," and that its contents were nothing but ideas formulated *a posteriori*, mere *flatus vocis*. His hope was to be able to produce a picture of the world that was entirely independent of the observer. This hope has been fulfilled only in part, as the findings of modern physics show: the observer cannot be finally eliminated, which means that the psychic premises remain operative.

379     In the case of Dorn we can see how the archetypal tree, which consisted of the ramifications of the bronchi, blood vessels, and veins of ore, was projected upon the empirical world and gave rise to a totalistic view which embraced the whole of organic and inorganic nature and the "spiritual" world as well. The fanatical defence of his standpoint shows that Dorn was gnawed by inner doubt and was fighting a lost battle. Neither he nor Fludd could hold up the march of events, and today we see how the spokesmen of so-called objectivity are defending themselves with similar outbursts of affect against a psychology that demonstrates the necessity of psychic premises.

## 6. DORN'S INTERPRETATION OF THE TREE

380     In his treatise "Congeries Paracelsicae chemicae de transmutatione metallorum" Dorn writes:[1]

On account of likeness alone, and not substance, the Philosophers compare their material to a golden tree with seven branches, thinking that it encloses in its seed the seven metals, and that these are hidden in it, for which reason they call it a living thing. Again, even as natural trees bring forth divers blossoms in their season, so

1 *Theatr. chem.*, I (1659), pp. 513ff.

the material of the stone causes the most beautiful colours to appear[2] when it puts forth its blossoms.[3] Likewise they have said that the fruit of their tree strives up to heaven, because out of the philosophic earth there arises a certain substance, like to the branches of a loathsome sponge.[4] Whence they have put forward the opinion that the point about which the whole art turns lies in the living things of nature [*in vegetabilibus naturae*] and not in the living things of matter; and also because their stone contains within it soul, body, and spirit, as do living things. From a likeness not altogether remote they have called this material virgin's milk and blessed rose-coloured blood, although that belongs only to the prophets and sons of God. For this reason the Sophists have supposed that the philosophic matter consists of animal or human blood.

381    Dorn then enumerates the substances with which "frivolous triflers" operate, such as urine, milk, eggs, hair, and various kinds of salts and metals. These "Sophists" take the symbolical names concretely and attempt to make the magistery out of the most unsuitable ingredients. They were obviously the chemists of those days, who, as a result of their concretistic misunderstanding, worked with common materials, whereas the philosophers

called their stone animate because, at the final operations, by virtue of the power of this most noble fiery mystery, a dark red liquid, like blood, sweats out drop by drop from their material and their vessel. And for this reason they have prophesied that in the last days a most pure[5] man, through whom the world will be freed, will come to earth and will sweat bloody drops of a rosy or red hue, whereby the world will be redeemed from its Fall. In like manner, too, the blood of their stone will free the leprous metals[6] and also men from their

[2] An allusion to the many colours of the *caudo pavonis* (peacock's tail), whose appearance heralds the attainment of the goal.
[3] Cf. the awakened dead in Hades, who grow like the flowers in spring. Berthelot, *Alch. grecs*, IV, xx, 9.
[4] The terrestrial equivalent of the sponge was said to be the puff-ball. Sponges could hear and were sentient. When torn up, they exuded a juice like blood. Cf. the mandrake, which shrieks when it is torn up. "When they are torn from their places, it is heard and there will be a great noise." (Calid, "Liber secretorum," *Art. aurif.*, I, p. 343.) For the sponge, see *Mysterium Coniunctionis*, p. 134 and n. 205.
[5] *Putus* can also mean 'genuine' or 'unadulterated.' *Argentum putum* is unalloyed silver. *Putus* instead of *purus* is significant, see next section.
[6] Impure metals, oxides, and salts.

diseases.[7] Wherefore they have said, not without good reason, that their stone is animate [*animalem*]. Concerning this, Mercurius speaks as follows to King Calid, "To know this mystery is permitted only to the prophets of God," [8] and that is the reason why the stone is called animate. For in the blood of this stone is hidden its soul. It is also composed of body, spirit, and soul. For a like reason they have called it their microcosm, because it contains the similitude of all things of this world, and therefore again they say that it is animate, as Plato calls the macrocosm animate. But now the ignorant have come, who believe that the stone is threefold and is hidden in threefold kind [*genere*], namely vegetable, animal, and mineral, whence it has come to pass that they themselves have sought for it in minerals.[9] But this teaching is far removed from the opinion of the Philosophers, who maintain that their stone is vegetable, animal, and mineral in one and the same form.

382     This remarkable text explains the tree as a metaphorical form of the arcane substance, a living thing that comes into existence according to its own laws, and grows, blossoms, and bears fruit like a plant. This plant is likened to the sponge, which grows in the depths of the sea and seems to have an affinity with the mandrake (n. 4). Dorn then makes a distinction between the "living things of nature" and those of matter. By the last-named are obviously meant concrete, material organisms. But it is not so clear what the former are meant to be. A sponge that

---

[7] Human diseases are the equivalent of the *leprositas* of the metals. The text has *liberabat*, but the sense requires *liberabit*, as the prophecy is not yet fulfilled.

[8] The quotation is not literal. Calid ("Liber secretorum," *Art. aurif.*, I, p. 325) says: "You must know, brother, that this magistery of ours concerning the secret stone, and our honoured office, is a great secret of God, which he has hidden from his people, and has willed to reveal to none save those who have faithfully deserved well as sons and have known his goodness and greatness." Dorn interprets the speaker, perhaps rightly, as Hermes (Trismegistus), who later on in the text speaks of "my own disciple, Musa." Moses, who was counted as an alchemist, was identified with Musaios, the teacher of Orpheus.

[9] Here too Dorn may be referring to Calid, who says (ibid., p. 342): "Take this stone that is no stone nor of the nature of stone. Moreover, it is a stone whose substance is generated on the top of the mountains [*in capite montium*], and the philosopher chose to say 'mountains' instead of 'living things' [*animalia*]." (The text is corrupt.) The stone is found in the head of a snake or a dragon, or is the "head-element" itself, as in Zosimos. World-mountain, world-axis, world-tree, and *homo maximus* are synonymous. Cf. Holmberg, *Der Baum des Lebens*, pp. 20, 21, 25.

bleeds and a mandrake that shrieks when pulled up are neither "vegetabilia materiae" nor are they found in nature, at least not in nature as we know it, though they may occur in that more comprehensive, Platonic nature as Dorn understood it, that is, in a nature that includes psychic "animalia," i.e., mythologems and archetypes. Such are the mandrake and similar organisms. How concretely Dorn visualized them is a moot point. At any rate the "stone that is no stone, nor of the nature of stone" (n. 9) comes into this category.

### 7. THE ROSE-COLOURED BLOOD AND THE ROSE

383    The mysterious rose-coloured blood occurs in several other authors. In Khunrath, for instance, the "lion lured forth from the Saturnine mountain" had rose-coloured blood.[1] This lion, signifying "all and conquering all," corresponds to the πᾶν or πάντα of Zosimos, i.e., totality. Khunrath further mentions (p. 276)

the costly Catholick Rosy-Coloured Blood and Aetheric Water that flows forth Azothically[2] from the side of the innate Son of the Great World when opened by the power of the Art. Through the same alone, and by no other means, are Vegetable, Animal, and Mineral things, by the ablution of their impurities, raised to the highest Natural perfection, in accordance with Nature and by the Art.

384    In the "Aquarium sapientum" the "son of the great world" (*filius macrocosmi,* the lapis) is correlated with Christ,[3] who is the *filius microcosmi,* and his blood is the quintessence, the red tincture. This is the

true and authentic duplex Mercurius or Giant[4] of twofold substance. . . .[5] God by nature, man, hero, etc., who hath the celestial

---

[1] *Von hylealischen Chaos,* p. 93; cf. also p. 197.
[2] For Azoth, see "The Spirit Mercurius," supra, par. 271.
[3] *Mus. herm.,* p. 118: "Christ is compared and united with the earthly stone . . . it is an outstanding type and lifelike image of the incarnation of Christ."
[4] Psalm 18 : 6: "he, as a bridegroom coming out of his bride chamber, hath rejoiced as a giant to run the way" was referred by the Church Fathers to Christ.
[5] The text refers here to Matth. 26, obviously meaning verses 26ff., the institution of the Last Supper. [The phrase "giant of twofold substance" (*geminae gigas substantiae*) seems to have been first used by St. Ambrose, in line 19 of his

Spirit in him, which quickeneth all things . . . he is the sole and perfect Healer of all imperfect bodies and men, the true and heavenly physician of the soul . . . the triune universal essence,[6] which is called Jehovah.[7]

385    These panegyrics of the alchemists have often been regretted as examples of bad taste or ridiculed as exuberant fantasies— most unfairly, it seems to me. They were serious people, the alchemists, and they can be understood only when taken seriously, however hard this may hit our own prejudices. It was never their intention to exalt their stone into a world saviour, nor did they purposely smuggle into it a whole lot of known and unknown mythology any more than we do in our dreams. They simply found these qualities in their idea of a body composed of the four elements and capable of uniting all opposites, and were just as amazed at this discovery as anyone would be who had a singularly impressive dream and then came across an unknown myth which fitted it exactly. No wonder, therefore, that they endowed the stone or the red tincture, which they really believed could be produced, with all the qualities they had discovered in their idea of such an object. This makes it easier for us to understand a statement that is entirely characteristic of the alchemical way of thinking. It occurs on the same page as the above quotation from "Aquarium sapientum" and runs:

Even as, I say, this earthly and philosophic stone, together with its material, has many different names, indeed it is said almost a thousand, for which reason it is also called wonderful, even so can these and other afore-mentioned names and titles be applied much more properly, and indeed in the highest degree, to Almighty God and the Supreme Good.

---

Christmas hymn beginning "Intende qui regis Israel." The relevant stanza is translated by J. M. Neale, *Collected Hymns, Sequences and Carols*, p. 104: "Proceeding from His chamber free,/The royal hall of chastity,/Giant of twofold substance, straight/His destined way He runs elate."—A.S.B.G.]

[6] The anonymous author of "Aquarium sapientum" was not altogether clear about the triune essence, for he says it is "of one, a divine essence, then of two, of God and man, that is, of three persons, of four, namely of three persons and one divine essence, as also of five, of three persons and two essences, namely one divine and one human" (p. 112). The *filius macrocosmi* seems to have loosened up the dogma quite considerably.

[7] "Aquarium sapientum," pp. 111f.

It obviously never occurred to the author, as we with our preju-
diced view are quick to assume, that he had simply transferred
God's attributes to the stone.

386    It is evident from this that the stone for the alchemists was
nothing less than a primordial religious experience which, as
good Christians, they had to reconcile with their beliefs. This
accounts for that ambiguous identity or parallelism between
Christ as the *filius microcosmi* and the *lapis philosophorum* as
the *filius macrocosmi*, or even the substitution of the one for the
other.

387    The lapis-Christ parallel was presumably the bridge by
which the mystique of the Rose entered into alchemy. This is
evident first of all from the use of "Rosarium" or "Rosarius"
(rose-gardener) as a book title. The first *Rosarium* (there are
several), first printed in 1550, is for the greater part ascribed to
Arnaldus de Villanova. It is a compilation whose historical components have not yet been sorted out. Arnaldus lived in the second half of the thirteenth century. He is also credited with the
*Rosarium cum figuris,* where the rose is the symbol of relationship between king and queen. The reader will find a detailed
account of this in my "Psychology of the Transference," which
reproduces the *Rosarium* illustrations.

388    The rose has the same meaning in Mechthild of Magdeburg.
The Lord spoke to her, saying: "Look at my heart, and see!" A
most beautiful rose with five petals covered his whole breast,
and the Lord said: "Praise me in my five senses, which are indicated by this rose." As is explained later, the five senses are the
vehicles of Christ's love for man (e.g., "through the sense of
smell he has always a certain loving affection directed towards
man").[8]

389    In the spiritual sense the rose, like the *hortus aromatum*
(garden of spices),[9] *hortus conclusus,*[10] and *rosa mystica,*[11] is
an allegory of Mary, but in the worldly sense it is the beloved,
the rose of the poets, the "fedeli d'amore" of that time. And just
as Mary is allegorized in St. Bernard[12] as the *medium terrae*

---

[8] *Liber gratiae spiritualis* (Venice, 1578), pp. 107f.

[9] Alan of Lille, *Elucidatio in Cant. Cant.* 6 (Migne, *P.L.,* vol. 210, col. 95).

[10] Ibid., col. 82.

[11] Litany of Loreto.

[12] *Sermo II in Festo Pentecostes* (Migne, *P.L.,* vol. 183, col. 327).

(centre of the earth), in Rabanus Maurus[13] as the "city," in God-frey, Abbot of Admont, as the "fortress" [14] and the "house of divine wisdom," [15] and in Alan of Lille as the *acies castrorum* (army with banners),[16] so the rose has the significance of a mandala, as is clear from the heavenly rose in Dante's *Paradiso*. Like its equivalent, the Indian lotus, the rose is decidedly feminine. In Mechthild of Magdeburg it must be understood as a projection of her own feminine Eros upon Christ.[17]

390    It seems as though the rose-coloured blood of the alchemical redeemer[18] was derived from a rose mysticism that penetrated into alchemy, and that, in the form of the red tincture, it expressed the healing or whole-making effect of a certain kind of Eros. The strange concretism of this symbol is explained by the total absence of psychological concepts. Dorn was therefore bound to understand the rose-coloured blood as a "vegetabile naturae," in contrast to ordinary blood, which was a "vegetabile materiae." As he says, the soul of the stone is in its blood. Since the stone represents the *homo totus*,[19] it is only logical for Dorn to speak of the "putissimus homo" when discussing the arcane substance and its bloody sweat, for that is what it is all about. *He* is the arcanum, and the stone and its parallel or prefiguration is Christ in the garden of Gethsemane.[20] This "most pure" or "most true" man must be no other than what he is, just as "argentum putum" is unalloyed silver; he must be entirely man, a man who knows and possesses everything human and is not adulterated by any influence or admixture from without. This man will appear on earth only "in the last days." He cannot be Christ, for Christ by his blood has already redeemed the world from the consequences of the Fall.[21] Christ may be the "purissi-

---

13 *Allegoriae in Sacram Scripturam* (Migne, *P.L.*, vol. 112, col. 897).

14 *Homilia III in Dominicam I Adventus* (Migne, *P.L.*, vol. 174, col. 32).

15 *Homilia LXIII in Vigiliam Assumptionis* (ibid., col. 957).

16 *Elucidatio* (Migne, *P.L.*, vol. 210, col. 94).

17 Cf. the chapter on the kiss of the Lord, where there is a similar projection (*Liber gratiae*, p. 90).

18 The blood, that is, of the lion, which is equated with the lion of the tribe of Judah (= Christ).

19 Cf. *Psychology and Alchemy*, "The Lapis-Christ Parallel," and *Aion*, ch. 5.

20 Luke 22 : 44: ". . . and his sweat was as it were great drops of blood falling down to the ground."

21 [The text continues: "and one has never heard that his blood was rose-coloured." There is, however, an interesting reference to "cruore ejus roseo

mus homo," but he is not "putissimus." Though he is man, he is also God, not pure silver but gold as well, and therefore not "putus." On no account is it a question here of a future Christ and *salvator microcosmi*, but rather of the alchemical *servator cosmi* (preserver of the cosmos), representing the still unconscious idea of the whole and complete man, who shall bring about what the sacrificial death of Christ has obviously left unfinished, namely the deliverance of the world from evil. Like Christ he will sweat a redeeming blood, but, as a "vegetabile naturae," it is "rose-coloured"; not natural or ordinary blood, but symbolic blood, a psychic substance, the manifestation of a certain kind of Eros which unifies the individual as well as the multitude in the sign of the rose and makes them whole, and is therefore a panacea and an alexipharmic.

391    The second half of the sixteenth century saw the beginning of the Rosicrucian movement, whose motto—*per crucem ad rosam*—was anticipated by the alchemists. Goethe caught the mood of this Eros very well in his poem "Die Geheimnisse." Such movements, as also the emergence of the idea of Christian charity with its emotional overtones,[22] are always indicative of a corresponding social defect which they serve to compensate. In the perspective of history, we can see clearly enough what this defect was in the ancient world; and in the Middle Ages as well, with its cruel and unreliable laws and feudal conditions, human rights and human dignity were in a sorry plight. One would think that in these circumstances Christian love would be very much to the point. But what if it is blind and without insight? Solicitude for the spiritual welfare of the erring sheep can explain even a Torquemada. Love alone is useless if it does not also have understanding. And for the proper use of understanding a wider consciousness is needed, and a higher standpoint to enlarge one's horizon. That is why Christianity as a historical force has not rested content with admonishing man to love his

gustando vivimus Deo" (by tasting his rosy blood we live to God) in a very well-known hymn, beginning "Ad coenam agni providi," formerly attributed to St. Ambrose, but though now denied him, known to date back to the 6th or early 7th century. For centuries past it has been the liturgical hymn sung at Vespers in the Easter season in the Roman church. Cf. Neale, *Collected Hymns*, p. 194. —A.S.B.G.]

22 Cf. I Cor. 13 : 4ff.

neighbour, but has also performed a higher cultural task which it is impossible to overestimate. It has educated man to a higher consciousness and responsibility. Certainly love is needed for that, but a love combined with insight and understanding. Their function is to illuminate regions that are still dark and to add them to consciousness—regions in the outside world as well as those within, in the interior world of the psyche. The blinder love is, the more it is instinctual, and the more it is attended by destructive consequences, for it is a dynamism that needs form and direction. Therefore a compensatory Logos has been joined to it as a light that shines in the darkness. A man who is unconscious of himself acts in a blind, instinctive way and is in addition fooled by all the illusions that arise when he sees everything that he is not conscious of in himself coming to meet him from outside as projections upon his neighbour.

## 8. THE ALCHEMICAL MIND

392    The alchemists seem to have had an inkling of this state of mind; at any rate it got mixed up with their opus. Already in the fourteenth century they had discovered that what they were searching for reminded them not only of all manner of mysterious substances, remedies, and poisons, but of various living things, plants and animals, and, finally, of some strange mythological figure, a dwarf, earth-spirit or metal-spirit, or even of something like a God-man. Thus in the first half of the fourteenth century, Petrus Bonus of Ferrara wrote that in a certain letter Rhazes had said:

With this red stone the philosophers exalted themselves above all others and foretold the future. They prophesied not only in general but also in particular. Thus they knew that the day of judgment and the end of the world must come, and the resurrection of the dead, when each soul will be united with its former body and will no more be separated from it for ever. Then each glorified body will be changed, possess incorruptibility and brightness, and an almost unbelievable subtlety, and it will penetrate all solids,[1] because its nature will then be of the nature of spirit as well as body. . . . It is

1 Allusion to "Tabula smaragdina": "This is the strong strength of all strength, for it will overcome every subtle thing, and penetrate every solid thing" (*De alchemia,* p. 363).

297

a nature which, when it is moistened and left for many nights in that condition, is like a dead man, and then that thing needs the fire, until the spirit of that body is extracted and left to stand through the nights, and falls to dust like a man in his grave. And when all this has happened, God will give it back its soul and its body, and take away its imperfection; then will that thing be strengthened and improved, as after the resurrection a man becomes stronger and younger than he was in this world. . . . Thus the philosophers have beheld the Last Judgment in this art, namely the germination and birth of this stone, which is miraculous rather than rational; for on that day the soul to be beatified unites with its former body through the mediation of the spirit, to eternal glory. . . . So also the old philosophers of this art knew and maintained that a virgin must conceive and bring forth, because in their art the stone conceives of itself, becomes pregnant, and brings itself forth. . . . And because they beheld the miraculous conception, pregnancy, birth, and nourishment of this stone, they concluded that a woman who is a virgin will conceive without a man, become pregnant and give birth in miraculous wise, and remain a virgin as before. . . . As Alphidius says, this stone is cast out into the streets, is lifted up into the clouds, dwells in the air, feeds in the streams and rests on the tops of the mountains. Its mother is a virgin, its father knows not woman. . . . The philosophers also knew that God must become man on the last day of this art, whereon is the fulfilment of the work; begetter and begotten become altogether one; old man and boy, father and son, become altogether one; thus all old things are made new.[2] God himself has entrusted this magistery to his philosophers and prophets, for whose souls he has prepared a dwelling place in his paradise.[3]

393     As this text makes very plain, Petrus Bonus discovered that the alchemical opus anticipated, feature for feature, the sacred myth of the generation, birth, and resurrection of the Redeemer, for he was quite convinced that the ancient authorities of the art, Hermes Trismegistus, Moses, Plato, and others knew the whole process long ago and consequently had prophetically anticipated the coming salvation in Christ. He was not in any

---

[2] Of Alphidius nothing is known. He is an oft-cited author, who may have lived in the 12th–13th cents. (Cf. Kopp, *Die Alchemie*, II, pp. 339, 363).

[3] "Pret. marg. nov.," *Bibliotheca chemica*, II, p. 30. Alleged date of composition is 1330. Janus Lacinius, who first printed the treatise in 1546, says (fol. 70r) that Bonus "was living in the city of Pola in Istria about the year 1338," and (fol. 46v) that he was a contemporary (*coaetaneus*) of Raymund Lully (1235–?1315).

way conscious that the situation might be the reverse and that the alchemists were drawing on ecclesiastical tradition and subsequently approximated their operations to the sacred legend. The degree of his unconsciousness is more than merely astonishing: it is instructive. This extraordinary blindness shows us that there must have been an equally powerful motive behind it. Bonus was not the only one to make this declaration, though he was the first; in the next three hundred years it became increasingly widespread and caused offence. Bonus was an erudite scholastic and, quite apart from his religious beliefs, was intellectually well in a position to recognize his error. But what impelled him to this view was the fact that he was indeed drawing on a source more ancient than ecclesiastical tradition: when contemplating the chemical changes that took place during the opus, his mind became suffused with archetypal, mythological parallels and interpretations, just as had happened to the old pagan alchemists, and as still happens today when the imagination is given free play in the observation and investigation of the products of the unconscious. Under these conditions forms of thought emerge in which one can afterwards discover parallels with mythological motifs, including Christian ones; parallels and similarities which perhaps one would never have suspected at first sight. So it was with the old adepts who, not knowing anything about the nature of chemical substances, reeled from one perplexity to the next: willy-nilly they had to submit to the overwhelming power of the numinous ideas that crowded into the empty darkness of their minds. From these depths a light gradually dawned upon them as to the nature of the process and its goal. Because they were ignorant of the laws of matter, its behaviour did not do anything to contradict their archetypal conception of it. Occasionally they made chemical discoveries in passing, as was only to be expected; but what they really discovered, and what was an endless source of fascination to them, was the symbolism of the individuation process.

394    Petrus Bonus could not but recognize that the alchemical symbols which had been discovered in an entirely different way agreed in a remarkable manner with those of the Christian story of salvation. In their efforts to fathom the secrets of matter the alchemists had unexpectedly blundered into the unconscious, and thus, without at first being aware of it, they became the

discoverers of a process which underlies Christian symbolism among others. It did not take more than a couple of centuries for the more reflective among them to realize what the quest for the stone was actually about. Hesitantly at first, hint by hint, and then with unmistakable clarity, the stone revealed to them its identity with man himself, with a supraordinate factor that could actually be found within him, with Dorn's "quid," which today can be identified without difficulty with the self, as I have shown elsewhere.[4]

395    In their various ways, the alchemists struggled to come to terms with the lapis-Christ parallel. They did not find a solution, nor was this possible so long as their conceptual language was not freed from projection into matter and did not become psychological. Only in the following centuries, with the growth of natural science, was the projection withdrawn from matter and entirely abolished together with the psyche. This development of consciousness has still not reached its end. Nobody, it is true, any longer endows matter with mythological properties. This form of projection has become obsolete. Projection is now confined to personal and social relationships, to political Utopias and suchlike. Nature has nothing more to fear in the shape of mythological interpretations, but the realm of the spirit certainly has, more particularly that realm which commonly goes by the name of "metaphysics." There mythologems claiming to utter the absolute truth still tumble over one another, and anyone who dresses up his mythologem in solemn enough words believes that he has made a valid statement, and even makes a virtue of not possessing the modesty becoming to our limited human intelligence, which knows that it does not know. Such people even think that God himself is menaced whenever anyone dares to interpret their archetypal projections for what they are, namely, human statements, which no reasonable person supposes signify nothing, seeing that even the most preposterous statements of the alchemists have their meaning, though not the one which they themselves, with but few exceptions, sought to give their symbols, but one which only the future could formulate. Whenever we have to do with mythologems it is advisable to assume that they mean more than what they appear to say. Just as dreams do not conceal something already known, or ex-

[4] *Aion*, pp. 164f.

press it under a disguise, but try rather to formulate an as yet unconscious fact as clearly as possible, so myths and alchemical symbols are not euhemeristic allegories that hide artificial secrets. On the contrary, they seek to translate natural secrets into the language of consciousness and to declare the truth that is the common property of mankind. By becoming conscious, the individual is threatened more and more with isolation, which is nevertheless the *sine qua non* of conscious differentiation. The greater this threat, the more it is compensated by the production of collective and archetypal symbols which are common to all men.

396    This fact is expressed in a general way by the religions, where the relation of the individual to God or the gods ensures that the vital link with the regulating images and instinctual powers of the unconscious is not broken. Naturally this is true only so long as the religious ideas have not lost their numinosity, i.e., their thrilling power. Once this loss has occurred, it can never be replaced by anything rational. Compensating primordial images then appear in the form of mythological ideas such as alchemy produced in abundance and as may also be found in our own dreams. In both cases, consciousness reacts to these revelations in the same characteristic way: the alchemist reduced his symbols to the chemical substances he worked with, while the modern man reduces them to personal experiences, as Freud also does in his interpretation of dreams. Both of them act as though they knew to what known quantities the meaning of their symbols could be reduced. And both, in a sense, are right: for just as the alchemist was caught in his own alchemical dream language, so modern man, caught in the toils of egohood, uses his personal psychological problems as a *façon de parler*. In both cases the representational material is derived from already existing conscious contents. The result of this reduction, however, is not very satisfactory—so little, in fact, that Freud saw himself obliged to go back as far as possible into the past. In so doing he finally hit upon an uncommonly numinous idea, the archetype of incest. He thus found something that to some extent expressed the real meaning and purpose of symbol production, which is to bring about an awareness of those primordial images that belong to all men and can therefore lead the individual out of his isolation. Freud's dogmatic rigidity is explained by the

fact that he succumbed to the numinous effect of the primordial image he had discovered. If we assume with him that the incest motif is the source of all modern man's psychological problems as well as of alchemical symbolism, this gets us nowhere as regards the *meaning* of the symbols. On the contrary, we have landed ourselves in a blind alley, for we shall only be able to say that all symbolism, present and future, derives from the primal incest. That is what Freud actually thought, for he once said to me: "I only wonder what neurotics will do in the future when it is generally known what their symbols mean."

397 Luckily for us, symbols mean very much more than can be known at first glance. Their meaning resides in the fact that they compensate an unadapted attitude of consciousness, an attitude that does not fulfil its purpose, and that they would enable it to do this if they were understood.[5] But it becomes impossible to interpret their meaning if they are reduced to something else. That is why some of the later alchemists, particularly in the sixteenth century, abhorred all vulgar substances and replaced them by "symbolic" ones which allowed the nature of the archetype to glimmer through. This does not mean that the adept ceased to work in the laboratory, only that he kept an eye on the symbolic aspect of his transmutations. This corresponds exactly to the situation in the modern psychology of the unconscious: while personal problems are not overlooked (the patient himself takes very good care of that!), the analyst keeps an eye on their symbolic aspects, for healing comes only from what leads the patient beyond himself and beyond his entanglement in the ego.

### 9. VARIOUS ASPECTS OF THE TREE

398 What the tree meant to the alchemists cannot be ascertained either from a single interpretation or from a single text. In order to discover this, a great many sources must be compared. We shall therefore turn to further statements about the tree. Pictures of the tree are often given in the medieval texts. Some of them are reproduced in *Psychology and Alchemy*. Sometimes the prototype is the tree of paradise, hung not with apples but

[5] As archetypal symbols are numinous, they have an effect even though they cannot be grasped intellectually.

with sun-and-moon fruit, like the trees in the treatise of Michael Maier in the *Musaeum hermeticum*,[1] or else it is a sort of Christmas tree, adorned with the seven planets and surrounded by allegories of the seven phases of the alchemical process. Standing beneath the tree are not Adam and Eve but Hermes Trismegistus as an old man and the adept as a youth. Behind Hermes Trismegistus is King Sol sitting on a lion accompanied by a fire-spitting dragon, and behind the adept is the moon goddess Diana sitting on a whale accompanied by an eagle.[2] The tree is generally in leaf and living, but sometimes it is quite abstract and expressly stands for the phases of the process.[3]

399    In the Ripley *Scrowle*[4] the serpent of paradise dwells in the top of the tree in the shape of Melusina—"desinit in [anguem] mulier formosa superne." [5] This is combined with a motif that is not in the least Biblical but is primitive and shamanistic: a man, presumably the adept, is halfway up the tree and meets Melusina, or Lilith, coming down from above. The climbing of the magical tree is the heavenly journey of the shaman, during which he encounters his heavenly spouse. In medieval Christianity the shamanistic anima was transformed into Lilith,[6] who according to tradition was the serpent of paradise and Adam's first wife, with whom he begot a horde of demons. In this picture primitive traditions cross with Judaeo-Christian ones. I have

---

1 P. 702. Cf. "Symbolum Saturni," in Mylius, *Phil. ref.*, p. 313: "Not far from there I was conducted to a meadow, in which was planted a remarkable garden with various kinds of trees, most excellent to behold. And among these trees he showed me seven that were distinguished by name; among these I perceived two outstanding ones, higher than the others, of which one bore a fruit like to the brightest and most refulgent sun, and its leaves were like gold. But the other brought forth the whitest fruits, more brightly shining than lilies, and its leaves were like quicksilver. They were named by Neptune the tree of the sun and the tree of the moon."

2 *Psychology and Alchemy*, Fig. 188.

3 Ibid., Figs. 122, 221.

4 Ibid., Fig. 257. [Cf. also supra, Fig. B5.]

5 "A beautiful woman in her upper part, she passes into a [snake]." ("Anguis" is my adaptation for "piscis.") A late Hellenistic statue of Isis shows her as a beautiful goddess wearing the mural crown and carrying a torch, but whose lower half changes into a *uraeus*.

6 The classic representation is to be found in the *Scrowle* of Sir George Ripley, Canon of Bridlington, probably the most important English alchemist (1415–90).

never come across the climbing of the tree in the pictures done by my patients, and have met it only as a dream motif. The motif of ascent and descent occurs in modern dreams chiefly in connection with a mountain or a building, or sometimes a machine (lift, aeroplane, etc.).

400    The motif of the leafless or dead tree is not common in alchemy, but is found in Judaeo-Christian tradition as the tree of paradise that died after the Fall. An old English legend [7] reports what Seth saw in the Garden of Eden. In the midst of paradise there rose a shining fountain, from which four streams flowed, watering the whole world. Over the fountain stood a great tree with many branches and twigs, but it looked like an old tree, for it had no bark and no leaves. Seth knew that this was the tree of whose fruit his parents had eaten, for which reason it now stood bare. Looking more closely, Seth saw that a naked snake without a skin [8] had coiled itself round the tree. It was the serpent by whom Eve had been persuaded to eat of the forbidden fruit. When Seth took a second look at paradise he saw that the tree had undergone a great change. It was now covered with bark and leaves, and in its crown lay a little new-born babe wrapped in swaddling clothes, that wailed because of Adam's sin. This was Christ, the second Adam. He is found in the top of the tree that grows out of Adam's body in representations of Christ's genealogy.

401    Another alchemical motif is the truncated tree. In the frontispiece to the French edition (1600) of Francesco Colonna's *Hypnerotomachia Poliphili* (Venice, 1499), it forms the counterpart to the lion with cut-off paws,[9] which appears as an alchemical motif in Reusner's *Pandora* (1588). Blaise de Vigenère (1523–?1569), who was influenced by the Cabala, speaks of the "caudex arboris mortis" (trunk of the tree of death) that sent out a red death-ray.[10] "Tree of death" is synonymous with "coffin." The strange recipe, "Take the tree and place in it a

[7] Horstmann, *Sammlung altenglischer Legenden*, I, pp. 124ff.
[8] The tree's lack of bark and the snake's lack of skin indicate the identity between them.
[9] *Psychology and Alchemy*, Fig. 4. The motif of mutilation occurs in "Allegoriae super librum Turbae," *Art. aurif.*, I, pp. 140, 151. These amputations have nothing to do with a so-called castration complex, but refer to the motif of dismemberment.
[10] "De igne et sale," *Theatr. chem.*, VI (1661), p. 119.

man of great age," [11] should probably be understood in this sense. This motif is a very ancient one, and occurs in the ancient Egyptian tale of Bata, preserved in a papyrus of the nineteenth dynasty. There the hero placed his soul on the topmost blossom of an acacia-tree. When the tree was cut down with treacherous intent, his soul was found again in the form of a seed. With this the dead Bata was restored to life. When he was killed a second time in the form of a bull, two persea trees grew out of the blood. But when these were cut down, a chip of the wood fertilized the queen, who bore a son: he was the reborn Bata, who then became Pharaoh, a divine being. It is evident that the tree here is an instrument of transformation. [12] Vigenère's "caudex" is similar to the truncated tree in Poliphilo. This image probably goes back to Cassiodorus, who allegorizes Christ as a "tree cut down in his passion." [13]

402 More frequently the tree appears bearing flowers and fruit. The Arabian alchemist Abu'l Qāsim (13th cent.) describes its four kinds of blossoms as red, midway between white and black, black, and midway between white and yellow. [14] The four colours refer to the four elements that are combined in the opus. The quaternity as a symbol of wholeness means that the goal of the opus is the production of an all-embracing unity. The motif of the double quaternity, the ogdoad, is associated in shamanism with the world-tree: the cosmic tree with eight branches was planted simultaneously with the creation of the first shaman. The eight branches correspond to the eight great gods. [15]

403 The *Turba* has much to say about the fruit-bearing tree. [16] Its fruits are of a special kind. The "Visio Arislei" speaks of "this most precious tree, of whose fruit he who eats shall never hunger." [17] The parallel to this in the *Turba* runs: "I say that that old man does not cease to eat of the fruits of that tree . . .

[11] Hoghelande (*Theatr. chem.*, I, 1659, p. 145), referring to *Turba*, Sermo LVIII (ed. Ruska, p. 161): "Take that white tree and build around it a round dark house covered with dew, and place in it a man of great age, a hundred years old," etc. The old man is Saturn = lead as prima materia.
[12] Flinders Petrie, *Egyptian Tales*, 2nd series, XVIIIth to XIXth dynasty, pp. 36ff.
[13] A parallel to the pine tree of Attis.
[14] *Kitāb al-'ilm al-muktasab*, ed. Holmyard, p. 23.
[15] Eliade, *Shamanism*, pp. 70–187.
[16] Pp. 127, 147, 162.
[17] Codex Q. 584 (Berlin), fol. 21ᵛ (Ruska, *Turba*, p. 324).

until that old man becomes a youth." [18] These fruits are here equated with the bread of life in John 6 : 35, but they go back beyond that to the Ethiopic Book of Enoch (second century B.C.), where it is said that the fruits of the tree in the Western Land will be the food of the elect.[19] This is a clear hint of death and renewal. It is not always the fruit of the tree, but of the *granum frumenti,* the grain of wheat, from which the food of immortality is prepared, as in *Aurora consurgens* I: "For from the fruits of this grain is made the food of life, which cometh down from heaven." [20] Manna, Host, and panacea form here an unfathomable mixture. The same idea of a miraculous spiritual food is mentioned in the Arisleus vision. There it is said that Harforetus (Harpokrates), a "disciple of Pythagoras" and the "author of nourishment," came to the help of Arisleus and his companions, evidently with the fruits of the tree that are mentioned in Ruska's edition of Berlin Codex Q. 584.[21] In the Book of Enoch the fruits of the tree of wisdom are likened to grapes, and this is of interest inasmuch as in the Middle Ages the philosophical tree was sometimes called a vine,[22] with reference to John 15 : 1, "I am the true vine." The fruits and seeds of the tree were also called sun and moon,[23] to which the two trees of paradise corresponded.[24] The sun-and-moon fruits presumably go back to Deuteronomy 33 : 13f. (DV): "[Blessed] of the Lord be his land . . . [for] the fruits brought forth by the sun and by the moon . . .[25] and [for] the fruits of the everlasting hills."

18 Sermo LVIII, Ruska, p. 161.
19 Charles, *Apocrypha and Pseudepigrapha,* II, pp. 204f. From the fruits of the sun-and-moon tree is prepared "the immortal fruit, which has life and blood." "The blood causes all unfruitful trees to bear fruit of the same nature as the apple" (Mylius, *Phil. ref.,* p. 314).    20 *Aurora Consurgens* (ed. von Franz), p. 143.
21 *Turba* p. 324. Cf. *Psychology and Alchemy,* par. 449 and n. 2.
22 As in Ripley's *Scrowle:* "vitis arborea."
23 Maier, *Symb. aur. mens.,* p. 269, also the "Secretum" of Greverus (*Theatr. chem.,* III, 1659, p. 700) and the "Summarium philosophicum" of Flamel (*Mus. herm.,* p. 175). Cf. Pordage, *Sophia,* p. 10: "Here I saw the fruits and herbs of paradise, whereof my eternal man should thenceforward eat, and live."
24 These trees also occur in the Romance of Alexander as the "most holy trees of the sun and moon, which will declare the future to you" (Hilka, *Der altfranzösische Prosa-Alexander-Roman,* p. 204).
25 Vulgate: "de pomis fructuum solis ac lunae." The alchemists naturally took this version as authoritative. The original text has, as in AV: ". . . The precious fruits brought forth by the sun, and the precious things put forth by the moon."

Laurentius Ventura[26] says: "Sweet of smell is this apple, rich in colour this little apple," and pseudo-Aristotle says in his "Tractatus ad Alexandrum Magnum":[27] "Gather the fruits, for the fruit of this tree has led us into the darkness and through the darkness." This ambiguous advice evidently alludes to a knowledge which was not on the best of terms with the prevailing world-view.

404      Benedictus Figulus calls the fruit "the golden apple of the Hesperides, to be pluck't from the blest philosophic tree," [28] the tree representing the opus and the fruit its results, i.e., the gold of which it is said: "Our gold is not the common gold." [29] A special light is thrown on the meaning of the fruit by a saying in "Gloria mundi": "Take the fire, or quicklime, of which the philosophers speak, which grows on trees, for in that [fire] God himself burns with divine love." [30] God himself dwells in the fiery glow of the sun and appears as the fruit of the philosophical tree and thus as the product of the opus, whose course is symbolized by the growth of the tree. This remarkable saying loses its strangeness if we remember that the goal of the opus was to deliver the *anima mundi,* the world-creating spirit of God, from the chains of Physis. Here this idea has activated the archetype of the tree-birth, which is known to us chiefly from the Egyptian and Mithraic spheres of culture. A conception prevalent in shamanism is that the ruler of the world lives in the top of the world-tree,[31] and the Christian representation of the Redeemer at the top of his genealogical tree might be taken as a parallel. In Figure 27, the woman's head rising "like the pistil of a flower" might be compared with the Mithras relief from Osterburken (Germany).[32]

---

[26] *Theatr. chem.,* II (1659), p. 241. ("Dulce pomum est odorum, floridus hic pomulus.")

[27] Ibid., V (1660), p. 790. ("Collige fructus quia fructus arboris seduxit nos in et per obscurum.")

[28] The title of this book runs in part: *Paradisus aureolus hermeticus . . . in cuius . . . offertur instructio, quomodo aureola Hesperidum poma, ab arbore benedicta philosophica sint decerpenda, etc.*

[29] Senior, *De chemia,* p. 92.

[30] *Mus. herm.,* p. 246.

[31] Eliade, *Shamanism,* pp. 70f.

[32] Cumont, *Textes et Monuments figurés relatifs aux mystères de Mithra,* II, p. 350, and Eisler, *Weltenmantel und Himmelszelt,* II, p. 519.

405     Sometimes the tree is small and young, something like the "grani tritici arbuscula" (little trees of wheat grains),[33] sometimes large and old, taking the form of an oak[34] or the world-tree, in so far as it bears the sun and moon as its fruits.

## 10. THE HABITAT OF THE TREE

406     The philosophical tree usually grows alone and, according to Abu'l Qāsim, "on the sea" in the Western Land, which presumably means on an island. The secret moon-plant of the adepts is "like a tree planted in the sea." [1] In a parable in Mylius[2] the sun-and-moon tree stands on an island in the sea and grows out of the wonderful water that is extracted by the power of the magnet from the rays of the sun and moon. Khunrath says: "From this little salty fountain grows also the tree of the sun and moon, the red and white coral tree of our sea." [3] Salt and sea-water signify in Khunrath among other things the maternal Sophia from whose breasts the filii Sapientiae, the philosophers, drink. Abu'l Qāsim might well have been acquainted with Persian traditions (his surname al-Iraqi also brings him geographically nearer to Persia), and more particularly with the legend of the tree in the Bundahish that grows in the sea named Vouru-kasha, or of the tree of life that grows in the fountain of Ardvī Sūra Anāhita.[4]

407     The tree (or wonderful plant) also has its habitat on the mountains. Since the imagery of the Book of Enoch was often taken as a model, it should be mentioned that there the tree in the Western Land stood on a mountain.[5] In the "Practica Mariae Prophetissae" [6] the wonderful plant is described as

---

[33] "Instructio de arbore solari," Theatr. chem., VI (1661), p. 168.
[34] Bernardus Trevisanus, Theatr. chem., I (1659), p. 706.
[1] "Allegoriae super librum Turbae," Art. aurif., I, p. 141. Evidently a reference to the tree of the Hesperides on an island, where also the fount of ambrosia and the dragon are found. Cf. the coral tree (ibid., p. 143) and Psychology and Alchemy, par. 449, n. 6. In the Livre d'Heures du Duc de Berry, Paradise is shown as a round island in the sea.
[2] Phil. ref., p. 313.          [3] Hyl. Chaos, p. 270.
[4] Windischmann, Zoroastrische Studien, pp. 90, 171.
[5] Perhaps in remembrance of the shrines of the Semitic Astarte on mountains. Cf. Charles, Apocrypha and Pseudepigrapha, II, pp. 204f.
[6] Art. aurif., I, p. 321.

"growing on hills." The Arabic treatise of Ostanes in the "Kitâb el Foçul" [7] says: "It is a tree that grows on the tops of mountains." The relation of tree to mountain is not accidental, but is due to the original and widespread identity between them: both are used by the shaman for the purpose of his heavenly journey.[8] Mountain and tree are symbols of the personality and of the self, as I have shown elsewhere; Christ, for instance, is symbolized by the mountain[9] as well as by the tree.[10] Often the tree stands in a garden, as an obvious reminder of Genesis. Thus the trees of the seven planets grow in the "private garden" of the blessed isles.[11] In Nicolas Flamel (1330?–?1418) the "most highly praised tree" grows in the garden of the philosophers.[12]

408    As we have seen, the tree has a special connection with water, salt, and sea-water, and thus with the *aqua permanens,* the true arcanum of the adepts. This as we know is Mercurius, who is not to be confused with Hg, the *mercurius crudus sive vulgaris.*[13] Mercurius is the tree of the metals.[14] He is the prima materia,[15] or else its source.[16] The god Hermes (= Mercurius) "watered his tree with that water, and with his glass made the flowers grow high." [17] I cite this passage because it expresses the subtle alchemical idea that the artifex and the arcanum are one and the same. The water that makes the tree grow but also consumes it[18] is Mercurius, who is called "duplex" because he

---

7 Berthelot, *Moyen âge,* III, p. 117.

8 Eliade, *Shamanism,* pp. 266f.

9 Epiphanius, *Ancoratus,* 40; St. Ambrose, *De interpellatione Job et David,* I, iv, 17 (Migne, *P.L.,* vol. 14, col. 818): "A mountain small and great."

10 St. Gregory the Great, *Moralia in Job,* XIX, 1 (Migne, *P.L.,* vol. 76, col. 97): "A fruitful tree to be cultivated in our hearts."

11 "Symposium Saturni," in Mylius, *Phil. ref.,* p. 313. Cf. the hymn for St. Paul of Constantinople in Theodore the Studite: "O most blessed one, from the cradle thou didst flourish like a comely plant in the ascetic garden; thou gavest forth a pleasant odour, bowed down with the finest apples of the Holy Spirit" (Pitra, *Analecta sacra,* I, p. 337).

12 *Mus. herm.,* p. 177.

13 Cf. "The Spirit Mercurius," supra, par. 255.

14 Flamel, *Mus. herm.,* p. 177, also p. 175.

15 "The Spirit Mercurius," supra, pars. 282ff.

16 Abu'l Qāsim, *Kitāb al-'ilm al-muktasab,* ed. Holmyard, p. 23.

17 Ripley, "Duodecim portarum," *Theatr. chem.,* II (1659), p. 113, and *Opera omnia,* p. 86.

18 The tree of Hermes is burnt to ashes with the "humiditas maxime permanens," as Ripley says (ibid., p. 39). Cf. p. 46: "That water has fire within it."

unites the opposites in himself, being both a metal and a liquid. Hence he is called both water and fire. As the sap of the tree he is therefore also fiery (cf. Fig. 15), that is to say the tree is of a watery and a fiery nature. In Gnosticism we encounter the "great tree" of Simon Magus, which consists of "supracelestial fire." "From it all flesh is fed." [19] It is a tree like the one that appeared to Nebuchadnezzar in a dream. Its branches and leaves are consumed, but "the fruit, when it is ready formed and has received its shape, is brought into a barn and not cast into the fire." [20] This image of the "supracelestial fire" accords on the one hand with the much earlier "ever-living fire" of Heraclitus, and on the other with the much later interpretation of Mercurius as fire and as the *spiritus vegetativus* that pervades the whole of nature, both animating and destructive. The fruit that is "not cast into the fire" is naturally the man who has stood the test, the "pneumatic" man of the Gnostics. One of the synonyms for the lapis, which likewise signifies the inner, integrated man, is "frumentum nostrum" (our grain).[21]

409      The tree is often represented as metallic,[22] usually golden.[23] Its connection with the seven metals implies a connection with the seven planets, so that the tree becomes the world-tree, whose shining fruits are the stars. Michael Maier attributes the woody parts to Mercurius, the (fourfold) flowers to Saturn, Jupiter, Venus, and Mars, and the fruits to Sol and Luna.[24] The tree with seven branches (= seven planets) is mentioned in *Aurora consurgens* II [25] and identified with the Lunatica or Berissa,[26] "whose root is the metallic earth, its trunk red tinged

---

[19] Hippolytus, *Elenchos*, VI, 9, 8ff. (Legge, II, p. 5).

[20] Ibid. Cf. the Indian parallel in Coomaraswamy, "The Inverted Tree," p. 126: "The tree is a fiery pillar as seen from below, a solar pillar as seen from above, and a pneumatic pillar throughout; it is a tree of light." The reference to the motif of the pillar is significant.

[21] "Gloria mundi," *Mus. herm.*, p. 240.

[22] Mercurius is named "arbor metallorum." For an interpretation of this symbol see Dorn, "Congeries Paracelsicae," *Theatr. chem.*, I (1659), p. 508.

[23] *Arbor aurea* in "Scriptum Alberti," ibid., II (1659), p. 456; also Abu'l Qāsim, ed. Holmyard, p. 54, and "Consilium coniugii," *Ars chemica*, p. 211.

[24] *Symb. aur. mens.*, p. 269, with reference to Greverus.

[25] *Art. aurif.*, I, p. 222.

[26] This plant derives ultimately from the Homeric μῶλυ (see *Mysterium Coniunctionis*, p. 133 and n. 200). Cf. Rahner, "Die seelenheilende Blume," *Eranos-Jahrbuch* XII (1945), 117ff.

with a certain blackness; its leaves are like the leaves of Marjoram, and are thirty in number according to the age of the moon in its waxing and waning; its flower is yellow." It is clear from this description that the tree symbolizes the whole opus. Accordingly Dorn says:[27] "Let therefore the tree [of the planets or metals] be planted and its root be ascribed to Saturn, and let that inconstant Mercurius and Venus, arising in the trunk and branches, offer to Mars[28] the leaves and fruit-bearing flowers." The relation to the world-tree is also apparent when Dorn says that "nature has planted the root of the [metallic] tree in the midst of her womb."[29]

## 11. THE INVERTED TREE

410      The tree is frequently called the "inverted tree" (arbor inversa).[1] Laurentius Ventura (16th cent.) says: "The roots of its ores are in the air and the summits in the earth. And when they are torn from their places, a terrible sound is heard and there follows a great fear."[2] Ventura is obviously thinking of the mandrake, which, when tied to the tail of a black dog, shrieks when it is torn out of the earth. The "Gloria mundi" likewise mentions that the philosophers had said that "the root of its minerals is in the air and its head in the earth."[3] Sir George Ripley says that the tree has its roots in the air and, elsewhere, that it is rooted in the "glorified earth," in the earth of paradise or in the future world.

411      Similarly, Vigenère states that a "Rabbi, the son of Josephus Carnitolus," had said: "The foundation of every lower structure is affixed above and its summit is here below, like an inverted

27 "De tenebris contra naturam," Theatr. chem., I (1659), p. 470. ("Plantetur itaque arbor ex eis [planetis s. metallis], cuius radix adscribatur Saturno, per quam varius ille Mercurius ac Venus truncum et ramos ascendentes, folia floresque fructum ferentes Marti praebent.")
28 That is, to Aries, whose ruler is Mars; hence to the first spring zodion.
29 "De genealogia mineralium," Theatr. chem., I (1659), p. 574.
1 Presumably Dante means this in Purgatorio, XXII, 131ff.
2 "Radices suarum minerarum sunt in aere et summitates in terra. Et quando evelluntur a suis locis, auditur sonus terribilis et sequitur timor magnus." ("De ratione conficiendi lapidis," Theatr. chem., II, 1659, p. 226.)
3 Mus. herm., pp. 240, 270.

tree." [4] Vigenère had some knowledge of the Cabala and is here comparing the philosophical tree with the tree of the Sefiroth, which is actually a mystical world-tree. But for him this tree also signifies man. He substantiates the singular idea that man is implanted in paradise by the roots of his hair with a reference to Song of Songs 7 : 5 (DV): "Thy head is like Carmel, and the hairs of thy head as the purple of the king bound in the channels" (. . . *comae capitis tui sicut purpura Regis vincta*[5] *canalibus*). The "canales" are little tubes, perhaps some kind of head ornament.[6] Knorr von Rosenroth is of the opinion that the "great tree" refers to Tifereth, the bridegroom of Malchuth.[7] The upper Sefira Binah is named the "root of the tree," [8] and in Binah is rooted the tree of life. Because this stood in the middle of the garden, it was called the *linea media* (middle line). Through this middle line, which was as it were the trunk of the Sefiroth system, it brought life down to earth from Binah.[9]

412      The idea that man is an inverted tree seems to have been current in the Middle Ages. The humanist Andrea Alciati (d. 1550) says in his *Emblemata cum commentariis:* "It pleased the Physicists to see man as a tree standing upside down, for what in the one is the root, trunk, and leaves, in the other is the head and the rest of the body with the arms and feet." [10] The link with Indian conceptions is provided by Plato.[11] Krishna says in the Bhagavadgītā (ch. 15): "I am the Himalaya among mountains and the *ashvattha* among trees." The *ashvattha* (*Ficus reli-*

---

[4] "Rabbi Josephi Carnitoli filius . . . inquit: fundamentum omnis structurae inferioris supra est affixum et eius culmen hic infra est sicut arbor inversa." ("De igne et sale," *Theatr. chem.*, VI, 1661, p. 39.) It is also said in the *Prodromus Rhodostauroticus* (fol. Vʳ) that the ancients called man an inverted tree.

[5] The text has, erroneously, "iuncta" for "vincta."

[6] More accurate translation, as in RSV: "your flowing locks are like purple; a king is held captive in the tresses."

[7] *Cabbala denudata*, I, p. 166.

[8] Ibid., p. 77.

[9] Ibid., p. 629.

[10] P. 888: "Inversam arborem stantem videri hominem placet Physicis, quod enim radix ibi, truncus et frondes, hic caput est et corpus reliquum cum brachiis et pedibus."

[11] Cf. Chwolsohn, *Die Ssabier und der Ssabismus*, II, p. 373. *Timaeus* 90A: ". . . seeing that we are not an earthly but a heavenly plant." Vettius Valens, *Anthologiarum* IX, p. 330, 23. Orphic fragment, Kern, No. 228a: "But the soul in man is rooted in the aether."

*giosa)* pours down from above the drink of immortality, soma.[12]
The Bhagavadgītā continues:

> There is a fig tree
> In ancient story,
> The giant Ashvattha,
> The everlasting,
> Rooted in heaven,
> Its branches earthward;
> Each of its leaves
> Is a song of the Vedas,
> And he who knows it
> Knows all the Vedas.
>
> Downward and upward
> Its branches bending
> Are fed by the gunas,
> The buds it puts forth
> Are the things of the senses,
> Roots it has also
> Reaching downward
> Into this world,
> The roots of man's action.[13]

413    The alchemical illustrations showing the opus as a tree and
its phases as the leaves[14] are very reminiscent of the Indian conception of deliverance through the Veda, i.e., through knowledge. In Hindu literature the tree grows from above downwards, whereas in alchemy (at least according to the pictures) it
grows from below upwards. In the illustrations to the *Pretiosa
margarita novella* of 1546,[15] it looks very like an asparagus
plant. Figure 27 in my picture series contains the same motif,
and indeed the upthrusting stalks of asparagus are a graphic representation of the way previously unconscious contents push
into consciousness. In East and West alike, the tree symbolizes

12 Chhāndogya Upanishad, VIII, 5, 3 (SBE, I, p. 131). Shatapatha-Brāhmana (SBE,
XLIV, p. 317): "The Nyagrodha with cups—for when the gods were performing
sacrifice, they tilted over those Soma cups, and turned downwards they took root,
whence the Nyagrodhas, when turned downwards (*nyak*) take root (*roha*)." The
*ashvattha* is the seat of the gods (*Hymns of the Atharva-Veda*, V, 4; SBE, XLII,
p. 4). Cf. Coomaraswamy, "The Inverted Tree," pp. 122f.
13 *The Song of God* (trans. Prabhamananda and Isherwood), pp. 146f.
14 *Psychology and Alchemy*, Figs. 122 and 221.
15 Fol. **vff.

a living process as well as a process of enlightenment, which, though it may be grasped by the intellect, should not be confused with it.

414    The tree as guardian of the treasure appears in the alchemical fairytale of "The Spirit in the Bottle." As it contains the treasure which appears in its fruit, the tree is a symbol of the *chrysopoea* (goldmaking) or *ars aurifera* in general, in accordance with the principle laid down by "Hercules":[16] "This magistery arises in the beginning from one root, which afterwards expands into several substances and then returns to the one." [17] Ripley likens the artifex to Noah cultivating the vine,[18] in Djābir the tree is the "mystic myrtle," [19] and in Hermes the "vine of the wise." [20] Hoghelande says: "But the fruits go forth from the most perfect tree in early spring and flower at the beginning of the end." [21] It is clear from this that the life of the tree represents the opus, which as we know coincides with the seasons.[22] The fact that the fruits appear in the spring and the flowers in the autumn may be connected with the motif of reversal (*arbor inversa!*) and the *opus contra naturam*. The "Allegoriae sapientum supra librum Turbae" give the following recipe: "Again, plant this tree on the stone, that it fear not the buffetings of the winds; that the birds of heaven may come and multiply on its branches, for thence cometh wisdom." [23] Here

16 The Byzantine emperor Heraclius (610–641).

17 Morienus, "De transmutatione metallorum," *Art. aurif.*, II, pp. 25f. "Hoc autem magisterium ex una primum radice procedit, quae postmodum in plures res expenditur et iterum ad unam revertitur."

18 *Opera omnia*, p. 46.

19 Berthelot, *Moyen âge*, III, pp. 214f.

20 Cited in Hoghelande, *Theatr. chem.*, I (1659), p. 147. The "vintage of Hermes" (*vindemia Hermetis*) goes back to an Ostanes quotation in Zosimos (Berthelot, *Alch. grecs*, III, vi, 5).

21 Loc. cit. "Quidem fructus exeunt a perfectissima arbore primo vere et in exitus initio florent." Hoghelande is referring to the *Turba*, Sermo LVIII, where Balgus is asked: "Why have you ceased to speak of the tree, of which he who eats its fruit shall never hunger?"

22 The opus begins in the spring, when the conditions are most favourable (cf. "Paracelsus as a Spiritual Phenomenon," supra, pars. 190ff.) and the "element of the stone is most abundant" (Ventura, *Theatr. chem.*, II, 1659, p. 253). The relation of the opus to the zodiac is shown in *Psychology and Alchemy*, Fig. 92.

23 *Theatr. chem.*, V (1660), p. 61. "Item planta hanc arborem super lapidem, ne ventorum cursus timeat, ut volatilia coeli veniant et supra ramos eius gignant, inde enim sapientia surgit."

too the tree is the true foundation and arcanum of the opus. This arcanum is the much-praised *thesaurus thesaurorum.* Just as the tree of the metals has seven branches, so also has the tree of contemplation, as a treatise entitled "De arbore contemplationis" shows.[24] There the tree is a palm with seven branches and on each branch sits a bird: "pavo, [illegible word], cignus, [h]arpia, filomena, hyrundo, fenix," and on each a flower: "viola, gladiola, lilium, rosa, crocus, solsequium, flos [. . . ?]," all of which have a moral significance. These ideas are very much like those of the alchemists. They contemplated their tree in the retort, where, according to the *Chymical Wedding,* it was held in the hand of an angel.[25]

## 12. BIRD AND SNAKE

415    Birds, as I have said, have a special relation to the tree. The "Scriptum Alberti" says that Alexander, on his great journey, found a tree which had its "glorious greenness" (*viriditas gloriosa*) within. On this tree sat a stork, and there Alexander built a golden palace to "set a fitting end to his travels." [1] The tree with the bird stands for the opus and its consummation. The motif also appears in picture form.[2] The fact that the leaves of the tree (the *viriditas gloriosa*) grew inwards is another instance of the *opus contra naturam* and at the same time a concrete expression of introversion in the contemplative state.

416    The snake, too, with obvious reference to the Bible story, is connected with the tree, first of all in a general way since it is properly speaking the mercurial serpent which, as the chthonic *spiritus vegetativus,* rises from the roots into the branches, and then more specifically because it represents the tree-numen and appears as Melusina.[3] The mercurial serpent is the arcane substance that transforms itself inside the tree and thus constitutes its life. This is substantiated by the "Scriptum Alberti." The text is probably a commentary on a picture which unfortunately

24 MS. in Basel University Library, AX. 128b.

25 Cf. supra, "Paracelsus as a Spiritual Phenomenon," par. 228.

1 *Theatr. chem.,* II (1659), p. 458.

2 *Psychology and Alchemy,* Fig. 231, and *Mus. herm.,* p. 201.

3 *Psychology and Alchemy,* par. 537, n. 58, and Figs. 10–12, 157, 257. Cf. also Jaffé, "Bilder und Symbole aus E. T. A. Hoffmanns Märchen 'Der Goldene Topf,' " p. 300ff.

is not given in the edition of 1602. It begins with the statement: "This is a picture of heaven, which is named the heavenly sphere, and contains eight most noble figures, viz., the first figure, which is named the first circle and is the circle of the Deity," etc.[4] It is clear from this that it was a picture of concentric circles. The first, outermost, circle contains the "verba divinitatis," the divine world order; the second the seven planets; the third the "corruptible" and "creative" elements (*generabilia*); the fourth a raging dragon issuing from the seven planets; the fifth "the head and the death" of the dragon. The head of the dragon "lives in eternity," is named the "vita gloriosa," and "the angels serve it." The *caput draconis* is here obviously identified with Christ, for the words "the angels serve it" refer to Matthew 4 : 11, where Christ has just repudiated Satan. But if the dragon's head is identified with Christ, then the dragon's tail must be identical with Antichrist or the devil. According to our text the whole of the dragon's body is absorbed by the head, so that the devil is integrated with Christ. For the dragon fought against the imago Dei, but by the power of God it was implanted in the dragon and formed its head: "The whole body obeys the head, and the head hates the body, and slays it beginning from the tail, gnawing it with its teeth, until the whole body enters into the head and remains there for ever."[5] The sixth circle contains six figures and two birds, namely storks. The figures are presumably human, for the text says one of them looked like an Ethiopian.[6] It appears that the stork is a *vas circulatorium* (a vessel for circular distillation), like the Pelican.[7] Each of the six figures represents three phases of transformation and together with the two birds they form an ogdoad as a symbol of the transformation process. The seventh circle, says the text, shows the relation of the "verba divinitatis" and the seven planets to the eighth circle, which contains the golden tree. The author states he would rather keep quiet about the content of the seventh circle, because this is where the great secret begins,

---

4 *Theatr. chem.*, II (1659), p. 456.

5 Ibid., p. 457.

6 Cf. von Franz, "Passio Perpetuae," pp. 463ff.

7 For the importance of the vessel in alchemy see *Psychology and Alchemy*, index, s.v. vas/vessel. The *ciconia vel storca* was a kind of retort (Rhenanus, *Solis e puteo emergentis*, Lib. I, 22). [Cf. supra, Fig. B7.]

which can be revealed only by God himself. Here is found the stone which the king wears in his crown. "Wise women hide it, foolish virgins show it in public, because they wish to be plundered." "Popes, certain priests, and monks revile it, because it was so commanded of them by God's law."

417    The golden tree in the eighth circle shines "like lightning." Lightning in alchemy, as in Jakob Böhme, signifies sudden rapture and illumination.[8] On the tree sits a stork. Whereas the two storks in the sixth circle represent the distilling apparatus for two transformations of three phases each, the stork sitting on the golden tree has a far wider significance. Since ancient times it was held to be the "pia avis" (devout bird), and appears as such in Haggadic tradition,[9] despite being listed among the unclean beasts in Leviticus 11 : 19. Its piety may go back to Jeremiah 8 : 7: "Yea, the stork in the heaven knoweth her appointed times . . . but my people know not the judgment of the Lord." In imperial Rome the stork was an allegory of piety, and in Christian tradition it is an allegory of Christ the judge, because it destroys snakes. Just as the snake or dragon is the chthonic numen of the tree, so the stork is its spiritual principle and thus a symbol of the Anthropos.[10] Among the forerunners of the alchemical stork must be counted the stork Adebar in Teutonic mythology, which brings back to earth the souls of the dead that were renewed in the fountain of Hulda.[11] The attribution of the "Scriptum" to Albertus Magnus is highly questionable. To judge by its style, its discussion of the philosophical tree can hardly be dated earlier than the sixteenth century.

### 13. THE FEMININE TREE-NUMEN

418    As the seat of transformation and renewal, the tree has a feminine and maternal significance. We have seen from Ripley's *Scrowle* that the tree-numen is Melusina. In *Pandora* the trunk of the tree is a crowned, naked woman holding a torch in each hand, with an eagle sitting in the branches on her head.[1] On

[8] Cf. "A Study in the Process of Individuation," pp. 295ff.
[9] Grünbaum, *Jüdisch-deutsche Chrestomathie,* p. 174.
[10] Picinellus, *Mundus symbolicus,* I, p. 281.
[11] Wünsche, "Die Sagen vom Lebensbaum und Lebenswasser," pp. 85f.
[1] *Psychology and Alchemy,* Fig. 231.

Hellenistic monuments Isis has the form of Melusina and one of her attributes is the torch. Other attributes are the vine and the palm. Leto and Mary[2] both gave birth under a palm, and Maya at the birth of the Buddha was shaded by the holy tree. Adam, "so the Hebrews say," was created out of the "earth of the tree of life," the "red Damascene earth." [3] According to this legend, Adam stood in the same relation to the tree of life as Buddha to the Bodhi tree.

419    The feminine-maternal nature of the tree appears also in its relation to Sapientia. The tree of knowledge in Genesis is in the Book of Enoch the tree of wisdom, whose fruit resembles the grape.[4] In the teachings of the Barbeliots, reports Irenaeus,[5] the Autogenes finally created "the man perfect and true, whom they also called Adamas." With him was created perfect knowledge: "From [the perfect] man and gnosis is born the tree, which they also call gnosis." [6] Here we find the same connection of man with the tree as in the case of Adam and the Buddha. A similar connection is found in the *Acta Archelai:* "But that tree which is in paradise, whereby the good is known, is Jesus and the knowledge of him which is in the world." [7] "For thence [i.e., from the tree] cometh wisdom," says the "Allegoriae sapientum." [8]

420    Similar ideas of the tree are found in alchemy. We have already met the conception of man as an inverted tree, a view found also in the Cabala. The *Pirke de Rabbi Eliezer*[9] says: "R. Zehira said, 'Of the fruit of the tree'—here 'tree' only means man, who is compared to the tree, as it is said, 'For man is the tree of the field' (Deuteronomy 20 : 19)." In the gnosis of Justin the trees in the Garden of Eden are angels, while the tree of knowledge of good and evil is the third of the motherly angels,

2 Cf. Koran, Sura XIX.

3 Steeb, *Coelum Sephiroticum,* p. 49.

4 Charles, *Apocrypha and Pseudepigrapha,* II, p. 207.

5 *Adversus haereses,* Lib. I, 29, 3.

6 "Ex Anthropo autem et Gnosi natum lignum, quod et ipsum Gnosin vocant."

7 "Illa autem arbor quae est in paradiso, ex qua agnoscitur bonum, ipse est Jesus et scientia eius quae est in mundo." Hegemonius, *Acta Archelai* (ed. Beeson), p. 18, lines 15ff.

8 *Theatr. chem.,* V (1660), p. 61.

9 Trans. and ed. Friedlander, p. 150. The *Pirke* dates from 7th–8th cents. Eliezer (ben Hyrcanus) lived in the 2nd cent.

the Naas.[10] This division of the tree-soul into a masculine and a feminine figure corresponds to the alchemical Mercurius as the life principle of the tree, for as an hermaphrodite he is duplex.[11] The picture in *Pandora*, where the tree trunk is a woman's body, refers to Mercurius in his feminine role of wisdom, who in his masculine aspect is symbolized by the figure of Mercurius Senex or Hermes Trismegistus.

### 14. THE TREE AS THE LAPIS

421    Just as the tree and man are central symbols in alchemy, so also is the lapis in its double significance as the prima and ultima materia. The above-mentioned quotation from the "Allegoriae sapientum"—"Plant this tree on the stone, that it fear not the buffetings of the winds"—seems to be an allusion to the parable of the house that was built on sand and fell when the floods came and the winds blew (Matthew 7 : 26–27). The stone might therefore mean simply the sure foundation afforded by the right prima materia. But the context points to the symbolic significance of the stone, as the preceding sentence makes clear: "Take wisdom with all thy power, for from it thou shalt drink eternal life, until thy [stone] is congealed and thy sluggishness depart, for thence cometh life." [1]

422    "The prima materia is an oily water and is the philosophic stone, from which branches multiply into infinity," says Mylius.[2] Here the stone is itself the tree and is understood as the "fiery substance" (the ὑγρὰ οὐσία of the Gnostics) or as the "oily water." As water and oil do not mix, this represents the double or contrary nature of Mercurius.

423    Similarly the "Consilium coniugii," commenting on Senior, says: "Thus the stone is perfected of and in itself. For it is the tree whose branches, leaves, flowers, and fruits come from it and

10 Hippolytus, *Elenchos*, V, 26, 6. Naas, the serpent, is the prima materia of the Naassenes, a "moist substance" like Thales' water. It is substantial to all things and contains all things. It is like the river of Eden, which divides into four streams (V, 9, 13ff.).
11 Cf. "The Spirit Mercurius," supra, pars. 268f.
1 "Item accipe sapientiam vi intensissima[m] et ex ea vitam hauries aeternam, donec tuus [lapis] congeletur ac tua pigredo exeat, tunc inde vita fit" (*Theatr. chem.*, V, 1660, p. 61).
2 *Phil. ref.*, p. 260. For "rami infiniti multiplicantur" I read "infinite."

through it and for it, and it is itself whole or the whole [*tota vel totum*] and nothing else." [3] Hence the tree is identical with the stone and, like it, a symbol of wholeness. Khunrath says:

Of itself, from, in, and through itself is made and perfected the stone of the wise. For it is one thing only: like a tree (says Senior), whose roots, stem, branches, twigs, leaves, flowers, and fruit are of it and through it and from it and on it, and all come from one seed. It is itself everything, and nothing else makes it. [4]

424    In the Arabic "Book of Ostanes" there is a description of the arcane substance, or the water, in its various forms, first white, then black, then red, and finally a combustible liquid or a fire which is struck from certain stones in Persia. The text continues:

It is a tree that grows on the tops of the mountains, a young man born in Egypt, a prince from Andalusia, who desires the torment of the seekers. He has slain their leaders. . . . The sages are powerless to oppose him. I can see no weapon against him save resignation, no charger but knowledge, no buckler but understanding. If the seeker finds himself before him with these three weapons, and slays him, he [the prince] will come to life again after his death, will lose all power against him, and will give the seeker the highest power, so that he will arrive at his desired goal. [5]

425    The chapter in which this passage occurs begins with the words: "The sage has said, what the student needs first of all is to know the stone, the object of the aspirations of the ancients." The water, the tree, the young Egyptian, and the Andalusian prince all refer to the stone. Water, tree, and man appear here as its synonyms. The prince is an important symbol that needs a little elucidation, for it seems to echo an archetypal motif that is found in the Gilgamesh epic. There Enkidu, the chthonic man and shadow of Gilgamesh, is created by the gods at the behest of the insulted Ishtar, so that he may kill the hero. In the same way the prince "desires the torment of the seekers." He is their enemy and "has slain their leaders," that is, the masters and authorities of the art.

426    This motif of the hostile stone is formulated in the "Alle-

3 *Ars chemica,* p. 160.
4 *Hyl. Chaos,* pp. 20f.
5 Berthelot, *Moyen âge,* III, p. 117.

goriae sapientum" as follows: "Unless thy stone shall be an enemy, thou wilt not attain to thy desire." [6] This enemy appears in alchemy in the guise of the poisonous or fire-spitting dragon and also as the lion. The lion's paws must be cut off,[7] and the dragon must be killed, or else it kills or devours itself on the principle of Democritus: "Nature rejoices in nature, nature rules over nature, and nature conquers nature." [8]

427    The slaying of the alchemical authorities cannot fail to remind us of the intriguing picture in *Pandora* of Melusina stabbing Christ's side with a lance.[9] Melusina corresponds to the Edem of the Gnostics and represents the feminine aspect of Mercurius, i.e., the female Nous (Naas of the Naassenes), which in the form of the serpent seduced our first parents. A parallel to this would be the aforementioned quotation from the "Tractatus ad Alexandrum Magnum": "Gather the fruits, for the fruit of the tree has led us into the darkness and through the darkness." [10] As this admonition clearly contradicts the authority of the Bible and the Church, one can only suppose that it was uttered by someone who was consciously opposed to the ecclesiastical tradition.

428    The connection with the Gilgamesh epic is of interest because Ostanes was thought to be a Persian and a contemporary of Alexander the Great. As a further parallel to the initial hostility of Enkidu and the Andalusian prince and of the stone in general we might cite the Khidr legend.[11] Khidr, the messenger of Allah, at first frightens Moses by his misdeeds. Considered as a visionary experience or as a didactic tale, the legend sets forth the relation of Moses on the one hand to his shadow, his servant Joshua ben Nun, and on the other hand to the self, Khidr.[12] The lapis and its synonyms are likewise symbols of the self. Psychologically, this means that at the first meeting with the self all

---

[6] "Nisi lapis tuus fuerit inimicus, ad optatum non pervenies" (*Theatr. chem.*, V, 1660, p. 59).

[7] See illustration in Reusner's *Pandora*, p. 227. Also *Psychology and Alchemy*, Fig. 4.

[8] Ἡ γὰρ φύσις τὴν φύσιν τέρπει, καὶ ἡ φύσις τὴν φύσιν κρατεῖ καὶ ἡ φύσις τὴν φύσιν νικᾷ (Berthelot, *Alch. grecs*, I, iii, 12).

[9] See supra, Fig. B4.

[10] *Theatr. chem.*, V (1660), p. 790.

[11] Koran, Sura XVIII.

[12] Cf. "Concerning Rebirth," pp. 135ff.

those negative qualities can appear which almost invariably characterize an unexpected encounter with the unconscious.[13] The danger is that of an inundation by the unconscious, which in a bad case may take the form of a psychosis if the conscious mind is unable to assimilate, either intellectually or morally, the invasion of unconscious contents.

### 15. THE DANGERS OF THE ART

429    *Aurora consurgens* I says in regard to the dangers which threaten the artifex: "O how many understand not the sayings of the wise; these have perished because of their foolishness, for they lacked spiritual understanding." [1] Hoghelande is of the opinion that "the whole art is rightly to be held both difficult and dangerous, and anyone who is not improvident will eschew it as most pernicious." [2] Aegidius de Vadis feels the same when he says: "I shall keep silent about this science, which has led most of those who work in it into confusion, because there are few indeed who find what they seek, but an infinite number who have plunged to their ruin." [3] Hoghelande, citing Haly, says: "Our stone is life to him who knows it and how it is made, and he who knows not and has not made it and to whom no assurance[4] is given when it will be born, or who thinks it another stone, has already prepared himself for death." [5] Hoghelande makes it clear that it is not just the danger of poisoning[6] or of

---

13 *Aion,* pp. 8ff.

1 *Aurora Consurgens* (ed. von Franz), p. 117. "This is therefore a great sign, in the investigation of which some have perished" (*Art. aurif.,* II, p. 264). "Know ye, who seek after wisdom, that the foundation of this art, on account of which many have perished, is a thing stronger and more sublime than all other things" ("Turba," in *Art. aurif.,* I, p. 83).

2 "De alchimiae difficultatibus," *Theatr. chem.,* I (1659), p. 131.

3 "Dialogus inter naturam et filium philosophorum," ibid., II (1659), p. 104.

4 Cf. Du Cange, *Glossarium,* II, p. 275, "certificatio."

5 "Lapis noster est vita ei qui ipsum scit et eius factum et qui nesciverit et non fecit et non certificabitur quando nascetur aut putabit alium lapidem, iam paravit se morti" (Hoghelande, *Theatr. chem.,* I, 1659, p. 182).

6 This danger was well known. "Because of the fires and sulphurous exhalations it brings with it, the opus is highly dangerous" (Dee, "Monas hieroglyphica," *Theatr. chem.,* II, 1659, p. 196). "I [the divine water] give them a blow in the face, that is a wound, which makes them toothless, and brings about many infirmities through the smoke" ("Rosinus ad Sarratantam," *Art. aurif.,* I, p. 293).

possible explosions but of mental aberrations: "Let him take care to recognize and guard against the deceptions of the devil, who often insinuates himself into the chemical operations, that he may hold up the laborants with vain and useless things to the neglect of the works of nature." [7] He authenticates this danger by a quotation from Alphidius: "This stone proceeds from a sublime and most glorious place of great terror, which has given over many sages to death." [8] He also cites Moyses: "This work comes about as suddenly as the clouds come from heaven," adding a quotation from Micreris: "If you should suddenly see this transformation, wonder, fear, and trembling will befall you; therefore work with caution." [9]

430    The danger of daemonic agencies is likewise mentioned in the "Liber Platonis quartorum": "At a certain hour during the preparation certain kinds of spirits will oppose the work, and at another time this opposition will not be present." [10] The clearest of all is Olympiodorus (sixth century): "And all the while the demon Ophiuchos instils negligence, impeding our intentions; everywhere he creeps about, within and without, causing oversights, fear, and unpreparedness, and at other times he seeks by harassments and injuries to make us abandon the work." [11] He also mentions that lead is possessed of a demon which drives men mad.[12]

431    The miracle of the stone which the alchemist expected or experienced must have been intensely numinous, and this would explain his holy dread of profaning the mystery. "No one can disclose the name of the stone without damning his soul, for

---

"From the beginning the opus is like a death-dealing poison" (Ventura, "De ratione conficiendi lapidis," *Theatr. chem.*, II, 1659, p. 258). The alchemists seem to have known about mercurial poisoning.

[7] "Cautus sit in diaboli illusionibus dignoscendis et praecavendis, qui se chemisticis operationibus saepius immiscet, ut operantes circa vana et inutilia detineat praetermissis naturae operibus" (Hoghelande, p. 126). *Aurora Consurgens* (ed. von Franz, p. 51) speaks of the "evil odours and vapours that infect the mind of the laborant."

[8] Hoghelande, p. 160. "Hic lapis a loco gloriosissimo sublimi maximi Terroris procedit, qui multos sapientes neci dedit."

[9] Ibid., p. 181.

[10] *Theatr. chem.*, V (1660), p. 126.

[11] Berthelot, *Alch. grecs*, II, iv, 28.

[12] Ibid., II, iv, 43 and 46.

he cannot justify himself before God," says Hoghelande.[13] This conviction should be taken seriously. His treatise is the work of an honest and reasonable man, and differs very much to its advantage from the pretentious obscurantism of other treatises, particularly those of Lully. Since the stone had "a thousand names," one only wonders which of them it was that Hoghelande did not wish to disclose. The stone was indeed a great embarrassment to the alchemists, for since it had never been made no one could say what it really was. The most probable hypothesis, it seems to me, is that it was a psychic experience, which would account for the repeatedly expressed fear of mental disturbance.

432    Wei Po-yang, the oldest Chinese alchemist known to us (2nd cent. A.D.), gives an instructive account of the dangerous consequences of making mistakes during the opus. After a brief résumé of the latter he describes the *chên-yên,* the true or complete man, who is the beginning and end of the work: "He is and he is not. He resembles a vast pool of water, suddenly sinking and suddenly floating." He appears as a material substance, like Dorn's *veritas,*[14] and in it are "mixed the squareness, the roundness, the diameter, and the dimensions, which restrain one another, having been in existence before the beginning of the heavens and the earth: lordly, lordly, high and revered."[15] This again conveys that impression of extreme numinosity which we found in Western alchemy.

433    The author goes on to speak of a region "closed on all sides, its interior made up of intercommunicating labyrinths. The protection is so complete as to turn back all that is devilish and undesirable. . . . Cessation of thought is desirable and worries are preposterous. The divine *ch'i* (air, spirit, ethereal essence) fills the quarters and it cannot be held back. Whoever retains it will prosper and he who loses it, will perish." For the latter will employ the "false method": he will direct himself in all things by the course of the sun and the stars, in other words will lead a rationally ordered life in accordance with the rules of Chinese conduct. But this is not pleasing to the *tao* of the feminine prin-

13 *Theatr. chem.,* I (1659), p. 160. "Nomen lapidis patefacere nemo potest sub animae suae condemnatione, quia coram Deo rationem reddere non posset."
14 *Aion,* pp. 161ff.
15 Wei Po-yang, "An Ancient Chinese Treatise on Alchemy," pp. 237ff.

ciple (*yin*), or, as we should say, the ordering principles of consciousness are not in harmony with the unconscious (which in a man has a feminine character). If the adept at this point orders his life according to rules traditionally regarded as rational he brings himself into danger. "Disaster will come to the black mass." The black mass is the *massa confusa*, the chaos or *nigredo* of Western alchemy, the prima materia, which is black outside and white inside, like lead. It is the *chên-yên* hidden in the darkness, the whole man, who is threatened by the rational and correct conduct of life, so that individuation is hindered or deflected into the wrong path. The *ch'i*, the quintessence (the rose-coloured blood of Western alchemy) cannot be "held back": the self struggles to make itself manifest and threatens to overpower consciousness.[16] This danger was particularly great for the Western alchemist, because the ideal of the *imitatio Christi* led him to regard the sweating out of the soul-substance in the form of the rose-coloured blood as a task that had actually been enjoined upon him. He felt morally obliged to realize the demands of the self regardless of whether these demands taxed him too highly. It seemed to him that God and his highest moral principles required this self-sacrifice. It is indeed a self-sacrifice, a true θυσία of the self, when a man gives way to the urgency of these demands and perishes, for then the self has lost the game as well, having destroyed the human being who should have been its vessel. This danger, as the Chinese Master rightly observes, occurs when the traditional, moral, and rational principles of conduct are put into force at a moment when something other than social life is in question, namely, the integration of the unconscious and the process of individuation.

434     Wei Po-yang gives a graphic description of the physiological and psychic consequences of error: "Gases from food consumed will make noises inside the intestines and stomach. The right essence (*ch'i*) will be exhaled and the evil one inhaled. Days and nights will be passed without sleep, moon after moon. The body will then be tired out, giving rise to an appearance of insanity. The hundred pulses will stir and boil so violently as to drive away peace of mind and body." Nor will it be of any avail (following conscious morality) to build a temple, to watch diligently and bring gifts to the altar morning and night. "Ghostly

16 *Aion*, pp. 23ff.

things will make their appearance, at which he will marvel even in his sleep. He is then led to rejoice, thinking that he is assured of longevity.[17] But all of a sudden he is seized by an untimely death." The author adds the moral: "A slight error has thus led to a grave disaster." The insights of Western alchemy did not penetrate to these depths. Nevertheless, the alchemists were aware of the subtle dangers of the work, and they knew that high demands were made not only on the intelligence of the adept but also on his moral qualities. Thus the invitation to the royal marriage in Christian Rosencreutz[18] runs:

> Keep watch, and ward,
> Thyself regard;
> Unless with diligence thou bathe,
> The Wedding can't thee harmless save;
> He'll damage have that here delays;
> Let him beware, too light that weighs.

435    It is clear from what happens in the *Chymical Wedding* that it was not concerned solely with the transformation and union of the royal pair, but also with the individuation of the adept. The union with the shadow and the anima is a difficulty not to be taken lightly. The problem of opposites that then makes its appearance and the unanswerable questions that this entails lead to the constellation of compensating archetypal contents in the form of numinous experiences. What complex psychology discovered only late was known long ago to the alchemists—*symbolice*—despite their limited intellectual equipment. Laurentius Ventura expresses this insight in a few succinct words: "The perfection of the work does not lie in the power of the artifex, but God the most merciful himself bestows it upon whom he will. And in this point lies all the danger." [19] We might add that the words "the most merciful" should probably be taken as an apotropaic euphemism.

---

[17] This is a typical symptom of inflation. A person with a famous name once assured me he would live a very long time; he needed at least 150 years. A year later he was dead. In this case the inflation was obvious even to a layman.

[18] *The Chymical Wedding* (trans. Foxcroft), p. 6.

[19] "(Operis perfectio) non est enim in potestate artificis, sed cui vult ipse Deus clementissimus largitur. Et in hoc puncto totum est periculum." *Theatr. chem.*, II (1659), p. 296.

### 16. UNDERSTANDING AS A MEANS OF DEFENCE

436    After this discussion of the dangers that threaten the adept, let us turn back to the Ostanes quotation in section 14. The adepts knew that they could offer no resistance to the lapis in the form of the Andalusian prince. It seemed to be stronger than they, and the text says that they had only three weapons—"resignation," the charger of "knowledge," and the buckler of "understanding." It is evident from this that on the one hand they thought themselves well advised to adopt a policy of non-resistance, while on the other they sought refuge in intelligence and understanding. The superior power of the lapis is attested by the saying: "The philosopher is not the master of the stone, but rather its minister."[1] Obviously they had to submit to its power, but with a reserve of understanding which would finally enable them to slay the prince. We shall probably not go wrong if we assume that the adepts tried as best they could to understand that apparently invincible thing and thereby break its power. It is not only a well-known fairytale motif (Rumpelstiltskin!) but also a very ancient primitive belief that he who can guess the secret name has power over its possessor. In psychotherapy it is a well-known fact that neurotic symptoms which seem impossible to attack can often be rendered harmless by conscious understanding and experience of the contents underlying them. This is obvious enough, because the energy which maintained the symptom is then put at the disposal of consciousness, causing an increase of vitality on the one hand and a reduction of useless inhibitions and suchlike disturbances on the other.

437    In order to understand the Ostanes text, one must bear such experiences in mind. They occur whenever previously unconscious, numinous contents emerge into consciousness either spontaneously or through the application of a method. As in all magic texts, it is supposed that the power of the conquered daemon will pass into the adept. Our modern consciousness can hardly resist the temptation to think in the same way. We readily assume that psychic contents can be completely disposed of by insight. This is true only of contents that do not mean very

1 "Philosophus non est magister lapidis, sed potius eius minister." *Ros. phil.* in *Art. aurif.*, II, pp. 356f.

much anyway. Numinous complexes of ideas may be induced to change their form, but since their content can take any number of forms it does not vanish in the sense of being rendered wholly ineffective. It possesses a certain autonomy, and when it is repressed or systematically ignored it reappears in another place in a negative and destructive guise. The devil whom the magician fancies he has bound to his service fetches him in the end. It is a waste of effort to try to use the daemon as a familiar for one's own purposes; on the contrary, the autonomy of this ambivalent figure should be religiously borne in mind, for it is the source of that fearful power which drives us towards individuation. Consequently the alchemists did not hesitate to endow their stone with positively divine attributes and to put it, as a microcosm and a man, on a par with Christ—"and in this point lies all the danger." We neither can nor should try to force this numinous being, at the risk of our own psychic destruction, into our narrow human mould, for it is greater than man's consciousness and greater than his will.

438     Just as the alchemists occasionally betrayed a tendency to use the symbols produced by the unconscious as spellbinding names, so does modern man make analogous use of intellectual concepts for the opposite purpose of denying the unconscious, as though with reason and intellect its autonomy could be conjured out of existence. Curiously enough, I have critics who think that I of all people want to replace the living psyche by intellectual concepts. I do not understand how they have managed to overlook the fact that my concepts are based on empirical findings and are nothing but names for certain areas of experience. Such a misunderstanding would be comprehensible if I had omitted to present the facts on which I base my statements. My critics assiduously overlook the obvious truth that I speak of the facts of the living psyche and have no use for philosophical acrobatics.

## 17. THE MOTIF OF TORTURE

439     The Ostanes text gives us valuable insight into the phenomenology of the individuation process as the alchemists experienced it. The reference to the "torment" which the prince desires for the artifex is particularly interesting. This motif appears in the Western texts but in inverse form, the tormented

one being not the artifex but Mercurius, or the lapis or tree. The reversal of roles shows that the artifex imagines he is the tormentor whereas in fact he is the tormented. This becomes clear to him only later, when he discovers the dangers of the work to his own cost. A typical example of the projected torture is the vision of Zosimos.[1] The *Turba* says: "Take the old black spirit and destroy and torture[2] with it the bodies, until they are changed." [3] Elsewhere a philosopher tells the assembled sages: "The tortured thing, when it is immersed in the body, changes it into an unalterable and indestructible nature." [4] Mundus in Sermo XVIII says: "How many there be who search out these applications[5] and [even] find some, but yet cannot endure the torments." [6]

440    These quotations show that the concept of torture is an ambiguous one. In the first case it is the bodies, the raw materials of the work, that are tormented; in the second case the tormented thing is without doubt the arcane substance, which is often called *res;* and in the third case it is the investigators themselves who cannot endure the torments. This ambiguity is no accident and has its deeper reasons.

441    In the old texts that are contemporaneous with the Latin translation of the *Turba* there are gruesome recipes in the manner of the Magic Papyri, as for instance the disembowelling[7] or plucking of a live cock,[8] the drying of a man over a heated stone,[9] the cutting off of hands and feet,[10] etc. Here the torture is applied to the body. But we find another version in the equally old "Tractatus Micreris." [11] There it is said that just as the Creator separates souls from bodies and judges and rewards them, "so we also must use flattery [*adulatio uti*] [12] on these souls

1 Cf. supra, pars. 86–87.    2 "Diruite et cruciate."    3 Ed. Ruska, p. 152.
4 Ibid., p. 168.
5 By "applicationes" are meant the arcane substances, such as the "gumma" (= *aqua permanens*) mentioned in the text.
6 *Poenas*, corresponding to the κολάσεις in Zosimos; supra, par. 86 (III, i, 2).
7 Preisendanz, *Pap. Graec. Mag.*, I, p. 79.
8 "Allegoriae sapientum," *Art. aurif.*, I, p. 140.
9 Ibid., p. 139.
10 "Visio Arislei," ibid., p. 151.
11 "Micreris" is a corruption of "Mercurius" due to Arabic transliteration.
12 *Adulatio* usually refers to the love-play of the royal marriage. Here it serves to extract the souls.

and condemn them to the heaviest punishments [*poenis,* with marginal note: *laboribus*]." At this point an interlocutor raises the doubt as to whether the soul can be treated in this way, since it is "tenuous" and no longer inhabits the body. The Master replies: "It must be tormented with the most subtle spiritual thing, namely with the fiery nature which is akin to it. For if its body were tormented, the soul would not be tormented, and the torment would not reach it; for it is of spiritual nature, to be touched only by something spiritual." [13]

442     Here it is not the raw material that is tortured but the soul which has been extracted from it and must now suffer a spiritual martyrdom. The "soul" corresponds as a rule to the arcane substance, either the prima materia or the means by which it is transformed. Petrus Bonus, who, as we have seen, was one of the first medieval alchemists to wonder about the scope of his art, says that just as Geber met with difficulties "we also were plunged into stupor [*in stuporem adducti*] for a long time and were hidden under the cloak of despair. But when we came back to ourselves and tormented our thoughts with the torment of unlimited reflection, we beheld the substances." He then cites Avicenna, who had said that it was necessary for us "to discover this operation [the *solutio*] through ourselves [*per nos ipsos*]." "These things were known to us before the experiment, as a consequence of long, intense, and scrupulous meditation." [14]

443     Petrus Bonus puts the suffering back into the investigator by stressing his mental torments. In this he is right, because the most important discoveries of the alchemists sprang from their meditations on their own psychic processes, which, projected in archetypal form into the chemical substances, dazzled their minds with unlimited possibilities. The same prior knowledge of the results is generally admitted, as when Dorn says: "It is not possible for any mortal to understand this art unless he is previously enlightened by the divine light." [15]

444     The tormenting of the substances also occurs in Sir George Ripley: "The unnatural fire must torment the bodies, for it is the dragon violently burning, like the fire of hell." [16] With

---

13 *Theatr. chem.,* V (1660), p. 93.     14 Lacinius, *Pret. marg. nov.,* fol. 45ᵛ.
15 "Physica Trismegisti," *Theatr. chem.,* I (1659), p. 366.
16 "Ignis contra naturam debet excruciare corpora, ipse est draco violenter comburens, ut ignis inferni" ("Duodecim portarum," *Theatr. chem.,* II, 1659, p. 113).

Ripley the projection of the torments of hell is explicit and complete, as with so many others. Only with the authors of the sixteenth and seventeenth centuries does the insight of Petrus Bonus break through again. Dorn's view is emphatic: "Wherefore the Sophists . . . have persecuted this Mercurius with various torments, some with sublimations, coagulations, precipitations, mercurial *aquae fortes,* etc., all of which are mistaken courses to be avoided." [17] Among the Sophists he reckons also Geber and Albertus, "surnamed the Great," as he mockingly adds. In his "Physica Trismegisti" he even declares that the time-honoured blackness (*melanosis, nigredo*) is a projection: "For Hermes saith, 'From thee shall all obscurity flee away,' [18] he saith not 'from the metals.' By obscurity naught else is to be understood save the darkness of disease, and sickness of body and mind." [19]

445    Many passages in *Aurora consurgens* I are significant in this respect. In the "Book of Ostanes" the philosophers shed tears over the stone, which is enclosed in another stone, so that, bedewed by their tears, it loses its blackness and becomes white as a pearl.[20] A Gratianus quotation in the *Rosarium* says: "In alchemy there is a certain noble substance . . . in the beginning whereof is wretchedness with vinegar, but in the end joy with gladness." [21] The "Consilium coniugii" equates the *nigredo* with melancholia.[22] Vigenère says of the Saturnine lead: "Lead signifies the vexations and aggravations with which God afflicts us and troubles our senses." [23] This adept was aware that lead, which had always been considered an arcane substance, was identical with the subjective state of depression. Similarly, the personified prima materia in the "Aurelia occulta" says of her brother Saturn that his spirit was "overcome by the passion of melancholy." [24]

---

17 "Congeries Paracelsicae," ibid., I (1659), p. 516.

18 Quotation from "Tab. smarag."

19 "(Hermes) dicit enim 'a te fugiet omnis obscuritas,' non dicit 'a metallis.' Per obscuritatem nihil aliud intelligitur quam tenebrae morborum et aegritudinem corporis atque mentis." (*Theatr. chem.,* I, 1659, p. 384.)

20 Berthelot, *Moyen âge,* III, p. 118.

21 "In Alchimia est quoddam corpus nobile, . . . in cuius principio erit miseria cum aceto, sed in fine gaudium cum laetitia" (*Art. aurif.,* II, p. 278).

22 *Ars chemica,* pp. 125f.    23 *Theatr. chem.,* VI (1661), p. 76.

24 Ibid., IV (1660), p. 505.

446    In this context of thought, where suffering and sadness play so great a role, it is not surprising that the tree was brought into connection with the cross of Christ. This analogy was supported by the old legend that the wood of the cross came from the tree of paradise.[25] Another thing that contributed to it was the quaternity, whose symbol is the cross;[26] for the tree possesses a quaternary quality by reason of the fact that it represents the process by which the four elements are united. The quaternity of the tree goes back beyond the Christian era. It is found in Zarathustra's vision of the tree with four branches made of gold, silver, steel, and "mixed iron." [27] This image reappears later in the alchemical tree of the metals, which was then compared with the cross of Christ. In Ripley the royal pair, the supreme opposites, are crucified for the purpose of union and rebirth.[28] "If I be lifted up, [as Christ says,] then I will draw all men unto me. . . . From that time forward, when both parts, having been crucified and exanimated, are espoused, man and woman shall be buried together and are afterward quickened again by the spirit of life." [29]

447    The tree also appears as a symbol of transformation in a passage in Dorn's "Speculativa philosophia," which is very interesting from the point of view of the psychology of religion: "[God] hath determined to snatch the sword of his wrath from the hands of the angel, substituting in place thereof a three-pronged hook of gold, hanging the sword on a tree: and so God's wrath is turned into love." [30] Christ as Logos is the two-edged sword, which symbolizes God's wrath, as in Revelation 1 : 16.

[25] Zöckler, *The Cross of Christ,* and Bezold, *Die Schatzhöhle,* pp. 5, 35.
[26] Dee, *Theatr. chem.,* II (1659), p. 202.
[27] Reitzenstein and Schaeder, *Studien zum antiken Synkretismus aus Iran und Griechenland,* p. 45.
[28] Cf. the oak in the fount of renewal in Trevisanus, "De chemico miraculo," *Theatr. chem.,* I (1659), pp. 683ff. [*Mysterium Coniunctionis,* pp. 70f.]
[29] Ripley, *Opera omnia,* p. 81. "Si exaltatus fuero, tunc omnes ad me traham. Ab eo tempore, quo partes sunt desponsatae, quae sunt crucifixae et exanimatae contumulantur simul mas et foemina et postea revivificantur spiritu vitae."
[30] *Theatr. chem.,* I (1659), p. 254. "(Deus) conclusit angelo gladium irae suae de manibus eripere, cuius loco tridentem hamum substituit aureum, gladio ad arborem suspenso: et sic mutata est ira Dei in amorem."

448    The[31] somewhat unusual allegory of Christ as the sword hanging on a tree is almost certainly an analogy of the serpent hanging on the cross. In St. Ambrose[32] the "serpent hung on the wood" is a "typus Christi," as is the "brazen serpent on the cross" in Albertus Magnus.[33] Christ as Logos is synonymous with the Naas, the serpent of the Nous among the Ophites. The Agathodaimon (good spirit) had the form of a snake, and in Philo the snake was considered the "most spiritual" animal. On the other hand, its cold blood and inferior brain-organization do not suggest any noticeable degree of conscious development, while its unrelatedness to man makes it an alien creature that arouses his fear and yet fascinates him. Hence it is an excellent symbol for the two aspects of the unconscious: its cold and ruthless instinctuality, and its Sophia quality or natural wisdom, which is embodied in the archetypes. The Logos-nature of Christ represented by the chthonic serpent is the maternal wisdom of the divine mother, which is prefigured by Sapientia in the Old Testament. The snake-symbol thus characterizes Christ as a personification of the unconscious in all its aspects, and as such he is hung on the tree in sacrifice ("wounded by the spear" like Odin).

449    Psychologically, this snake sacrifice must be understood as an overcoming of unconsciousness and, at the same time, of the attitude of the son who unconsciously hangs on his mother. The alchemists used the same symbol to represent the transformation of Mercurius,[34] who is quite definitely a personification of the unconscious, as I have shown.[35] I have come across this motif several times in dreams, once as a crucified snake (with conscious reference to John 3 : 14), then as a black spider hung on a pole which changed into a cross, and finally as the crucified body of a naked woman.

31 [In the Swiss edn., this and the following par. were given at the end of sec. 18.—Editors.]
32 *De XLII Mansionibus Filiorum Israel,* XXXV (Migne, *P.L.,* vol. 17, col. 34).
33 In his hymn to the Mother of God: "Ave praeclara maris Stella." Cf. Gourmont, *Le Latin mystique,* p. 150. [Also *Psychology and Alchemy,* par. 481 and Fig. 217.]
34 See illustration in Eleazar, *Uraltes chymisches Werck,* facing p. 26. The book is a forgery of Flamel's "Rindenbuch." [Cf. *Mysterium Coniunctionis,* p. 410.]
35 "The Spirit Mercurius," pars. 284ff.

## 18. THE RELATION OF SUFFERING TO THE CONIUNCTIO

450     In the above quotation from Dorn, the three-pronged hook of gold refers to Christ, for in medieval allegory the hook with which God the Father catches the Leviathan is the crucifix. The golden trident is, of course, an allusion to the Trinity, and the fact that it is "golden" is an alchemical *sous-entendu,* just as the idea of God's transformation in this strange allegory of Dorn's is intimately bound up with the alchemical *mysterium.* The notion of God throwing out a hook is of Manichaean origin: he used the Primordial Man as a bait for catching the powers of darkness. The Primordial Man was named "Psyche," and in Titus of Bostra he is the world soul ($\psi\nu\chi\grave{\eta}$ $\dot{\alpha}\pi\acute{\alpha}\nu\tau\omega\nu$).[1] This psyche corresponds to the collective unconscious, which, itself of unitary nature, is represented by the unitary Primordial Man.

451     These ideas are closely related to the Gnostic conception of Sophia-Achamoth in Irenaeus. He reports that

> the Ἐνθύμησις [reflection] of the Sophia who dwells above, compelled by necessity, departed with suffering from the Pleroma into the darkness and empty spaces of the void. Separated from the light of the Pleroma, she was without form or figure, like an untimely birth, because she comprehended nothing [i.e., became unconscious]. But the Christ dwelling on high, outstretched upon the cross, took pity on her, and by his power gave her a form, but only in respect of substance, and not so as to convey intelligence [i.e., consciousness]. Having done this, he withdrew his power, and returned [to the Pleroma], leaving Achamoth to herself, in order that she, becoming sensible of the suffering caused by separation from the Pleroma, might be influenced by the desire for better things, while possessing in the meantime a kind of odour of immortality left in her by Christ and the Holy Spirit.[2]

452     According to these Gnostics, it was not the Primordial Man who was cast out as a bait into the darkness, but the feminine figure of Wisdom, Sophia-Achamoth. In this way the masculine element escaped the danger of being swallowed by the dark powers and remained safe in the pneumatic realm of light, while Sophia, partly by an act of reflection and partly driven by necessity, entered into relation with the outer darkness. The suffer-

[1] Bousset, *Hauptprobleme der Gnosis,* p. 178.
[2] *Adversus haereses,* I, 4.

ings that befell her took the form of various emotions—sadness, fear, bewilderment, confusion, longing; now she laughed and now she wept. From these affects (διαθέσεις) arose the entire created world.

453 This strange creation myth is obviously "psychological": it describes, in the form of a cosmic projection, the separation of the feminine anima from a masculine and spiritually oriented consciousness that strives for the final and absolute victory of the spirit over the world of the senses, as was the case in the pagan philosophies of that epoch no less than in Gnosticism. This development and differentiation of consciousness left a literary deposit in the *Metamorphoses* of Apuleius, and more particularly in his tale of *Amor and Psyche,* as Erich Neumann has shown in his study of that work.

454 The emotional state of Sophia sunk in unconsciousness (ἄγνοια), her formlessness, and the possibility of her getting lost in the darkness characterize very clearly the anima of a man who identifies himself absolutely with his reason and his spirituality. He is in danger of becoming dissociated from his anima and thus losing touch altogether with the compensating powers of the unconscious. In a case like this the unconscious usually responds with violent emotions, irritability, lack of control, arrogance, feelings of inferiority, moods, depressions, outbursts of rage, etc., coupled with lack of self-criticism and the misjudgments, mistakes, and delusions which this entails.

455 In such a state a man soon loses touch with reality. His spirituality becomes ruthless, arrogant, and tyrannical. The more unadapted his ideology is, the more it demands recognition and is determined to gain it if necessary by force. This state is a definite πάθος, a suffering of the soul, though at first it is not perceived as such because of lack of introspection, and only gradually comes to consciousness as a vague malaise. Eventually this feeling forces the mind to recognize that something is wrong, that one is indeed suffering. This is the moment when physical or psychological symptoms appear which can no longer be banished from consciousness. Expressed in the language of myth, Christ (the principle of masculine spirituality) perceives the sufferings of Sophia (i.e., the psyche) and thereby gives her form and existence. But he leaves her to herself so that she should feel the full force of her sufferings. What this means psychologically is that

the masculine mind is content merely to perceive psychic suffering, but does not make itself conscious of the reasons behind it,
and simply leaves the anima in a state of *agnoia*. This process is
typical and can be observed today not only in all masculine
neuroses but among so-called normal people who have come into
conflict with the unconscious thanks to their one-sidedness (usually intellectual) and psychological blindness.

456    Although, in this psychologem, the Primordial Man (Christ)
is still the means for conquering the darkness, he nevertheless
shares his role with a feminine being, Sophia, who coexisted with
him in the Pleroma. Moreover, the Crucified no longer appears
as the bait on God's fishing rod; instead, he "takes pity" on the
formless feminine half, revealing himself to her outstretched
upon the cross. The Greek text uses here a strong expression:
ἐπεκταθέντα, which lays particular emphasis on stretching and extension. This image of torment is held before her so that she may
recognize his sufferings, and he hers. But before this recognition
can take place, Christ's masculine spirituality withdraws into
the world of light. This dénouement is typical: as soon as the
light catches a glimpse of the darkness and there is a possibility
of uniting with it, the power drive that is inherent in the light
as well as in the darkness asserts itself and will not budge from
its position. The one will not darken its radiance, and the other
will not give up its gratifying emotions. Neither of them notices
that their suffering is one and the same and is due to the process
of becoming conscious, whereby an original unity is split into
two irreconcilable halves. There can be no consciousness without this act of discrimination, nor can the resultant duality be
reunified without the extinction of consciousness. But the original wholeness remains a desideratum (ὀρεχθῇ τῶν διαφερόντων) for
which Sophia longs more than does the Gnostic Christ. It is still
the case today that discrimination and differentiation mean
more to the rationalistic intellect than wholeness through the
union of opposites. That is why it is the unconscious which produces the symbols of wholeness.[3]

457    These symbols are usually quaternary and consist of two
pairs of opposites crossing one another (e.g., left/right, above/
below). The four points demarcate a circle, which, apart from

[3] *Psychology and Alchemy*, pars. 122ff., and "A Study in the Process of Individuation."

the point itself, is the simplest symbol of wholeness and therefore the simplest God-image.[4] This reflection has some bearing on the emphasis laid on the cross in our text, since the cross as well as the tree is the medium of conjunction. Hence St. Augustine likened the cross to a bridal bed, and in the fairytale the hero finds his bride in the top of a great tree,[5] where also the shaman finds his heavenly spouse, as does the alchemist. The coniunctio is a culminating point of life and at the same time a death, for which reason our text mentions the "fragrance of immortality." On the one hand the anima is the connecting link with the world beyond and the eternal images, while on the other hand her emotionality involves man in the chthonic world and its transitoriness.

### 19. THE TREE AS MAN

458 Like the vision of Zarathustra, the dream of Nebuchadnezzar, and the report of Bardesanes (A.D. 154–222) on the god of the Indians,[1] the old Rabbinic idea that the tree of paradise was a man[2] exemplifies man's relationship to the philosophical tree. According to ancient tradition men came from trees or plants.[3] The tree is as it were an intermediate form of man, since on the one hand it springs from the Primordial Man and on the other hand it grows into a man.[4] Naturally the patristic

[4] "God is a circle whose centre is everywhere and the circumference nowhere." [Cf. *Mysterium Coniunctionis*, p. 47.]

[5] [Cf. "The Phenomenology of the Spirit in Fairytales," pp. 231ff.]

[1] Stobaeus, I, 3 (ed. Wachsmuth, I, pp. 67f.), referring to a wooden statue in a cave, with outstretched arms (like one crucified), the right side male, the left side female. It could sweat and bleed.

[2] " 'Of the fruit of the tree'—here tree only means man, who is compared to a tree" (*Pirke de Rabbi Eliezer*, trans. Friedlander, p. 150). "As is a tree, just such as is the Lord of Trees, so indeed is man" (Coomaraswamy, "The Inverted Tree," p. 138).

[3] In Iranian tradition the seven metals flowed into the earth from the body of Gayomart, the Primordial Man. Out of them grew the *reivas* plant, from which the first men, Mahrya and Mayryana, sprang. (Cf. Ask and Embla, the first men in the Edda.) Christensen, *Les Types du premier homme et du premier roi dans l'histoire légendaire des Iraniens*, p. 35. In the Gilbert Islands, men and gods come from the primordial tree.

[4] Ibid., p. 18, and the Bundahish, 15, 1. The cedar and persea tree play the same role in the ancient Egyptian tale of Bata. Cf. Jacobsohn, *Die dogmatische Stellung des Königs in der Theologie der alten Aegypter*, p. 13. It is to be regretted that

conception of Christ as a tree or vine[5] exerted a very great influence. In *Pandora,* as we have said, the tree is represented in the form of a woman, in agreement with the pictures reproduced in the first part of this essay, which, unlike the alchemical pictures, were done mostly by women. This raises the question of how the feminine tree-numen should be interpreted. The results of our investigation of the historical material have shown that the tree can be interpreted as the Anthropos or self. This interpretation is particularly obvious in the symbolism of the "Scriptum Alberti" [6] and is confirmed by the fantasy material expressed in our pictures. The interpretation of the feminine tree-numen as the self therefore holds good for women, but for the alchemists and humanists the feminine representation of the tree is an obvious projection of the anima figure.[7] The anima personifies the femininity of a man but not the self. Correspondingly, the patients who drew Figures 29 and 30 depict the tree-numen as the animus. In all these cases the contrasexual symbol has covered up the self. This is what regularly happens when the man's femininity, the anima, or the woman's masculinity, the animus, is not differentiated enough to be integrated with consciousness, so that the self is only potentially present as an intuition but is not yet actualized.

459     In so far as the tree symbolizes the opus and the transformation process "tam ethice quam physice" (both morally and physically), it also signifies the life process in general. Its identity with Mercurius, the *spiritus vegetativus,* confirms this view. Since the opus is a life, death, and rebirth mystery, the tree as well acquires this significance and in addition the quality of wisdom, as we have seen from the view of the Barbeliots reported in Irenaeus: "From man [= Anthropos] and gnosis is born the

---

these transformation processes, which are of great interest as regards the psychology of religion, are omitted in Pritchard's recension of the Bata fairytale in his *Ancient Near Eastern Texts.*

5 "Fruitful tree" in St. Gregory the Great, *Super Cant. Cant.,* II, 4 (Migne, *P.L.,* vol. 79, col. 495). Cf. also supra, par. 407, n. 10. As vine in John 15 : 1. The Buddha, like Christ (supra, par. 419), was named the tree of paradise (*Buddha-Carita* of Ashvaghosha: SBE, XLIX, p. 157).

6 Supra, section 12.

7 Cf. Aldrovandus (1522–1605) and his interpretation of the "Enigma of Bologna" (*Dendrologia,* I, p. 211), in *Mysterium Coniunctionis,* pp. 68ff.

tree, which they also call gnosis." [8] In the Gnosis of Justin, the angel Baruch, named the "wood of life," [9] is the angel of revelation, just as the sun-and-moon tree in the Romance of Alexander foretells the future.[10] However, the cosmic associations of the tree as world-tree and world-axis take second place among the alchemists as well as in modern fantasies, because both are more concerned with ,the individuation process, which is no longer projected into the cosmos. An exception to this rule may be found in the rare case, reported by Nelken,[11] of a schizophrenic patient in whose cosmic system the Father-God had a tree of life growing out of his breast. It bore red and white fruits, or spheres, which were worlds. Red and white are alchemical colours, red signifying the sun and white the moon. On the top of the tree sat a dove and an eagle, recalling the stork on the sun-and-moon tree in the "Scriptum Alberti." Any knowledge of the alchemical parallels was quite out of the question in this case.

460    On the evidence of the material we have collected, we can see that the spontaneous products of the unconscious in modern man depict the archetype of the tree in a way that brings out quite plainly the historical parallels. So far as I can judge, the only historical models of which my patients might have made conscious use are the Biblical tree of paradise and one or two fairytales. But I cannot recall a single case in which it was spontaneously admitted that the patient was consciously thinking of the Bible story. In every case the image of the tree presented itself spontaneously, and whenever a feminine being attached itself to the tree, none of the patients associated it with the snake on the tree of knowledge. The pictures show more of an affinity with the ancient idea of the tree nymph than with the Biblical prototype. In Jewish tradition the snake is also interpreted as Lilith. There is a strong prejudice in favour of the assumption that certain forms of expression exist only because a pattern for them may be found in the respective sphere of culture. If that were so in the present instance, all expressions of this type

8 *Adversus haereses*, I, 29, 3. The fire-tree of Simon Magus is a similar conception (Hippolytus, *Elenchos*, VI, 9, 8).
9 Ibid., V, 26, 6.
10 See supra, par. 403, n. 24.
11 "Analytische Beobachtungen über Phantasien eines Schizophrenen," p. 541.

would have to be modelled on the tree of paradise. But that, as we have seen, is not the case: the long obsolete concept of the tree nymph predominates over the tree of paradise or Christmas tree; in fact there are even allusions to the equally obsolete cosmic tree and even to the *arbor inversa,* which, although it found its way into alchemy via the Cabala, nowhere plays a role in our culture. Our material is, however, fully in accord with the widespread, primitive shamanistic conceptions of the tree and the heavenly bride,[12] who is a typical anima projection. She is the *ayami* (familiar, protective spirit) of the shaman ancestors. Her face is half black, half red. Sometimes she appears in the form of a winged tiger.[13] Spitteler also likens the "Lady Soul" to a tiger.[14] The tree represents the life of the shaman's heavenly bride,[15] and has a maternal significance.[16] Among the Yakuts a tree with eight branches is the birthplace of the first man. He is suckled by a woman the top part of whose body grows out of the trunk.[17] This motif is also found among my examples (Figure 22).

461    As well as with a feminine being, the tree is also connected with the snake, the dragon, and other animals, as in the case of Yggdrasil,[18] the Persian tree Gaokerena in the lake of Vourukasha, or the tree of the Hesperides, not to mention the holy trees of India, in whose shadow may often be seen dozens of *naga* (= snake) stones.[19]

462    The inverted tree plays a great role among the East Siberian shamans. Kagarow has published a photograph of one such tree, named Nakassä, from a specimen in the Leningrad Museum. The roots signify hairs, and on the trunk, near the roots, a face has been carved, showing that the tree represents a man.[20] Pre-

12 Eliade, *Shamanism,* pp. 73f., 142, 344, 346.

13 Ibid., p. 72.

14 *Prometheus and Epimetheus* (trans. Muirhead), p. 38. (Cf. *Psychological Types,* trans. Baynes, p. 212.) In China, the tiger is a symbol of *yin.*

15 Eliade, p. 75.

16 Pp. 117–18.

17 P. 272.

18 Squirrel, stag. Yggdrasil means "Odin's horse." (Ninck, *Götter und Jenseitsglauben der Germanen,* p. 191.) For the feminine significance of Yggdrasil see *Symbols of Transformation,* p. 296.

19 For instance, before the gate of the fort at Seringapatam. Cf. Fergusson, *Tree and Serpent Worship.*

20 Kagarow, "Der umgekehrte Schamanenbaum," p. 183.

sumably this is the shaman himself, or his greater personality. The shaman climbs the magic tree in order to find his true self in the upper world. Eliade says in his excellent study of shamanism: "The Eskimo shaman feels the need for these ecstatic journeys because it is above all during trance that he becomes truly himself: the mystical experience is necessary to him as a constituent of his true personality." [21] The ecstasy is often accompanied by a state in which the shaman is "possessed" by his familiars or guardian spirits. By means of this possession he acquires his " 'mystical organs,' which in some sort constitute his true and complete spiritual personality." [22] This confirms the psychological inference that may be drawn from shamanistic symbolism, namely that it is a projection of the individuation process. This inference, as we have seen, is true also of alchemy, and in modern fantasies of the tree it is evident that the authors of such pictures were trying to portray an inner process of development independent of their consciousness and will. The process usually consists in the union of two pairs of opposites, a lower (water, blackness, animal, snake, etc.) with an upper (bird, light, head, etc.), and a left (feminine) with a right (masculine). The union of opposites, which plays such a great and indeed decisive role in alchemy, is of equal significance in the psychic process initiated by the confrontation with the unconscious, so the occurrence of similar or even identical symbols is not surprising.

### 20. THE INTERPRETATION AND INTEGRATION OF THE UNCONSCIOUS

463     It has not yet been understood in many quarters—nor, I am sorry to say, by my medical colleagues—how a series of fantasies such as I have described comes into existence in the first place, and secondly why I concern myself so much with comparative research into a symbolism that is unknown to them. I am afraid that all sorts of uncorrected prejudices still impede understanding, above all the arbitrary assumption that neuroses as well as dreams consist of nothing but repressed infantile memories and wishes, and that psychic contents are either purely personal or, if impersonal, are derived from the collective consciousness.

[21] *Shamanism,* p. 293.
[22] Ibid., p. 328.

464    Psychic disturbances, like somatic disturbances, are highly complex phenomena which cannot be explained by a purely aetiological theory. Besides the cause and the unknown X of the individual's disposition, we must also take into account the teleological aspect of fitness in biology, which in the psychic realm would have to be formulated as *meaning*. In psychic disturbances it is by no means sufficient in all cases merely to bring the supposed or real causes to consciousness. The treatment involves the integration of contents that have become dissociated from consciousness—not always as a result of repression, which very often is only a secondary phenomenon. Indeed, it is usually the case that, in the course of development following puberty, consciousness is confronted with affective tendencies, impulses, and fantasies which for a variety of reasons it is not willing or not able to assimilate. It then reacts with repression in various forms, in the effort to get rid of the troublesome intruders. The general rule is that the more negative the conscious attitude is, and the more it resists, devalues, and is afraid, the more repulsive, aggressive, and frightening is the face which the dissociated content assumes.

465    Every form of communication with the split-off part of the psyche is therapeutically effective. This effect is also brought about by the real or merely supposed discovery of the causes. Even when the discovery is no more than an assumption or a fantasy, it has a healing effect at least by suggestion if the analyst himself believes in it and makes a serious attempt to understand. If on the other hand he doubts his aetiological theory, his chances of success sink at once, and he then feels compelled to look at least for real causes which would be convincing to an intelligent patient as well as to himself. If he is inclined to be critical, this task may become a heavy burden, and often he will not succeed in overcoming his doubts. The success of the treatment is then in jeopardy. This dilemma explains the fanatical doctrinairism of Freudian orthodoxy.

466    I will illustrate the problem by means of an example which I came across recently. A certain Mr. X, who was unknown to me, wrote that he had read my book *Answer to Job,* which had interested him very much and put him in a great commotion. He had given it to his friend Y to read, and Y had thereupon had the following dream: *He was back in the concentration camp and*

*saw a mighty eagle circling above it, looking for prey. The situation became dangerous and frightening, and Y wondered how he was to protect himself. He thought he might be able to fly up in a rocket-propelled aircraft and shoot down the eagle.* X described Y as a rationalistic intellectual who had spent a long time in a concentration camp. X and Y both referred the dream to the affects that had been released by the reading of my book on the previous day. Y went to X for advice about the dream. X was of the opinion that the eagle spying on Y referred to himself, whereupon Y rejoined that he didn't believe it, but thought the eagle referred to me, the author of the book.

467    X now wanted to hear my opinion. It is in general a tricky business to try to interpret the dreams of people one does not know personally, and in the absence of amplificatory material. We must therefore content ourselves with asking a few questions which are suggested by what material there is. Why, for instance, should X think he knew that the eagle referred to himself? From what I could gather from the letter, it appeared that X had imparted a certain amount of psychological knowledge to his friend and therefore felt himself in the role of a mentor who could, as it were, see through his friend's game from above. At any rate he was toying with the idea that it was disagreeable for Y to be spied upon by him, the psychologist. X was thus in the position of a psychotherapist who by means of the sexual theory knows in advance what is lurking behind neuroses and dreams, and who, from the lofty watch-tower of superior insight, gives the patient the feeling that he is being seen through. In the dreams of his patient he always expects himself to appear in whatever disguise may be invented by the mystic "censor." In this way X readily came to conjecture that he was the eagle.

468    Y was of a different opinion. He seems not to have been conscious of being invigilated or seen through by X, but, reasonably enough, went back to the obvious source of his dream, namely my book, which had evidently made an impression on him. For this reason he named me the eagle. We can conclude from this that he felt he was being somehow meddled with, as though someone had found him out, or had put his finger on a sore spot in a way that wasn't entirely to his liking. There was no need for him to be conscious of this feeling, for otherwise it would hardly have been represented in a dream.

469    Here interpretation clashes against interpretation, and the one is as arbitrary as the other. The dream itself does not give the least indication in either direction. One might perhaps hazard the view that Y was rather afraid of the superior insight of his friend and therefore disguised him under the façade of the eagle so as not to recognize him. But did Y himself make his dream? Freud supposes the existence of a censor who is responsible for these transmogrifications. As against this I take the view, reinforced by experience, that a dream is quite capable, if it wants to, of naming the most painful and disagreeable things without the least regard for the feelings of the dreamer. If the dream does not in fact do so, there is no sufficient reason for supposing that it means something other than what it says. I therefore maintain that when our dream says "eagle" it means an eagle. Thus I insist on the very aspect of dreams which makes them appear so nonsensical to our reason. It would be so much simpler and more reasonable if the eagle meant Mr. X.

470    In my view, then, the task of the interpretation is to find out what the eagle, aside from our personal fantasies, might mean. I would therefore advise the dreamer to start investigating what the eagle is *qua* eagle, and what general meanings may be attributed to it. The solution of this task leads straight into the history of symbols, and here we find the concrete reason why I concern myself with researches which are apparently so remote from the doctor's consulting room.

471    Once the dreamer has established the general meanings of the eagle which are new and unknown to him (for he will have been familiar with many of them from literature and common speech), he must investigate in what relationship the experience of the previous day, namely the reading of my book, stands to the symbol of the eagle. The question is: what was it that affected him so much that it gave rise to the fairytale motif of a great eagle capable of injuring or making off with a grown man? The image of an obviously gigantic (i.e., mythical) bird, circling high in the sky and surveying the earth with all-seeing eye, is indeed suggestive in view of the content of my book, which is concerned with the fate of man's idea of God.

472    In the dream Y is back in the concentration camp, which is supervised by an "eagle eye." This points clearly enough to a situation which is feared by the dreamer and which makes his

energetic defence measures seem plausible. In order to shoot down the mythical bird, he wants to employ the most advanced technological invention—a rocket-propelled aircraft. This is one of the greatest triumphs of the rationalistic intellect and is diametrically opposed to the mythical bird, whose menacing presence is to be averted with its help. But what kind of danger lurks in my book for such a personality? The answer to this is not difficult when one knows that Y is a Jew. At all events a door is opened to problems that lead into regions that have nothing to do with personal resentments. It is rather a question of those principles, dominants, or ruling ideas which regulate our attitude to life and the world, of convictions and beliefs which, as experience shows, are indispensable psychic phenomena. Indeed they are so indispensable that when the old systems of thought collapse new ones instantly take their place.

473     Neuroses, like all illnesses, are symptoms of maladjustment. Because of some obstacle—a constitutional weakness or defect, wrong education, bad experiences, an unsuitable attitude, etc.—one shrinks from the difficulties which life brings and thus finds oneself back in the world of the infant. The unconscious compensates this regression by producing symbols which, when understood objectively, that is, by means of comparative research, reactivate general ideas that underlie all such natural systems of thought. In this way a change of attitude is brought about which bridges the dissociation between man as he is and man as he ought to be.

474     Something of the sort is taking place in our dream: Y may well be suffering from a dissociation between a highly rationalistic, intellectualized consciousness and an equally irrational background which is anxiously repressed. The anxiety appears in the dream and should be acknowledged as a real fact belonging to the personality, for it is nonsense to assert that one has no anxiety only because one is incapable of discovering the reason for it. Yet that is what one generally does. If the anxiety could be accepted, there would also be a chance of discovering and understanding the reason. This reason is vividly portrayed by the eagle in the dream.

475     Assuming that the eagle is an archaic God-image whose power a person cannot escape, then it makes very little difference in practice whether he believes in God or not. The fact that

his psyche is so constituted as to produce such phenomena should be enough for him, for he can no more get rid of his psyche than he can get rid of his body, neither of which can be exchanged for another. He is a prisoner of his own psychophysical constitution, and must reckon with this fact whether he will or no. One can of course live in defiance of the demands of the body and ruin its health, and the same can be done in regard to the psyche. Anyone who wants to live will refrain from these tricks and will at all times carefully inquire into the body's and the psyche's needs. Once a certain level of consciousness and intelligence has been reached, it is no longer possible to live one-sidedly, and the whole of the psychosomatic instincts, which still function in a natural way among primitives, must consciously be taken into account.

476    In the same way that the body needs food, and not just any kind of food but only that which suits it, the psyche needs to know the meaning of its existence—not just any meaning, but the meaning of those images and ideas which reflect its nature and which originate in the unconscious. The unconscious supplies as it were the archetypal form, which in itself is empty and irrepresentable. Consciousness immediately fills it with related or similar representational material so that it can be perceived. For this reason archetypal ideas are locally, temporally, and individually conditioned.

477    The integration of the unconscious takes place spontaneously only in rare cases. As a rule special efforts are needed in order to understand the contents spontaneously produced by the unconscious. Where certain general ideas, which are regarded as valid or are still efficacious, already exist, they act as a guide to understanding, and the newly acquired experience is articulated with or subordinated to the existing system of thought. A good example of this is afforded by the life of the patron saint of Switzerland, Niklaus von der Flüe, who, by dint of long meditation and with the help of a little book written by a German mystic, gradually turned his terrifying vision of God into an image of the Trinity. Or again, the traditional system may be understood in a new way as a result of the new experiences.

478    It goes without saying that all personal affects and resentments participate in the making of a dream and can therefore be read from its imagery. The analyst, especially at the beginning

346

of a treatment, will have to be satisfied with this, since it seems reasonable to the patient that his dreams come from his personal psyche. He would be completely bewildered if the collective aspect of his dreams were pointed out to him. Freud himself, as we know, tried to reduce myth motifs to personal psychology, in defiance of his own insight that dreams contain archaic residues. These are not personal acquisitions, but vestiges of an earlier collective psyche. There are, however, not a few patients who, as if to prove the reversibility of psychological rules, not only understand the universal significance of their dream symbols but also find it therapeutically effective. The great psychic systems of healing, the religions, likewise consist of universal myth motifs whose origin and content are collective and not personal; hence Lévy-Bruhl rightly called such motifs *représentations collectives*. The conscious psyche is certainly of a personal nature, but it is by no means the whole of the psyche. The foundation of consciousness, the psyche *per se*, is unconscious, and its structure, like that of the body, is common to all, its individual features being only insignificant variants. For the same reason it is difficult or almost impossible for the inexperienced eye to recognize individual faces in a crowd of coloured people.

479     When, as in the dream of the eagle, symbols appear which have nothing about them that would point to a particular person, there is no ground for assuming that such a person is being disguised. On the contrary, it is much more probable that the dream means just what it says. So when a dream apparently disguises something and a particular person therefore seems indicated, there is an obvious tendency at work not to allow this person to appear, because, in the sense of the dream, he represents a mistaken way of acting or thinking. When, for instance, as not infrequently happens in women's dreams, the analyst is represented as a hairdresser (because he "fixes" the head), the analyst is being not so much disguised as devalued. The patient, in her conscious life, is only too ready to acknowledge any kind of authority because she cannot or will not use her own head. The analyst (says the dream) should have no more significance than the hairdresser who puts her head right so that she can then use it herself.

480     If, therefore, instead of reducing the dream symbols to circumstances, things, or persons which the analyst presumes to

know in advance, we regard them as real symbols pointing to something unknown, then the whole character of analytical therapy is altered. The unconscious is then no longer reduced to known, conscious factors (this procedure, incidentally, does *not* abolish the dissociation between conscious and unconscious) but is recognized as in fact unconscious, and the symbol is not reduced either but is amplified by means of the context which the dreamer supplies and by comparison with similar mythologems so that we can see what the unconscious intends it to mean. In this way the unconscious can be integrated and the dissociation overcome. The reductive procedure, on the other hand, leads away from the unconscious and merely reinforces the one-sidedness of the conscious mind. The more rigorous of Freud's pupils have failed to follow up the Master's lead with a deeper exploration of the unconscious and have remained satisfied with reductive analysis.

481     As I have said, the confrontation with the unconscious usually begins in the realm of the personal unconscious, that is, of personally acquired contents which constitute the shadow, and from there leads to archetypal symbols which represent the collective unconscious. The aim of the confrontation is to abolish the dissociation. In order to reach this goal, either nature herself or medical intervention precipitates the conflict of opposites without which no union is possible. This means not only bringing the conflict to consciousness; it also involves an experience of a special kind, namely, the recognition of an alien "other" in oneself, or the objective presence of another will. The alchemists, with astonishing accuracy, called this barely understandable thing Mercurius, in which concept they included all the statements which mythology and natural philosophy had ever made about him: he is God, daemon, person, thing, and the innermost secret in man; psychic as well as somatic. He is himself the source of all opposites, since he is duplex and *utriusque capax* ("capable of both"). This elusive entity symbolizes the unconscious in every particular, and a correct assessment of symbols leads to direct confrontation with it.

482     As well as being an irrational experience, this confrontation is a process of realization. Accordingly the alchemical opus consisted of two parts: the work in the laboratory, with all its emotional and daemonic hazards, and the *scientia* or *theoria*, the

348

guiding principle of the opus by which its results were interpreted and given their proper place. The whole process, which
today we understand as psychological development, was designated the "philosophical tree," a "poetic" comparison that
draws an apt analogy between the natural growth of the psyche
and that of a plant. For this reason it seemed to me desirable to
discuss in some detail the processes which underlie both alchemy
and the modern psychology of the unconscious. I am aware, and
hope I have also made it clear to the reader, that merely intellectual understanding is not sufficient. It supplies us only with
verbal concepts, but it does not give us their true content, which
is to be found in the living experience of the process as applied
to ourselves. We would do well to harbour no illusions in this
respect: no understanding by means of words and no imitation
can replace actual experience. Alchemy lost its vital substance
when some of the alchemists abandoned the laboratorium for
the oratorium, there to befuddle themselves with an ever more
nebulous mysticism, while others converted the oratorium into
a laboratorium and discovered chemistry. We feel sorry for the
former and admire the latter, but no one asks about the fate of
the psyche, which thereafter vanished from sight for several
hundred years.

# BIBLIOGRAPHY

# BIBLIOGRAPHY

The items of the bibliography are arranged alphabetically under two headings: *A*. Ancient volumes containing collections of alchemical tracts by various authors; *B*. General bibliography, including cross-references to the material in section *A*. Short titles of the ancient volumes are printed in capital letters.

## *A*. COLLECTIONS OF ALCHEMICAL TRACTS BY VARIOUS AUTHORS

*ARS CHEMICA, quod sit licita recte exercentibus, probationes doctissimorum iurisconsultorum.* . . . Argentorati [Strasbourg], 1566.

*Contents quoted in this volume:*

i Septem tractatus seu capitula Hermetis Trismegisti aurei [pp. 7–31; usually referred to as "Tractatus aureus"]
ii Hortulanus: Commentariolum in Tabulam Smaragdinam [pp. 33–47]
iii Studium Consilii coniugii de massa solis et lunae [pp. 48–263; usually referred to as "Consilium coniugii"]

*ARTIS AURIFERAE quam chemiam vocant.* . . . Basileae [Bascl], [1593]. 2 vols.

*Contents quoted in this volume:*

### VOLUME I

i Allegoriae super librum Turbae [pp. 139–45]
ii Aenigmata ex visione Arislei philosophi et allegoriis sapientum [pp. 146–54; usually referred to as "Visio Arislei"]
iii In Turbam philosophorum exercitationes [pp. 154–82]
iv Aurora consurgens, quae dicitur Aurea hora [pp. 185–246]
v [Zosimos:] Rosinus ad Sarratantam episcopum [pp. 277–319]
vi Maria Prophetissa: Practica . . . in artem alchemicam [pp. 319–24]
vii Calid: Liber secretorum alchemiae [pp. 325–51]

353

viii   Opusculum authoris ignoti [pp. 389–92]
  ix   Tractatulus Avicennae [pp. 405–37]
   x   Liber de arte chymica [pp. 575–632]

VOLUME II

  xi   Morienus Romanus: Sermo de transmutatione metallorum
       [pp. 7–54]
 xii   Scala philosophorum [pp. 107–70]
xiii   Rosarium philosophorum [pp. 204–384]
 xiv   Arnold of Villanova: Flos florum [pp. 470–88]

*AUREUM VELLUS, oder Güldin Schatz und Kunstkammer . . .
von dem . . . bewehrten Philosopho Salomone Trismosino.* Rorschach, 1598.

*Contents quoted in this volume:*

   i   Trismosin: Splendor solis [Tract. III, pp. 3–59]
  ii   Melchior, Cardinal Bishop of Brixen; Vom dem Gelben und
       Roten Mann [Tract. III, pp. 177–91]

*DE ALCHEMIA.* Nuremberg, 1541.

*Contents quoted in this volume:*

   i   Geber: Summae perfectionis metallorum sive perfecti magis-
       terii libri duo [pp. 20–205]
  ii   Tabula smaragdina [p. 363]
 iii   Hortulanus: Super Tabulam Smaragdinam Commentarius
       [pp. 364–73]

*DE ALCHIMIA opuscula complura.* Frankfurt a. M., 1550. 2 vols.

*Contents quoted in this volume:*

VOLUME II

Rosarium philosophorum [whole volume]

MANGETUS, JOHANNES JACOBUS (ed.). *BIBLIOTHECA CHEMICA
CURIOSA, seu Rerum ad alchemiam pertinentium thesaurus in-
structissimus.* . . . Geneva, 1702. 2 vols.

*Contents quoted in this volume:*

VOLUME I

   i   Hermes Trismegistus: Tractatus aureus [pp. 400–45]
  ii   Dicta Belini [pp. 478–79]

iii  Lully: Codicillus seu vade mecum aut Cantilena [pp. 880–911]

iv  Braceschus: Lignum vitae [pp. 911–38]

v  [Altus:] Mutus liber [pp. 938–53]

### VOLUME II

vi  Bonus: Margarita pretiosa novella correctissima [pp. 1–80]

vii  Rosarium philosophorum [pp. 87–119; a second version, pp. 119–33]

viii  Sendivogius: Parabola, seu Aenigma philosophicum [pp. 474–75]

*MUSAEUM HERMETICUM reformatum et amplificatum . . . continens tractatus chimicos XXI praestantissimos . . .* Francofurti [Frankfurt a. M.], 1678. For translation, see ARTHUR EDWARD WAITE (ed. and trans.). *The Hermetic Museum restored and enlarged.* London, 1893. 2 vols.

*Contents quoted in this volume:*

(The entries in parentheses show the title and pagination of the treatises in the Waite translation)

i  [Hermes Trismegistus:] Tractatus aureus de lapide philosophorum [pp. 1–52] ("The Golden Tract," I, 7–50)

ii  [Siebmacher:] Hydrolithus sophicus, seu Aquarium sapientum [pp. 73–144] ("The Sophic Hydrolith," I, 71–120)

iii  Flamel: Tractatus brevis seu Summarium philosophicum [pp. 172–79] ("A Short Tract, or Philosophical Summary," I, 141–47)

iv  Via veritatis unicae [pp. 181–202] ("The Only True Way," I, 151–64)

v  [Barcius (F. von Sternberg):] Gloria mundi [pp. 203–304] ("The Glory of the World," I, 167–243)

vi  Lambspringk: De lapide philosophico figurae et emblemata [pp. 337–72] ("The Book of Lambspring," I, 273–306)

vii  Basilius Valentinus: Practica [pp. 377–432] ("Practica," I, 312–57)

viii  Norton: Crede mihi, seu Ordinale [pp. 433–532] ("Believe-Me, or The Ordinal of Alchemy," II, 2–67)

ix  Sendivogius: Novum lumen chemicum [pp. 545–600] ("The New Chemical Light," II, 81–158)

x  Philalethes: Introitus apertus [pp. 647–700] ("An Open Entrance to the Closed Palace of the King," II, 163–98)

xi  Maier: Subtilis allegoria super secreta chymiae [pp. 701–40] ("A Subtle Allegory Concerning the Secrets of Alchemy," II, 201–23)

xii  Philalethes: Metallorum metamorphosis [pp. 741–74] ("The Metamorphosis of Metals," II, 225–45)

xiii  Philalethes: Brevis manuductio. ad rubinum caelestem [pp. 775–98] ("A Brief Guide to the Celestial Ruby," II, 246–60)

xiv  Philalethes: Fons chymicae veritatis [pp. 799–814] ("The Fount of Chemical Truth," II 261–69)

*THEATRUM CHEMICUM, praecipuos selectorum auctorum tractatus . . . continens.* Argentorati [Strasbourg], Vols. I–IV, 1659; Vol. V, 1660; Vol. VI, 1661.

*Contents quoted in this volume:*

356

xvii    Ventura: De ratione conficiendi lapidis (De lapide philo-
        sophico) [pp. 215–312]
xviii   Albertus Magnus: De alchemia [pp. 423–58]
 xix    Albertus Magnus: Scriptum super arborem Aristotelis [in
        ibid.]

### VOLUME III

 xx     Jodocus Greverus: Secretum nobillisimum et verissimum
        [pp. 699–722]
 xxi    Melchior Cibinensis: Addam et processum sub forma missae
        [pp. 758–61]

### VOLUME IV

xxii    Artefius: Clavis maioris sapientiae [pp. 198–213]
xxiii   Happelius: Aphorismi Basiliani [pp. 327–30]
xxiv    Sendivogius: Dialogus Mercurii alchymistae et naturae [pp.
        449–56]
 xxv    Aenigma philosophorum sive symbolum Saturni [pp. 457–
        61]
xxvi    [Beatus:] Aurelia occulta [pp. 462–512]
xxvii   Hermes Trismegistus: Tractatus aureus cum scholiis [pp.
        592–705]

### VOLUME V

xxviii  Allegoriae sapientum supra librum Turbae [pp. 57–89]
xxix    Tractatus Micreris [pp. 90–101]
 xxx    Platonis liber quartorum [pp. 101–85]
xxxi    Tractatus Aristotelis alchymistae ad Alexandrum magnum
        [pp. 787–98]
xxxii   Epistola ad Hermannum [pp. 799–805]

### VOLUME VI

xxxiii  Vigenerus: De igne et sale [pp. 1–139]
xxxiv   Anonymi Galli Instructio de arbore solari [pp. 166–94]
xxxv    Orthelius: Epilogus et recapitulatio in Novum lumen chym-
        icum Sendivogii [pp. 430–58]

*THEATRUM CHEMICUM BRITANNICUM. Containing Sev-
erall Poeticall Pieces of Our Famous English Philosophers, Who
Have Written the Hermetique Mysteries in Their Owne Ancient
Language.* Collected with annotations by Elias Ashmole. London,
1652.

*Contents quoted in this volume:*

i   Norton: The Ordinall of Alchemy [pp. 1–106]
ii  Ripley: Verses belonging to an Emblematicall Scrowle [pp. 375–79]
iii Ripley: Preface to "Medulla" [pp. 389–92]


# B.  GENERAL BIBLIOGRAPHY

ABU'L QĀSIM MUHAMMAD IBN AHMAD AL-'IRĀQĪ. *Kitāb al-'ilm al-muktasab* (Book of knowledge acquired concerning the cultivation of gold). Edited and translated by E. J. Holmyard. Paris, 1923.

*Acta S. Hildegardis.* In MIGNE, *P.L.,* Vol. 197, cols. 9–90.

ADLER, GERHARD. *Studies in Analytical Psychology.* London and New York, 1948.

AEGIDIUS DE VADIS. "Dialogus inter naturam et filium philosophiae." See (*A*) *Theatrum chemicum,* xiii.

"Aenigma philosophicum." See (*A*) MANGETUS, *Bibliotheca chemica curiosa,* viii.

"Aenigma philosophorum sive symbolum Saturni." See (*A*) *Theatrum chemicum,* xxv.

"Aenigmata ex visione Arislei et allegoriis sapientum." See (*A*) *Artis auriferae,* ii.

AGRICOLA, GEORG(IUS). *De animantibus subterraneis.* Basel, 1549.

AGRIPPA VON NETTESHEIM, HEINRICH CORNELIUS. *De incertitudine et vanitate scientiarum.* Cologne, 1584. For translation, see: *The Vanity of Arts and Sciences.* London, 1684.

———. *De occulta philosophia libri tres.* Cologne, 1533.

ALAN OF LILLE (Alanus de Insulis). *Elucidatio in Cantica Canticorum.* In MIGNE, *P.L.,* vol. 210, cols. 51–110.

ALBERTUS MAGNUS. "De alchemia." See (*A*) *Theatrum chemicum,* xviii.

———. "De mineralibus et rebus metallicis" ("Mineralium libri quinque"). In: AUGUSTE AND EMIL BORGNET (eds.). *Beati Alberti Magni Opera omnia.* Paris, 1890–99. 38 vols. (Vol. 5, pp. 1–103.)

———. "Scriptum super arborem Aristotelis." See (*A*) *Theatrum chemicum,* xix.

ALCIATI, ANDREA. *Emblemata cum commentariis.* Padua, 1621.

ALDROVANDUS, ULYSSES. *Dendrologiae libri duo.* Bologna, [1667]. 2 vols.

AL-'IRĀQĪ. See ABU'L QĀSIM.

"Allegoriae sapientum supra librum Turbae XXIX distinctiones." See (*A*) *Theatrum chemicum,* **xxviii.**

"Allegoriae super librum Turbae." See (*A*) *Artis auriferae,* **i.**

[ALTUS.] *Mutus liber.* La Rochelle, 1677. See also (*A*) MANGETUS, *Bibliotheca chemica curiosa,* **v.**

AMBROSE, SAINT. *De interpellatione Job et David.* In MIGNE, *P.L.,* vol. 14, cols. 798–850.

———. *De XLII mansionibus filiorum Israel.* In MIGNE, *P.L.,* vol. 17, cols. 9–40.

APASTAMBA. In: *Sacred Laws of the Āryas.* Translated by G. Bühler Part I: Apastamba and Gautama. (Sacred Books of the East, 2.) Oxford, 1879.

Apocalypse of Elias. See STEINDORFF, GEORG.

APULEIUS, LUCIUS. *The Golden Ass.* Translated (1566) by William Adlington and revised by Stephen Gaselee. London and New York (Loeb Classical Library) 1915. Another version: Translated by Robert Graves. (Penguin Classics.) Harmondsworth, 1954.

"Aquarium sapientum." See (*A*) *Musaeum hermeticum,* **ii.**

[ARISLEUS.] "Aenigmata ex visione Arislei et allegoriis sapientum." See (*A*) *Artis auriferae,* **ii.**

[ARISTOTLE, PSEUDO-.] "Tractatus Aristotelis alchymistae ad Alexandrum magnum de lapide philosophico." See (*A*) *Theatrum chemicum,* **xxxi.**

ARNOLD OF VILLANOVA (Arnaldus). "Flos florum Arnaldi." See (*A*) *Artis auriferae,* **xiv.**

ARTEFIUS. "Clavis maioris sapientiae." See (*A*) *Theatrum chemicum,* **xxii.**

ASHVAGHOSHA. "Buddha-carita." Translated by E. B. Cowell. In: *Buddhist Mahayana Texts.* (Sacred Books of the East, 49.) Oxford, 1894.

Atharva-Veda. See *Hymns of the Atharva-Veda.*

AUGUSTINE, SAINT. *The Confessions.* Translated by Francis Joseph Sheed. London and New York, 1943.

————. *De civitate Dei*. In Migne, *P.L.*, vol. 41. For translation, see: *The City of God*. Translated by Marcus Dods et al. (The Works of Aurelius Augustine, 2.) Edinburgh, 1872.

————. *Liber de Spiritu et Anima*. In Migne, *P.L.*, vol. 40, cols. 779–832.

————. *De vera religione*. In Migne, *P.L.*, vol. 34, cols. 121–72. For translation, see: "Of True Religion," in J. H. S. Burleigh (ed. and trans.). *Augustine: Earlier Writings*. (Library of Christian Classics, 6.) London and Philadelphia, 1953.

————. *Dialogus Quaestionum LXV*. In Migne, *P.L.*, vol. 40, cols. 733–52.

————. *Enarrationes in Psalmos*. In Migne, *P.L.*, vols. 36, 37. For translation, see: S. Hobgin and F. Corrigan (trans.). *St. Augustine on the Psalms*. Westminster (Md.) and London, 1960– . 2 vols. published.

"Aurea hora." See "Aurora consurgens."

"Aurelia occulta." See (*A*) *Theatrum chemicum,* **xxvi.**

"Aurora consurgens." See (*A*) *Artis auriferae,* **iv;** Codices and MSS., **xvii;** Franz, M.-L. von.

Avalon, Arthur, pseud. (Sir John Woodroffe) (ed. and trans.). *The Serpent Power* (Shat-cakra-nirūpana and Pādukāpañchaka). (Tantrik Texts.) London, 1919.

Avicenna. See "Tractatulus Avicennae," in (*A*) *Artis auriferae,* **ix.**

Baring-Gould, Sabine. *Curious Myths of the Middle Ages*. London, 1869.

Barnabas, Epistle of. See Lake, Kirsopp.

Baynes, Charlotte Augusta. *A Coptic Gnostic Treatise contained in the Codex Brucianus—Bruce MS. 96, Bodleian Library, Oxford*. Cambridge, 1933.

Belletête, ———— (trans.). *Contes turcs en langue turque, extraits du roman intitulé "Les Quarante Vizirs."* [By Shaikh-zadah or Şeyhzada.] Paris, 1812.

Benoit, Pierre. *Atlantida*. Translated by M. C. Tongue and Mary Ross. New York, 1920.

Bernard, Saint. *Sermones de tempore*. In Migne, *P.L.*, vol. 183, cols. 35–359.

BERNARDUS TREVISANUS. "De chemico miraculo (De alchimia)." See (A) Theatrum chemicum, xii.

BÉROALDE DE VERVILLE, FRANÇOIS (trans.). Le Tableau des riches inventions couvertes du voile des feintes amoureuses, qui sont représentées dans le Songe de Poliphile. . . . Paris, 1600.

BERTHELOT, MARCELLIN. La Chimie au moyen âge. (Histoire des sciences.) Paris, 1893. 3 vols.

——. Collection des anciens alchimistes grecs. Paris, 1887–88. 3 vols.

——. Les Origines de l'alchimie. Paris, 1885.

BEZOLD, CARL (ed. and trans.). Mĕ'arrath Gazzē. Die Schatzhöhle. Leipzig, 1883–88. 2 parts.

[Bhagavadgītā.] The Bhagavadgītā, with the Sanatsugātiya and the Anugītā. Translated by Kashinath Trimbak Telang. (Sacred Books of the East, 8.) Oxford, 1882. Another version: SWAMI PRABHAVANANDA and CHRISTOPHER ISHERWOOD (trans.). The Song of God. London, 1947. (Also, with differing pagination, Hollywood, 1944.)

BODENSTEIN, ADAM VON. Onomasticon. See: Dictionarium Theophrasti Paracelsi . . . a Gerardo Dorneo collectum. Frankfurt a. M., 1583.

[BÖHME, JAKOB.] XL Questions concerning the Soule. Propounded by Dr. Balthasar Walter. And answered, by Jacob Behmen. [Translated by John Sparrow.] London, 1665.

BONUS, PETRUS. Pretiosa margarita novella de thesauro ac pretiosissimo philosophorum lapide. . . . Edited by Janus Lacinius. Venice, 1546. For translation, see: A. E. WAITE. The New Pearl of Great Price. London, 1894. See also (A) MANGETUS, Bibliotheca chemica curiosa, vi.

BOUSSET, WILHELM. Hauptprobleme der Gnosis. (Forschungen der Religion und Literatur des Alten und Neuen Testaments, 10.) Göttingen, 1907.

BRACESCHUS, JOHANNES. "Lignum vitae." See (A) MANGETUS, Bibliotheca chemica curiosa, iv.

"Brevis manuductio." See (A) Musaeum hermeticum, xiii.

Brihadāranyaka Upanishad. See HUME.

BUDGE, ERNEST ARTHUR WALLIS. *Amulets and Superstitions.* London, 1930.

——— (ed. and trans.). *The Book of the Dead.* An English translation of the Theban Recension. (Books on Egypt and Chaldaea, 6, 7, 8.) 2nd edn., London, 1909. 3 vols.

———. *The Gods of the Egyptians.* London, 1904. 2 vols.

Bundahish. In: E. W. WEST (trans.). *Pahlavi Texts,* Vol. I (Sacred Books of the East, 5.) Oxford, 1880–97.

CAESARIUS OF HEISTERBACH. *Dialogus miraculorum.* Edited by Joseph Strange. Cologne, 1851. For translation, see: H. VON E. SCOTT and C.C.S. BLAND (trans.). *Dialogue on Miracles.* London, 1929.

CALID. "Liber secretorum." See (*A*) *Artis auriferae,* **vii.**

"Canticum de creatione." See HORSTMANN.

CARTER, JAMES BENEDICT. *Epitheta Deorum quae apud Poetas Latinas leguntur. (Ausführliches Lexikon der griechischen und römishcen Mythologie,* ed. W. H. Roscher, Supplement.) Leipzig, 1902.

CASSIODORUS, MARCUS AURELIUS. *Historia Tripartita.* In MIGNE, *P.L.,* vol. 70, cols. 879–1214.

CHARLES, ROBERT HENRY (ed.). *The Apocrypha and Pseudepigrapha of the Old Testament in English.* Oxford, 1913. 2 vols.

CHAUCER, GEOFFREY. *The Complete Works.* Edited by F. N. Robinson. (Student's Cambridge Edition.) Boston, 1933.

Chhāndogya Upanishad. In: *The Upanishads.* Translated by F. Max Müller. (Sacred Books of the East, 1, 15.) Oxford, 1900. 2 vols. (Vol. 1, 1–144.)

CHRÉTIEN DE TROYES. See HILKA.

CHRISTENSEN, ARTHUR (EMANUEL). *Les Types du premier homme et du premier roi dans l'histoire légendaire des Iraniens.* (Archives d'études orientales, 14.) Stockholm, 1917, 1934. 2 parts.

CHWOLSOHN, DANIEL (Khwol'son, Daniil Avraamovich). *Die Ssabier und der Ssabismus.* St. Petersburg, 1856. 2 vols.

CIBINENSIS (SZEBENY), NICHOLAS MELCHIOR. "Addam et processum sub forma missae." See (*A*) *Theatrum chemicum,* **xxi.**

CICERO, MARCUS TULLIUS. *De natura deorum.* In: *M. Tullii Ciceronis Scripta quae manserunt omnia,* ed. C. F. W. Müller, Part IV, vol. 2. Leipzig, 1878. (pp. 1–142.)

Codices and Manuscripts.

   i    Basel. University Library. AX. 128b. Contains "De arbore contemplationis."

   ii   ——. ——. "Alchymistisches MS."

  iii   Berlin. Codex Berolinensis Latinus 532.

  iv   ——. Codex Berolinensis Latinus Q. 584.

   v    Leiden. University Library. Codex Vossianus Chemicus 520 (29). 16th cent.

  vi   London. British Museum. MS. Additional 10302. 16th cent.

 vii   ——. ——. MS. Sloane 5025. 1588. "Four Rolls Drawn in Lübeck" (The Ripley Scrowle).

viii   ——. ——. MS. Additional 15268. 13th cent. "Le Livre des Ansienes Estoires."

  ix   Munich. Staatsbibliothek. Codex Germanicus 598. 1420. "Das Buch der heiligen Dreifaltigkeit und Beschreibung der Heimlichkeit von Veränderung der Metallen."

ix-a  New Haven. Yale University Library. German alchemical ms. (Mellon Coll.). *c.* 1600.

   x    Paris. Bibliothèque nationale. MS. gr. 2250.

  xi   ——. ——. MS. gr. 2252.

 xii   ——. ——. MS. gr. 2419.

xiii   ——. Bibliothèque Ste. Geneviève. MS. 2263–64. "Lapidis philosophorum nomina."

xiv   St. Gall. Codex N. Vadiensis 390. 15th cent. Contains the "Turba philosophorum."

 xv   ——. Codex Germanicus Alchemicus Vadiensis. 16th cent.

xvi   Vatican. Codex Vaticanus Latinus 7286. 17th cent.

xvii  Zurich. Zentralbibliothek. Codex Rhenoviensis 172. 15th cent. "Aurora consurgens."

COLONNA, FRANCESCO. *Hypnerotomachia Poliphili* . . . Venice, 1499. For French translation, see BÉROALDE DE VERVILLE; for English paraphrase, see FIERZ-DAVID.

"Consilium coniugii." See (*A*) *Ars chemica*, **iii.**

COOMARASWAMY, ANANDA K. "The Inverted Tree," *Quarterly Journal of the Mythic Society* (Bangalore), XXIX (1938–39), 111–49.

Corpus Hermeticum. See SCOTT, *Hermetica.*

CRAWLEY, ALFRED ERNEST. *The Idea of the Soul.* London, 1909.

CUMONT, FRANZ. *Testes et monuments figurés relatifs aux mystères de Mithra.* Brussels, 1894–99. 2 vols.

"De arte chymica." See (*A*) *Artis auriferae*, **x.**

*De chemia.* See ZADITH SENIOR.

"Declaratio et explicatio Adolphi." See "Aurelia occulta."

DEE, JOHN. "Monas hieroglyphica." See (*A*) *Theatrum chemicum*, **xvi.**

DEURSEN, ARIE VAN. *Der Heilbringer.* (Dissertation.) Groningen, 1931.

DEUSSEN, PAUL. *Allgemeine Geschichte der Philosophie.* Leipzig, 1894–1917. 2 vols. in 6 parts.

"Dicta Belini." See "Allegoriae sapientum." See also (*A*) MANGETUS, *Bibliotheca chemica curiosa*, **ii.**

DIETERICH, ALBRECHT. *Eine Mithrasliturgie.* Leipzig, 1903.

[DIOSCORIDES.] *Petri Andreae Matthioli Medici Senensis Commentarii in libros sex Pedacii Dioscoridis Anazarbei de medica materia.* Venice, 1554.

DJĀBIR IBN HAYYĀN. "Le Livre du Mercure oriental. . . ." In BERTHELOT, *Moyen âge*, vol. 3, pp. 214f.

DORN, GERARD. "Congeries Paracelsicae chemicae." See (*A*) *Theatrum chemicum*, **ix.**

———. "De tenebris contra naturam et vita brevi." See (*A*) *Theatrum chemicum*, **vii.**

———. "Duellum animi cum corpore." See (*A*) *Theatrum chemicum*, **viii.**

———. "De genealogia mineralium." See (*A*) *Theatrum chemicum*, **x.**

———. "Philosophia chemica." See (*A*) *Theatrum chemicum*, **vi.**

———. "Physica genesis." See (*A*) *Theatrum chemicum*, **iii.**

———. "Physica Trismegisti." See (*A*) *Theatrum chemicum*, **iv.**

———. "Physica Trithemii." See (*A*) *Theatrum chemicum*, **v.**

———. "Speculativa philosophia." See (*A*) *Theatrum chemicum*, **ii.**

———. See also PARACELSUS, *De vita longa.*

DOZY, REINHART, and DE GOEJE, M. J. "Nouveaux documents pour l'étude de la religion des Harraniens." *Actes du sixième congrès international des Orientalistes, 1883.* London, 1885.

Du Cange, Charles du Fresne. *Glossarium ad scriptores mediae et infimae Latinitatis.* 1733–36. 6 vols. New edn., Graz, 1954. 10 vols. in 5.

Eisler, Robert. *Weltenmantel und Himmelszelt.* Munich, 1910. 2 vols.

Eleazar, Abraham. *Uraltes chymisches Werck.* Leipzig, 1760. (Part II has separate pagination.)

El-Habib, Book of. See Berthelot, *Chimie au moyen âge,* III.

Eliade, Mircea. *Shamanism: Archaic Techniques of Ecstasy.* Translated from the French by Willard R. Trask. New York (Bollingen Series) and London 1964.

[Eliezer ben Hyrcanus.] *Pirkê de Rabbi Eliezer.* Translated and edited by Gerald Friedlander. London and New York, 1916.

Elijah, Apocalypse of. See Apocalypse of Elias.

Enoch, Book of. See Charles, *Apocrypha and Pseudepigrapha.*

Epiphanius. *Ancoratus und Panarium.* Edited by Karl Holl. (Griechische Christliche Schriftsteller.) Leipzig, 1915–33. 3 vols. (*Ancoratus,* vol. I, pp. 1–149; *Panarium,* vol. I, p. 169 through vol. III).

"Epistola ad Hermannum." See (*A*) *Theatrum chemicum,* **xxxii.**

Eucherius, Bishop of Lyons. *Liber formularum spiritalis intelligentiae.* In Migne, *P.G.,* vol. 50, cols. 727–72.

Euripides. "The Cretans" (fragment). In Dieterich, q.v.

Euthymios Zigabenos. *Panoplia dogmatica.* In Migne, *P.G.,* vol. 130, cols. 129ff.

Eutychius, Patriarch of Alexandria. *Annales.* In Migne, *P.G.,* vol. 111, cols. 907–1156.

Evans-Wentz, W. Y. (ed.). *The Tibetan Book of the Dead.* With a Psychological Commentary by C. G. Jung. 3rd edn., London and New York, 1957.

"Exercitationes in Turbam." See (*A*) *Artis auriferae,* **iii.**

Ezra, Fourth Book of. See Charles, *Apocrypha and Pseudepigrapha.*

Ferguson, John. *Bibliotheca chemica.* Glasgow, 1906. 2 vols.

Fergusson, James. *Tree and Serpent Worship.* London, 1868.

Ficino, Marsilio. *De vita libri tres.* Basel, 1549.

Fierz-David, Linda. *The Dream of Poliphilo.* Translated by Mary Hottinger. New York (Bollingen Series) and London, 1950.

FIGULUS, BENEDICTUS. *Paradisus aureolus hermeticus.* . . . Frankfurt a. M., 1608.

———. *Rosarium novum olympicum et benedictum.* Basel, 1608.

FIRMICUS MATERNUS, JULIUS. *Liber de errore profanarum religionum.* See: *M. Minucii Felicis Octavius et Julii Firmici Materni Liber de errore profanarum religionum.* Ed. Karl Halm. (Corpus scriptorum ecclesiasticorum latinorum, 2.) Vienna, 1867.

FLAMEL, NICOLAS. "Summarium philosophicum." See *(A) Musaeum hermeticum,* iii.

"Fons chymicae veritatis." See *(A) Musaeum hermeticum,* **xiv.**

FRANZ, MARIE-LOUISE VON (ed.). *Aurora Consurgens: A Document Attributed to Thomas Aquinas on the Problem of Opposites in Alchemy.* Translated by R. F. C. Hull and A. S. B. Glover. New York (Bollingen Series) and London, 1966.

———. "Die Passio Perpetuae." In: C. G. JUNG. *Aion.* (Psychologische Abhandlungen, 8.) Zurich, 1951.

FRAZER, JAMES G. *The Golden Bough.* London, 1911–15. 12 vols. (Part I: *The Magic Art,* vols. 1 and 2. Part IV: *Adonis, Attis, Osiris,* vols. 5, 6.)

———. *Totemism and Exogamy.* London, 1910. 4 vols.

FROBENIUS, LEO. *Das Zeitalter des Sonnengottes.* Vol. I (no more published). Berlin, 1904.

GALEN, CLAUDIUS. *De simplicium medicamentorum facultatibus libri XI.* Lyons, 1561.

GAUDENTIUS, SAINT. *Sermo XIX.* In MIGNE, *P.L.,* vol. 20, cols. 981–93.

GEBER. *Summae perfectionis.* See *(A) De alchemia* (1541), **i.**

[GESSNER, CONRAD.] *Epistolarum medicinalium Conradi Gesneri, philosophi et medici . . . Libri III.* Tiguri [Zurich], 1577.

"Gloria mundi." See *(A) Musaeum hermeticum,* **v.**

GODFREY (GODEFRIDUS), ABBOT OF ADMONT. *Homilia III in Dominica I Adventus.* In MIGNE, *P.L.,* vol. 174, cols. 32–36.

———. *Homilia LXIII in Vigiliam Assumptionis.* In MIGNE, *P.L.,* vol. 174, cols. 957–59.

GOETHE, JOHANN WOLFGANG VON. *Faust.* An abridged version. Translated by Louis MacNeice. London, 1951.

————. *Faust: Part Two.* Translated by Philip Wayne. Harmondsworth, 1959.

GOURMONT, RÉMY DE. *Le Latin mystique.* 4th edn., Paris, 1930.

GRAY, RONALD D. *Goethe the Alchemist.* Cambridge, 1952.

GREGORY THE GREAT, SAINT. *Moralia in Job.* In MIGNE, *P.L.,* vol. 75, col. 509–vol. 76, col. 782.

————. *In septem Psalmos penitentiales expositio.* In MIGNE, *P.L.,* vol. 79, cols. 549–658.

————. *Super Cantica Canticorum expositio.* In MIGNE, *P.L.,* vol. 79, cols. 471–548.

GREVERUS, JODOCUS. "Secretum." See (A) *Theatrum chemicum,* **xx.**

GRIMM, JACOB. *Teutonic Mythology.* Translated by James Steven Stallybrass. London, 1880–88. 4 vols.

[GRIMM, JACOB AND WILHELM.] *Grimm's Fairy Tales.* Translated by Margaret Hunt and revised by James Stern. New York, 1944.

GRÜNBAUM, MAX. *Jüdisch-deutsche Chrestomathie.* Leipzig, 1882.

HAGGARD, HENRY RIDER. *She.* London, 1887.

HAPPELIUS, NICOLAUS NIGER. "Aphorismi Basiliani." See (A) *Theatrum chemicum,* **xxiii.**

HASTINGS, JAMES (ed.). *Encyclopaedia of Religion and Ethics.* Edinburgh and New York, 1908–27. 13 vols.

HEGEMONIUS. *Acta Archelai.* Edited by Charles Henry Beeson. (Griechische Christliche Schriftsteller.) Leipzig, 1906.

HERMES TRISMEGISTUS. "Tabula smaragdina." See (A) *De alchemia* (1541), **ii.**

————. "Tractatus aureus." See (A) *Ars chemica,* **i;** MANGETUS, *Bibliotheca chemica curiosa,* **i;** *Musaeum hermeticum,* **i;** *Theatrum chemicum,* **xxvii.**

HERMOLAUS BARBARUS. *Corollarium in Dioscoridem.* See MAIER, *Symbola aureae mensae.*

HILDEGARD OF BINGEN. *Acta.* In MIGNE, *P.L.,* vol. 197, col. 18.

HILKA, ALFONS. *Der altfranzösische Prosa-Alexander-Roman nach der Berliner Bildenhandschrift.* Halle, 1920.

———— (ed.). *Der Percevalroman (Li Contes del Graal).* Von Christian von Troyes. (Christian von Troyes, Sämtliche erhaltene Werke, ed. Wendelin Foerster, 5.) Halle, 1932.

HIPPOLYTUS. *Elenchos.* See: *Hippolytus' Werke.* Vol. III. Edited by Paul Wendland. (Griechische Christliche Schriftsteller.) Leipzig, 1916. For translation, see: *Philosophumena, or, The Refutation of All Heresies.* Translated by Francis Legge. (Translations of Christian Literature.) London and New York, 1921. 2 vols.

HOGHELANDE, THEOBALD DE. "De alchemiae difficultatibus." See (*A*) *Theatrum chemicum,* i.

HOLMBERG, UNO. *Der Baum des Lebens.* In: *Annales Academiae Scientiarum Fennicae,* Series B, vol. 16. Helsinki, 1922–23.

HOLMYARD, ERIC JOHN. See ABU'L QĀSIM.

HONORIUS OF AUTUN. *Speculum de mysteriis ecclesiae.* In MIGNE, *P.L.,* vol. 172, cols. 807–1108.

HORACE. *Epistola* I.

[HORAPOLLO NILIACUS.] *The Hieroglyphics of Horapollo.* Translated by George Boas. New York (Bollingen Series), 1950.

HORSTMANN, CARL. *Sammlung altenglischer Legenden.* Heilbronn, 1878–81. 2 vols. ("Canticum de creatione," vol. I, pp. 124–38.)

HORTULANUS. "Commentarius" or "Commentariolum." See (*A*) *Ars chemica,* ii; *De alchemia* (1541), iii.

HUME, ROBERT ERNEST (trans.). *The Thirteen Principal Upanishads.* 1921.

*Hymns of the Atharva-Veda.* Translated by M. Bloomfield. (Sacred Books of the East, 42.) Oxford, 1897.

HYSLOP, JAMES H. *Science and a Future Life.* Boston, 1905.

*I Ching, or Book of Changes.* The Richard Wilhelm [German] translation rendered into English by Cary F. Baynes. New York (Bollingen Series), 1950; London, 1951. 2 vols.; 3rd edn. in 1 vol., 1967.

[——.] *The Yi King.* Translated by James Legge. (Sacred Books of the East, 16.) 2nd edn., Oxford, 1899.

[IGNATIUS LOYOLA, SAINT.] *The Spiritual Exercises of St. Ignatius Loyola.* Edited and translated by Joseph Rickaby, S.J. 2nd edn., London, 1923.

"Instructio de arbore solari." See (*A*) *Theatrum chemicum,* xxxiv.

"Introitus apertus." See (*A*) *Musaeum hermeticum,* x.

IRENAEUS. *Adversus* [or *Contra*] *haereses libri quinque.* In MIGNE, *P.G.,* vol. 7, cols. 433–1224. For translation, see: *The Writings of*

*Irenaeus.* Translated by Alexander Roberts and W. H. Rambaut. (Ante-Nicene Christian Library, 5, 9.) Edinburgh, 1868–69. 2 vols.

"Isis to Horus." See SCOTT, *Hermetica.*

JACOBSOHN, HELMUTH. *Die dogmatische Stellung des Königs in der Theologie der alten Aegypter.* (Aegyptologische Forschungen, herausgegeben von Alexander Scharff, 8.) Gluckstadt, Hamburg, and New York, 1939.

JAFFÉ, ANIELA. "Bilder und Symbole aus E. T. A. Hoffmanns Märchen 'Der Goldne Topf.'" In: C. G. JUNG. *Gestaltungen des Unbewussten.* (Psychologische Abhandlungen, 8.) Zurich, 1950.

JUNG, CARL GUSTAV. *Aion: Researches into the Phenomenology of the Self. Collected Works,\** vol. 9, part ii.

————. "Answer to Job." In: *Collected Works,* vol. 11.

————. "The Archetypes of the Collective Unconscious." In: *Collected Works,* vol. 9, part i.

————. "Concerning Mandala Symbolism." In: *Collected Works,* vol. 9, part i.

————. "Concerning Rebirth." In: *Collected Works,* vol. 9, part i.

————. *Memories, Dreams, Reflections.* Recorded by Aniela Jaffé. Translated by Richard and Clara Winston. New York and London, 1963.

————. *Mysterium Coniunctionis. Collected Works,* vol. 14.

————. "On the Nature of the Psyche." In: *Collected Works,* vol. 8.

————. "Paracelsus the Physician." In: *Collected Works,* vol. 15.

————. "The Phenomenology of the Spirit in Fairytales." In: *Collected Works,* vol. 9, part i.

————. *Psychiatric Studies. Collected Works,* vol. 1.

————. "A Psychological Approach to the Dogma of the Trinity." In: *Collected Works,* vol. 11.

————. *Psychological Types. Collected Works,* vol. 6. Alternative source: Translation by H. G. Baynes. New York and London, 1923.

————. *Psychology and Alchemy. Collected Works,* vol. 12.

---

\* For details of the *Collected Works of C. G. Jung,* see announcement at the end of this volume.

———. "The Psychology of Dementia Praecox." In: *Collected Works*, vol. 3.

———. "Psychology and Religion." In: *Collected Works*, vol. 11.

———. *Psychology and Religion: West and East. Collected Works*, vol. 11.

———. "The Psychology of the Transference." In: *Collected Works*, vol. 16.

———. "Richard Wilhelm: In Memoriam." In: *Collected Works*, vol. 15.

———. *The Spirit in Man, Art, and Literature. Collected Works*, vol. 15.

———. "A Study in the Process of Individuation." In: *Collected Works*, vol. 9, part i.

———. *Symbols of Transformation. Collected Works*, vol. 5.

———. "Transformation Symbolism in the Mass." In: *Collected Works*, vol. 11.

———. *Two Essays on Analytical Psychology. Collected Works*, vol. 7.

———. See also PAULI; WILHELM.

KAGAROW, EUGEN. "Der umgekehrte Schamanerbaum," *Archiv für Religionswissenschaft* (Leipzig and Berlin), XXVII (1929), 183–85.

KERN, OTTO (ed.). *Orphicorum fragmenta*. Berlin, 1922.

KHUNRATH, HENRICUS (HEINRICH). *Amphitheatrum sapientiae aeternae*. Hanau, 1609.

———. *Von hylealischen Chaos*. Magdeburg, 1597.

KIRCHER, ATHANASIUS. *Mundus subterraneus*. Amsterdam, 1678. 2 vols.

KNORR VON ROSENROTH, CHRISTIAN. *Kabbala Denudata*. Sulzbach and Frankfurt a. M., 1677–84. 2 vols.

KNUCHEL, EDUARD FRITZ. *Die Umwandlung in Kult, Magie und Rechtsbrauch*. (Schriften der Schweizerischen Gesellschaft für Volkskunde, 15.) Basel, 1919.

KOMARIOS. See BERTHELOT, *Collection des anciens alchimistes grecs*, Treatise IV.

KOPP, HERMANN. *Die Alchemie in älterer und neuerer Zeit*. Heidelberg, 1886. 2 vols.

Koran. Translated by N. J. Dawood. Harmondsworth, 1956.

Krates, Book of. See BERTHELOT, *La Chimie au moyen âge*, vol. III.

KRICKEBERG, W. (ed. and trans.). *Indianermärchen aus Nordamerika.* (Die Märchen der Weltliteratur.) Jena, 1924.

———. *Märchen der Azteken, Inka, Maya und Muiska.* (Die Märchen der Weltliteratur.) Jena, 1928.

KRUEGER, GUSTAV. *Das Dogma von der Dreieinigkeit und Gottmenschheit in seiner geschichtlichen Entwicklung dargestellt.* (Lebensfragen; Schriften und Reden, edited by Heinrich Weinel.) Tübingen, 1905.

LACINIUS. See BONUS.

LAKE, KIRSOPP (ed. and trans.). *The Apostolic Fathers.* (Loeb Classical Library.) London and New York, 1914. 2 vols. ("Epistle of Barnabas," I, 340–409.)

"Lambspringk, The Book of." See (*A*) *Musaeum hermeticum*, vi.

LASZLO, VIOLET S. DE (ed.). *Psyche and Symbol: A Selection from the Writings of C. G. Jung.* Garden City, N.Y., 1958.

[LAZARELLO, LUDOVICUS.] *Contenta in hoc volumine: Pimander Mercurii Trismegisti . . . Asclepius ejusdem Mercurii . . . item Crater Hermetis a Lazarelo Septempedano.* (No date or place.) (Folios 32–42$^r$.)

LÉVY-BRUHL, LUCIEN. *Primitive Mentality.* Translated by Lilian A. Clare. London and New York, 1923.

"Lignum vitae." See BRACESCHUS.

LIPPMANN, EDMUND O. VON. *Entstehung und Ausbreitung der Alchemie.* Berlin, 1919–54. 3 vols.

LULLY, RAYMOND. "Codicillus." See (*A*) Mangetus, *Bibliotheca chemica curiosa*, iii.

MAIER, MICHAEL. *De circulo physico quadrato.* Oppenheim, 1616.

———. *Secretioris naturae secretorum scrutinium chymicum.* Frankfurt a. M., 1687.

———. "Subtilis allegoria super secreta chymiae." See (*A*) *Musaeum hermeticum*, xi.

———. *Symbola aureae mensae duodecim nationum.* Frankfurt a. M., 1617.

MAITLAND, EDWARD. *Anna Kingsford: Her Life, Letters, Diary, and Work.* London, 1896. 2 vols.

Maitrayana-Brāhmana Upanishad. In: *The Upanishads.* Translated by F. Max Müller. (Sacred Books of the East, 1, 15.) Oxford, 1900. 2 vols. (Vol. 2, pp. 287–346.)

MARIA PROPHETISSA. "Practica." See (*A*) *Artis auriferae,* vi.

MARSILIO FICINO. *De vita libri tres.* Basel, 1549.

MARTIAL (Marcus Valerius Martialis). *Epigrammata.* Edited by Walter Gebert. Leipzig, 1896.

MATTHEWS, WASHINGTON. "The Mountain Chant: A Navajo Ceremony." *Fifth Annual Report of the Bureau of Ethnology, 1883–84.* Washington, 1887. (Pp. 385–467.)

MEAD, G. R. S. *The Doctrine of the Subtle Body in Western Tradition.* London, 1919.

MECHTHILD OF MAGDEBURG. *Liber gratiae spiritualis.* Venice, 1578.

MELCHIOR OF BRIXEN. "Vom dem Gelben und Rotten Mann." See (*A*) *Aureum vellus,* ii.

MELCHIOR CIBINENSIS (SZEBENY), NICHOLAS. "Addam et processum sub forma missae. See (*A*) *Theatrum chemicum,* xxi.

MICHELSPACHER, STEFFAN. *Cabala, speculum artis et naturae, in alchymia.* Augsburg, 1654. (German version: *Cabala, Spiegel der Kunst und Natur: in Alchymia.* Augsburg, 161, 1616.)

MIGNE, JACQUES PAUL (ed.). *Patrologiae cursus completus.*
    [*P.L.*] Latin series. Paris, 1844–64. 221 vols.
    [*P.G.*] Greek series. Paris, 1857–66. 166 vols.
    (These works are referred to as "Migne, *P.L.*" and "Migne, *P.G.*" respectively.)

[Missal.] *The Missal in Latin and English.* Edited by J. O'Connell and H.P.R. Finberg. London, 1949.

MORIENUS ROMANUS. "De transmutatione metallorum." See (*A*) *Artis auriferae,* xi.

MÜLLER, MARTIN. . . . *Paracelsus Sämtliche Werke: Erste Abteilung. Registerband.* (Nova Acta Paracelsica, Supplementum.) Einsiedeln, 1960.

"Mutus liber." See ALTUS.

MYLIUS, JOHANN DANIEL. *Philosophia reformata.* Frankfurt a. M., 1622.

NAZARI, GIOVANNI BATTISTA. *Della tramutatione metallica sogni tre.* Brescia, 1599.

NEALE, J. M. *Collected Hymns, Sequences and Carols.* London, 1914.

NELKEN, JAN. "Analytische Beobachtungen über Phantasien eines Schizophrenen," *Jahrbuch für psychoanalytische und psychopathologische Forschungen* (Vienna and Leipzig), IV (1912), 504–62.

NEUMANN, ERICH. *Amor and Psyche: The Psychic Development of the Feminine.* A Commentary on the tale by Apuleius. Translated by Ralph Manheim. New York (Bollingen Series) and London, 1956.

NIETZSCHE, FRIEDRICH WILHELM. *Thus Spake Zarathustra.* See: *The Portable Nietzsche.* Selected and translated by Walter Kaufmann. New York, 1954.

NINCK, MARTIN. *Götter und Jenseitsglauben der Germanen.* Jena [1937].

NORTON, THOMAS. "The Ordinal of Alchemy." See (*A*) *Musaeum hermeticum,* **viii;** (*A*) *Theatrum chemicum britannicum,* **i.**

"Novum lumen chemicum." See (*A*) *Musaeum hermeticum,* **ix.**

OLYMPIODORUS. See BERTHELOT, *Collection des anciens alchimistes grecs,* Treatise II.

ONIANS, RICHARD BROXTON. *The Origins of European Thought.* 2nd edn., Cambridge, 1954.

"Opusculum authoris ignoti." See (*A*) *Artis auriferae,* **viii.**

ORTHELIUS. "Epilogus." See (*A*) *Theatrum chemicum,* **xxxv.**

OSTANES. See BERTHELOT, *La Chimie au moyen âge,* vol. III; *Collection des anciens alchimistes grecs,* Treatises III, IV.

PANTHEUS. *Ars transmutationis metallicae.* Venice, 1519.

PARACELSUS (Theophrastus Bombast of Hohenheim). *Theophrast von Hohenheim genannt Paracelsus Sämtliche Werke.* First section: *Medizinische, naturwissenschaftliche und philosophische Schriften.* Edited by Karl Sudhoff and Wilhelm Matthiessen. Munich and Berlin, 1922–33. 14 vols. Second section: *Theologische und religionsphilosophische Schriften.* Edited by Karl Sudhoff, Wilhelm Matthiessen, and K. Goldammer. Munich and Wiesbaden, 1923–    . 5 vols. published. (In the references below, this edn. is cited as "Sudhoff"; all vols. are in the first section except "De religione perpetua.")

————. *Aureoli Philippi Theophrasti Bombasts von Hohenheim Paracelsi . . . Philosophi et Medici Opera Bücher und Schrifften.* Strasbourg, 1603–16. 2 vols. (In the references below, this edn. is cited as "Huser.")

————. "Archidoxis magicae." In: Huser, II, 544–73.

————. *Astronomia magna.* In: Sudhoff, XII, 1–444.

————. "Das Buch Meteorum." In: Huser, II, 69–96.

————. "Caput de morbis somnii." In: Sudhoff, IX, 359–62.

————. "De caducis." In: Sudhoff, VIII, 263–308; Huser, I, 589–607.

————. "De morbis amentium." In: Huser, I, 486–506.

————. "De natura rerum." In: Sudhoff, XI, 309–403.

————. "De nymphis." In: Sudhoff, XIV, 115–51; see also "De pygmaeis," below.

————. "De pestilitate." In: Huser, I, 326–56.

————. "De podagricis." In: Huser, I, 563–77.

————. "De pygmaeis." See "Liber de nymphis, sylphis, pygmaeis, et salamandris, et de caeteris spiritibus," in Huser, II, 180–92.

————. "De religione perpetua." In: Sudhoff, Part 2, I, 89–107.

————. "De sanguine ultra mortem." In: Huser, II, 267–71.

————. "De tartaro: Fragmenta anatomiae." In: Sudhoff, III, 461–76.

————. *De vita longa.* In: Sudhoff, III, 249–92. Other editions: (1) Edited by Adam von Bodenstein. Basel, 1562. (2) *Theophrasti Paracelsi Libri V de Vita Longa.* Edited by Gerard Dorn. Frankfurt a. M., 1583.

————. "Fragmenta." In: Sudhoff, III, 292–308.

————. "Fragmenta medica." In: Huser, I, 131–69.

————. "Labyrinthus medicorum errantium." In: Sudhoff, XI, 161–221.

————. "Liber Azoth." In: Huser, II, 519–43.

————. *Das Buch Paragranum.* Edited by Franz Strunz. Leipzig, 1903.

————. *Paramirum primum.* In: Sudhoff, I, 163–239.

————. "Philosophia ad Athenienses." In: Huser, II, 1–19.

————. "Von der Astronomey." In: Huser, I, 212–18.

————. "Von den dreyen ersten essentiis." In: Huser, I, 323–26.

————. "Von Erkantnus des Gestirns." In: Sudhoff, XII, 495–98.

————. *The Hermetical and Alchemical Writings of Aureolus Philippus Theophrastus Bombast of Hohenheim, called Paracelsus the Great.* Translated by A. E. Waite. London, 1894. 2 vols.

PAULI, W. "The Influence of Archetypal Ideas on the Scientific Theories of Kepler." Translated by Priscilla Silz. In: C. G. JUNG and W. PAULI, *The Interpretation of Nature and the Psyche.* New York (Bollingen Series) and London, 1955.

PAULINUS OF NOLA. *Poemata.* In MIGNE, *P.L.,* vol. 61, cols. 437–710.

PAUSANIAS. *Descriptio Graeciae.* Edited by Friedrich Spiro. Leipzig, 1903. 3 vols.

PENOTUS. "De medicamentis chemicis." See (*A*) *Theatrum chemicum,* **xi.**

————. Table of Symbols. See (*A*) *Theatrum chemicum,* **xiv.**

PERNETY, A. J. *Dictionnaire mytho-hermétique.* Paris, 1787.

————. *Les Fables égyptiennes et grecques.* Paris, 1758. 2 vols.

PETRIE, WILLIAM FLINDERS. *Egyptian Tales, translated from the Papyri.* London, 1895. 2 series.

PHILALETHES, EIRENAEUS. "Brevis manuductio ad rubinum caelestem." See (*A*) *Musaeum hermeticum,* **xiii.**

————. "Fons chymicae veritatis." See (*A*) *Musaeum hermeticum,* **xiv.**

————. "Introitus apertus." See (*A*) *Musaeum hermeticum,* **x.**

————. "Metallorum metamorphosis." See (*A*) *Musaeum hermeticum,* **xii.**

PHILO. "De opificio mundi" ("On the Account of the World's Creation given by Moses"). In: *Works,* translated by T. H. Colson and G. H. Whitaker. (Loeb Classical Library.) New York and London, 1929– . 10 vols. (I, 6–137.)

PICINELLUS, PHILIPPUS. *Mundus symbolicus.* Cologne, 1687. 2 vols.

PICO DELLA MIRANDOLA, JOANNES. "De arte cabalistica." In *Opera omnia,* I.

————. *Heptaplus.* In *Opera omnia,* I.

————. *Opera omnia.* Basel, 1572–73. 2 vols.

PIERRE, NOËL. *Soleil noir.* Paris, 1952.

*Pirkê de Rabbi Eliezer.* See ELIEZER BEN HYRCANUS.

PITRA, JEAN-BAPTISTE (ed.). *Analecta sacra Spicilegio Solesmensi praeparata.* Paris, 1876–91. 8 vols.

"Platonis liber quartorum." See (*A*) *Theatrum chemicum,* **xxx.**

POMPONIUS MELA. *Chronographia.* Edited by Carl Frick. Leipzig, 1880.

PORDAGE, JOHN. *Ein gründlich philosophisch Sendschreiben von rechten und wahren Stein der Weisheit.* In FRIEDRICH ROTH-SCHOLTZ (ed.). *Deutsche Theatrum Chemicum.* Nürnberg, 1728–32. 3 vols. (I, 557–96.)

———. *Sophia.* Amsterdam, 1699. (In German: translated from English MS.)

"Practica Mariae." See (*A*) *Artis auriferae,* **vi.**

PREISENDANZ, KARL. *Papyri Graecae Magicae: Die griechischen Zauberpapyrien.* Berlin, 1928–31. 2 vols.

PRELLER, LUDWIG. *Griechische Mythologie.* Leipzig, 1854. 2 vols.

PREUSCHEN, ERWIN. *Antilegomena.* Giessen, 1901.

[PRISCILLIAN.] *Priscilliani quae supersunt.* Edited by Georg Schepss. (Corpus Scriptorum Ecclesiasticorum Latinorum, 18.) Vienna, Prague, Leipzig, 1889.

PRITCHARD, JAMES B. (ed.). *Ancient Near Eastern Texts relating to the Old Testament.* 2nd edn., Princeton, 1955.

*Prodromus Rhodostauroticus, Parergi philosophici.* . . . . n.d., 1620. (Contains *Verus Hermes.*)

PSELLUS, MICHAEL. *De daemonibus.* Translated by Marsilio Ficino. 1497.

RABANUS MAURUS. *Allegoriae in Sacram Scripturam.* In MIGNE, *P.L.,* vol. 112, cols. 850–1088.

RAHNER, HUGO. "Die seelenheilende Blume." In *Eranos-Jahrbuch XII,* Festgabe für C. G. Jung, Zurich, 1945. (Pp. 117–239.)

REINACH, SALOMON. *Cultes, mythes, et religions.* Paris, 1905–23. 5 vols.

REITZENSTEIN, RICHARD. *Alchemistische Lehrschriften und Märchen bei den Arabern.* (Religionsgeschichtliche Versuche und Vorarbeiten, 19, part 3.) Giessen, 1923.

———. *Poimandres: Studien zur griechisch-ägyptischen und frühchristlichen Literatur.* Leipzig, 1904.

———— and SCHAEDER, H. *Studien zum antiken Synkretismus aus Iran und Griechenland*. (Studien der Bibliothek Warburg, 7.) Berlin, 1926.

REUSNER, HIERONYMUS. *Pandora: Das ist, die edelst Gab Gottes, oder der Werde und heilsame Stein der Weysen*. Basel, 1588.

RHENANUS, JOANNES (ed.). *Solis e puteo emergentis sive dissertationis chymotechnicae libri tres*. Frankfurt a. M., 1613.

RIPLEY, GEORGE. *Opera omnia chemica*. Cassel, 1649.

————. *Chymische Schrifften*. Erfurt, 1624.

————. "Duodecim portarum axiomata philosophica." See (*A*) *Theatrum chemicum*, **xv**.

————. Preface to "Medulla." See (*A*) *Theatrum chemicum britannicum*, **iii**.

————. "Verses belonging to an Emblematicall Scrowle." See (*A*) *Theatrum chemicum britannicum*, **ii**.

"Rosarium philosophorum." See (*A*) *Artis auriferae*, **xiii**; (*A*) *De alchimia* (1550); (*A*) MANGETUS, *Bibliotheca chemica curiosa*, **vii**.

ROSCHER, W. H. (ed.). *Ausführliches Lexikon der griechischen und römischen Mythologie*. Leipzig, 1884–1937. 6 vols.

ROSENCREUTZ, CHRISTIAN (pseud. of Johann Valentin Andreae). *Chymische Hochzeit*. Strasbourg, 1616. For translation, see: *The Hermetick Romance, or The Chymical Wedding*. Translated by E. Foxcroft. London, 1690.

"Rosinus ad Sarratantam Episcopum." See (*A*) *Artis auriferae*, **v**.

RULAND, MARTIN. *Lexicon alchemiae sive Dictionarium alchemisticum*. Frankfurt a. M., 1612. For translation, see: *A Lexicon of Alchemy*. London, 1892.

RUPESCISSA, JOHANNES DE (JEAN DE ROCHETAILLADE OR ROQUETAILLADE). *La Vertu et propriété de la quinte essence de toutes choses*. Lyons, 1581.

RUSKA, JULIUS (ed.). *Turba Philosophorum*. (Quellen und Studien zur Geschichte der Naturwissenschaften und der Medizin, 1.) Berlin, 1931.

"Scala philosophorum." See (*A*) *Artis auriferae*, **xii**.

SCALIGER, JOSEPH JUSTUS. *Animadversiones in Chronologia Eusebii*. In his: *Thesaurus temporum, Eusebii . . . chronicorum canonum . . . libri duo*. 1606.

SCHEVILL, MARGARET E. *Beautiful on the Earth*. Santa Fe (New Mexico), 1945.

SCHOPENHAUER, ARTHUR. "On the Fourfold Root of the Principle of Sufficient Reason." In: *Two Essays by Arthur Schopenhauer*. Translated anonymously. (Bohn's Philosophical Library.) London, 1889. (Pp. 1–189.)

SCHREBER, DANIEL PAUL. *Memoirs of My Nervous Illness*. Translated by Ida Macalpine and Richard A. Hunter. (Psychiatric Monograph Series, 1.) London, 1955.

SCHWEITZER, BERNHARD. *Herakles*. Tübingen, 1922.

SCOTT, WALTER (ed.). *Hermetica*. Oxford, 1924–36. 4 vols.

SENDIVOGIUS, MICHAEL (Michal Sendiwoj). "Dialogus Mercurii alchymistae et naturae." See (*A*) *Theatrum chemicum*, **xxiv**.

———. "Novum lumen chemicum." See (*A*) *Musaeum hermeticum*, **ix**.

———. "Parabola, seu Aenigma philosophicum." See (*A*) MANGETUS, *Bibliotheca chemica curiosa*, **viii**.

———. *Tripus chemicus*. Strasbourg, 1628.

SENIOR. See ZADITH.

ŞEYHZADE. See BELLETÊTE.

*Shatapatha-Brāhmana*. Translated by Julius Eggeling. (Sacred Books of the East, 12, 26, 41, 43, 44.) Oxford, 1882–1900. 5 vols.

SPENCE, LEWIS. *The Gods of Mexico*. London, 1923.

SPENCER, SIR WALTER B., and GILLEN, FRANCIS JAMES. *The Northern Tribes of Central Australia*. London, 1904.

SPIELREIN, SABINA. "Über den psychologischen Inhalt eines Falls von Schizophrenie." *Jahrbuch für psychoanalytische und psychopathologische Forschung* (Leipzig and Vienna), III (1912), 329–400.

SPITTELER, CARL. *Prometheus and Epimetheus*. Translated by James Fullarton Muirhead. London, 1931.

STEEB, JOHANN CHRISTOPH. *Coelum Sephiroticum Hebraeorum*. Mainz, 1679.

STEINDORFF, GEORG (ed.). *Die Apokalypse des Elias*. (Texte und Untersuchungen, N. S., 2, part 3a.) Leipzig, 1899.

STEINEN, KARL VON DEN. *Unter den Naturvölkern Zentral-Brasiliens*. Berlin, 1894.

STEVENSON, JAMES. "Ceremonial of Hasjelti Dailjis and Mythical Sand Painting of the Navajo Indians." *Eighth Annual Report of the Bureau of Ethnology, 1886–87.* Washington, 1891. (Pp. 235–85.)

STOBAEUS, JOHN. *Anthologium.* Edited by Kurt Wachsmuth and Otto Hense. Berlin, 1884–1912. 5 vols.

SZEBENY. See CIBINENSIS.

TABERNAEMONTANUS, JACOBUS THEODORUS. *Kräuterbuch.* [*Herbal.*] Basel, 1731. 2 vols.

"Tabula smaragdina." See HERMES TRISMEGISTUS.

TALBOT, AMAURY. *In the Shadow of the Bush.* London, 1912.

TODD, RUTHVEN. "Coleridge and Paracelsus, Honeydew and LSD," *London Magazine,* March 1967.

"Tractatulus Avicennae." See (*A*) *Artis auriferae,* ix.

"Tractatus Aristotelis." See (*A*) *Theatrum chemicum,* xxxi.

"Tractatus aureus." See (*A*) *Ars chemica,* i; (*A*) MANGETUS, *Bibliotheca chemica curiosa,* i; *Musaeum hermeticum,* i.

"Tractatus Micreris." See (*A*) *Theatrum chemicum,* xxix.

TRISMOSIN, SALOMON. "Splendor solis." See (*A*) *Aureum vellus,* i. For translation, see: *Splendor solis: Alchemical Treatises of Salomon Trismosin.* With explanatory notes by J. K. London, 1920.

"Turba philosophorum." See RUSKA.

USENER, HERMANN. *Das Weihnachtsfest.* 2nd edn., Bonn, 1911.

VALENTINUS, BASILIUS. "Practica." See (*A*) *Musaeum hermeticum,* vii.

VECERIUS, CONRADUS. "De rebus gestis Imperatoris Henrici VII." In: *Germaniae Historicorum . . .* Edited by Christianus Urstisius (Wurstisen) of Basel. Frankfurt a. M., 1585. 2 vols. (Vol. II, pp. 63–64.)

*Vedanta-Sutras.* Translated by G. Thibaut. (Sacred Books of the East, 34, 38, 48.) Oxford, 1890–1904. 3 vols.

VENTURA, LAURENTIUS. "De ratione conficiendi lapidis." See (*A*) *Theatrum chemicum,* xvii.

*Verus Hermes.* See *Prodromus Rhodostauroticus.*

VETTIUS, VALENS. *Anthologiarum libri.* Edited by Wilhelm Kroll. Berlin, 1908.

"Via veritatis unicae." See (*A*) *Musaeum hermeticum*, **iv**.

VIGENERUS, BLASIUS. "De igne et sale." See (*A*) *Theatrum chemicum*, **xxxiii**.

"Visio Arislei." See ARISLEUS.

WALDE, ALOIS. *Lateinisches Etymologisches Wörterbuch*. Edited by J. B. Hofmann. 3rd edn., Heidelberg, 1938–54. 2 vols.

*Wasserstein der Weysen, Der*. Frankfurt a. M., 1619.

[WEI PO-YANG.] "An Ancient Chinese Treatise on Alchemy entitled Ts'an T'ung Ch'i, written by Wei Po-yang about 142 A.D." (translated by Lu-ch'iang Wu and Tenney L. Davis), *Isis* (Bruges), XVIII (1932), 210–89.

WELLS, HERBERT GEORGE. *Christina Alberta's Father*. London, 1925.

WILHELM, RICHARD, and JUNG, C. G. *The Secret of the Golden Flower: A Chinese Book of Life*. Translated by Cary F. Baynes. London and New York, 1931; new edn., 1962.

WINDISCHMANN, FR. *Zoroastrische Studien*. Berlin, 1863.

WÜNSCHE, AUGUST. "Die Sagen von Lebensbaum und Lebenswasser," *Ex Oriente Lux* (Leipzig), I (1905), parts 2, 3.

ZADITH SENIOR (Zadith ben Hamuel). *De chemia Senioris antiquissimi philosophi libellus*. Strasbourg, 1566.

ZÖCKLER, OTTO. *The Cross of Christ*. Translated by Maurice J. Evans. London, 1877.

INDEX

# INDEX

Under alchemical collections, when cross reference is made to "individual treatises in Bibl. A," see above pp. 353ff, where names of these and their authors are listed.

## A

Aaron, 130
aberrations, mental, 323
*ablutio*, 68
ablution, 292
abortifacient, 135n
above and below, 104n, 140, 233, 264, 336; growth from, 272
Abraham le Juif, 213, 220; *see also* Eleazar
Abu'l Qāsim al-'Irāqī, 139n, 226n, 305, 308, 309n, 310n
acacia tree, 305
Achamoth, 283, 334
action and non-action, 16n, 25
Adam, 81n, 94, 113n, 131&n, 137n, 139, 143, 146, fig. B4, 166, 169, 219, 220, 318; earthly, 169n; and Eve, fig. 32, 303; first wife of, 303; genitals of, 143; heavenly, 169n; man of light imprisoned in, 130; mystic, 139; Old, 80; parable, 83n; second, 80; —, Christ as, 304; —, Mercurius as, 235; sin of, 304; tree of paradise of, 138; true hermaphroditic, 219; with Venus in bath, 226n
Adam Kadmon, 130, 220, 220n
Adamas, 283n, 318
Adam von Bodenstein, *see* Bodenstein
adaptation, lack of, 12
adaptedness, 18
Adebar (stork), 317

Adech, 131&n, 164, 165&n, 166, 169, 172; difficult, 170, 171, 173, 174, 179; great, 170, 171; *homo maior*, 182
adept(s), 126, 139, 151, 171f, 172n, 179f, 231, 275, 299, 302f, 309, 327, 331; individuation of, 326; moon-plant of, 308
Adhvaryu, 267
Adityas, 267
Adler, Gerhard, xiv
Admont, Godfrey Abbot of, *see* Godfrey
*adulatio*, 329n
Aegidius de Vadis, 217n, 322
"Aenigma VI," 68n, 93n, 105n; *see also* "Visio Arislei"
"Aenigma Bononiense," 199n
"Aenigma philosophorum," 227n
Aeons, 162
*aer elementalis*, 136n
aerial life, 163
aesthetic experiment, 45
*aestphara*, 134n
aether, 76, 162, 176; soul rooted in, 312n
aetiology, 108, 342
affect(s), 12, 15, 34, 35, 41, 45, 82, 334, 343; autonomous character of, 39; outbursts of, 289; personal, 346; uncontrollable, 50
affective: nature of man, Mars characterizes, 141n; states, 39
Agathodaimon (good spirit), 62, 67n, 74n, 104, 333
age, old, 272
aggregation, gaseous, 212

## D

I

317f; as fiery pillar, fig. 313, 310n; fire-, 258, 339n; with four metallic/branches, 89, 332; fruit-, 166, 305; as gnosis, 318; golden, 289, 310, 316f; as guardian of treasure, 314; and heavenly bride, 340; of Hermes, 309n; of Hesperides, 256; holy, of India, 340; identity of, with Mercurius, 338; immortal, 67n; individuality of, 194; inverted (arbor inversa), 311, 314, 318, 340; —, man as, 312n; as Jesus, 318; of knowledge, 318, 339, fig. 11; as lapis, 319; leafless or dead, 256, 264, 268, 304; of life, 83, 196n, 274, 308, 312, 318, 339; — and death, 271; —, rooted in Binah, 312; life principle of, 196; of light, 255; Lord of, 337n; magic(al), 303, 341; as man, 337; maternal significance of, 261; medium of conjunction, 337; Mercurius and, see Mercurius; metallic, 286, 310, 311, 315, 332; —, of alchemy, 89; modern fantasies of, 341; of moon, 303n; on mountaintop, 308, 320; -numen, 195, 315, 317, 318; nymph, 262, 265, 339; —, witchlike, 260; oji, 199; opus as, 313, 338; of paradise/paradisal, 143, 199, 257, 302, 304, 318, 332, 339f; —, Buddha/Christ named, 338n; —, of knowledge, 240; —, as man, 337; —, two, 306; personal atman of, 239; personification of, 194n;* philosophical, 230, 240, 253, 287; planted in sea, 308; as pneumatic pillar, 310n; primordial, 337n; projection into, 200; —, of anima figure, 338; quaternity of, 332; rebirth mystery, 338; relation of, to mountain, 309; —, to Sapienta, 318; in the retort, 315; in Ripley Scrowle, 199n; rooted in air, 311; as seat of transformation and renewal, 317; secret in roots of, 195; of Sefiroth, 312; and seven metals, 310; of seven planets, 309; shaman(ist)ic, fig. 2, 272; snake, 241, 315; —, chthonic numen of, 317; and —, union of, fig. 12; as solar pillar, 310n; -soul, divi-

sion of into masculine/feminine, 319; spirit in, see spirit; is spiritual principle of stork, 317; of sun, 303n; — and moon, 306n, 308, 339; sword hanging on the, 333; symbol(s), 195n, 253, 270, 272; —, of chrysopoea (gold-making), 314; —, of enlightenment, 313f; —, of personality and self, 309; —, of transformation, 332; —, of whole opus, 311; as system of blood vessels, 287; truncated, 304f; or vine, Christ as, 338; visible sign of realization of self, 196; -voice, 199; and water, 309; in Western Land, 306; white, 305n; of wisdom, 258, 306, 318; as woman, 338; world-, see world; Zarathustra's vision of, 332; see also acacia; almond; ash; ashvattha; baobab; Bodhi; cedar; fig; forest; Gaokerena; myrtle; nettle; oak; olive; palm; persea; pine; plants

tremendum, 200

Trevisanus, Bernardus, see Bernardus

triad(s), 151, 221, 241; of animals, 141n; chthonic, fig. B2, 223; indivisible, 221n; lower, 141n, 183n; Paracelsan, 277; sun/moon/Mercurius, 277; upper, 165, 167

triadic: character of gods of underworld, 221; nature of Mercurius, 221

triangle, 224

trident, golden, 334

Trinity, 35, 103n, 151n, 166, 222, 241, 277, 334, 336; Holy, 221, 276; —, union of persons in, 277; masculine, 96; Mercurius as, see Mercurius; totality of, 96; union of, 278n; upper, 141n, 183n

Trismegistos, 221n; see also Hermes Trismegistus

Trismosin, Salomon, 68n, 219; see also Splendor solis

triune essence, 293

triunus, Mercurius, see Mercurius

truth, 77, 249n, 301; absolute, 300; divine body of, 35; living, 162; psychic, 171; revealed, 160; seekers after, 160;

The Collected Works of C. G. Jung

Editors: Sir Herbert Read, Michael Fordham, and Gerhard Adler; executive editor, William McGuire. Translated by R.F.C. Hull, except where noted.

*In the following list, dates of original publication are given in parentheses (of original composition, in brackets). Multiple dates indicate revisions.*

Psychophysical Investigations with the Galvanometer and Pneumo-
graph in Normal and Insane Individuals (by F. Peterson and
Jung)
Further Investigations on the Galvanic Phenomenon and Respira-
tion in Normal and Insane Individuals (by C. Ricksher and Jung)
Appendix: Statistical Details of Enlistment (1906); New Aspects of
Criminal Psychology (1908); The Psychological Methods of Inves-
tigation Used in the Psychiatric Clinic of the University of Zurich
(1910); On the Doctrine of Complexes ([1911] 1913); On the
Psychological Diagnosis of Evidence (1937)

3. THE PSYCHOGENESIS OF MENTAL DISEASE (1960)
The Psychology of Dementia Praecox (1907)
The Content of the Psychoses (1908/1914)
On Psychological Understanding (1914)
A Criticism of Bleuler's Theory of Schizophrenic Negativism
(1911)
On the Importance of the Unconscious in Psychopathology
(1914)
On the Problem of Psychogenesis in Mental Disease (1919)
Mental Disease and the Psyche (1928)
On the Psychogenesis of Schizophrenia (1939)
Recent Thoughts on Schizophrenia (1957)
Schizophrenia (1958)

4. FREUD AND PSYCHOANALYSIS (1967)
Freud's Theory of Hysteria: A Reply to Aschaffenburg (1906)
The Freudian Theory of Hysteria (1908)
The Analysis of Dreams (1909)
A Contribution to the Psychology of Rumour (1910–11)
On the Significance of Number Dreams (1910–11)
Morton Prince, "The Mechanism and Interpretation of Dreams": A
Critical Review (1911)
On the Criticism of Psychoanalysis (1910)
Concerning Psychoanalysis (1912)
The Theory of Psychoanalysis (1913)
General Aspects of Psychoanalysis (1913)
Psychoanalysis and Neurosis (1916)
Some Crucial Points in Psychoanalysis: A Correspondence between
Dr. Jung and Dr. Lo ̈y (1914)
Prefaces to "Collected Papers on Analytical Psychology" (1916,
1917)

Four Papers on the Psychological Typology (1913, 1925, 1931, 1936)

7. TWO ESSAYS ON ANALYTICAL PSYCHOLOGY (1953; 2d ed., 1966)
On the Psychology of the Unconscious (1917/1926/1943)
The Relations between the Ego and the Unconscious (1928)
Appendix: New Paths in Psychology (1912); The Structure of the Unconscious (1916) (new versions, with variants, 1966)

8. THE STRUCTURE AND DYNAMICS OF THE PSYCHE (1960; 2d ed., 1969)
On Psychic Energy (1928)
The Transcendent Function ([1916] 1957)
A Review of the Complex Theory (1934)
The Significance of Constitution and Heredity in Psychology (1929)
Psychological Factors Determining Human Behavior (1937)
Instinct and the Unconscious (1919)
The Structure of the Psyche (1927/1931)
On the Nature of the Psyche (1947/1954)
General Aspects of Dream Psychology (1916/1948)
On the Nature of Dreams (1945/1948)
The Psychological Foundations of Belief in Spirits (1920/1948)
Spirit and Life (1926)
Basic Postulates of Analytical Psychology (1931)
Analytical Psychology and Weltanschauung (1928/1931)
The Real and the Surreal (1933)
The Stages of Life (1930–1931)
The Soul and Death (1934)
Synchronicity: An Acausal Connecting Principle (1952)
Appendix: On Synchronicity (1951)

9. PART I. THE ARCHETYPES AND THE COLLECTIVE UNCONSCIOUS (1959; 2d ed., 1968)
Archetypes of the Collective Unconscious (1934/1954)
The Concept of the Collective Unconscious (1936)
Concerning the Archetypes, with Special Reference to the Anima Concept (1936/1954)
Psychological Aspects of the Mother Archetype (1938/1954)
Concerning Rebirth (1940/1950)
The Psychology of the Child Archetype (1940)

Good and Evil in Analytical Psychology (1959)
Introduction to Wolff's "Studies in Jungian Psychology"(1959)
The Swiss Line in the European Spectrum (1928)
Reviews of Keyserling's "America Set Free" (1930) and "La Révolution Mondiale" (1934)
The Complications of American Psychology (1930)
The Dreamlike World of India (1939)
What India Can Teach Us (1939)
Appendix: Documents (1933–38)

11. PSYCHOLOGY AND RELIGION: WEST AND EAST (1958; 2d ed., 1969)
    WESTERN RELIGION
    Psychology and Religion (The Terry Lectures) (1938/1940)
    A Psychological Approach to Dogma of the Trinity (1942/1948)
    Transformation Symbolism in the Mass (1942/1954)
    Forewords to White's "God and the Unconscious" and Werblowsky's "Lucifer and Prometheus" (1952)
    Brother Klaus (1933)
    Psychotherapists or the Clergy (1932)
    Psychoanalysis and the Cure of Souls (1928)
    Answer to Job (1952)
    EASTERN RELIGION
    Psychological Commentaries on "The Tibetan Book of Great Liberation" (1939/1954) and "The Tibetan Book of the Dead" (1935/1953)
    Yoga and the West (1936)
    Foreword to Suzuki's "Introduction to Zen Buddhism" (1939)
    The Psychology of Eastern Meditation (1943)
    The Holy Men of India: Introduction to Zimmer's "Der Weg zum Selbst" (1944)
    Foreword to the "I Ching" (1950)

12. PSYCHOLOGY AND ALCHEMY ([1944] 1953; 2d ed., 1968)
    Prefatory Note to the English Edition ([1951?] added 1967)
    Introduction to the Religious and Psychological Problems of Alchemy
    Individual Dream Symbolism in Relation to Alchemy (1936)
    Religious Ideas in Alchemy (1937)
    Epilogue

# THE COLLECTED WORKS

## OF

# C. G. JUNG

*VOLUME 13*

### EDITORS

SIR HERBERT READ

MICHAEL FORDHAM, M.D., M.R.C.P.

GERHARD ADLER, PH.D.

WILLIAM MCGUIRE, *executive editor*